How Should We Talk about

RELIGION?

Erasmus Institute Books

How Should We Talk about
RELIGION?

Perspectives, Contexts, Particularities

edited by
JAMES BOYD WHITE

University of Notre Dame Press
Notre Dame, Indiana

Manufactured in the United States of America

Library of Congress Cataloging-in-Publication Data

How should we talk about religion? : perspectives, contexts,
particularities / [edited] by James Boyd White.
p.   cm. — (Erasmus Institute books)
Includes bibliographical references.
ISBN-13: 978-0-268-04407-7 (pbk. : alk. paper)
ISBN-10: 0-268-04407-4 (pbk. : alk. paper)
1. Religion—Congresses.   I. White, James Boyd, 1938–   II. Series.
BL21.H69   2006
200—dc22

2006008040

CONTENTS

INTRODUCTION

James Boyd White

This book had its genesis in a faculty summer seminar held in the year 2000 at the University of Notre Dame, under the auspices of the Erasmus Institute. Our topic was the subject of the present book, which asks, as the title suggests, how we should talk about religion, especially in the languages of our various academic disciplines. The idea of the seminar was to collect a dozen people from very different fields and backgrounds, each of whom in his or her professional work has faced this question in a significant way. Each member of the seminar was responsible for leading a two-hour session on his or her work, beginning with a presentation that was then the subject of questions and comments. As we proceeded we found ourselves engaged in a conversation with its own shape and life, which continues today.

The purpose of the seminar was not to produce a book, but to educate ourselves and each other, expanding in various ways our sense of the reality and complexity of religious experience and intensifying our awareness of the difficulty and necessity of talking about it. When we finished our work together, we looked back over what we had done, saw certain common themes and interests, and concluded that we did have at least the beginnings of a book. There followed years of rewriting, editing, and conversation of other kinds, until we had the book before you, which can be conceived of as a kind of extension of the seminar itself.

These chapters should not be read as a series of unrelated essays aimed at distinct professional audiences—historians or psychologists, say, or philosophers—but as composed for the diverse audience to which they were originally given and then rewritten for the even more diverse audience we hope this book reaches. While each of the writers speaks from a disciplinary base, each of them also questions the nature and limits of that base, both as an independent matter and in connection with the other essays in this book. The writers of these essays know that they speak in different ways, and that these differences are an important part of our subject.

Our experience, supported we think by that of others, is that it is in fact quite difficult to talk about religion in a satisfactory way, whether we are trying to do so within a discipline such as law or psychology or anthropology, or while speaking in more informal ways with our friends and colleagues. There are many reasons for this: it is in the nature of religious experience to be ineffable or mysterious, at least for some people or in some religions; different religions imagine the world and its human inhabitants, and their histories, in ways that are enormously different and plainly unbridgeable; and there is no super-language into which all religions can all be translated, for purposes either of comparison or of mutual intelligibility. What is more, it seems to be nearly always the case that one religion's deepest truths and commitments, its fundamental narratives, appear simply irrational, even weird, to those who belong to another tradition, or are themselves simply without religion. This means that in any attempt to study and talk about a religion other than one's own there is a necessary element of patronization, at least whenever we are studying beliefs we could not imagine ourselves sharing.

Yet it is of enormous importance to attempt to learn to talk about religion well, if we possibly can, if only for the obvious political and practical reason that religious divisions, both within nations and among them, are often intractable and bitter, and mutual understanding very difficult to attain. Yet it is hard even to imagine an intellectually respectable way of doing this. Think of the anthropologist of religion for example: is he or she to assume that there is a cross-cultural phenomenon called "religion," and if so on what basis? "Religion" is our word, and why should we assume that the Cheyenne, say, or the Hindus of the Indian subcontinent have practices or beliefs that parallel what we know in the West? (Perhaps we should use their words, and see what happens.) Or consider the psychologist, say the psychotherapist working on analytic principles: is he or she to regard the religious beliefs and experiences of a patient as fantasies and wishes of a pathological kind, of which the patient should be cured? Or as healthy formations? If the latter, how can that position possibly be explained in the language of psychology?

Or think of the historian of the Middle Ages, interested perhaps in architecture or philosophy: how is she to come to understand the world of religious meaning in which the people whose work she is describing lived, and how can she represent it in anything other than reduced terms? Or, to shift to another field, how is the economist to think about the tensions between the premises of his economic thought and those of his religious life, or the religious lives of his culture? And how is the political theorist or scientist to resist the tendency of the field to reduce religion to its merely civic utility, or to a social formation that can be discussed in purely sociological terms? Such were the questions that brought us together.

Our diversity of discipline and background, of age and nationality, was a great virtue of our work together, but it is true nonetheless that certain common themes and questions emerged from what we did. I sketch out some of these below, very briefly, as an introduction to the much fuller and richer treatment of these ideas in the chapters that follow, presenting them in the form of questions, most of which each of our writers has in some way addressed.

1. *Is what we call "reason" sufficient for a full intellectual, practical, and imaginative life? To the extent it is not sufficient, what else is required, and what relation should it have to reason?* This is obviously a crucial question in the academic study of religion, which almost by definition involves the assertion and use of capacities of the mind, or self, that cannot sensibly be included in any definition of "reason." Yet as academics we are committed to reason as our primary instrument of thought and conversation; as members of democratic polities we believe in reasoned deliberation as a central political activity; and so on. If we seek to talk about religion as academics, then, our subject challenges our own habits of thought and expression. The question of the limits of rationality thus naturally arises whenever one studies a religion, or thinks about the connection between religious and secular parts of the culture. (This question figures largely in the essays by Ruth Abbey, Luis Bacigalupo, Patrick Deneen, Javier Iguíñiz, and Sol Serrano.)

2. *How adequate are our languages of description and analysis as ways of representing religion?* This question is present in every effort to talk about the religions of others, beginning with the word "religion" itself. Why should Westerners assume that the Japanese or Indonesians, say, have any cultural formation that parallels what we call "religion"? Or think of our religious terms: "god" or

"priest" or "ritual" or "ceremony." Why should we think any of these apply without great difficulty to another world?

It is obvious that in talking about the religions of others we should make a constant effort to be conscious of the implications of our own language, and aware of what is possibly misleading and incomplete in it. But that is much easier said than done. It is insufficient simply to say such a thing as a general matter, and then forget it; our answer must not be stated but performed, enacted in the way we ask questions, respond to them, seek more general truths—in a sense in every sentence we utter on the subject. (This question is addressed particularly by Clifford Ando, Scott Appleby, and Sabine MacCormack.)

3. *To what degree will any serious confrontation with the religious experience of others be a challenge to our own deepest commitments—whether these are theistic or agnostic or atheistic?* The difficulty here is an obvious one: if you insist on maintaining without change your own worldview—your own sense of the way things are, your own sense of yourself as neutral and objective observer—you may not ever really understand what it is like for other people to imagine the world as they do and to live on those terms. One common response to this gap between worlds is to reduce the religion of others to a list of beliefs, and beliefs that you cannot imagine yourself ever sharing—that the gods live on Olympus, that Apollo represents reason, Dionysus passion, that Zeus is the most powerful, and so on—all of which tells you very little of what it would be like to live in such a world. But as you come to extend yourself and your imagination into the other world, to begin to live on its terms, you begin to accept what at the outset you knew you could never accept. The extreme limit of this movement is to "go native," and begin to think of yourself as a Hindu, say, or an animist, maybe even converting to the religion in question. So where can one stand between the two points defined by the icy objectivist, who can actually see and understand rather little, and the convert who accepts it all as living truth?

This difficulty is exacerbated by the fact that, for many people who live in a particular religious world, their particular religion is not just one among many equally valid systems or forms, but represents the absolute, unique, and eternal truth. All other religions are false. This position is I think impossible for the person who engages seriously with the religious life of others, which means that there is in this sense too a profound tension between the worldview of the comparatist and that of the people she is studying. This tension is a necessary part of our subject, and we need to find ways to think about it. My own sense is that it cannot be resolved; what we need to learn is particular ways of living with the tension in particular contexts. (The essays by Jeffrey Kripal and Bilinda Straight in particular speak to this difficulty.)

4. This brings us to the next question: *can there be a pluralism that does not dissolve into universal relativism?* This question runs through almost everything we did in the seminar. Indeed, it is the necessary consequence of thoughtful comparative work of any kind. How are we to face the enormous diversity of serious belief, seriously engaged in, that characterizes the human world?

One instinct is to seek a larger or more general framework in which two religious systems both have a place, or more general principles of which each can be instances; but this has the double vice of claiming a coherence that may be false and of creating a language that claims to be a super-language into which each religion can be translated. Another approach would be to seek a sharpened sense of differentiation among religions, coupled, one would hope, with an increase in respect for and appreciation of what is distinctive in each. The idea would be that to see our own position more clearly from the point of view of others does not necessarily lead to its dilution, but perhaps to its intensification, though in a context in which fuller recognition of its relation to others becomes possible.

If I may give an example from my personal experience: for many years I attended a church that shared its building with a Jewish synagogue. When people drove by and saw the Cross and the Star of David side by side, they thought something weird indeed must be going on—the creation of some diluted form of nonreligion in which we all participated together. But in fact the experience of the two congregations was the opposite: not that we became more alike, but that we became more different, or at least more aware of our differences. As the rabbi put it, "When we joined up with you we became more Jewish." Over the years the main lesson for both congregations was how surprisingly different the other one is; but that was coupled, I believe on both sides, with an increase not only in acceptance but appreciation of the other. (The question of pluralism is the particular concern of the essays by Ruth Abbey, Wayne Booth, and Ebrahim Moosa.)

5. *To what degree must any attempt to talk seriously and deeply about religion be communal, rather than simply the voice of an individual speaking to the world?* The suggestion here is that the kind of thought and conversation that will most advance understanding, especially across lines of difference, can only take place under conditions of trust and respect. If this is right, a part of talking about religion well is thinking about the conditions under which it takes place. I think the performance of the seminar as a whole demonstrates the truth

of the principle that talk about religion, to be successful, should be both sharply diverse and deeply communal. Of course one cannot state a set of rules for the successful intellectual community: it is all a matter of tone and style, the effort to recognize and respect particularities of difference. (The essay by Eugene Garver deals explicitly with one aspect of this question.)

6. *What is the significance of the fact that for many people religious experience is deep and individuated, involving the most complete resources of the soul and reflecting profound differences in the structure and motives of the personality?* The point here is that, although religion obviously has its public face—as a branch of culture, as a system of thought, and as a set of practices—it also has a private face, in the world and mind of the individual person, for whom the meaning of what he or she does and believes may be quite different from that of a neighbor whose stated beliefs and external practices may seem virtually identical. This difficulty runs through every effort to talk about religion. How are we to reflect the fact that for one adherent or practitioner a religion may all be a matter of surface obligation, while for another it may call upon and shape and give life to the very deepest aspects of the self or soul? (In this book, the essay by Carol Bier speaks particularly to this question.)

It should be clear by now that the title of our seminar and this book—*How Should We Talk about Religion?*—is to be taken as a statement of the problem we collectively addressed, not as the promise of a prescriptive answer offered by any individual or by us collectively. Each of the authors had his or her own way of talking about religion, and the merit of this collection lies in large part in the diversity of approach—of discipline and background, age and nationality, religious outlook and intellectual commitment—reflected here. Yet perhaps there is something of an answer to our question that can be found in this collection of essays, for we found that we talked together much better—more fully, more deeply, more intelligently—than any of us did alone. To build on one of the themes identified above, if we have an answer to the question "How to talk about religion?" it is this: in intellectual and personal community.

In talking to one another over two intense weeks we found, not surprisingly, that our conversation improved enormously. We came to know each other better, and responded to each other more fully; and as we came to know and trust one another, we discovered that a wider range of sentences became sayable by the speakers, comprehensible by the listeners. (Perhaps a wider range of sentences became unsayable as well.) In some sense a larger part of the mind of each of us came to be engaged in this conversation than is normally the case in academic life. As we proceeded, the particularities of each person—in training, commitment, experience, disposition—came to be acknowledged as a necessary part of the conversation itself, for they were what we brought to it, and what we were responding to in each other. We were engaged in a kind of collective thought, which over time became richer and deeper. One way to put this is to say that the question for each of us became not only how to talk, but how to listen to each other talk, about religion.

None of this is surprising, I think, but it is different from much discourse about religion. Compare with the kind of conversation I am describing, for example, a standard academic attempt to speak on the subject of religion—as a psychologist, say, or anthropologist or theologian or sociologist—beginning, as Plato somewhere has Socrates advise us to begin every intellectual exercise, with a definition: "By *religion* I mean," or "By *Protestantism* I mean," or "By *textualism* I mean . . . ." Here one would be attempting to speak in a universal voice to a universal audience, or if not quite universal, in the voice of a discipline to all members of the discipline. This kind of talk is driven by understandable and meritorious impulses toward clarity, rationality, and neutrality, and of course the enterprise can have great value. But we need to recognize that we may get farther in a different direction working in a different mode, the heart of which is the recognition of particularity: the particularity of the speaker and the audience, the particularity of their context, and the particularity of their subject—which is not religion as a whole, but this or that practice or belief, these sentences or actions, this or that way of imagining the world and acting within it, and as seen from this or that perspective, as the object of this or that question cast in this or that language.

The very fact that we were talking across lines of discipline and language, which was from some perspectives frustrating—none of us could assume that the others in the seminar knew what we could expect everyone in our disciplinary audience to know—had the virtue, among other things, of leading us to think and talk not only about our subject, religion, but also about how we were talking: about the assumptions we were making and about the terms in which we cast our thought. All this gave rise to valuable, if imperfect, self-consciousness about our own disciplinary assumptions and habits, what they were and how they differed from others.

This context made it harder than it often is in an academic setting for each of us to come with hardened positions we were prepared to explicate and defend to the last. And even if we had had such positions, the disciplinary context in which they would have been framed would have been largely meaningless to the others in the group. We were thus forced as it were into a terrain between the languages of our disciplines, or among them, where none of us claimed to know much and all of us were ready to learn. This was an accident of our organization, but one that may have larger lessons for all of us as a general matter.

Our hope in putting together this book is that the reader will have some of the sense that we had, of collective thought taking place across real differences of training, experience, and disposition, and something like our experience of listening to different minds, working independently and together on different versions of the same deep problems of thought and life.

We do not reproduce here the conversation in which we discussed each other's work and the larger issues it presented, but this book does offer the reader the basis for that conversation—the material that gave rise to it—and this should make it possible for him to construct, in his own way, at least the beginnings of such conversation. If that happens the major purpose of the book will have been achieved. This is especially true if our effort to ask how we should talk about religion across lines of disciplinary difference can be seen as related to a larger problem: how to talk about religion across lives of religious difference. In both situations acceptance of difference, willingness to learn, and trust in each other are crucial to any hope of success.

NOTE

A word about the authors, and the point of view from which each proceeded, is presented here not alphabetically but in the order in which their work appears in this book.

- Luis Bacigalupo teaches medieval philosophy at the Catholic University of Peru. His essay deals with the way in which a narrow conception of scientific rationality that entered Western thought in the Middle Ages has distorted much of our thinking both about religion and about rationality itself.
- Clifford Ando, a classicist at the University of Southern California, treats the puzzle of a single event, the transfer of the statue of the goddess known as the Great Mother from Asia Minor to Rome. At every turn he faces up to the opacity of that event, and the inadequacy of our own language of description to comprehend and represent it.

- Scott Appleby, an historian at Notre Dame, addresses the intellectual and imaginative difficulties involved in thinking about fundamentalism as a cross-cultural category. To use this category, or something like it, seems compelled by the facts of recent history; but at the same time it involves us in the deepest puzzles of intercultural and inter-religious thought.
- Sabine MacCormack, from the classics and history departments of the University of Notre Dame, traces out important aspects of the complex relation between Christianity and the religion of the Incas in the Peruvian Andes as it developed over the past five hundred years.
- Bilinda Straight, an anthropologist at Western Michigan University, focuses on difficulties inherent in trying to understand, imagine, and talk about the religion of another culture—in this case that of the Samburu, who live in what is now Kenya.
- Patrick Deneen, a political theorist at Georgetown, uses the work of Tocqueville to trace the complex and paradoxical relation between faith and democracy in America.
- Wayne Booth (1921–2005), who taught in the English department and the Committee on Ideas and Methods at the University of Chicago, argues that a certain kind of rhetorical method can establish a common ground for science and religion—with the aim not of obliterating their differences but rather of enabling more fruitful conversation to take place between them.
- Eugene Garver, a philosopher from St. John's University in Minnesota, addresses the question "When and why should we listen to arguments based on a religion we do not share?" His answer draws on Aristotle, and a conception of rationality that connects reason to the degree of trust between speaker and audience; in the doing so he raises an issue large in all religious discourse.
- Javier Iguíñiz, an economist at the Catholic University of Peru, traces similarities in the premises, methods, and conclusions of Amartya Sen and Gustavo Gutiérrez in their work on economic development.
- Ruth Abbey, a political theorist at Notre Dame, analyzes the work of Charles Taylor, with a particular interest both in the kind of pluralism he recommends and in his intellectual methods, which are opposed to the schematic rationality of much modern philosophy.
- Sol Serrano, an historian from the Catholic University of Chile, writes of the complex relation between Catholicism and modernity in the history of that country.

- Carol Bier, a research associate at The Textile Museum in Washington, D.C., analyzes the geometric basis and theological significance of pattern and design in Islamic art and architecture, connecting them both to Greek philosophy, especially Plato's *Timaeus,* and to Indian arithmetic.
- Jeffrey Kripal, who teaches religious studies at Rice University, writes about the problems and possibilities of talking about religion in the classroom.
- Ebrahim Moosa, who teaches at Duke, was trained as a Muslim theologian. His essay explores the work of Al Ghazālī (1058–1111), whose theory of language and meaning has current relevance in the effort to establish the possibility of more comprehensive and open religious thought, in Islam and elsewhere.

CHAPTER ONE

Talking about Religion in Philosophy

Luis E. Bacigalupo

Luis Bacigalupo, whose field is medieval philosophy, argues that a certain conception of rationality and science entered Western thinking in the late Middle Ages, with the reception of Aristotle, and that this way of thinking has ever since had serious and negative consequences for theology. For a contrasting model he turns to Augustine, who worked in a different way, quite skeptical of the claims of theoretical reason to reach irrefutable truth. Augustine's way of responding to the inadequacy of this kind of reason and science was to focus on questions of conduct and practice, to be governed by wisdom, or on practical reason, to be guided by revelation.

Our own thought about these matters tends to be skewed by the effort of the medieval theologians to achieve in the field of theology and religion the kind of perfect rationality promised by Aristotelian science, an effort that not only failed but led to misperceptions of the nature of religious truth and rationality. All this has real consequences, for a return to the Augustinian mode of thought would lead to a theology that focuses not so much on the ontological perfection of an unknowable God as upon his justice, and upon his demand that we and our conduct be just.

My concern in this essay is the relationship between contemporary understandings of Christian religion and late medieval theology. In every Christian confession we are used to thinking about religion in direct contrast to a modern conception of science, which we tend to identify with reason itself. I think this tendency produces misinterpretations of religion, both when theology tries to harmonize with reason, as in Catholicism, and when theology tries to separate from reason, as is apparently the case in some Protestant trends.

It is thus important to examine the transformation of the notion of "science" in Western history, from its broad premodern version to the more rigidly defined modern conception. This modern understanding has had negative implications for religious thought, for the prestige accorded science and the scientific method has resulted in their being identified with reason, rationality, and even reasonableness. One of the primary effects of this transformation has been to drive a wedge between rational thought and theology, which leaves believers with only two options: they can attempt to narrow the gap, and in the process rescue religion from irrationality, by pursuing theological inquiry in as scientific-like a way as possible. Or they can not only acknowledge the gap but seek to widen it, by making theology as little scientific-like as possible, with the object of challenging scientific rationality through faith. The problem with this second alternative is that, since the equation between reason and science persists, religious discourse tends toward irrationality or emotivism, in the sense for which it is criticized by Alasdair MacIntyre.[1]

To demonstrate the substantive changes in religious thought made in response to the link between science and rationality, I focus here on the conception of "God" itself. This concept serves not only as an instance of late medieval and early modern "theological rationality," but also represents the most significant effect that the modern rise of scientific thought has had on theology. For theology itself has been transformed from a rationalization of religious experience, which included the human being and God in their particular relations, into an analysis of the sort of "scientific" understanding the human being may have of the concept "God." As a consequence, the way in which traditional religious thought expressed God's presence in the lives of believers—namely, in terms of an interpersonal relationship—has been subsumed by the transformation of "God" into an object for intellectual analysis and understanding.

In this essay I try to elucidate premodern religious thought by working out the similarities between radical skepticism and Christianity. I argue that radical skepticism has always been a sort of antidote to the overwhelming authority often granted theoretical rationality—as embodied in science—by those who consider it to be the supreme and ruling expression of Reason. For skeptics traditionally have thought it possible for individuals to be strictly rational in everyday conduct, without having to consult any theoretical science for guidance. We can recognize a similar conviction during premodern Christianity by exploring the influence of Augustine's thought on matters of reason and faith.

Traditional religious rationality is thus understood in this essay as essentially concerned with the singular, personal relation between the individual and God. Skepticism, in its turn, is understood to be concerned with practical issues as they are encountered by the individual, not with the broad generalizations of science. I hope to show that the transformation of premodern Christian theology under the influence of late medieval scientific rationality displaced both the approach to God in terms of singular, personal relationship and the skeptical frame of mind I describe.

Why was this transformation a major loss for Western Christian religion? Part of the answer has to do with the biblical character of Christianity, which offers clues to the religion's spiritual rationality. This is the rationality of hermeneutics, by the authority of which the Christian tradition is seen by its adherents to stand on some fundamental prejudgments. One of the first and most important of these prejudgments is that Revelation is given by God to the human being in the expectation that he or she will understand it. This means that Revelation itself is rational, and that the believer must receive it rationally, not only emotionally. Religious discourse is from the first not a matter of *pathos* alone, but rather of *logos* and *ethos* as well.

The question is, of course, what "rationality" is proper for religion? After "reason" in modern times became equated with analytical science, the putative rationality of Revelation was challenged. Why? Because the *logos* implied in scientific rationality is knowledge of reality acquired by means of a scientific method — that is, it discovers on the basis of its own authority what is real and how that reality works — leading to a collision with the "given" truths of Revelation. But the *logos* implied in nonscientific, skeptical rationality creates no theoretical knowledge of its own, but rather works methodically on the doctrines of Revelation.

What then is the problem of talking about religion in modern times? Once scientific rationality came to monopolize the idea of Reason itself, believers were left to decide between two conflicting worldviews — one "rational" and the other "religious." In time this polarization would lead to a split among Christian believers: those who tried to reconcile the two and those who realized that any such reconciliation was a hopeless task. My suggestion is that both groups were confronted with a false problem.

WHAT RELIGION IS ABOUT: QUESTIONING THE PERVASIVENESS OF MODERN THEOLOGY

For all its diversity, the shape of Western Christian religion in our day has been significantly affected by the way in which modern Christian theology, modern philosophy, and modern culture more broadly were prefigured by the evolution of thought in the late Middle Ages, in both theoretical and practical aspects. Scholastic philosophy played a leading role in that process: with respect to the transformation of the understanding of religion, it took a first decisive step toward modernity in response to its encounter with Aristotle's concept of science, which it sought to make compatible with theology. As a result, some scholastic philosophers and theologians began to think about religion and religious issues in new terms.

The Premodern Concept of Science and Its Relation to Religion

Latin medieval culture between the sixth and early twelfth centuries used the word *scientia* to refer to sources of knowledge transmitted by several encyclopedic works such as Pliny's *Historia naturalis* and Martianus Capella's *De nuptiis Mercurii et Philologiae*. Works like these contained wide-ranging information on diverse matters, and had their remote origins rooted in the great Greek authors of the past.[2] In this context, *scientia* meant a pattern of true knowledge of reality that could be obtained in diverse settings by observing some more or less well-defined procedures. Accordingly, it is understandable that theologians of the day would have hoped their reflections on faith and religious experience would achieve a kind of "scientific" status. Nevertheless, they did not ignore the fact that "science" of God, meaning knowledge of his nature, could not be their ultimate goal insofar as direct knowledge of God was something reserved to the very few, and not in this but in the coming life.

I call this a "premodern" concept of science not only because it was shared by such different theologians as Augustine of Hippo, John Scott Eriugena, Anselm of Canterbury, and Peter Abelard, but also because all these thinkers were active in the period before theology came to be dominated by the works of Aristotle. Hence they thought of science in a non-Aristotelian way. For example, lacking a comprehensive definition of science as such, the attempt was made to conceive the unity of science in terms of the unity of its teaching. From Alcuin of York in the early ninth century, educators elaborated formats of scholarly organization in which different sciences were displayed as if they formed an organic whole,[3] regardless of the variety of the methods of knowledge involved.

In the later years of the premodern period, the sciences generally were divided into five different fields. The first and most important was *scientiae sermocinalis*—that is, the sciences of words—referred to as the *trivium*, where logic played a fundamental role. Then there was *scientiae realis*—the sciences of things—referred to as the *quadrivium,* which importantly was the domain of mathematics. After that came *scientia naturalis,* the natural sciences and physics, which were scarcely developed beyond the encyclopedic sources until the twelfth century. A prominent place was also assigned to *scientia fidei,* the science of faith or theology, which involved a complex set of procedures leading to the true interpretation of the Bible. Finally theologians recognized *scientia Dei*—God's science—meaning the knowledge he has of his creation, that is only indirectly known by the human being through the science of faith.

As we can see, this was a rather wide-ranging use of the term "science," and we may assume that its meaning across the fields was not a very technical one. It referred basically to true knowledge of some aspect of reality acquired through some sort of traditional method. Besides its external unity, obtained by means of scholarly organization, the only commonality we can find among these various uses of *scientia* is that each relies on logical reasoning.

This premodern concept of science did not at all collide with the religious thought of the day. As a part of reality, faith itself could be thought of scientifically without compromising its nature or the nature of scientific thought. Moreover, in Western theology at least since Augustine, it was a traditional assignment put upon theologians to offer in their writings a "scientific" view of faith. Here the sense of "scientific" was as a logical explanation of Christian beliefs (*ratio fidei*), that is, a true knowledge of faith as discovered by the rationality embedded in it (*credo ut intelligam*).

The act of faith present in the first encounter of the believer with God's Word was expected to evolve into a complete and clear knowledge: an understanding of faith (*fides qua creditur*), and a progressive knowledge or understanding of its contents (*fides quae creditur*). No one in this cultural context would claim that such an understanding of faith wasn't *scientia* in the same profound religious sense ascribed to *sapientia Dei rerum.* This term did not mean God's wisdom about things nor human knowledge of God's wisdom as such, but rather human wisdom about the things of God that directly concern human life. It was science "of the faith" in God precisely because humans have no access to God's wisdom directly.

The Modern Concept of Science and Its Influence on the Understanding of Religion

Beginning around the middle of the twelfth century, *scientia* gradually took on a more technical meaning. Philosophers active in the urban schools of the day began to conceive science as true and warranted universal knowledge of the necessary causes of beings, orderly set out in terms of genera and species. Here, one immediately recognizes Aristotle's concept of science, the adoption of which would drastically affect the medieval concept of true human knowledge as well as true divine knowledge, turning both into knowledge of universal necessary objects. There are systematic and historical connections between this Aristotelian concept of *scientia* and later developments in modern times under the new mathematical paradigm. Copernicus's heliocentric cosmos and Galileo's mathematical "perfect mind of God" are perhaps the most renowned of such developments.

What were the implications of the Aristotelian concept of science for the understanding of religion? Science, of course, has to have a subject (*subiectum*), that is, as we would now say, an object of knowledge. But can faith *qua creditur* and religious experience continue to be the subject of theology if theology is to be thought of as a science in Aristotelian terms? Is it possible to know the faith of the believer and his or her religious experience in their universality, as effects of certain necessary causes? All theologians writing after the reception of Aristotle were concerned with questions of this sort. Foremost among them was the question regarding the proper *subiectum* of theology.[4] But the Aristotelian challenge was already set forth: science is only possible of a universal object, whereas faith and religious experience are personal objects.

If we focus on the traditional medieval understanding of religion, this development of scientific knowledge can be seen as a sort of side step that skirts some important aspects of religious thought. For instance, in stating that God is the proper subject of theology instead of faith in Christ and the religious experience embedded in that faith, Christian theologians were forced to make further distinctions in their object of knowledge. So they distinguished between God's essence, unreachable in its singularity, and his virtue and operation, both of which could be known by scientific reason in its generality. That is, the theologians considered the subject of their science in a threefold manner: theoretically postulating (not knowing) the divine substance, and theoretically knowing both Christ and the works of reparation. In this, they could hardly be indifferent to humankind, since Christ and the works of reparation have meaning only in the context of human lives. But the religious person as such was no longer the principal subject of theology.

Therefore one of the first consequences of the new concept of science in religious thought was a reappraisal of the problem of God's threefold nature as it was revealed to humankind. Dogmatic theology had to develop from its metaphysical notion of God's "substance," which it conceived of simply as an eternal and unchangeable nature. To this Platonic characterization of Supreme Being, the notion of God as "pure act" and the concept of an "immovable mover" were added from Aristotelian sources. Therefore, the Christian God was understood as eternal substance, unchangeable and unmoved—as pure act that has complete and necessary knowledge of its proper object of knowledge, which of course includes his creation. The concept of perfection breaks into this logic and stands for all the divine attributes, one of which is God's necessary existence. But the supplanting of the personal ("ethical" and "pathetic") role God played in premodern religious life by this "logical" concept of a perfect God was not without problems.

How, for instance, can we ascribe *pathos*—feeling—to God if he is conceived as perfect: a complete, nonmutable being who neither needs nor is affected by anything external to himself. Must *pathos* and divine substance be so utterly separate? I am unaware of any Western medieval theologian for whom these were not striking questions.[5] Because the logic of its discourse was not conceived in terms of a direct or even indirect "scientific" analysis of the nature of God, premodern religious discourse took the *pathos* of God for granted. It was directly devoted to discovering the ultimate ethical dimension of human life through understanding the mutual *pathos,* divine and human, as revealed to humankind through God's Word.

So long as they remained under the spell of the new notion of science, however, theologians were forced to search for solutions to the puzzling problems it raised. Their main task was to save the unity of theology by reconciling the human experience of God as Love with the concept of God as a perfect, immutable being. These efforts eventually reached so great a sophistication that the gulf between theology and religious faith in everyday life could hardly be bridged. I believe that the Reformation was the first—but certainly not the last—reaction against this neglect of religion by theological sophistication.

Some Questions That Philosophy of Religion Might Settle: What Is Theology About? Is It about Religion?

Was medieval theology bound to operate at such a high level of sophistication, but at such high costs? I am convinced that scholastic theology and philosophy, no matter which particular school of thought we might consider, helped clear the way for some decisive intellectual achievements of modernity, such as international law and economics. Nevertheless, as we have just seen, and as may be the case with all sophistication, one legacy of modernity was the widening gap between intellectual considerations and simple, everyday life. In order to fill that gap, we can now raise a number of questions, some of which were not likely to have been welcomed in the cultural milieu of medieval or modern Europe, or even in the context of contemporary Catholic conservative theology.

The questions I have in mind challenge some of the most deeply rooted presuppositions concerning the comprehension of God. For instance, why is perfection assumed to be an attribute of God? When and why did it become a divine attribute and on what religious basis? Was it theologically necessary as a guard against anthropomorphizing the concept of God? Or was the assumption of divine perfection equivalent to the need of some modern philosophers who constructed metaphysical systems as a way of sustaining a comprehensive picture of reality? Of course I do not have final answers to these questions, but I believe that talking about religion in philosophy should pursue inquiries of this kind.

Let's follow some clues about the assumption of God's perfection to clarify the point I am trying to make. Suppose that two medieval theologians are chatting about the nature of God while walking through a cloister. When the topic of feelings such as love or anger is broached, the theologians are uncomfortable, though they realize that such emotions cannot be excluded from any analysis of God's nature. Searching for a solution one of them recalls that God created humans in his own image, to which the other would probably ask if they are talking of the human being resembling God or God resembling the human being? Peering into the mirror of God that humans were believed to be, one of them finally mentions those aspects of human reason that were perfect or almost perfect. "Such as, you would say?" "Such as the analytical character of scientific reasoning, so well revealed to humankind by God through the Philosopher in his *Posterior Analytics*." "Although never strictly applied to positive knowledge, even by him."[6]

Now, when theologians undertook analyses such as the one above, they inevitably came into conflict with biblical language, which is supported by a completely different rationality. Perceiving the explosive problems this line of thinking posed for theology, other influential thinkers of the thirteenth and fourteenth centuries, like William of Ockham, rejected the rationalistic approach to God of mainstream Scholasticism and adopted a more skeptical theological rationality. According to Ockham, theology cannot be conceived as science at all. But basing their arguments on Aquinas's reputed synthesis of Aristotelianism and Christian belief, hard-line Thomists of the Counter-

Reformation fought back in an effort to gain worldwide acceptance of their comprehensive, scientific Christian theology.

These were modern thinkers already: theologians whose conceptions of religion were affected by the growing prestige accorded to the analytic notion of science. Modern scholasticism was enormously fruitful in many fields of modern European culture, particularly in the development of logic, but also in law, political economy, and ethics, where the teachings of Thomas Aquinas were crucial. But as to metaphysics and epistemology, Thomism struggled to repair a collapsing structure of increasingly conflicting propositions in the effort to preserve an ideal of unity that was in fact quite alien to religious experience. This was the architectural unity of human knowledge, at the top of which theology was placed as the perfect human as well as divine science of God. For their part, Protestant theologies seem to have worked in the direction of separating theological and scientific propositions completely, deconstructing as it were the Thomistic metaphysical efforts and searching for a different understanding of God by means of a revitalized exegetical tradition.

If, as I say, early Christian thinkers expressed little interest in theoretical insights about the nature of God as the Supreme Being, then medieval Aristotelians and modern Thomists might have simply missed the point of that earlier religious thinking. In fact, it does not seem to me that Christian believers of any time would be very much interested in imagining God in terms that pertain to the noblest aspects of the human being: his being, his unity, nor even his truth, reason, or spirit. Do believers really care whether such attributes properly characterize God's nature? I think that religion works exactly the other way round: it cares about the human being as God sees the human being. Or, to put it slightly differently, religion is the effort on the part of human beings to understand themselves as God understands them.

As for the definition of God, "perfection" is not used in the Bible as a divine attribute,[7] whereas divine *pathos* is illustrated throughout the Scriptures. I do not mean that the idea of "perfection" is not to be found in the Bible in any significant sense. But when we read that the work of God is perfect,[8] it means that he is faithful, righteous, and just, which we understand in the first place to be ethical attributes directly connected to human life. When we read that the law of the Lord is perfect,[9] we realize that this means that the law is complete, whole, true, real, genuine—because that is how the law is experienced by this or that individual to heal his or her soul.

As far as I know, there is only one verse in the Bible where perfection is mentioned as an attribute of God himself,[10] but what does Jesus mean when he says:

"Therefore you are to be perfect, as your heavenly Father is perfect"? He surely does not mean "Take a profound intellectual look into God's nature in order to see how far humanity is from being nonmutable, and then use this insight as the cornerstone of your system of beliefs." I believe the passage is better understood to say "Become full-grown, mature persons by listening to this astonishing command my Father is giving to you—'love your enemy'—believing that it is possible, and then fighting against your own mental and moral habits in order to perform it." And the Apostle Paul sounds that same ethical note when he exhorts the members of the church at Rome not to conform to this world, but to be transformed by the renewing of their minds, "so that you may prove what the will of God is, that which is good and acceptable and perfect."[11]

Why, then, must a religious, intellectually cultivated woman or man of our day—Catholic, Protestant, or Jewish—think of the "native" God of the Scripture as a kind of Perfect God of the theologians, that is, as the "imported" Perfect Being of early Greek and modern philosophers, governing the whole of creation, from celestial spheres to subatomic structures, by his nonmutable thought? Why must today's believer, faced with an internal inconsistency in his or her system of beliefs, be left to either ignore the inconsistency—which is what normally happens with theological discourse—or declare it a mystery? And if someone is lucky enough to have resolved all internal inconsistencies within their own system of beliefs, what would they think about religion practiced by people who do not share those beliefs? What I am suggesting, in other words, is that we all would benefit from a profound, well-mediated revision of our own theological heritage.

Searching for the Sense of Our Religious Traditions

Could it be that we lack full understanding both of the so-called secularization process and of our own religious traditions because of a few particular features of modern theological thinking, such as the unquestioned assumption that "perfection = nonmutability" and that perfection is an attribute of God? When we think of God's perfect nature "negatively," in terms that are opposite to the characterizations used to describe human being—for example, that God is *un*changeable because we are changeable—does it really help us better understand ourselves as God's creatures? Are we not doing exactly what Ludwig Feuerbach and many other critics of religion have charged, making it the worship of an idealized Self and thinking of God as the sort of perfect human mind we long for? And, anyway, what does that attribute of God—

his nonmutability—have to say about our imperfect, mutable real lives, beside the implicit message: "Listen, I'm sorry, but you're not like me," which we already knew?

I do not say that we should look at God as "imperfect," whatever that may mean. I only want to raise a simple question: why should we care about those attributes of God that seem so utterly irrelevant for religious life? Now, as a Catholic I have to insist on the fact that putting science aside does not mean that we are not rationally concerned with faith. We are strictly rational in our concern with it. Why then is "agnosticism" such a bad word in the theological tradition of Roman Catholicism? The reason, it seems to me, has to do with the distinction between two different features of rationality: understanding and theoretical knowledge. To say that you do not "know" God in any theoretical sense does not mean that you do not understand him or even that you do not know him in some other sense.

From a more theologically driven perspective, I think that Catholic theologians have traditionally been unreceptive to agnosticism in view of their interest in establishing an organic connection between the metaphysical attributes of God, obtained by theoretical insight into the nature of Being as such, and the ethical implications of the faith of Christ as gleaned from Revelation. This is a need that derives from the late medieval assumption of the unity of theoretical and practical sciences as an organic whole. That is all right so far as it goes, but nobody needs to profess this unity in order to be a Christian. Rational discourse about God need not include the construction and maintenance of this huge scientific, metaphysical structure, nor does it compel belief in the doctrine that postulates it.

Regardless of the points at which we differ, all Christian traditions and schools of thought share a common conviction—namely, that the best source of our understanding, we might even say knowledge, of God is undoubtedly the Bible. Moreover, it is proper to see Scripture not so much as the ground for a rational (or irrational) theology than as the Revelation to reason of God's anthropology. That is, the Bible contains God's anthropology insofar as it depicts man in his nature, and states the pattern of his conduct, and we believe it to be God's Word.[12] Let me again stress the point that it is Revelation to reason in a very strong sense, so that if we were to abandon the scientific method, or whatever other paradigm of science we may have been relying on, this does not mean that we are abandoning strict reasoning at all.

If we actually do as I suggest, we might say we are thinking religiously. Is this the goal of Christian theology, to think religiously about religion? Does

Christian theology include within its ambit the understanding of the nature of faith? If the answers to these questions are "yes"—as I think they once were—then theology should turn away from the scientific, theoretically oriented search for the "knowledge of God," which is so characteristic of the Catholic modern tradition, and regain the much more spiritual and ethical character it had in *premodern* times. For the same reason, it should also abandon the pointless conflict with scientific knowledge. The logic and methodologies underlying scientific theories are properly not shared by religious belief.

Scientific knowledge about the origin of the world can be accepted by the faithful because it does not compete with faith at all. The "science" of faith—if we wish to retain use of the word—need not to be thought of as universal knowledge of abstract necessary causes and beings. The science of faith is not about the nature and status of the physical world; rather, it seeks an understanding of the human being, a coherent discourse about persons enlightened by the presence of God. And there is no need to consider this discourse irrational or emotive because it does not seem to match some kind of scientific paradigm. This would be to concede to the modern prejudice that reason is ultimately a synonym for scientific rationality.

THE THERAPEUTIC ROLE OF SKEPTICISM

How then to talk about religion in philosophy? I assume that the task of philosophers is not to understand religion by describing its function in society and culture, but rather to discern the sorts of claims made in religious discourse and to explore their meanings. I do not presume to have a full understanding of how best to go about this, but propose the following example as a possible starting point: what would follow if Christianity—and perhaps all other religions—were, in the first place, understood to concern the human being, not as seen by humans themselves but rather as seen by God or the gods? What I am suggesting is that religion is not about the nature of divinity but about human life as filtered through what we accept as divine Revelation, which of course implies that divinity cares about humanity. To work out the implications of this hypothesis, we need a heuristic strategy to serve as a touchstone for the project, and I propose for that purpose that we turn to the role radical skepticism has played in Western understandings of Christianity.[13]

Radical Skepticism and Augustine's Conception of Christian Philosophy

In spite of the common assumption to the contrary, I want to suggest that there have been important points of contact between skepticism and Christianity, and point as an example to Augustine's understanding of philosophy as *sacrosanta philosophia*[14] or *nostra philosophia christiana*.[15] Augustine, writing during late antiquity, conceived true philosophy to be identical with true Christian religion,[16] and that non-Christian philosophy is essentially unable to provide knowledge of truth by its own means, although it can occasionally discover some truths by luck.[17] For Augustine, philosophy can be the bearer of truth only because of God's Revelation of himself as the Truth.[18]

Augustine's assertion that a non-Christian philosophy or natural theology is essentially incapable of embodying anything more than a mere approximation of the truth[19] stands on a common epistemological ground with radical skepticism. In spite of the most obvious difference between them, both views share a basic epistemic structure as to whether truth can fully be attained by the human mind. Concerning theoretical knowledge, both Augustine and radical skeptics would accept that human minds could reach partial truths by chance. As a Christian, however, Augustine goes beyond this bare assertion to acknowledge that humans may be in possession of practical truth in the form of true belief, though only with divine assistance.

To make this point differently, a radical skeptic would never judge the truth value of propositions, whether the truth claimed is theoretical or practical. Augustine pronounces his outlook openly, arguing that theoretical truth of the sort appropriate to science can be attained by chance, but that practical truths can be reached by human beings only with the assistance of God. So what radical skeptics and Augustine do have in common is that they doubt the mind's capability of reaching practical truth on its own.

I propose that this limitation on the operations of reason is an essentially skeptical feature of Augustine's thought. This is not to say, of course, that Augustine himself was a skeptic. He obviously cannot be considered as such because of his conviction that God has revealed himself as Truth to humankind, which is capable of partially knowing that Truth in this life, and entirely in Eternity. Moreover, unlike the skeptics, he does not reject science as a pointless endeavor, though he assigns it a clearly subordinate position in relation to wisdom.[20] Wisdom results from the true opinion about God's revelation that is inspired in the minds of the faithful. These true beliefs enable the partial knowledge of God, but a fuller understanding of human life gleaned from the rational interpretation of God's revealed Word and Will. The divine Revelation reveals more about humanity as creatures of God than about the nature of divinity itself.

Evidence for this skeptical matrix as a feature of Augustine's thought can be found in two of his well-known theses. The first one is that wisdom does not imply the kind of complete and direct knowledge of its object that is claimed by theoretical sciences such as natural theology, physics, or mathematics, since wisdom is knowledge of God through Christ[21]—that is, at least during one's present life, it is always *interposita persona*. The second thesis is that there cannot be science of spiritual things because science is a *ratio inferior*,[22]—that is, rationality applied exclusively to temporal objects. On the basis of these two theses, Augustine can be seen to be making a rather complicated separation between temporal and spiritual objects of knowledge, turning on its head the way these are normally related, both now and in classical epistemology (Plato and Aristotle).

Temporal objects are the subject matter of theoretical sciences, whereas spiritual objects are the proper subject of wisdom or religion. Augustine at this juncture does not dwell so much on temporal objects, and he is highly skeptical of the mind's ability to achieve true knowledge of spiritual objects on its own. Like the Apostle Paul, Augustine entirely rejects all worldly wisdom's claim of truth. Divine wisdom or true religion involves essentially practical knowledge, that is, knowledge in the form of beliefs about how humans should conduct their lives in order to gain happiness or salvation. Augustine's epistemic levels are therefore arranged as follows: at the top of the scheme is heavenly wisdom, which consists of true belief or true practical knowledge of spiritual things; and on the bottom is science, which consists of theoretical knowledge of temporal objects or worldly wisdom.

In turning the common hierarchical order of theoretical and practical reason on its head, and in setting clear limits to the role and capacity of reason in both domains, Augustine is standing on a common ground with radical skeptics. In relegating science to the lower epistemic level, they both discard scientific, theoretical doctrines as incapable of producing knowledge of any significance for practical life. They reject the assumption in Platonic epistemology that any well-cultivated individual could derive true rational knowledge to guide her praxis from a theoretical knowledge of the Good. In other words, Augustine and radical skeptics do not believe that practical reasoning depends on any kind of theoretical insight into reality.

Once theoretical knowledge was put aside as a source for truth in practical matters, radical skeptics sought an alternative form of reasoning directly devoted to the unavoidable matters of everyday life. This other kind of rationality had to be dialectical rather than analytical, probable rather than conclusively true (as the theoretical sciences claimed their knowledge to be). In any case practical reason ought not depend on any theoretical doctrine, which means that it can stand by itself without the support of a full-blown, rationalistic depiction of the cosmic order. Consequently radical skeptics pursued a pragmatic interpretation of sense data in order to reach rationality in practical matters. This was their worldly wisdom.

Augustine's Christian philosophy achieves nearly the same. In a very Pauline fashion, it discards worldly science as incapable of leading the way to salvation.[23] But, here unlike the skeptics, rather than engaging entirely on a pragmatic reading of sense data, Augustine focuses on the rationality of the narrative that emerges from biblical hermeneutics. Of course, this narrative constitutes itself as a doctrine that is part of God's unfolding Revelation, and therefore produces a kind of knowledge from which morals are to be derived. But it is not primarily or essentially theoretical knowledge. Although not as strictly pragmatic as that of the skeptics, for Augustine Christian doctrine is nevertheless essentially practical rationality.

Some Consequences for Medieval Philosophy

Having sketched in broad outline the basic Augustinian understanding that Christian doctrine and belief fundamentally—although not exclusively—pertain to practical, not theoretical or scientific, rationality, I now move to some issues of medieval philosophy concerning the nature of religion. For obviously, if this epistemological common ground between radical skepticism and Christian religion really obtains, we should be able to find traces of it in the Middle Ages, since Saint Augustine was one of the most influential thinkers during that time. In this part of the essay, then, I suggest that this implicit relation between such different philosophies—radical skepticism and Augustinism—did indeed fruitfully operate in the minds of medieval theologians for centuries. It came dramatically to an end in the twelfth century, however, with the reception of Aristotle's work in logic, where his concept of science is found.

Thus I come to the two different moments of this process that I usually refer to in my teaching as "before" and "after" the Latin reception of Aristotle.

In the BA period (meaning "Before Aristotle") I focus on the pre-Scholastic understanding of philosophy and theology, particularly on the use of crucial concepts like "reason" and "faith" by such authors as Anselm of Canterbury and Peter Abelard. The relationship between Christian religion and philosophy during this period is very much the same as the one established by Augustine, except for the much more subtle use of logic by the medieval authors. Incorporating this increased emphasis on logic, pre-Scholastic philosophy can be seen as *ancilla theologiae* in the sense of using logical reasoning to expose the logic of faith in a nondoctrinal and therefore nonconflicting manner.

Theoretical science in this context, as said, plays no significant part. All doctrines about God, the soul, and the world needed for religious life come from Revelation and tradition, mediated of course by philosophical concepts, but not dependent on any one body or school of philosophical work. This nondoctrinal philosophy—that is, the rules of logic and their embodiment into the art of interpretation—had the task of giving the religious doctrines a kind of "scientific" or rational status, which means it had to make its truth logically manifest.

In the period after the reception of Arisotle, the Aristotelian notion of analytical science brought an abrupt end to the pre-Scholastic conception of Christian philosophy. From an epistemological point of view, the important difference between the two is that in the later period philosophy becomes substantially doctrinal—which is to say that it embodies knowledge about the nature of things—and therefore becomes profoundly anti-skeptical. In the wake of this change, a conflict between the practical rationality of the skeptics and theoretical knowledge claimed by the Scholastics was inevitable.

The conflicts surrounding the reason of faith (*ratio fidei*) and faith understood as a set of rational beliefs concerning the condition and conduct of human life would dominate the work of medieval theologians. With the ascendance of Aristotelien modes of thought, however, an assertion of the earlier rational pragmatism could not meet the new standards for scientific rationality and truth now imposed by Aristotle in order to harmonize with reason. As we know, Dominicans and Franciscans disputed because some of the Grey Friars were able to perceive the destructive consequences of this enormous transformation of Christian rationality.[24]

Thomas Aquinas searched for a solution to the problems produced by the attempt to transform revealed theology into an analytical, theoretical science in Aristotelian terms. His main contribution in this task was to locate faith at a higher epistemological position than either mere belief or mere human scientific knowledge. Faith became equal to the "science God has"; equal in its contents, but viewed only partially by man during this life—thus, "faith." Thomism is an impressive achievement, to be sure, yet it is heavily burdened with philosophical doctrines alien to faith itself. For example, you must believe in a world made of substances, and these as made of matter and form, and so on.

It is important to point out that the rejection of skepticism and the ascendancy of strict Aristotelian modes of scientific and analytic rationality was contested within the Catholic tradition itself. In fact, skepticism and rationalism would at some level remain engaged in a fruitful, dialectical tension in other contexts, particularly those concerning the development of natural science. Thus, in speaking about religion, we should be careful not to talk in terms that exclude or diminish the roles of both rationalism and faith.

Some Political Implications: Practical Skepticism and Christian Faith

What political developments are implied in this evolving relation between reason and religion during the Middle Ages? In the classroom study of political thought during that period, using such leading works as that by the historian Walter Ullmann,[25] I call the attention of my students to the medieval origins of political liberalism. For that purpose I concentrate on philosophers of the late thirteenth century such as Aquinas and Dante, and of the early fourteenth century such as Marsilius of Padova and Ockham. The goal is to uncover the roots of Michael Oakeshott's thesis regarding the dichotomy characterizing modern political philosophy.[26]

Oakeshott argues that Western political thought oscillates between the politics of faith and the politics of skepticism. In the first of these, political views rest on a strong doctrinal basis; the politics of skepticism, however, is driven by a dialectical, nondoctrinal confrontation with what are seen to be unique historical and political circumstances, a confrontation that is nevertheless supported by a strong traditional basis. It's the difference between saying: "This is how things should be done because it follows from our doctrine of human nature as social being" and "This is how things were done till now and we'll see if it still works or if we have to make some arrangements based on some traditional principles." The interesting point here is that Oakeshott admitted to not extending his research to look for medieval antecedents of his thesis, and assumed in particular that the nondoctrinal confrontation of the sort just mentioned was essentially a modern development of European (Western) political thought.

In my research and teaching I try to sort through medieval political theology, using as a framework Oakeshott's thesis regarding the dichotomy of modern political philosophy. Of course, understanding the political doctrines of late medieval philosophers is far more complicated than merely arranging them along a bipolar scheme, but an illuminating starting point is always helpful. Thus guided by the Oakeshottian thesis, I start with Augustine, of course, then move forward to the popes Gelasius I and Gregory the Great, followed at the end of the great medieval Reformation period by the political implications of Peter Abelard's ethics, finally reaching Scholasticism.

For what am I searching? My quest is for medieval political doctrines we could understand to be both liberal and ethical. Moreover, these doctrines must also be "skeptical" in the sense I've been using that term in this essay: they are not to be deduced from philosophical doctrines (that is, from theoretical knowledge about the human being), nor from political theories rooted in principles other than those of our religious tradition. In other words, I'm after one or more ethical principles sustaining moral-political doctrines about what God demands from the human being "as an individual" living in a particular society.[27] Here my goal is to overturn Oakeshott's insistence that only doctrinal grounds for the politics of skepticism can be found to operate during the Middle Ages.

As for political liberalism, my goal is to find whether some of the principal characteristics of liberal thought are reflected in medieval thinkers. There are basically two such characteristics with which I am concerned here: first, radical individualism, in the sense that practical reasoning places the dignity of the individual person above any other interest, and second, the intention to universalize this individualism as an absolute ethical principle.[28] Both liberal characteristics are supposed to have played an essential role in the modern development of such concepts as freedom, justice, government, and social order.

My hypothesis is that a number of medieval thinkers can be grouped together as evincing a certain liberal sense of justice—skeptical in Oakeshott's terms,[29] biblical or prophetic from a religious point of view. It is a sense of justice that is fundamentally ethical in character, and therefore contrary to the mainly political and judicial view of justice characteristic of Aristotle and Roman law as inherited by the Christian West during the Middle Ages. The results of this inheritance are not so much the coercive rationality of theoretical science as they are the systematic and comprehensive doctrines regarding the individual person.

The questions that arise at this juncture include the following: What has political skepticism to do with Christianity? Is it only coincidence that both liberalism and a certain understanding of Christianity focus on the dignity of the person when they seek to discern good and evil in human conduct and action? Is it only coincidence that both reject comprehensive political doctrines—ideologies—because they underlie most misinterpretations of human nature and misuse of political power?

In pondering these questions, I have found a clue for the direction this inquiry might best take. It is a verse in Matthew—indeed, I call it the "Matthew Principle." As a principle of moral justice, I find it to be of the utmost significance that precisely the same verse is explicitly misused today by the apostles of cynicism who preach the gospel of economic rationality called "neoliberalism": "For to everyone who has, more shall be given, and he will have in abundance; but from the one who does not have, even what he does have shall be taken away."[30]

THINKING RELIGIOUSLY ABOUT JUSTICE

To a significant extent, Christianity today may be understood to remain captive to the thought patterns rooted in the late medieval period that came to dominate modern philosophy and theology—namely, those that privilege science and the scientific method. The primary danger of this tendency lies in what it leads us to forget, but what I call the "Matthew Principle" is meant to counter that forgetfulness. This principle prompts us to remember that when talking about religion or, even better, when thinking religiously about justice, it is not that God should be understood to be like humans (though perfected in all attributes) but that human beings must become like God. This means that God's Word does not consist of logical arguments leading to scientific knowledge. We must learn to think differently—to think like God—if we are to hear his Word.

For instance, God does not conceive of justice in the way most of humanity does. This is what we learn from Matthew 25:29, where Jesus' words would hardly be judged fair by human standards: "For to everyone who has, more shall be given, and he will have in abundance; but from the one who does not have, even what he does have shall be taken away." So the human being who seeks to become more like God has to overcome his or her own concept of justice. "Try to think like God" means "try *not* to think as men and women usually do." But is that really possible? Our religious tradition, predating the modern era, provides an answer: we are to believe it is. The implicit message of that tradition is "Do not pretend to know what God thinks, because that's to think like humans usually do." To believe in God, to have faith in his will and therefore to be certain of it, does not consist of any kind of direct knowledge. It implies a rational praxis.

We ordinarily think there is no difference between being certain of something and knowing it directly. But in light of the skeptical outlook we considered earlier, we should realize that in this, at least, we are wrong. Recall also the example of Job. He does not pretend to know that God is being just with him. How could he "know" that after all he's been through? Yet he "believes with all certainty" and counter to everyday common sense that God is just, and that makes him just before God. Is Job acting irrationally? Not at all, because it is reason of a kind—a rational skepticism—that calls into question the possibility for direct and theoretical knowledge of God's justice. It is that same reason that sustains his faith and provides the nonrefutable truth that he does not know his ultimate destiny, which rests in God's power.

As I noted earlier, the pervasive modern conception of science has greatly influenced religious thought and led us to ask the wrong questions. We have sought a scientific understanding of that which cannot be defined or measured by the scientific method. What is the point of asking about the nature of God? What is the point of the theological determination of his nature as "perfect," eternal and nonmutable. These may go some of the way toward satisfying the modern human longing to "know" that which, in the end, it cannot know. In this light, I suggest that if we only liberate ourselves from this modern pattern of thinking, we can see that rationality of a different sort leads us to think of God as absolutely just rather than perfect. Why justice? Why not continue to focus on and refine the "perfected" attributes of God? The answer is that pursuing an understanding of justice makes sense in view of its many connections to our everyday practical lives, whereas God's perfection as nonmutable tells us nothing about the relations between God and humanity. Religious experience is not subject to the scientific method. It is the belief in God as just, then, that reveals God's sharing our joy and suffering.

In this essay I have warned against the tendency, which can be traced from the modern era to the present day, to understand God in terms of the "perfection" of attributes that in reality pertain only to humans. This has been the theological legacy of the overwhelming power of theoretical reason as embodied in science and the scientific method—that God mirrors human being. As an antidote to counter this ascendency of the theoretical, I have proposed a return to radical skepticism as practiced inadvertently by Augustine and others, for whom human beings mirror God, however darkly. But note that reason nonetheless plays a signficant role in that mirroring, the concern of which is practical rather than theoretical. It is a religious rationality that never divorces *logos* from *ethos* and *pathos,* and that furthermore relies on the results of biblical hermeneutics to deepen our (nonscientic, but rational) faith in the justice of God.

NOTES

1. See Alasdair MacIntyre, *After Virtue* (Notre Dame, Ind.: University of Notre Dame Press, 1984), 23 ff.

2. See Edward Grant, *The Foundations of Modern Science in the Middle Ages: Their Religious, Institutional and Intellectual Contexts* (Cambridge: Cambridge University Press, 1996), 9–14.

3. For an overview of all these schemes, see Celina A. Lértora Mendoza, "El concepto y la clasificación de la ciencia en el Medioevo (SS. VI–XV)," in *A Ciência e a Organização dos Saberes na Idade Média,* ed. Luiz Alberto de Boni (Porto Alegre: EDIPUCRS, 2000), 57–83.

4. See Ulrich Köpf, *Die Anfänge der theologischen Wissenschaftstheorie im 13. Jahrhundert* (Tübingen: Mohr, 1974), 79 ff.

5. Early Christian theologians in the East avoided much of the predicament by dividing theology in two, reserving metaphysical and mystical insights into the nature of divinity for the few capable of understanding such high-flung speculation. The other kind of theology—which was not considered secondary in rank—used metaphorical, allegorical language and was practiced for the benefit of a less sophisticated audience.

6. See Grant, *Foundations of Modern Science,* 142–44.

7. Abraham Heschel, *Between God and Man: An Interpretation of Judaism* (New York: Free Press, 1965), 97–98.

8. Deuteronomy 32:4.

9. Psalm 19:7.

10. Matthew 5:48.

11. Romans 12:2.

12. See Heschel, *Between God and Man.*

13. The following sketch of radical skepticism is based on Sextus Empiricus's *Outlines of Pyrrhonism.*

14. *De ordine* I, XI 31.

15. *Contra Iulianum* IV 14.

16. *De vera religione* V 8, 25.

17. *De Civitate Dei* VIII 1.

18. *De doctrina christiana* II 18, 28.

19. *De Civitate Dei* VIII 9.

20. *De diversis quaestionibus octaginta tribus* q. 81.

21. *De beata vita* IV 34.

22. *De Trinitate* XII 15, 25.

23. *De Civitate Dei* VIII 11.

24. See David Knowles, *The Evolution of Medieval Thought* (Harlow [UK]: Longman, 1998), 213 ff.

25. Walter Ullmann, *A History of Political Thought: The Middle Ages* (Harmondsworth: Penguin Books, 1965).

26. See Michael Oakeshott, *The Politics of Faith and the Politics of Scepticism* (New Haven: Yale University Press, 1996).

27. See Oakeshott's Harvard lecture entitled "The Religious Version [of the Political Theory of Collectivism]," in Oakeshott, *Morality and Politics in Modern Europe* (New Haven: Yale University Press, 1993), 89 ff.

28. See John Gray, *Liberalisms: Essays in Political Philosophy* (London: Routledge, 1991).

29. See also Richard E. Flathman, *Toward a Liberalism* (Ithaca: Cornell University Press, 1989).

30. Matthew 25:29.

CHAPTER TWO

Idols and Their Critics

Clifford Ando

How is one to understand the rituals, practices, and beliefs of another people or culture, especially one located in the past and thus not open to questioning in the usual ways? Clifford Ando here addresses this general issue in a highly specific context, asking what the Romans can possibly have meant when they spoke about the signal event in which the goddess Cybele was transferred from Pessinus, in Asia Minor, to Rome. What physical object was transferred and what relation did it have to the goddess? Was it only an image, and if so, why was its transfer a matter of any particular moment? Or was the goddess herself somehow present in the object, and if so, exactly how was this presence imagined? Is she present, for example, only in this unique material manifestation? If so, what happens if it is lost at sea or otherwise destroyed?

In his exploration of these matters Ando discovers and examines a marked contrast between two different ways of imagining the act of representation—indeed different ways of imagining matter and materiality—both of which have ancient roots. One of them but not the other continues into our own day and thus clouds our perception of the past. Only by reviving relevant ancient understandings on these points can we begin to understand events such as the "transfer" of the "goddess" to Rome. In all of this Ando establishes an attitude and method, a set of questions, that could be of real value in any investigation of the religious life of others.

The critique of idolatry has a long and distinguished history in the philosophical and religious literatures of Greece and Rome, and indeed of Christian Europe.[1] The sophistication of that tradition, and of its modern students, has in many ways overdetermined the study of idolatry itself, as though ancient philosophers or medieval or early-modern Christians could be expected to describe accurately and faithfully the workings and presuppositions of Greco-Roman religiosity.[2] This essay explores the impact of that tradition in one area of inquiry: the metaphysical status and representational function of the idols themselves. Simply stated, Plato advanced a philosophy of representation that has required scholars to treat idols as either being or representing gods; the cogency of this polarity depends, I shall argue, on a theory and theology of matter at odds with ones widely accepted in the ancient world.

THE STONE THAT WAS THE GODDESS

Our ability to recognize the strangeness of Greco-Roman religion and to comprehend its rituals depends in large measure on our understanding of its idols.[3] Reconstructions of Greek and Roman rituals reveal that virtually all included the gods as participants.[4] Indeed, the few rituals held without the gods inevitably observed their absence: the *sellisternium,* for example, consisted in part of a parade of empty chairs, in direct contrast to the *lectisternium,* a feast at which wicker representations of the heads of gods rested on couches and shared a meal.[5] Richard Gordon called attention to this problem in a famous article on religious art, in which he observed that Pausanias was as likely to refer to "Athena" as to "a statue of Athena" when he described any given temple.[6] At one level, Gordon did no more than revisit a long-standing puzzle, namely, the tendency of participants in Greek and Roman cult to confuse "image and prototype, represented and representation."[7] As Johannes Geffcken observed long ago, this charge had been the mainstay of rationalizing critics of idolatry throughout antiquity; Geffcken could do little more than document that fact, however, because he affirmed it. According to him, this confusion of categories was symptomatic of the "simplistic habits and superstitions *des Volkes.*"[8]

Few recent scholars have taken up the challenge presented by Gordon's observation, namely, that of explaining the seeming confusion of ontological categories implied by Pausanias's diction, in large measure because they, like Geffcken, unwittingly subscribe to a theory of representation incompatible with pagan religiosity. For example, although several scholars have catalogued rituals in which idols were treated as gods and fed, washed, and clothed, none of them sought to explain the philosophical or theological underpinnings of this behavior.[9] Scholarship on rituals in which humans took the place of gods has with few exceptions been similarly abortive: extensive research has revealed that such rituals continued to be performed well into the Christian era, but they are labeled the relics of earlier religiosity and their survival evidence of institutional formalism.[10] Jas Esner's discussion of "image as ritual," in his essay arguing for a "religious way of viewing images," and Greg Woolf's kindred study of the Jupiter columns, constitute two important exceptions to these generalizations, both explicitly indebted to Gordon's work.[11]

Research in other areas of Greek and Roman religion has made significant advances in unpacking ancient descriptions of religious art. For example, Greek and Latin terminology for statuary always reflected the ontological status of the individual depicted and could record whether or not a given statue had been ritually consecrated.[12] Similarly, Greeks brought to the appreciation of religious art a complex aesthetic that distinguished it from other forms of artistic production and assimilated it to a specifically literary theological discourse.[13] For their part, the Romans positioned artwork in their temples in patterns that reflected ontological hierarchies, from god to human, whose appreciation might well aid modern investigations of Roman theological literature and imperial cult.[14] But this ancient sophistication in marking and observing metaphysical boundaries—through language, ritual, and law—has not elicited a correspondingly sophisticated and sympathetic explanation for the theology of idols and sacrality of material objects.[15]

Let me start with an episode from the history of Rome, whose narratives, ancient and modern, neatly illustrate my concerns. In the last years of the Hannibalic war, the Romans were told to bring Cybele, the mother of the gods, from Pessinus to Rome.[16] Rejoicing in the many omens and prophecies that presaged its ultimate victory, the Senate gathered to deliberate "by what means the goddess should be transported to Rome" (*quae ratio transportandae Romam deae esset*).[17] It is not mere captiousness that leads me now to quote the Penguin translation of Aubrey de Sélincourt, who wrote for this clause, "the best means of transferring the *image* of the Goddess to Rome."[18] For the anxiety felt by the twentieth-century translator when confronted by a goddess who was a rock, which led him to replace the goddess with her image, was shared by Livy himself, and it is the history of that anxiety, as much as anything, that requires, indeed, demands elucidation.

I say that Livy shared this anxiety because he vacillated in his estimation of the metaphysical or existential status of Cybele's *baitulos* (her sacred—possibly meteoric—stone). In Livy's narrative, the Senate sent legates to Attalus of Pergamum and sought his aid in obtaining the goddess. "Attalus received the Romans amicably, led them to Pessinus in Phrygia, gave them the sacred stone which the natives said *was* the mother of the gods, and ordered them to take it to Rome."[19] The qualms reflected in the diction of that sentence had disappeared by the time the *lapis niger* arrived in Rome: there Publius Cornelius Scipio was ordered to meet the *goddess* at Ostia; there he received *her* from the ship; and in the temple of Victory on the Palatine he installed the *goddess* on the day before the Ides of April, 204.[20]

Ovid's narrative of Cybele's arrival shares this feature with Livy's history: he referred to the stone as the goddess at every opportunity but one, when he described Claudia Quinta fixing her gaze "on the image of the godess" (*in imagine divae*).[21] But not everyone felt this need to distance themselves from those who identified idol and goddess. Writing four centuries later in defense of the altar and statue of Victory in the Senate house, Quintus Aurelius Symmachus asked the emperor, "Where shall we swear to obey your laws and decrees? By what scruple will the deceitful mind be terrified, lest it perjure itself under oath? To be sure, all things are full of god, nor is any place safe for perjurers. Nevertheless, the *praesentia numinis,* the presence of the goddess, is a powerful inducement to a fear of wrong-doing."[22] It is, I think, insufficient to say that Symmachus has done no more than elide a distinction between image and prototype, even in the service of a psychological or emotional understanding of religious art. For what was at stake for him in his quarrel with Ambrose, bishop of Milan, who wished to remove the altar and statue, was a great deal more than a philosophy of representation.

Let me provide two more examples to further define my aim in this essay. In the first chapter of *Mimesis,* Erich Auerbach famously contrasts Homeric and biblical narratives in their strategies for "representing reality." The episodes he recounts in that chapter are Eurykleia's recognition of Odysseus's scar and the sacrifice of Isaac in Genesis 22. He identifies the impulse of Homeric style as a desire "to represent phenomena in a fully externalized form, visible and palpable in all their parts, and completely fixed in their spatial and temporal relations."[23] Of course, the interaction between two metaphysically equivalent subjects lends itself to this reading; the question is why Auerbach contrasts the one encounter between two humans with another between God and a man. Although he alludes in a single line to the occasional arrival of Zeus or Poseidon from feasts of the Aethiopians, he refrains from suggesting that Homeric poetry and its representational impulses could have theological implications, as the representation of God in Genesis surely does; indeed, by refusing to select true comparanda, he denies the texts equivalent sacrality. Classical literature is, on his reading, not religious literature at all.

Second, in a homily delivered late in the 390s, Augustine berates his audience for celebrating the birthday of Carthage in a public feast for the Genius of the city. Had they not known that they were practicing idolatry? "It is no god, someone says, because it is the genius of Carthage. As though, were it Mars or Mercury, it would be a god. But learn how it is regarded by them: not for what it is. For you and I know that it is a stone. . . . But they regard [the genius] as a *numen,* and they accept that statue in the place of the *numen;* the altar testifies to this. What is the altar doing there, if the genius is not regarded as a *numen?* Let no one tell me, 'It is not a *numen;* it is not a god.' I have already said, 'Would that they knew this, as we all do.' But that altar testifies to their belief concerning the genius and the statue and to their practice. It convicts the minds of those who worship it; let it not convict those who recline before it."[24]

To the evident concern of an Ovid or a Livy with the representational capacity of religious art, Augustine added an indictment against the materiality of the idols themselves—he and his fellow Christians knew that the statue was merely a stone—as well as a denial that pagan divinities had a metaphysical status equivalent to that of the true god.[25] These related concerns, the seemingly irreducible materiality of idols, on the one hand, and the seeming impossibility of representing anything invisible and incorporeal in or through matter, on the other, formed the basis of all critiques of idolatry in Greco-Roman literature. I want now selectively to review that tradition, in perhaps more philosophical terms than is customary, for what it can reveal about the problems of writing about religion in the ancient and modern worlds, and of reading what has been written.

IDOLS AS (MIS)REPRESENTATIONS: PLATO AND THE TRADITION OF CRITIQUE

Even the limited fragments that we now possess reveal that Presocratic philosophers were preoccupied with the issues that were later to exercise Augustine. Xenophanes' famous attack on anthropomorphism, for example, censured it as more than a strategy of representation. Of course, cattle that could draw would draw gods that looked like cattle, as humans drew gods with human forms; but anthropomorphism also concretized theological and metaphysical presuppositions of far greater moment, of which the joke about cattle and horses and lions was merely a *reductio ad absurdum.*[26] And although Heraclitus attacked the forms of contemporary religious ritual with particular vehemence, like Xenophanes he did so because he believed that ritual expressed beliefs that he found insupportable. Insisting that idols as material objects had the same metaphysical status as other such objects—he likened praying to a statue to conversing with one's house—he lamented that devotees of idols did not understand the true nature of the gods.[27]

It was Plato, not surprisingly, who exercised the greatest influence on the critique of idolatry. He might have been expected to do so through his attack on the immorality of traditional mythopoesis, but those sections of the *Republic* were largely ignored until their arguments were appropriated by Christian apologists of the second century and beyond.[28] Rather, it was his complex subordination of representation and epistemology to metaphysics that sounded the death knell for sympathetic appreciations of idolatrous religiosity among later intellectuals, both pagan and Christian.[29]

Of course, Plato had severe misgivings about the status of images depicting even material objects. Early in the *Cratylus,* for example, he drew an analogy between producing images of Cratylus and reproducing the number ten. Take anything away from ten and it is no longer ten. So, a perfect image of Cratylus would be another Cratylus. What, then, is the principle of correctness with which we can judge images?[30] Where representation as such was concerned, Plato answered this question most fully early in the *Sophist.* Writing there of the art of image making, which he called ἡ εἰδωλοποιικὴ or εἰκαστική τέχνη, Plato argued that artists must necessarily leave behind the truth in order to give their creations not the actual proportions of their exemplars, but such proportions as *seem* to be beautiful. For this reason, plastic images, which are called "likenesses" because they are "like" their prototypes, do not even deserve that name, but should be called φάντασμα, appearances.[31]

In the *Cratylus,* the quest for a provisional principle of correctness by which to judge images soon yields to a very different question, one framed as a choice between starkly opposed alternatives. Is it better to learn about the truth of things from images of them, and from those images to conjecture about the accuracy of the image itself? Or is it better to learn the truth from the truth, and on that basis to judge its representations?[32] By equating paradigm or prototype with truth, Plato transformed a problem of representation into one of epistemology. This argumentative sleight of hand has its analog in the *Sophist* too. In that work, Theaetetus and the Stranger had reached a seeming paradox, that insofar as being belongs to that which is true, and images are inherently false because inaccurate, neither images or idols nor appearances can exist at all, in any way, at any time.[33] But they soon satisfied each other that both false speech and false opinion were possible, and this allowed them to concede a form of existence to imitations of things that really are.[34]

Plato has shifted ground once again. For what are these things that really are? Not Cratylus, of course, nor any corporeal object: for all such things are subject to generation and corruption, and insofar as they are always in flux, no knowledge of them is possible. What had seemed an argument about epistemology has its foundation in a simple, indeed simplistic, ontology. It informed much of Plato's work, including analogies he drew with image making. So, for example, he likened the particular examples used by geometricians to so many images in water, εἰκόνες ἐν ὕδασιν, used for seeking realities that are visible only through intellection.[35]

These varied strands of argument find their nexus in the *Timaeus*. Early in that work, Plato distinguished between two kinds of things: those that are and have no origin, and those that are always in a process of becoming but never are. The former are apprehended by intelligence along with reason; the latter by opinion with the aid of sense perception.[36] Understood in these terms, he observed, the world itself is an object of sense perception and must have been created through participation in some object of intellection: the world, in other words, is a copy of something.[37] But applying words like "image" and "paradigm" to cosmogonic processes made Plato uneasy. He had earlier deliberated whether to designate the universe by οὐρανός or κόσμος or some other name, and lamented that it would be impossible to speak even the little that one might know of the father and maker of the world.[38] He no longer hesitated. In speaking in this way, he continued, we must assume that words are akin to that which they describe: when they relate to the lasting and permanent and intelligible, they ought to be irrefutable and unalterable; but when they express only likeness, words need only be similar or analogous to what they describe. The problem of representation was thus resolved by the paradoxical assertion that the words of discursive language can represent the truly existent more accurately than objects of like metaphysical status to themselves, namely, those subject to generation and decay. "As being is to becoming," Plato could then conclude, "so truth is to belief."[39]

Plato had begun by positing a direct connection between a particular ontology and a set of epistemological distinctions, and only a few pages later used the same two assertions, before either had been proved, to complete a syllogism about representation. Later in the *Timaeus* he returned to problems of representation, asking whether one can designate corporeal objects using ταὐτόν, since doing so would make a complex assertion about the identity and ontological integrity of the object in question. Plato concluded that only that which receives all bodies and all forms can be so designated, because it never departs from its own nature and never participates in any way in any form. It is the mother and receptacle of all created and visible and sensible things, and yet it cannot be called "earth" or "air" or "fire" or "water," but is an invisible and shapeless form; all-receiving, it participates in some way in the intelligible and is itself utterly incomprehensible.[40]

So far, so good. But Plato closed this section by turning once again to epistemology. "There: I have put forth my argument. If mind and correct opinion are two different categories, then there must be self-existent ideas, which are not susceptible to sense perception but are apprehended only by the mind."[41] Only Plato would state this last argument as a conditional. It only begins to make sense if one remembers (as any Platonist would, I suppose) that the epistemological distinction between knowledge and belief rests on a metaphysical hierarchy conceived in ontological terms.

ART AS ALLEGORY

What has all this to do with idols? A great deal. In what follows, I shall follow modern trends in the study of ancient philosophy and treat the twin foundations of idolatry critique separately, concentrating first on representation and then materiality.[42] But these two cannot be entirely divorced. On the contrary, I argue in closing that it is presuppositions about materiality and metaphysics that lead us, as they led Augustine, to insist that idols must be—indeed, can only be—idols of something. Pagan understandings of the representational capacity of idols and the ontological premises of pagan ritual turn out to be far more fluid, complex, and potentially conflicting than any interpretation consistent with a Platonic metaphysics would allow.

Philosophizing defenses of idolatry existed in a variety of forms, but they all accepted the premise that the function of idols was *to represent*, and not in any way *to be*, the god. I label these texts "philosophizing" in part because their authors are demonstrably familiar with Plato, but especially because defending idolatry by recourse to theories of representation itself takes place only within a particular intellectual and discursive tradition.

The problem for idolatry's champions was twofold: first, to defend the use of images and only secondarily to defend anthropomorphism. As so often, we know the most influential defense of images in the Western tradition only from its opponents. For it was the first-century Roman polymath Varro who introduced the Latin-speaking world to the allegorical interpretation of religious statuary, and we know his work on religion almost exclusively through the extracts of them quoted by Augustine. We are, therefore, in no position to say whether Varro developed this theory of religious art himself, on analogy with Stoic allegorizing interpretations of Hesiod, although it seems clear that both he and Cicero knew Zeno's reading of Hesiod's *Theogony*. In any event, according to Augustine, Varro argued that the material objects used in religious rituals served to draw the attention of the eyes to themselves in order to direct the sight of the mind to invisible things.[43] Augustine placed a terse formulation of Varro's argument in the mouth of a fictive pagan in a sermon delivered during the closing years of the fourth century: "Suppose some debater stands forth, one who seems learned, and says: 'I do not worship the stone. I merely venerate what I see, but I worship him whom I do not see.' Who is this? An invisible *numen*, he says, which presides over that idol. People who defend the use of images in this way seem learned only to themselves: they may not worship idols, but they still worship demons."[44]

Other advocates for idolatry similarly accepted the premise that idols had to be defended as *representing* something. Although both Dio Chrysostom and Porphyry ultimately defended anthropomorphism, each began his defense of religious art by reflecting on its function and power. Dio admitted that it was difficult for humans to gain access to and secure knowledge about the divine. He identified four sources of accurate information: poets, lawgivers, artists, and philosophers. Although he knew the story that Pheidias had been inspired by Homer, he also insisted that artists could become the rivals and peers of the poets, as "through their eyes they interpreted the divine for their numerous and less experienced spectators."[45] By allowing that artists "interpret the divine" (ἐξηγούμενοι τὰ θεῖα), Dio implicitly elevated them to rivalry with the philosophers, as he had explicitly compared them with the poets, for it is the philosopher, according to Dio, "who interprets the divine in speech and most truthfully and perfectly proclaims its immortal nature."[46] In *On Images*, Porphyry followed Varro and Dio in construing the interpretation of statues as material objects on analogy with the reading of words as material signs. In the preface to that work, Porphyry promised "to those who have learned to read from statues as from books what is written about the gods" that he would reveal "the thoughts of wise theology, in which men have revealed God and God's powers through images susceptible to sense perception, by rendering the invisible in visible forms."[47]

All these authors shared with Plato the basic metaphysical assumption that incorporeal deities and, indeed, incorporeal ideas existed not simply on a different but on a higher plane than embodied humans; it was this assumption that triggered the need for the divine to be interpreted rather than merely depicted and that required artists to render the divine not from a corporeal model, but from some outstanding form of the beautiful that existed in their minds.[48] The philosophical basis of these debates is nowhere more apparent than in Origen's refutation of Celsus or the first book of John of Damascus's *On Images*.[49] Celsus had argued that Christians were both idolators and poor metaphysicians because they believed humans had been created in every way similar to God. Did they not depict God saying, "Let us create man in our image and resemblance" (κατ᾽ εἰκόνα καὶ ὁμοίωσιν ἡμετέραν)?[50] This was impossible, Celsus continued, because God did not make humans in his image, nor does God resemble any other visible being.[51] Origen defended Christians first with a specious semantic argument, insisting that God only made man in his image but not in his resemblance, a claim for which he offers no proof. But he also undertook a more rigorous defense of Christian metaphysics. Celsus has clearly misrepresented the Christians, Origen wrote, when he suggests that we think that which is made "after the image of God" is the body, while the soul, which is better, is deprived of that which is "after his image." For none of us, Origen asserted, thinks that your idols are actually images of gods, as you do, as though such things could depict the shape of an invisible and incorporeal deity; still less do we imagine that anything created after God's image could be "in a corruptible body" (ἐν τῷ φθαρτῷ σώματι).[52]

THE MATTER AND MATERIALITY OF RELIGIOUS ART

What is a corruptible body? Are there incorruptible bodies? These questions return us to theories of matter and to the reception of Plato's *Timaeus*. A modern reader might well respond that the *Timaeus* is not about physics, but in the ancient world it was always read as though it were. What is more, its most influential reader was also its most powerful critic. I refer, of course, of Aristotle.

In his engagement with Plato's physics, Aristotle reacted above all to two related problems. First, Plato offered no theory of matter. Aristotle asked, for example, whether Plato's universal receptacle or his so-called space might be prime matter but declared Plato insufficiently precise to allow any certainty.[53] Second, Plato wanted his Forms to preexist, to be prior to corporeal matter. But Plato's own illustration of formation—that of a goldsmith imposing a design on previously unformed gold—did not require that the design exist before the gold, nor, in fact, could it explain the existence of the gold at all.[54]

I do not want to belabor the details of Aristotle's reading of Plato. It is, however, crucial to understand two things, both connected to the paradoxical reception of Aristotle's critique among later Platonists. The first has to do with elaborate connection Aristotle drew between forms and particulars, on the one hand, and the ontological status of the different kinds of matter from which each is made, on the other; the second principally with the tools for discussing materiality that Aristotle bequeathed to Greco-Roman posterity. First, although Aristotle insisted that prime matter existed prior to its formation only in potentiality and not in actuality—only, that is, logically and not temporally—he did concede to Plato that the metaphor of the goldsmith may have been useful as a narrative representation of processes that were themselves atemporal.[55] Writing in the *Metaphysics* of the making of a bronze sphere from unformed bronze, Aristotle observed that we call the particular and the form by the same name, and yet that which we call the form cannot have any existence, is not, in his terms, a self-subsistent substance, merely because we have a name for it.[56]

If Aristotle resembles Plato in connecting problems of epistemology, representation, and metaphysics, he did so in radically different ways. So, for example, he conceded that most people defined processes of generation and corruption, γένεσις καὶ φθορά, by drawing an incorrect ontological distinction between perceptible and imperceptible matter.[57] Aristotle, on the other hand, insisted, first, that some matter was potentially not susceptible to sense perception, but only to intellection; and, second, that both kinds of matter were properly speaking unknowable prior to their formation. That is why we assign the same name to both forms and particulars.[58]

The second crucial legacy of Aristotle's critique of Plato is more subtle. It consists of the conceptual and terminological apparatus that Aristotle developed to correct Plato, which was appropriated by later Platonists merely to supplement him. Of particular importance were the assimilation of Aristotle's logically and potentially extant matter, what he calls the πρώτη ὕλη, to Plato's universal receptacle, on the one hand, and the complex belief that "intelligible" particulars had some form of imperceptible matter, different in kind from ὕλη γεννητὴ καὶ φθαρτή, sense-perceptible matter subject to generation and corruption, increase and change. This endowed Plato's ontological framework with a form of underlying and unchanging ὕλη νοητή, intelligible matter, that could be the object of reason and νόησις, to correspond to the corruptible matter that was the object of opinion and sense perception.[59]

I do not want to spend more than a few paragraphs on the history of middle Platonic physics; we need only to examine the articulation of first principles insofar as these affect pagan and Christian theorizing about idolatry. Here the testimony of Cicero's *Posterior Academics* is crucial, both for its account of the thought of Antiochus of Ascalon and for its explicit discussion of problems of translation. These issues became intertwined when Cicero turned to ὕλη, matter, because in brief compass he equated Aristotelian prime matter with Platonic space, called them both *materia,* and identified *corpus,* or body, as the product of this matter and Stoic ποιότης, which he rendered with *qualitas.*[60] Cicero implicitly acknowledged the eclecticism of this brief essay on *initia,* first principles, when he assigned authority for its various components to Antiochus, Aristotle, or the Stoics, but he often labeled the whole as the thought of the Greeks.

I here skip several interesting moments in the history of philosophical literature, not without some regret. Seneca's extended meditation on first principles, for example, would repay careful study, both for its Platonic smith who imposes form on Aristotelian bronze, and for its vocabulary, which is largely independent of Cicero. Indeed, Seneca's language reveals just how fluid the Latin philosophical tradition remained in the middle of the first century.[61]

But the full extent of Aristotle's influence on Platonic physics emerges with particular clarity in the philosophical handbooks of Alcinous and Apuleius. Alcinous took from Plato his correlations between knowledge and intellection, on the one hand, and sense perception and opinion, on the other.[62] Indeed, like Plato, Alcinous accepted this distinction as axiomatic: it is because intellection and opinion are categorically different that their objects possess differential ontological status. There must be primary objects of intellection, πρῶτα νοητά, as there are primary objects of sense perception, πρῶτα αισθητά.[63]

Post-Aristotelian metaphysicians, lacking the courage of that philosopher's rigorous empiricism and adhering to a Platonizing physics that would have dismayed Plato and Aristotle alike, concluded quite naturally that objects of intellection and sense perception each require their own kind of matter. What Alcinous provided, therefore, is a thoroughly Aristotelianized account of the *Timaeus.* Not only did he accept without hesitation that the universal receptacle, the mother and nurse of all things, and space are one and the same, but he equated them with an Aristotelian substratum inaccessible to sense perception and consisting of matter.[64] This substratum is neither corporeal nor incorporeal, but is body in potentiality.[65] I need not remind you that the words for "substratum," "matter," and "potentiality" do not occur in Plato. Next, adapting an argument from Aristotle's *Metaphysics,* Alcinous identified matter as a first principle, from which the world was created, and he proceeded to ask by whom and with reference to what it was fashioned.[66] The answers to those questions are, of course, God and the Forms, the former imposing the latter on a chaotic, imperceptible preexistent substratum of matter.[67]

Apuleius provides our best glimpse into the Latin reception of Plato between Cicero and Lactantius. In book 1 of *On Plato* he described Plato's first principles: God, matter, and the forms. According to Apuleius, prime matter is *improcreabilem incorruptamque,* by which he meant it is not subject to λένεσις καὶ φθορά, generation and corruption.[68] This matter is potentially recipient of form and is the substratum of creation. It is, finally, indeterminate and imperceptible: it is infinite insofar as its magnitude is indeterminate; it is neither corporeal or incorporeal. It cannot be body since it lacks form, but without body it cannot be said to exist.[69]

Alcinous drew his correspondences between epistemology and metaphysics in a section of his handbook separate from that on first principles. Apuleius, for his part, understood that knowledge of first principles was inseparable from its representation. So, for example, he tentatively concluded that prime matter was unsusceptible to sense perception but accessible to intellection.[70] He grew more certain when he turned to the distinction between objects of intellection and their essence, and objects of sense perception and their essence. The former are visible to the eyes of the mind and exist always in the same way, equal to themselves; the latter must be judged by opinion, whether rational or irrational, because they are created and pass away. What is more, the essence of objects of intellection, insofar as it is the subject of discourse, offers grounds for rational and abiding true statements; the essence of objects of sense perceptions, which are like the shadows and images of true things, offers ground for disputation and words that are inherently inconstant.[71]

It would be interesting to trace the development of this conceptual framework in greater detail, for its influence on theology and the exegesis of creation narratives from the Jewish diaspora to late antiquity, from Philo to Hermogenes and Tertullian, to Calcidius, Proclus, and John Philoponus. In this area as in so many others, Plotinus broke with his predecessors: his model of divine immanence, that of a mirror reflecting images, created conceptual space for growth in new directions.[72] Julian the Apostate's writings on embodiment similarly allowed for new understandings of ritual practice, which have been largely ignored by those convinced that paganism was on the wane by the mid-fourth century.[73] At present, however, I want only to return to the problem of gods and idols, and I do so by way of Augustine.

AUGUSTINE, IDOLS, AND THE AFFECTIONS OF THE MISERABLE

In his great commentary on Genesis, written early in the fifth century, Augustine was concerned to reconcile his own form of a Christian Platonizing metaphysics with a narrative of Creation that rather unfortunately concretized very different theological presuppositions.[74] Yet analysis of and writing about such issues raised irresolvable problems of representation, ones that Augustine sought to explain by appeal to the very metaphysical postulates that had motivated his project in the first place.[75]

When, therefore, Augustine asked how it was that God had said, "Let there be light," he wavered between two possibilities: God had either spoken in time or in the eternity of his Word. The first option he dismissed: *si temporaliter, utique mutabiliter,* if God had spoken in time, then his words would have been subject to change, for material words inevitably sound and pass away; their matter is subject to generation and corruption.[76] "But this is an absurd and fleshly way of thinking and speculating."[77] Augustine's diction, *carnalis,* "fleshly," invoked two closely related problems. As embodied souls, humans not only interacted with the world through sense perception, but their language and their physics had developed to explain the physical and not the intelligible world. Genesis had, therefore, to accommodate its narrative to the limitations of discursive speech and the patterns and habits of thought that human speech could articulate. Genesis 1.2, for example, represented the "waters" as preexistent not because matter participated in God's eternity in any way, but because God had *to be said* to be stirring above something: in actuality, Augustine insisted, the verse referred not to spatial relations, but to God's powers, which were transcendent over all things.[78]

As this example indicates, Augustine took pains throughout the commentary to be as precise as possible in matters of priority, both logical and temporal, and never more so than in matters of matter. Unformed matter, he insisted, was created at the same time as the things made from it: just as a speaker does not utter sound and then fashion words from it, so God did not first make unformed matter and then impose form upon it. Unformed matter is thus not prior in time, but in origin; and Scripture has, in narrating with the material words of discursive language, separated into a temporal sequence actions that God did not separate in time in the act of creation.[79] Augustine extended his concern for precision about materiality to the theology of demons and angels: demons may be animals, but they are ethereal ones. Their ethereal bodies remain ever strong and do not suffer corruption in death.[80] Formed not from corporeal matter but from what Augustine called "spiritual substance" or what Apuleius might have called "intelligible matter," the bodies of demons were not susceptible to sense perception. The anthropomorphism of their idols was thus doubly corrupting: the familiarity of their appearance was as reassuring as it was deceptive, and it granted to them such power as they had over the affections of the miserable.[81]

The particular metaphysics and theory of matter that underpinned Augustine's understanding of Genesis and the bodies of demons also framed his view of idolatry. In a sermon delivered in Carthage in 404, he once again posited a fictive interlocutor as a learned defender of pagan practice. "When I worship Mercury," he says, "I worship talent. Talent cannot be seen; it is something invisible. We readily concede that talent is something invisible (*aliquid inuisibile*), and insofar as it is invisible it is better than sky, or earth or sea or anything visible. Indeed, invisible substances (*substantia inuisibilis*), such as life, are better than every visible substance, since everything visible is a physical thing (*quia omne uisibile corpus est*), and talent is indeed a great thing. Nevertheless, if you were to consider that talent which they say they worship, what does it do? For do not many with great talent err? Perhaps they err greatly who think that talent is to be worshiped using an image of Mercury."[82]

What, then, of Cybele? Was the black stone really the goddess? Did the Romans get the one and only black stone that may have been the goddess? Might they, in fact, have received a duplicate of the stone housed at Pessinus, or even one copy among many? Let me suggest one way to answer these questions without looking at the history of Pessinus.

Plato's metaphysics of representation has influenced the reading of this episode and others like it in two ways. On the one hand, because we assume that copies are not only different from but inferior to their exemplars, we insist that religious artifacts cannot be duplicated. Hence the Romans must have received the one and only black stone. Paradoxically, because we assume that the divine exists on a higher plane than the corporeal, we also believe that the black rock must have *represented*, rather than *been*, the goddess. But surely a sign or a symbol or an image can be reproduced?

I suggest that ancient understandings of materiality, and the philosophy of representation underlying religious ritual, provide the means to obviate this most Platonic of false binarisms. Recognizing further hypostases beyond or between the divine and the corporeal, people in the ancient world might well have understood that Cybele somehow was, and yet was not coextensive with, their black stone; and in that way, she might also have been, but not been identical with, other black stones.

I do not know what the Romans brought from Pessinus to the Palatine in 204 B.C. But I suspect that the metaphysical and epistemological doctrines bequeathed to us from Plato are not going to help us find an answer. What I do know is that Cybele's shrine in Pessinus remained an active site of cult and focus for pilgrimage for at least five hundred and sixty years after her *baitulos* went to Rome. For that reason alone, I suspect that Lucius Cornelius Scipio received both more and less than the black rock that was the goddess in the port of Ostia twenty-two hundred years ago.

NOTES

For comments and conversation, my thanks to Ruth Abbey, Sabine MacCormack, Ebrahim Moosa, Bilinda Straight, and Jim White. The completion of this essay was supported by a fellowship from the American Council of Learned Societies.

1. Besançon 2000 provides a wide-ranging overview. Bevan 1940 and Barash 1992 survey attitudes to religious art in the ancient Mediterranean. On Greek and Roman critics of idolatry, see Clerc 1915; Borries 1918; Geffcken 1916/19. On iconoclasm in Byzantium, see Hennephof 1969; Pelikan 1990.

2. Pietz 1985, 1987, and 1988 explore from this perspective the development of the modern anthropological category of the "fetish." For other recent histories of religious historiography, see Ando 2003a, sec. I, and 2003b, 220–22, 373.

3. I would not follow Vernant (1985, 325–51) in arguing that the converse was true, that idols functioned as idols rather than *objets d'art* only insofar as they were used in rituals (see esp. 337, 343–45). If that were true, one would expect many more cult statues to perform miracles, and one might expect famously beautiful statues by renowned artists to account for a disproportionate number of such miracles. But famous Greek sculptures were rarely more than sculptures. Roman anxieties about the efficacy of ritual in desacralizing objects also suggests that Vernant's association of image and ritual needs modification.

4. Gladigow 1985/6 and 1994 survey the use of cult statues in Greek and Roman ritual; cf. Estienne 1997.

5. On the *lectisternium*, see esp. Festus s.v. *struppi* 472L and *capita deorum* 56L (capita deorum appellabantur fasciculi facti ex verbenis); cf. s.v. *stroppus* 410L, together with Livy 40.59.7 (terra movit; in fanis publicis, ubi lectisternium erat, deorum capita, qui in lectis erant, averterunt se, lanxque cum integumentis, quae Iovi adposita fuit, decidit de mensa); Pseudoacro on Horace *Carm.* 1.37.3 (PULVINAR DEORUM pulvinaria dicebantur aut lecti deorum aut tabulata, in quibus stabant numina, ut eminentiora viderentur). On the *sellisternium*, see Taylor 1935, correcting a long tradition of overreliance on Valerius Maximus 2.1.2.

6. Gordon 1979, 7–8; cf. Schnapp 1994; Burkert 1970, 360.

7. Geffcken 1916/19, 286: "Für das ursprüngliche Gefühl, den naiven Glauben, fallen Bild und Original, Darstellendes und Dargestelltes, jederziet zu einer gewissen Einheit zusammen."

8. Ibid., 287; cf. Link 1910, 34: "Antiquissima enim aetate simulacra sunt di ipsi, cuius opinionis recentiore quoque aetate reliquiae manserunt, quoniam auxilii numinis participes esse, si eius simulacrum possiderent, opinabantur. Cuius vetustioris sententiae reliquias ognoscimus ex eo, quod vivendi signa simulacra dedisse feruntur: rident, loquuntur, se avertunt, sudant, se movent, quin etiam ulciscuntur iniurias sibi illatas."

9. Kuhnert 1883; Gladigow 1985/6 und 1994. Vernant 1985, 333, constitutes an important exception, observing of the colossos in the archaic Greek world that one swore "by the stone." It was, as Vernant shows, a double in this world for something invisible, associated alike with the soul and with εἴδωλα (325–38; cf. MacCormack 1975 on the *genius*). But Vernant merely records rather than explains the disappearance of the conceptual framework that underpinned the use of such doubles, and so he does not ask what had to be believed of both visible and invisible things in order to assert their identity.

10. Back 1883 concludes a fascinating chapter with the judgment: "Hae actiones, quas proprie sacerdotales dixerim, non ab ipsius religionis initiis repetendae sunt, sed manifesto pertinent ad id tempus quo cultus deorum patriarchico illo statu relicto jam suae potestatis factus erat atque ad maximam partem in sacerdotum manus pervenerat. Attamen demonstrant, quamtum antiquitus apud homines Graecos ipsa, ad quorum similitudinem illae celebrabantur, spectacula floruerint. Recte igitur Augustinus civ. 7.18: ex cuiusque dei ingenio moribus actibus casibus sacra ete sollemnia instituta sunt" (28–29).

Kiechle 1970 ends a similar survey with the judgment that humans replacing gods in rituals was a feature of "der magischen Vorstellungswelt früher Religiosität." Scheid 1986 constitutes a very important exception to the scholarship in this area, as in many ways does Link 1910, esp. 46–48 and 55–56.

11. Elsner 1996; Woolf 2001.

12. Schubart 1866; Estienne 1997.

13. Madyda 1939; Gladigow 1990.

14. Among earlier work, I single out Link 1910. Link investigated the term "sanctus" and had to confront its application to widely disparate things: gods, places, and people. His argument about the chronological development of Roman belief does not persuade—his chronology is in any event indistinct—but his work is conspicuously free of the anachronisms that cloud much work of that era, and his insistence that pagan gods dwelled in particular locations is welcome. See also Scheid 1996 and 1999; Ando 2003a.

15. On the sacrality of objects, see Whitehouse 1996, esp. 13, 19; Glinister 2000; Ando 2001a and 2003a.

16. Beard, North, and Price 1998, 96–98, discuss this episode and cite earlier literature.

17. Livy 29.10.8.

18. De Sélincourt 1965, 579 (emphasis added).

19. Livy 29.11.7 (emphasis added).

20. Livy 29.14.10–14.

21. Ovid *Fasti* 4.317.

22. Symmachus *Relatio* 3.5.

23. Auerbach 1953, 6.

24. Augustine *Serm.* 62.6.10.

25. Ando 2001b, 26–30

26. Xenophones frr. 166–69 KRS, esp. 167 (Clement *Strom.* 5.109.2): mortals think the gods are born and have clothes and voice and bodies like their own.

27. Heraclitus fr. 241 KRS.

28. Weinstock 1926.

29. Vernant 1979, 105–37, provides an exceptionally useful overview of Plato's theory of representation but does not consider its connection to materiality nor its specific connection to religious art. Osborne 1987 offers a trenchant reading of Plato's criticism of mimesis in *Republic* 10, but her discussion of its "repercussions" is deeply ahistorical, leaping from Plato to Byzantine iconoclasm, and she is in any event not concerned with cult practice. Her choice of "incarnation" as a term in discussing mimesis in religious art was unfortunate: it seems implicitly to justify (or it simply reflects) a decision not to come to grips with the materiality of gods and idols outside Christian thought.

30. *Cratylus* 432b–d.

31. *Sophist* 235d–236c.

32. *Cratylus* 439a–b.

33. *Sophist* 264c–d: ὡς οὔτε εἰκὼν οὔτε εἴδωλον οὔτε φάντασμα εἴη τό παράπαν οὐδὲν διά τό μηδαμῶς μηδέποτε μηδαμοῦ ψεῦδος εἶναι....

34. *Sophist* 264d: ἐγχωρεῖ δή μιμήματα τῶν ὄντων εἶναι.

35. *Republic* 510d–e.

36. *Timaeus* 27d–28a.

37. *Timaeus* 29a.

38. *Timaeus* 28b–c.

39. *Timaeus* 29b–c.

40. *Timaeus* 50b–51a.

41. *Timaeus* 51d.

42. Cf. Ando 2001a, which attempts to break down the distinctions drawn by modern scholars between Christian and pagan theories of the sacralization of space. Pagan rituals of sacralization, and Christian reliance on sacred narratives and the contingent location of holy relics, presuppose very similar theories of divine immanence.

43. Varro *Ant. Div.* fr. 225; Augustine *Civ.* 7.5.

44. Augustine *En. Ps.* 96.11. On Augustine's critique of idolatry and its philosophical bases, see Ando 2001b, 26–30.

45. Dio *Or.* 12.46.

46. Dio *Or.* 12.47; Madyda 1939, 9, 38–39.

47. Porphyry Περὶ ἀγαλμάτων fr. 351 Smith (fr. 1 Bidez). See also fr. 353: Ἀλλ᾽ ἐπεὶ πάντα τὸν περὶ τούτων ἀπόρρητον δὴ καὶ μυστικώτερον λόγον εἰς ἀσωμάτους δυνάμεις μεταφορικῶς ἀνῆγον, ὥστε δοκεῖν μηκέτ᾽ ἐπὶ τὰ ὁρώμενα μέρη τοῦ κόσμου τὴν θεοποιίαν αὐτῶν ουντείνειν, ἀλλ᾽ ἐπί τινας ἀοράτους καὶ ἀσωμάτους δυνάμεις, σκεψώμεθα εἰ μὴ καὶ οὕτως μίαν χρὴ τὴν θείαν δύαμιν ἀποθαυμάζειν, ἀλλ᾽ οὐ πολλὰς ἡγεῖσθαι....

48. Cicero *Orator* 2.8–9; Madyda 1939, 16, 27–29.

49. See esp. John 1.7.

50. Origen *Cels.* 4.30; cf. 7.62.

51. Origen *Cels.* 6.63.

52. Ibid., 7.66.

53. Plato *Timaeus* 51e–52b; Aristotle *De generatione et corruptione* 329a5–24, with Joachim 1922, 194–95; cf. *Metaphysics* 1035b31–1036a13, 1028b33–1029b13; Ross 1960, 565.

54. Plato *Timaeus* 49a–50b; Aristotle *De generatione et corruptione* 329a5–24; cf. *Metaphysics* 1033a24–1034a8, 1050b6–28.

55. On the logical priority of prime matter, see Aristotle *De generatione et corruptione* 329a24–b2, with Joachim 1922, 198–99, as well as Ross 1960, 47, 50, on *Physics* 206b12–16.

56. Aristotle *Metaphysics* 1033a24–1034a8.

57. Aristotle *De generatione et corruptione* 318b18–27; cf. *Metaphysics* 1036b32–1037a5.

58. Aristotle *Metaphysics* 1035b31–1036a13, 1036b32–1037a10.

59. As both Joachim 1922, xxxiv, 143–44, and Bostock 1994, 156–57, 165–66, make clear, Aristotle regarded intellectual matter as nothing more than an imaginary logical postulate, useful for discussing the application of concepts like "place" and "touch" to τὰ γεωμετρικά.

60. Cicero *Acad. Post.* 24–27.

61. Seneca *Ep.* 58.16–31; cf. ibid., 65.8–9, 90.28–29.
62. Alcinous 4.3–4.
63. Alcinous 9.4; cf. *Timaeus* 51d–52a.
64. Alcinous 8.2: Καὶ πρῶτόν γε περὶ ὕγης λέγωμεν. Ταύτην τό´ νυν ἐκμαγῖόν τε καὶ πανδεχὲς καὶ τιθήνην καὶ μητέρα καὶ χώραν ὀνομάζει καὶ ὑποκείμενον ἁπτόν τε μετά ἀναισθησίας καὶ νόθῳ λιγσμῷ ληπτόν. . . .
65. Alcinous 8.3.
66. Alcinous 9.3, following Aristotle *Metaphysics* 1032a12 ff.
67. Alcinous 12.2.
68. Apuleius *De Platone* 1.5.
69. Ibid.
70. Ibid.
71. Apuleius *De Platone* 1.6.
72. Plotinus 4.3.
73. See, e.g., Julpian *Ep.* 89.293a–d.
74. The following paragraphs treat material studied in depth in Ando 2001b.
75. Ando 1994; cf. Ando 2001b.
76. Augustine *Gen. litt.* 1.2.4.
77. Augustine *Gen. litt.* 1.2.5.
78. Augustine *Gen. litt.* 1.7.13.
79. Augustine *Gen. litt.* 1.15.29.
80. Augustine *Gen. litt.* 3.10.14.
81. Augustine *En. Ps.* 113.2.6. Augustine regarded Plato's inability to conceive of "spiritual substance" as the principal failing of Platonic theology; on this problem, see Ando 2001b, 38–43.
82. Augustine *S. Dolbeau* 26.24; cf. *En. Ps.* 113.2.4.

WORKS CITED

Ando, C. 1994. "Augustine on Language." *Revue des Études Augustiniennes* 40:45–78.

———. 2001a. "The Palladium and the Pentatuch: Towards a Sacred Topography of the Later Roman Empire." *Phoenix* 55:369–410.

———. 2001b. "Signs, Idols and the Incarnation in Augustian metaphysics." *Representations* 73:24–53.

———. 2003a. "A Religion for the Empire." In *Flavian Rome: Culture, Image, Text,* ed. A. J. Boyle and W. Dominik, 323–44. Leiden: E. J. Brill. Reprinted in Ando 2003b, 220–43.

———. 2003b. *Roman Religion.* Edinburgh: Edinburgh University Press.

Auerbach, E. 1953. *Mimesis. The Representation of Reality in Western Literature.* Trans. W. R. Trask. Princeton: Princeton University Press.

Back, F. 1883. *De Graecorum caerimoniis in quibus homines deorum vice fungebantur.* Berlin: Schade.

Barasch, M. 1992. *Icon: Studies in the History of an Idea*. New York: New York University Press.

Beard, M., J. North, and S. Price. 1998. *Religions of Rome*. Vol. 1: *A History*. Cambridge: Cambridge University Press.

Besançon, A. 2000. *The Forbidden Image: An Intellectual History of Iconoclasm*. Trans. J. M. Todd. Chicago: University of Chicago Press.

Bevan, E. 1940. *Holy Images: An Inquiry into Idolatry and Image-Worship in Ancient Paganism and in Christianity*. London: George Allen and Unwin.

Borries, Bodo de. 1918. *Quid veteres philosophi de idololatria senserint*. Göttingen: Officina Academica Dieterichiana.

Bostock, D. 1994. *Aristotle, Metaphysics Books Z and H*. Oxford: Clarendon Press.

Burkert, W. 1970. "Buzyge und Palladion: Gewalt und Gericht in altgriechischem Ritual." *Zeitschrift für Religions- und Geistesgeschichte* 22:356–68.

Clerc, C. 1915. *Les théories relatives au culte des images chez les auteurs grecs du IIme siècle après J.-C.* Paris: Fontemoing.

Elsner, J. 1996. "Image and Ritual: Reflections on the Religious Appreciation of Classical Art." *Classical Quarterly* 46:513–31.

Estienne, S. 1997. "Statues de dieux 'isolées' et lieux de culte: l'exemple de Rome." *Cahiers du Centre Gustave Glotz* 8:81–96.

Geffcken, J. 1916/19. "Der Bilderstreit des heidnischen Altertums." *Archiv für Religionswissenschaft* 19:286–315.

Gladigow, B. 1985/6. "Präsenz der Bilder—Präsenz der Götter. Kultbilder und Bilder der Götter in der griechischen Religion." *Visible Religion* 4/5:114–33.

———. 1990. "Epiphanie, Statuette, Kultbild. Griechische Gottesvorstellungen im Wechsel von Kontext und Medium." *Visible Religion* 7:98–121.

———. 1994. "Zur Ikonographie und Pragmatik römischer Kultbilder." In *Iconologia Sacra. Mythos, Bildkunst und Dichtung in der religions- und sozialgeschichte Alteuropas. Festschrift für Karl Hauck*, ed. H. Keller and N. Staubach, 9–24. Berlin: de Gruyter.

Glinister, F. 2000. "Sacred Rubbish." In *Religion in Archaic and Republican Rome and Italy*, ed. E. Bispham and C. Smith, 54–70. Edinburgh: Edinburgh University Press.

Gordon, R. L. 1979. "Production and Religion in the Graeco-Roman World." *Art History* 2:5–34.

Hennephof, H. 1969. *Textus Byzantini ad iconomachiam pertinentes*. Byzantina Neerlanica, Series A, Fasc. 1. Leiden: E. J. Brill.

Joachim, H. H. 1922. *Aristotle on Coming-to-Be and Passing-Away (De generatione et corruptione)*. Oxford: Clarendon Press.

Kiechle, F. K. 1970. "Götterdarstellung durch Menschen in den altmediterranen Relitionen." *Historia* 19:259–71.

Kuhnert, E. 1883. *De cura statuarum apud Graecos*. Berlin: S. Calvary et Socium.

Link, W. 1910. *De vocis "sanctus" usu pagano quaestiones selectae*. Königsburg: Hartung.

MacCormack, S. 1975. "Roma, Constantinopolis, the Emperor, and His Genius." *Classical Quarterly* 25:131–50.

Madyda, L. 1939. *De pulchritudine imaginum deorum quid auctores Graeci saec. II. p. Chr. n. iudicaverint.* Arciwum Filologiczne nr. 16. Cracow: Polska Akademia Umierjetnosci.

Osborne, C. 1987. "The Repudiation of Representation in Plato's *Republic* and Its Repercussions." *Proceedings of the Cambridge Philological Society* 33:53–73.

Pelikan, J. 1990. *Imago Dei: the Byzantine Apologia for Icons.* Washington, D.C.: National Gallery of Art; Princeton: Princeton University Press.

Pietz, W. 1985. "The Problem of the Fetish, I." *Res* 9:5–17.

———. 1987. "The Problem of the Fetish, II. The Origin of the Fetish." *Res* 13:23–45.

———. 1988. "The Problem of the Fetish, IIIa. Bosman's Guinea and the Enlightenment Theory of Fetishism." *Res* 16:105–23.

Ross, W. D. 1960. *Aristotle's Physics.* Oxford: Clarendon Press.

Scheid, J. 1986. "Le flamine de Jupiter, les Vestales, et général triomphant. Variations romaines sur le thème de la figuration des dieux." In *Corps des Dieux,* ed. C. Malamoud and J.-P. Vernant, 213–29. Paris: Gallimard.

———. 1996. "Pline le jeune et les sanctuaires d'Italie. Observations sur les lettres IV, 1, VII, 8 et IX, 39." In *Splendidissima civitas: Études d'histoire romaine en hommage à François Jacques,* ed. A. Chastagnol, S. Demougin, and C. Lepelley, 241–58. Paris: Publications de la Sorbonne.

———. 1999. "Hiérarchie et structure dans le polythéisme romain. Façons romaines de penser l'action." *Archiv für Religionsgeschichte* 1(2):184–203. Translated by Philip Purchase in Ando 2003b, 164–89.

Schnapp, A. 1994. "Are Images Animated? The Psychology of Statues in Ancient Greece." In *The Ancient Mind: Elements of Cognitive Archaeology,* ed. C. Renfrew and E. B. W. Zubrow, 40–44. Cambridge: Cambridge University Press.

Schubart, A. 1866. "Die wörter ἄγαλμα, εἰκών, ξόανον, ἀνδριὰς und verwandte, in ihren verschiedenen beziehungen. Nach Pausanias." *Philologus* 24:561–87.

Sélincourt, A. de. 1965. *The War with Hannibal: Books XXI–XXX of Livy's History of Rome from its Foundation.* Baltimore: Penguin.

Taylor, L. R. 1935. "The Sellisternium and the Theatrical Pompa." *Classical Philology* 30:122–30.

Vernant, J.-P. 1979. *Religions, histoires, raison.* Paris: Maspero.

———. 1985. *Mythe & pensée chez les Grecs.* Paris: Éditions la Découverte.

Weinstock, S. 1926. "Die platonische Homerkritik und ihre Nachwirkung." *Philologus* 82:121–53.

Whitehouse, R. D. 1996. "Ritual Objects: Archaeological Joke or Neglected Evidence?" In *Approaches to the Study of Ritual: Italy and the Ancient Mediterranean,* ed. J. Wilkins, 9–30. London: Accordia Research Center.

Woolf, G. 2001. "Representation as Cult: The Case of the Jupiter Columns." In ed. W. Spickermann, 117–34. Tübingen: Mohr Siebeck.

CHAPTER THREE

A House of Many Mansions

Aspects of Christian Experience in Spanish America

Sabine MacCormack

How are we to think about the process of conversion from one religion to another, especially when it is an entire continent that is being converted? In this essay Sabine MacCormack pursues this question in a rich and particular historical context, that of Peru and Mexico after the Spanish conquest. What emerges from her account of the complex interactions between indigenous practices and beliefs and those of Christianity is not a picture of one religion simply replacing another, either in individuals or in communities, but a series of remarkable cultural meldings and transformations. These are significant in their own terms, both for the participants and for those interested in the nature of religious forms of life; and they are of real consequence too, for out of them has emerged the movement we know as liberation theology.

Christianity in Spanish America was, in the first instance, a by-product of invasion and conquest. Most of the exploratory and military expeditions that criss-crossed the continent during the sixteenth and seventeenth centuries were accompanied by clerics to care for the group's spiritual welfare, to endow the undertaking with an aura of legality, and to begin the conversion of indigenous peoples. Military and spiritual conquests were thus intimately intertwined, and this correlation of purposes has shaped Christian experience in Latin America to the present day.[1] On the one hand, the Christian social order that was implanted in Spanish America was a hierarchical one, consisting—as it did in Spain—of bishops, priests, religious orders, and laity. Alongside this ecclesiastical hierarchy, and interpenetrating it, there was the peninsular social and political hierarchy of birth and status. In the Americas, these hierarchies were reinforced by the realities of invasion and settlement: Spanish newcomers and their descendants who claimed to understand the true religion encountered an indigenous people and African slaves who were without that knowledge and were therefore in need of instruction.[2] But on the other hand, as I hope to show, the Scriptures and the Christian doctrine based upon them, as articulated by some early modern Spanish theologians and missionaries, and also by Indian Christians, provided resources for radical critiques of inequality and injustice that were sustained over generations and are still alive and strong.

Another theme that is explored in this essay is the tension between the Christian claim of universality as expressed in the precept of Jesus to "go into all the world and preach the gospel to every creature,"[3] and the way this missionary credo was met and accommodated at the local level. In one sense, the Christian message is the same wherever and whenever it is preached. But in another sense, no message, however universal, can be separated from the particular cultural environments in which it is articulated and lived. As a result, the purpose of conversion and the forms of life that could be expected to result, and did result, from conversion have varied over five centuries of Christian experience in Spanish America. Within such diversity, however, there are also overarching continuities in the story here sketched. Among these continuities I highlight Spanish American expressions of the communal dimension in the lives of the faithful that continues to distinguish Catholic Christianity from the Christian traditions that emerged from the Reformation. It is no accident that the theology of liberation, with its "preferential option for the poor" and its emphasis on shared, communal Christian experience, originated in Latin America.

In January 1599, the friar Diego de Ocaña set out on a journey to Spanish America in order to collect alms for the sanctuary of Our Lady of Guadalupe in Extremadura.[4] Landing in Puerto Rico, he traveled overland to Peru and Chile, spent over three years in the Andean highlands, in Potosi, Chuquisaca, Arequipa, and Cuzco, and in 1606 reached Mexico City, where he died two years later.[5]

Hernán Cortés had invaded and conquered Mexico in 1519, and Francisco Pizarro began the invasion of Peru in 1529. From Cortés himself, and from the men who fought with him and with Pizarro, we have descriptions of these campaigns and of the religious and cultural life of the polities that were being conquered. Priests, consecrated women, diviners, and ritual specialists (devoted to the service of supernatural presences of gods and deceased ancestors) were to be found everywhere, along with temples and shrines, whether in the small towns and villages of Mexico and the Andes, or in the great imperial cities of Tenochtitlan and Cuzco. The Spanish were convinced that their invasion had succeeded thanks in part to their valor and in part to the protection of both Saint James, the patron of the reconquest of the Peninsula from the Muslims, and of the Virgin Mary, "la Conquistadora."[6] For their part, many Indians felt abandoned by their gods. Thus, some decades after the invasion, people in Mexico remembered that their diviners had said that "perhaps it was the disposition of Huitzilopochtli that nothing more should happen,"[7] while in Peru people were wondering whether the Andean creator Viracocha had helped the Spanish.[8] In any event, the Spanish had come to stay, and when Diego de Ocaña traveled through these far-flung lands during the early years of the seventeenth century, he barely noticed a trace of the old gods. What he found instead were Christian buildings, institutions, and civic communities, and wherever he went he could stay in a monastery or priest's house, just as he would have done had he been traveling in Spain. In some sense, therefore, America was like home for him.

This was precisely what the first invaders had hoped to achieve. Their purpose was indeed set on conquest, but the activities of waging war, gaining power, and becoming rich were in their minds inseparable from founding cities and establishing Christian civic communities, just as their forebears had done when conquering the Muslim kingdoms of the Peninsula. In Protestant Europe, and thus in Protestant English-speaking America, the choice of religious allegiance has always been conceived primarily as a matter of inner orientation and of individual volition, in which society and the state should not interfere. But in Catholic Europe, reaching back through the European Middle Ages, and even to the Christian Roman Empire, the assumption was and remains that Christian identity is rooted in community as much as in the individual. The history of the early church as described in the New Testament is, after all, a history of Christian communities; where the texts speak about individuals, it is in terms of their relation with specific groups of believers. Conversion to Christianity was therefore seen as a social as well as an individual act, which figured significantly in how the church was founded and built in Spanish America.[9]

Community is rooted in a shared sense of identity. It also depends on and expresses a particular organization of space, whether, for example, the imagined space of the City in Heaven that is so frequent a theme in the visual arts of the Counter Reformation, or the concrete physical space of life on earth. This is why, all over the Americas, the invaders and their successors founded and planned cities with Christian topographies, where people like Diego de Ocaña and the many other men and women who settled in the Americas during the sixteenth century could feel at home. Take Lima, the city that Francisco Pizarro, the conqueror of the Incas, founded on the Pacific coast of Peru in 1535. Land was taken from the local Andean lord, and Pizarro marked on the ground the dimensions of Lima's central square: on one side would be the church, while arranged along the other three sides would be his own dwelling and those of other Spaniards, as well as the seat of the town council.[10] Subsequently, 117 blocks were outlined in a chess-board pattern, and were to be assigned to present and future settlers, with some blocks being reserved for churches and religious orders.[11] Both the sequence of events and the subdivision of space served to express and convey to others the beliefs that were central to the invaders' self-perception. The location of the church was the first to be determined "because the beginning of any settlement or city must be in God and for God, and in his name;"[12] next, the members of the city council were chosen and a site where they would meet was selected because "a people without justice, government and just and good laws deserves neither the name of a republic nor that of a political body, but rather, they are a mere stump without life or soul."[13]

Before the Spanish arrived, the site where Lima now sits was relatively empty. Not so Cuzco, the ancient capital of the Incas, which Francisco Pizarro and his followers refounded in 1534. But the invaders' concept of what a city ought to be—its foundational sequence and its distribution of space—was the same as in Lima. The center of Inca Cuzco was taken up by a large square surrounded by the palaces of various Inca rulers. Of these palaces the Spanish in due course obliterated almost every trace. But they could make sense of the square, the *plaza de armas* of our own day. On its upper end, land was set aside for the cathedral, and the seat of the town council was "on an agricultural terrace above the square."[14] Francisco Pizarro received a residence along the northeast side of the square, and at its far end was (and is) the convent and church of the Franciscans. Religious orders that came later, like the two women's congregations of Santa Clara and Santa Catalina, received land at some small distance from the square, while the Jesuits managed to acquire a magnificent location on the square itself, and several parish churches were erected elsewhere in the city. Such distributions of space were ubiquitous in colonial Latin America, whether in the great centers such as Lima, Cuzco, Quito, and Mexico City, or in small villages and missionary settlements throughout Central America and the Andes.[15] Moreover, even after the upheavals of indigenous rebellions, the wars of independence, and the profound institutional transformations of the republican and contemporary periods, much of this basic spatial pattern remains intact, even though the church on the main square of some small Andean towns is now a Protestant, not a Catholic, church.

This spatial order the Spanish brought with them implemented designs of the ideal city that Renaissance artists and architects derived from classical antiquity, in particular from the Roman architect Vitruvius. Throughout Latin America, the ideal became reality in that buildings were erected, each in its place, to articulate a concept not just of urban space and human community, but also of political and religious order, aspects of which endure to this day.[16] In Lima, Francisco Pizarro's dwelling first became the palace of the viceroy and later the seat of Peru's government. The archbishop's palace likewise is still situated in its original location, next to the cathedral, and the *audiencia*, Spanish Peru's highest court of appeal, had its seat nearby. During the colonial period, this central part of Lima was the core setting for the ongoing drama of viceregal politics, much of which revolved around relations between church and state, viceroy and archbishop, just as the city's topography suggested should be the case.

What the founders envisioned, or at least hoped for, was peaceable relations between church and state that were to be proclaimed periodically in rituals of ceremonial cooperation. Thus, in 1557, the cathedral chapter and town council of Cuzco came together in the city's main square to listen to the official announcement of Charles V's resignation and the succession of his son Philip II. No competing interests of rival dignitaries or friction over secular and ecclesiastical precedence disrupted the protracted solemnities, which began with bell ringing and a nocturnal illumination of the city and ended the next day with a tournament and bull fight.[17] Friction and competition, however, became all too frequent on other such occasions and over time produced embittered discussion. This was why in 1656, Gaspar de Villarroel, a learned Augustinian friar and bishop of Santiago de Chile and later of Arequipa, published two large volumes on *Peaceful Ecclesiastical Government,* in which he made many suggestions about how to avoid conflict between the two swords, the pontifical and the royal, between church and state. It was in considerable part a matter of ritual, of public representation, and thus of community formation, given that the rituals in question were inconceivable without spectators.

For example, a bishop newly appointed to a Peruvian bishopric traditionally began his duties by visiting Lima to meet the viceroy. But during those meetings, who had greater authority, viceroy or bishop? In practical terms, ought the bishop to pay the first call on the viceroy, or the other way round? And what if the new appointee was the archbishop of Lima? The official ceremonial of the Catholic Church decreed that sacred power always had precedence, but in the Spanish world, matters were somewhat more nuanced. Decorum did indeed demand, so Villarroel believed, that the viceroy should pay the first call on a newly arrived archbishop, but not so with other bishops. Hence, when Villarroel himself visited Lima to take up his bishopric of Santiago, before anything else he called on the viceroy Conde de Chinchón, who amply repaid the courtesy. In Villarroel's account, the viceroy

> alerted the gentlemen of his household to await me at the bottom of the stairs, and himself received me near the door of the first reception hall. We were seated on two equal seats, and he treated me with great benevolence, speaking to me with admirable openness and discretion. When I departed, he accompanied me a few steps beyond the place where he had received me. When he in turn visited me, I came out to receive him as far as the first cloister of our convent, and when I bid him good bye, I went out as far as the porter's lodge, and I would have accompanied him as far as his carriage if he had permitted it.[18]

Such ceremonial dramas, whether acted out against the grand architectural backdrop of Mexico City, Lima, or Cuzco, or in the more humble setting of towns and villages where the local governor paid his respects to a newly arrived parish priest, or *vice versa,* punctuated and spiced daily life in settlements both large and small throughout central and South America. In effect, every single parish and missionary parish, *doctrina,* was a miniature universe with its own life cycle.[19] In some ways, the smaller the place, the more powerful an impact ceremonial events had on the inhabitants, for, as Villarroel observed, "in small places, people talk a lot."[20] But even in Lima, people talked incessantly about ritual events. Did the countenance and manner that a newly appointed viceroy displayed during the protracted ceremonial of his arrival betoken an accommodating or an irascible temper?[21] Or had the Archbishop of Lima committed a serious blunder of etiquette in watching a bull fight in the main square from the balcony of his palace, seated under a canopy? For were not canopies reserved for the viceroy alone when a secular holiday was being celebrated?[22] The possibilities for ceremonial cooperation and unceremonial friction seemed almost infinite, and could make or break a man's career and reputation.

Reputation and career were not, however, all that was at stake, because a dignitary of church or state indeed stood not only for himself, but more importantly, for his office. Francisco Pizarro and in a more formal and absolute sense the viceroys who succeeded him were tantamount to the king, and bishops represented Christ's apostles, or even Peter, the prince of the apostles, and hence the pope. Ritual actions thus took place not so much among particular individuals as among individuals who represented certain transcendent realities. The point was well understood by the Andean lord Don Joan Santacruz Pachacuti Yamqui, who in the early seventeenth century wrote a short history of Peru. In concluding this work, Don Joan cast his mind back to the time when, amid warfare and destruction, the Spanish had occupied and refounded Cuzco. But that was not how Don Joan imagined this event to have taken place. Instead, he described the "great royal display and pomp of great majesty" of a formal ceremony of arrival.[23] With Francisco Pizarro representing Emperor Charles V and friar Vicente de Valverde, missionary and future bishop of Cuzco, representing the pope, they entered the city in peace, side by side with the Inca ruler Manco Inca. Next, Valverde converted Coricancha, the "enclosure of gold," the central shrine of the Inca empire and temple of the Sun, into a Christian place of worship. Neither Pizarro nor Valverde were in any sense exemplary personages, something Pachacuti Yamqui might have known, but that was not the issue. What mattered was that in the presence of "the Spanish and of the Andean lords," as Pachacuti Yamqui imagined it,[24] a ceremonial of foundation had been performed that accomplished the conversion of the empire of the Incas to Christianity.

Such, at any rate, was the ideal. In reality, however, ritual action was not necessarily the same as peaceful action, which the history of the evangelization of Spanish America makes clear. The aim of evangelization was, in part at least, the conversion of individuals, but more importantly, evangelization had the broader purpose of creating a Christian society. This is why the invaders and the missionary friars who accompanied them frequently did not begin by teaching the gospel, but by trying to change the religious meanings of cityscapes

and landscapes. In this sense, Pachacuti Yamqui's imagined Christian recon-
secration of Cuzco's Coricancha enshrined an important core of reality, even
if that reality was often more violent and less dignified than he seems to have
believed. The pattern of such reconsecrations was established early, during the
invasion of the Aztec empire. In June 1519, near the beginning of his march to
the Aztec capital, Hernan Cortés and his followers were received by the people
of Cempoallan, who offered their alliance and friendship, and, meaning to
confirm their offer, eight nobly born ladies. But none of this was acceptable
to the Spanish until the local temple pyramid had been cleansed of its "idols."
Over fifty Spanish soldiers clambered up the pyramid steps and overthrew
"the idols which came rolling down the steps shattered to pieces," while the
Cempoallans stood by helplessly weeping and covering their eyes. Still not content, the Spanish burnt the idols, ordered the temple to be cleaned and white-
washed, and then installed in it an image of the Virgin Mary along with a Christian altar. A priest then said Mass at this altar, the ladies were baptized, and the
Spanish proceeded on their campaign.[25] A little later, they repeated the procedure at Tlaxcala,[26] and subsequently elsewhere.

The Tlaxcalans were faithful allies of the Spanish throughout the period of
conquest and beyond. The Franciscan order founded one of their first Mexican convents there, and in 1536, only seventeen years after the invasion, one
of the friars described how the Tlaxcalans celebrated Corpus Christi. "If the
pope, and the emperor with his court had been present in the festival," the
friar wrote,

> they would have been very pleased to see it. Although the Tlaxcalans did
> not have many jewels and brocades, they did have other finery worthy
> of being seen, especially of flowers and roses such as God is clothed in,
> and they grow on the trees and in the fields, so that not even Solomon in
> all his glory was dressed like one of them. . . . There were banners and
> twelve men attired in the insignia of the apostles. . . . The procession was
> accompanied by many people who walked with lighted candles . . . and
> there were seven or eight different kinds of dances which added much
> lustre to the procession.[27]

Two years later, Bartolomé de las Casas, the defender of the Indians and the
most famous of all missionaries in the Americas, sang the High Mass for the
festival of the assumption of Mary in Tlaxcala. On that occasion, there was a
play about the death of Mary and how she was assumed into heaven. The ac-

tors were all Tlaxcalans, and amid singing, organ playing, and the music of flutes they represented the apostles and the Virgin so convincingly that all who watched were profoundly moved.[28] Las Casas may not have been the most impartial of witnesses, but his testimony does express the hope of several among the early missionaries that conversion would proceed apace and that in effect, the Indians were natural Christians. By 1584, the city of Tlaxcala possessed its fine church and principal square, somewhat in the Spanish manner, and it had long had its elected government of mayor, aldermen, and notaries, all exactly as befit a Christian and political society.[29] Elsewhere in Central America, especially in Mexico City, where the cathedral was erected on top of the ruins of the main Aztec temple, the evolution was similar.

The conquest of Peru took longer than that of Mexico, and it was much more destructive. Christianizing the population was more difficult and intermittent, but here also the aim was less the conversion of individuals than the creation of local topographies that articulated a Christian public and ceremonial life such as had been known to the invaders in the Peninsula. The difficulty was that these recreations of Spanish perceptions of space and sacred space in the Andes frequently conveyed to indigenous people a message that differed profoundly from the one that the invaders and their heirs had in mind. For where the latter created a version of Spain in the Americas, the former became aliens in their own land.

Throughout the Andes, Inca and regional shrines were looted and destroyed by the Spanish and holy objects of all kinds were systematically rounded up and burnt in many a public *auto de fé* that was watched by appalled Andean people.[30] These rituals of extirpation continued well into the seventeenth century. They polarized Peruvian society into disempowered and dispossessed Indians on the one hand, and overmighty Creoles and peninsular Spaniards on the other, with an increasing number of mestizos occupying an uncomfortable middle ground, not to mention the African slaves who at first did not seem to fit anywhere in this diverse spectrum of humanity. In Central America, the contrasts between victors and vanquished were less harsh, but they were nonetheless present. The surprising thing in this context is that the project of creating a Christian society did not simply flounder and fail. Quite the opposite.

The initial reshaping of urban topographies was accomplished, as we have seen, when the invading Spaniards desecrated, and often destroyed, existing sacred buildings. Replacing these structures with Christian ones not only required a host of architects and artists who initially came from the Peninsula while their successors were trained locally, it also required daunting amounts of labor, almost all of which was performed by Indians. Much of this labor formed part and parcel of Indian tribute obligations, and was thus involuntary. Often, however, the Indians volunteered their labor for the construction of churches and other Christian buildings, as they did in the case of the church of the Jesuits in Cuzco, the foundations of which were laid, at a depth of nearly eight meters, in 1579. The building blocks for the church were transported from earlier Inca structures to their new site by Indian workers amid song and rejoicing. As the Jesuit José de Acosta wrote in his annual letter to Rome:

> The Indians join together by kin groups to transport stones for our church, and are dressed as for a festival, and with their feathers and fineries they all come singing through the city.... The Incas ... work at the project with most eagerness, and another group of Indians, the Cañari ... who pride themselves on having always been loyal to the Spanish, come in competition bringing blocks with singing and (adorned in) their feather-work, and even the women transport stones and set to work with song. Someone asked one of these, who is a nobly born lady, why she lowered herself to do such humble work when she could pay someone else. She said she could easily pay for much more, but that he who worked for her money would not give her the merit of contributing to God's work.[31]

What Acosta perhaps failed to realize was that in thus contributing labor to the Jesuit project, the Indians were perpetuating an old established Andean and Inca practice. It is a practice that still lives on, and has been described by José Maria Arguedas in his novel *Yawar Fiesta* about the highland town of Puquio. Arguedas describes how in the 1920s the Indians, *comuneros,* of Puquio built a road of 180 kilometers down to the coastal lowlands in just under a month. Led and guided by their *varayok*, "staff bearers," that is their elected civic officials, they worked all day and long into the night, and the sound of their singing and flute playing was heard over great distances in the valleys, and on the small farms and in the villages near Puquio and down to the hills near the coast.[32]

This is how we can imagine the work of building early colonial churches to have been accomplished, for the construction of the Jesuit church in Cuzco was far from unique in receiving substantial and indeed decisive Indian help. In the late sixteenth and earlier seventeenth centuries, the Franciscan order supervised the construction of an entire string of churches in the Collca valley near Arequipa. These churches served village communities that had been brought together in the Andean-wide resettlement program organized by the Viceroy Toledo: each village had its central square, its church and public buildings. Similar building projects were undertaken in the villages that ring Lake Titicaca, in the Bolivian Andes, in the Quito region and New Granada, and throughout Central America.[33] Spanish law mandated that the Crown defray half the cost of such construction. Although these payments often served as an initial stimulus, they tended to lapse with time, leaving the responsibility for maintaining and adorning churches in the hands of Indian communities, who came together in this task and expressed their shared purpose and identity in it much as Arguedas's *comuneros* did in the building of their road. This sense of shared purpose can be read from the decoration of these churches, especially in the religious paintings and sculpture, where motifs were incorporated that appear only rarely if at all in European sacred contexts. In Mexico, representations of indigenous plants, birds, fish, and quadrupeds brought the concept of paradise close to Indian worshipers,[34] while the Christian battle against evil and sin was made a reality on a painted church wall showing Aztec tiger and eagle warriors contending with monsters.[35] In Peru, charango-playing[36] *sirenas,* water spirits, whose job it is to sweeten a young man's song when in pursuit of his beloved, ply their trade above church portals. Elsewhere on church façades, monkeys and birds of the tropics frolic amid verdure that trails around solomonic columns; and above the altar, the Virgin Mary appears as an ensouled holy mountain, or perhaps as the Andean Pachamama, Mother Earth.[37]

In short, throughout Spanish America, the Indians appropriated Christian architectural forms, motifs in Christian art, and European topographies as their own and enlivened them in accord with their own American environment and culture. The Christian societies that Cortés and Pizarro and their contemporaries established thus became a much more colorful and vivacious reality than those men of steel could ever have envisioned. Just as in Spain, babies were baptized at the church door; once grown up, they received the sacrament of confirmation and later, were joined as couples in marriage while standing before their priest at the main altar. Finally, once more at the main altar, their mortal remains were blessed for burial in consecrated ground.[38] Yet, these ancient rituals that had been shaped by centuries of acculturation on the missionary frontiers of late Roman and medieval Europe were now acculturated in a radically new sense. Take the sacrament of confirmation, which marked a person's spiritual maturity as a full member of the Christian community. This maturity was expressed by some missionaries in sixteenth-century Mexico in terms of young men growing into the aristocratic status of a soldier of Christ, on whom the sacrament of confirmation bestowed, figuratively speaking, the regalia that had formerly graced the Aztec warrior nobility.[39]

By the end of the sixteenth century, Spanish America observed the Catholic calendar: from Advent to Christmas, Lent, Easter and Pentecost, on to the festival of the Assumption of Mary and those of All Saints and All Souls, this calendar celebrated the lives of Jesus, of his mother and the apostles, and also the experience of the church at large. The agricultural and imperial calendars of an earlier day were thus supplanted by the calendar of the Catholic Church. And yet, many difficulties were latent in this success story.

Church architecture, ecclesiastical ritual, and the dances and music that were performed to honor God and his saints continued to express, however distantly, theological ideas and religious expectations that had formerly been tied to very different gods. For this reason, they appeared not wholly foreign to the native Indians, and thus played a role in convincing many to convert. But the religion of Jesus had from its inception required the complete assent of its followers. "Sell all and follow me," Jesus had said, and Paul saw no difference between "Jew or gentile, slave or free, male or female" among Christians,[40] since they had all become incorporated into the new Christian covenant that superceded all earlier sense of belonging and canceled all earlier religious obligations. In the ancient Mediterranean, the point often did not sink in at all or only with considerable difficulty. Thus, in Roman Spain, Christians who before their conversion had served their cities as priests of pagan deities saw no conflict between their new Christian identity and continuing to offer pagan sacrifice, just as their forebears had done.[41] In sixteenth-century Spain, where Muslims and Jews had been confronted with the alternative of leaving Spain or converting to Christianity, such issues were highly topical. For the many who chose to remain, was observance of the Sabbath compatible with being a Christian? Did wearing Muslim dress and speaking Arabic undermine or compromise Christian identity?[42] And in the Americas, were indigenous hairstyles and clothes, not to mention music and ways of dancing, in effect clandestine methods of continuing to worship the old gods? In the Peninsula and the Americas alike, many Spaniard officials took a rigorist position on such questions, and in the New World men of the church devoted much effort toward ensuring that pagan thought and practice did not survive in Christian guise. But survive they did, and not just in the form of buildings, music, clothes, and hairstyles.[43] Even in the later seventeenth century, many Andean Indians asked permission of the old gods before embarking on the celebration of Christian festivals, they quietly and secretly deposited figurines of sacred presences and other holy objects in churches, and they worshiped the mummified bodies of their ancestors.[44] Within the household, holy objects of indigenous origin were cherished side by side with Christian images and statuettes, as in many places they still are today.

During much of the seventeenth century, Catholic Church officials reacted decisively to this state of affairs by launching campaigns of "extirpating idolatries" that matched the violence and destruction of the early years following the invasion. In a sense, ecclesiastics were now expecting from indigenous Christians what had never been theirs: a clarity of religious identity that could only arise from the profound inner reorientation that was a product of personal conversion. There had been such conversions in the Americas: inner upheavals— sometimes accompanied by visions of heaven or hell, or of angels, Jesus, the Virgin Mary, or even of the devil and the pains of hell—that led a person to a complete turning around, an abandonment of all earlier experience. Such was the experience, in about 1550, of an Andean lord from Lampa who, while praying in an Andean holy place, had a vision of an angel in shining raiment. As a result, he was baptized, and then

> went where his house was and burnt it down, and his women and herds he distributed among his brothers and kinsfolk, and betook himself to the church where he always was preaching to the Indians about what they needed to do to be saved. . . . This he did with great fervour, like someone who had been illumined by the Holy Spirit.[45]

But such conversions were rare. Most Indians had become Christians in a public, social, and political sense. They had adapted Spanish institutions of local governance for their own use, they constructed and maintained churches that were adorned with paintings depicting Andean and Nahua lords as donors and patrons of pious works, and they celebrated the seasons of the Christian year by organizing processions, festivals, and public displays. It was in part by means of such shared activities that Indians were able to overcome the upheaval and destruction of invasion and conquest: they reconstituted their public identities within the new Christian framework that the invaders had brought with them. Within this framework, however, much scope was left for cultural and religious diversity and even dissent, which in due course offended Spanish and Creole men of the church. These people, among them the Jesuit

José de Arriaga, the Archbishop of Lima Pedro de Villagomez, and the extirpator of idolatries Francisco de Avila, looked back to the church of the apostles and martyrs as a model, and found their own church wanting by comparison. But where the early Christians had spoken the same language and lived in the same cultural nexus, Christianity in the Americas was a foreign implant that spanned an immense cultural distance between missionaries and their public, not to mention the distance of privilege and the unequal distribution of resources and obligations that separated Indians from Spaniards and Creoles. Indians and mestizos paid tribute and fulfilled heavy labor obligations, while Spaniards and Creoles paid little and did nothing: this state of affairs was taken so much for granted that the imposition of a modest sales tax, *alcabala,* in 1592, during a period of great financial difficulty throughout the Spanish Empire, generated a rebellion in Quito.[46] In such a world, the extirpation of idolatries that occupied so much ecclesiastical attention during the seventeenth century served to sharpen the divide between the privileged descendants of the invaders, among them the clergy, and the underprivileged and often terribly poor Indian majority.

In effect, Creoles and Spaniards lived in a different Christian universe from Indians, for apart from material and political privilege, they were separated by profoundly different forms of religious expression and experience. For Indians, Christian identity was one of many tokens of their conquered condition, a condition that could be temporarily suspended when Indian communities celebrated the festivals of their patron saints and of the Christian calendar with music, dance, and public feasting. Outward celebration, however, was and continues to be matched by an inward experience of lost love, sorrow, and homelessness that pervades Quechua poetry, and is present even in poems of Christian celebration, as in this liturgical hymn to Mary:

> Look at the splattered tears,
> To the crier of bitter tears,
> To the contrite broken-hearted,
> Turn your eyes
> Let me see your face,
> Mother of God . . .
> Joys of the angels,
> Light with which all see themselves.[47]

In one sense, we can read these verses as an Andean version of general Catholic sentiment as expressed, for example, in the prayer *Salve Regina* from the Roman liturgy: "Hail, Holy Queen, Mother of Mercy . . . to thee we cry, exiled children of Eve, to thee we send up our sighs, mourning and weeping in this vale of tears."[48] But in another sense, when contextualized in the Andes, where the most popular song style, the *waynu,* most often dwells on sorrow and loss,[49] liturgical prayer about these themes resonates in a way that is at once more universal and more intimate.

The privileged also expressed their piety in exuberant public display, and sometimes repented of their sins, as Indians did. But beyond that, members of privileged society were able to explore their inner lives and their identification with Jesus in ways not available to everyone else. This was the case especially for Spanish and Creole women, but not only for them. In late antiquity, Antony and Paul, Hilarion and Saint Mary of Egypt along with many others had sought out secluded places in order to find there, and in the recesses of the soul, converse with and closeness to Jesus. In Spanish America, painters, sculptors, and authors of devotional manuals recreated these experiences to serve as examples for new generations of searchers after God. Closer in time, in sixteenth-century Spain, Fray Luis de Granada, Teresa of Avila, and John of the Cross had described in their own inimitable Castilian how God might be found, and many copies of their books were shipped to the New World.[50] "En una noche obscura (On a dark night)," John of the Cross had written, he, his soul, set out for the beloved and found him:

> Oh night my guide,
> Night dearer than dawn,
> Oh night that joined
> Lover and loved,
> The loved in lover transformed.[51]

For these mystics, the language of secular love was really the language of the love of God, and the street songs of Madrid and Mexico City, of Lima and Quito, echoed in hearts whom no earthly lover could satisfy. One night, for example, in Lima in the early 1600s, the young nun Rosa in her Dominican convent was thinking:

> Midnight has struck,
> My Jesus has not come,

Who is the lucky one
Who is holding him up?[52]

A little later, similar thoughts went through the mind of the ascetic Mariana de Jesús in Quito, and at century's end in Mexico City, the learned and beautiful Sor Juana Inés de la Cruz, who wore the habit of the Order of Saint Jerome, wrote a poem for the veiling of a fellow nun:

Come to the wedding, hasten my lords,
A girl is to marry, she marries for love![53]

Santa Rosa de Lima became the patron of Peru in 1669, and nowadays her festival is a national holiday, while in Mexico, Sor Juana is celebrated not just for her sanctity and learning but especially as one of the nation's greatest poets.

While these women and some of their less famous sisters were passionately and persistently seeking union with the human and the divine Christ, a union in which the mortal self would be swept up in the infinity of God, they were not usually living alone or in isolation, but as members of religious communities. A number of small convents existed; many of them, like the religious communities of men, were miniature cities within the city, with their own streets, and bakeries, workshops, infirmaries, and pharmacies. Here also, as throughout colonial Spanish America, architecture gave visible shape to the order of society; in this instance, it helped to seclude the sacred from the secular without separating the two completely. Nevertheless, in becoming a member of such a community, one did enter a distinct society that lived by its own rule: whether this was the monastic rule that in the late fourth century Augustine had written for his own small monastery in Hippo, and that continued being observed in the great Augustinian monasteries of the Americas, or whether it was one of the later monastic rules, such as those of Saint Francis or Saint Dominic. The purpose of obeying such a rule was to live a holy and devout life, but beyond that, what these rules accomplished was to forge groups of individuals into communities that acted as such. Ideally, a religious community by virtue of its distinctness set a standard to aspire to for secular society.

But distinctness had its limits. Ties of family and friendship continued to link the lives of monks and nuns to the surrounding society; moreover, thanks to the numerous and often substantial pious bequests that were left to religious communities in return for their prayers, they became landowners on a large scale, financed loans, and participated in urban and regional economies.[54] In joining a religious community, one thus entered a society that enjoyed a certain privilege—a society, according to the laws that governed it, in which only whites were included. This did not prevent Martín de Porras, a mulatto lay brother and servant of the Dominican convent in Lima, from becoming one of Peru's most beloved saints, and from acquiring, even in life, a reputation for unperturbable moral authority and a sweetness of temper that embraced all living things: from the friars down to the convent's pack animals, dogs, and cats.[55] But Martín de Porras was an exception, and his sainthood represented and still represents a reality as much as a longing: the reality of his holy life, and the longing of those who come to him for relief from their burdens while hoping for a juster, more equitable society.

If, then, it was primarily people of European descent who could travel along the paths leading to financial gain, political power, and social privilege in both church and state, representatives of all of Spanish America's diverse humanity came together in pilgrimage sanctuaries and before the miracle-working images of Mary and of Christ and the saints. In 1582, the parish priest of Copacabana on Lake Titicaca allowed an image of Mary holding the Christ child that had been carved by the Inca sculptor Titu Yupanqui to be set up in the local church. This alone was a most unusual event because, even at this time, most Christian images were still made by Spanish artists. But before long, this Andean Mary, present to her worshipers through Titu Yupanqui's image, began restoring sight to the blind, making the lame walk, and curing all manner of diseases. In Mexico also, the Virgin manifested herself to Indians as when, so tradition recounts, she appeared to the poor Indian Juan Diego, filled his cloak with roses and ordered him to inform the archbishop to build her a church. After some hesitation the archbishop complied, but not before the "precious image of Saint Mary always Virgin, Mother of God" appeared imprinted on Juan Diego's cloak of simple Indian cloth.[56] This image exists in countless copies throughout the Americas, and each year thousands of pilgrims gather in the sanctuary of Our Lady of Guadalupe in Mexico. Like other sacred images, those of the Virgin of Guadalupe and the Virgin of Copacabana are no respecters of persons. The Virgin blesses with her miracles those whom she chooses regardless of wealth, status, or race. One might even conclude that miracles happen especially for the poor, the outcast, the helpless: for example, the Indian miners in colonial Potosi, who time and again, when a mining shaft collapsed or a mining tunnel flooded, were convinced that their lives had been saved by the intervention of the Mother of God.

Miracles remedied some of the inescapable pains and sorrows of the human condition, and they set things right that human frailty or sin had done amiss. But in themselves, miracles have not been a vehicle for social change, or even a stimulus for it. The poor and the disadvantaged journeyed to the great healing shrines like Copacabana or Guadalupe, or to some more humble miracle-working image, and at times, just like other suppliants, they found healing: even so, they left the sanctuary as poor and disadvantaged as they came. Not that there has been no Christian social consciousness in Spanish America, but it has flown and flows through other channels.

In telling a story, as I have done to this point, about the formation of Christian communities and of Christian inner experience in Spanish America, I have mainly drawn on texts composed by people who felt that they could work with, and even identify to some extent with the powers that be. These people include Spaniards, Creoles, and even some Indians, men and women practicing the devout life, bishops, clergy, officials, viceroys, notaries, and historians. However, if we are to more fully understand this story of formation and creative cultural unfolding, we must also account for the violence, death, and destruction that preceded and accompanied it. Throughout the Americas, European diseases for which indigenous people had no antibodies brought about unprecedented rates of mortality, which were aggravated by decades of warfare and exploitation. The deadly impact of European diseases on entire New World populations was not fully understood before our own time, but the impact of warfare and exploitation was understood very well indeed in the sixteenth century by some missionary friars who realized that they must address their message as much to Spaniards as to Indians. Insofar as the *conquistadores* acted under the stimulus of Christian motivation, which many of them did, they felt called on to spread the name of God, to defend his honor and that of his mother and the saints by force of arms. Concurrently, they were ready and even eager to honor God's ministers. When the first Franciscans arrived in Mexico, Hernán Cortés kissed their hands and knelt on the ground to greet them. He did so in part to impress on indigenous nobles the importance of Christian decorum, but he also meant to declare his own reverence for God's servants. To honor the friars and other clerics was a way to honor God, which was also expressed, as we have seen, in erecting cathedrals and churches—in giving the divine name a visible expression.

In the eyes of some of the missionary friars, however, such gestures, whether sincere or not, were quite simply beside the point. In 1511, on the island of Santo Domingo, the friar Antón Montesinos preached a sermon to Spanish settlers on one of the readings for Advent, about John the Baptist, "the voice of one crying in the wilderness." He himself was that voice, the friar declared:

> [A]nd it tells you that you are all in mortal sin. You are living and dying in it because of the cruel tyranny which you inflict on these innocent people. Tell me, with what right, what justice, do you keep these Indians in . . . servitude? With what authority have you made . . . war on these . . . people who were peacefully living in their lands? . . . Do they not have rational souls? Are you not obligated to love them as yourselves? Don't you understand this, or feel it? How can you be so abjectly caught in the sleep of moral lethargy?[57]

Further sermons by Montesinos and other Dominicans followed, and produced such outrage among Caribbean settlers that they pressed the king of Spain and his advisors to silence the friars. The king tried, but to no avail. What even the king had encountered was a perennial, perplexing, and fruitful tension in Catholic Christianity: to "render unto Caesar," to respect the powers that be because they were, as Paul had said, appointed by God, and at the same time to seek justice and equality for those who are in no position to seek these things for themselves. In 1513, Bartolomé de Las Casas gave up his Cuban grant of *encomienda*, of Indian labor services, and later he joined the Dominican order so as to devote the rest of his long life to defending the rights of indigenous people. His message was taken up in Spanish universities, especially at Salamanca, and by clerics and lay people throughout the Americas, and, as we shall see, it lives on today.[58]

For Montesinos and for Las Casas and his followers in Mexico and Peru, the task of honoring God could only be accomplished by treating Indians as fellow human beings in accord with the command to love one's neighbor as oneself. This was the one and essential precondition for preaching the Christian message.[59] "What nation," Las Casas asked, "does not admire courteous and benevolent conduct, an agreeable temper and other qualities of this kind? And what nation does not hate and despise proud people, evil doers, men who are cruel, malevolent and overbearing?" Christian conviction had to be arrived at by persuasion and under peaceful conditions:

If non-Christians are first . . . afflicted and anguished . . . by the calamities of war, and are mourning the loss of their children, their possessions and their freedom . . . , how can they possibly be moved to embrace voluntarily whatever they might be told about the faith, about religion, justice, and truth?[60]

Leaving aside these obstacles to evangelization, Las Casas, like some other Spaniards, thought that the Indians already possessed many of the virtues that were inculcated by the gospel. More often than not they lived in charity with one another; they had created civilized polities; and they had mastered the visual, musical, and mechanical arts. In effect, the Indians had much to teach the Spanish. "In monastic, economic and political life, many of them would be able to govern us, lead us into good customs and rule us by natural reason."[61] Europeans, who had been privileged to hear the Christian message earlier than the indigenous peoples of the Americas, ought therefore to share the message of the Gospel and live according to its precepts. The ethical imperative, which urgently called forth the evangelical way of life in the here and now, was reinforced by the conviction, held by many late medieval and early modern Europeans, that they were witnessing signs that indicated the completion of worldly history and the return of the Messiah. Columbus thought that his voyages would facilitate the recovery of Jerusalem by the Catholic kings, Ferdinand and Isabel, which was one such sign prophesied in John's Revelation. Two generations later, the Ottoman Sultan Suleiman the Magnificent and his advisers were convinced that it was their empire, not a Christian one, that would pave the way to the culmination of historical time. In Mexico, meanwhile, some missionaries thought that the millennial kingdom would emerge in the Christian Indian societies that they themselves were bringing into existence.[62]

This did not happen, but the idea of Las Casas that even before the Spanish first arrived Indians had lived and governed themselves in exemplary fashion—that somehow, Indians were natural Christians and that Amerindian societies enshrined the seeds of millennial perfection—has lived on in a variety of guises. Some early modern Europeans believed that the Christian message had been preached throughout the world during the lifetimes of the apostles: for had not Christ himself commanded them to "go and preach the gospel to all the world?" In accord with this theory, traces of an apostle were discovered by missionaries in India, in Brazil, and also in Mexico and Peru. The notion that the Indians had been taught Christianity during those early years of the church helped to explain why they governed themselves in the peaceable manner that

Las Casas and others so much admired. It also helped to explain the account that Indians gave of certain of their deities. In Mexico, missionaries heard that the beneficent creator deity Quetzalcóatl had left, but would one day return; a similar story was told about the creator Tunupa in the Andes. Were such stories, some Spaniards asked themselves, distant memories of an apostle who had visited these remote parts? Suggestions of this kind were eagerly taken up by Indians. In the early seventeenth century, the Andean historian Guaman Poma de Ayala was convinced that the Apostle Bartholomew had taught his people and had left, as a testimony of his message, the Cross of Carabuco, which was "rediscovered" and installed in a church in Guaman Poma's own day. A little later, Don Joan Santacruz Pachacuti Yamqui held similar convictions, but thought the apostle who had come to the Americas was Saint Thomas, known to Andean people as Tunupa, while in Mexico, the deity who represented Saint Thomas was Quetzalcóatl.[63]

More was at stake here than tying up loose ends of American and European sacred history, because stories about the apostle enabled Indians to declare that they needed no Spaniards to explain Christianity to them, given that they had understood and put it into practice long ago. Already in ancient times, Guaman Poma wrote, the Indians had worshiped one God. And in the time of the Incas, they had lived in an exemplary society where poverty was unknown; throughout the Andes, communities cared for those among them who were sick, and for widows, orphans, and the old. Guaman Poma may not have read any of the writings of Las Casas, but the ideas for which Las Casas fought throughout his life do speak in his pages. Repeatedly, Guaman Poma listed the many ills of his time: slow and expensive justice, excessive tribute payments, and corvée labor, all made worse by the corruption of Spanish officialdom. These ills, unheard of in the time of the Incas, forced many Indians to flee from their homes, leaving villages underpopulated and impoverished. In the Andes, as in Mexico, the response of the indigenous peoples went beyond a nostalgic yearning for a past paradise, and included political action and, often, revolt.

In 1712 in the village of Cancuc in Chiapas, where Las Casas had been bishop, the young Indian girl Maria López saw the Virgin Mary in a vision: "a very lovely and very white lady," who asked that a shrine be built for her so that she could live among the villagers. Once there was the shrine, a cult developed. The people of Chiapas were unhappy over the recent tribute payments they had been forced to make, and had more generally been discontented during these uncertain years after the Bourbon succession and the twelve years of warfare that accompanied it. In the wake of this discontent, the message that Maria López announced to the province reflected these circumstances, but from a local, Indian point of view. "Believe and follow me," she said, "because there will be no more tribute, king, bishop, or district magistrate, and you need do no more than follow and believe in this Virgin." "The time span and prophecy for them to throw off the yoke, and restore their lands and liberty had come," and

> it was the will of God that the Virgin of Cancuc should come for her children the Indians to free them from the captivity of the Spanish and lackeys of the church and that the angels would come and sow and guard their maize fields, and that by the signs there were in the sun and the moon the king of Spain had already died and it was necessary to name another.

Finally, "the king who was to rule them would be elected by themselves, and they would be free of the labor they were enduring and of paying tribute."[64]

The Mexican authorities succeeded in defeating this uprising in Chiapas, and throughout Spanish America during the later seventeenth and eighteenth centuries, numerous other indigenous uprisings, some small and others significant and well organized, were beaten down, often with great ferocity. Although prompted by local circumstances, the Indian rebels shared certain principles and concerns. Thus, whereas they all took for granted the Christianity the missionaries had taught, the facets of Christianity that most inspired their attempted revolts were the ethical and social ones. Take the edicts issued in 1781 by Tupac Amaru, the Inca leader of the most far-reaching indigenous Peruvian movement of independence. Reiterating an image that had been used by St. Paul, Tupac Amaru wrote repeatedly that all Peruvians, Spaniards, Creoles, blacks and Indians should live "like brothers, gathered together in one body." Elsewhere, he wrote that the depredations that representatives of the Spanish Crown were inflicting on those Indians who were least able to defend themselves required "the strictest restitution" of everything that had been taken[65]—just what Las Casas had urged so insistently in his day. In the face of such pressing material and political needs, Christian metaphysics and the explorations of the heart that so absorbed the Creole poets mattered little; indeed, the Christian decorum that had shaped political and urban life in Spanish America, and to some extent still does so, mattered hardly at all.

This is particularly pronounced in modern and contemporary movements. "The Church and the word of God have told us things to save our souls," a rural catechist in Chiapas said at one point during the 1960s,

> but we don't know how to save our bodies. While we're working for our salvation and that of everyone else, we suffer from hunger, illness, poverty and death.... We already know the Bible, the authors, the number of the books . . . we sing and pray every Sunday . . . but hunger, illness and poverty do not look as though they are going to end.[66]

Las Casas and the friars who worked with him would have understood exactly what the catechist meant, and many contemporary Latin American Christians are aware of this connection. Among indigenous people, the Columbian peasant leader and theologian Quintín Lame, who died in 1967, viewed his own struggles for his people and their land as a direct continuation of the work of Las Casas four centuries earlier.[67]

Contemporary Latin American theologians speak of the need to anchor their work in interpretations of the Bible that arise from the experience of Latin Americans, and most especially from that of the poor and dispossessed, instead of allowing priorities to be dictated by those speaking from the very different perspective of the developed world. As Gustavo Gutiérrez has written in his foundational book *The Theology of Liberation*, first published in 1970, the task is to read "the signs of the times,"[68] whether these signs are identified, as when the book was written, as the oppressive impact of neocolonialism on the poorer countries, or whether they are, as today, understood to point toward the oppressive effects of international development.[69]

The Spanish missionaries who in the sixteenth century saw signs of the fulfillment of the times looked to the millennial kingdom that had been prophesied in the *Apocalypse* as the sign that applied to their time. But they also looked to the ethical precepts of the prophets and the New Testament by way of implementing their message: a message, in the last resort, of social justice, of neighborly love committed to saving the body with the soul, and of forging communities on that basis.[70] This is what Indian Christians, from colonial times down to the present day, have seized on and made their own. Hence, in accounting for the experience and hopes of the poor and dispossessed, in describing the ethical basis of community, whether local or global, and in seeking the realization of a truly Christian society, the theologians of liberation have created a Latin American theology of their continent's historical experience, as well as a theology of daily practice for the here and now. The pursuit of this theology has in many instances led to a rupture in the relations between church and state, the maintenance of which had been so important a concern of missionaries and clerics like Gaspar de Villarroel during the colonial and even the republican periods.[71]

I have tried in this essay to convey a sense of the Christian experience in Spanish America, both its diversity and its coherence, over half a millennium. The search for a Christian society worthy of the name and for individual fulfillment within that framework, in preference to making individual aspirations a primary goal, has been central from the beginning of Christianity's history in Spanish America, and still is, even though the terms of this search, and the reasons for it, have changed profoundly. During the last forty years or so, the theology of liberation has brought this search, so characteristic of Latin American Christianity, to the attention of the world at large, so that a Christian tradition that has long been on the periphery is now on the periphery no longer.

NOTES

1. The best known accounts of the conquests of Mexico and Peru are by William Prescott in his now classic works *History of the Conquest of Mexico,* completed in 1843, and *History of the Conquest of Peru,* completed in 1847. More recent are two masterly narratives: Hugh Thomas, *Conquest: Montezuma, Cortés and the Fall of Old Mexico* (New York, 1993); John Hemming, *The Conquest of the Incas* (New York, 1973). A comparison of these accounts reveals how profoundly the understanding of the events described has changed over time. This is especially true with respect to the broadly cultural, religious, and political lives of the indigenous peoples of Central and South America.

2. See N. Sanchez-Albornoz, *La población de América Latina: Desde los tiempos precolumbinos al año 2025,* 2d ed. (Madrid, 1994), chaps. 3–4, on the catastrophic decline of indigenous populations and the immigration of Europeans, Africans, and some Asians during the sixteenth and seventeenth centuries. See also Serge Gruzinski and Nathan Wachtel, "Cultural Interbreedings: Constituting the Majority as a Minority," in *The Construction of Minorities: Cases for Comparison Across time and Around the World,* ed. André Burguière and Raymond Grew (Ann Arbor, 2001), 171–93, with comment by S. MacCormack at 194–212. A brief, somewhat episodic survey of the history of the Catholic Church in Spanish America is provided by León Lopetegui, "La iglesia española y la hispanoamericana de 1493 a 1810," in *Historia de la Iglesia en España III-2: La Iglesia en la España de los*

siglos XV y XVI, ed. Ricardo García-Villoslada (Madrid, 1980), 363–441; for a quite different vantage point, cf. note 71. *The Cambridge History of Latin America*, edited by Leslie Bethell, 10 vols. (Cambridge, 1984–95), contains several good chapters on the history of the church: Josep Barnadas, "The Catholic Church in Colonial Spanish America," vol. 1: *Colonial Latin America* (Cambridge, 1984), 511–40; 616–20; John Lynch, "The Catholic Church in Latin America 1830–1930," vol. 4: *C. 1870–1930* (Cambridge, 1986), 527–95, 656–60; Enrique Dussel, "The Catholic Church in Latin America since 1930," vol. 6: *Latin America since 1930: Economy, Society, Politics. Part 2, Politics and Society* (Cambridge, 1994), 547–82, 697–704; José Miguez Bonino, "The Protestant Churches in Latin America since 1930," ibid., 583–604; 204–77 (this latter topic, deserving of research, is left aside in this present essay). The survey of art and architecture, including ecclesiastical art and architecture, by George Kubler and Martin Soria, *Art and Architecture in Spain and Portugal and their American Dominions, 1500–1800* remains useful. See also Gauvin Alexander Bailey, *Art on the Jesuit Missions in Asia and Latin America 1542–1773* (Toronto, 1999).

3. Mark 16:15.

4. The cult of the Virgin of Guadalupe spread widely in America. See Sebastián García, *Guadalupe de Extremadura en América* (Guadalupe, 1990).

5. Diego de Ocaña, *A través de la America del Sur*, ed. Arturo Alvarez (Madrid, 1969), with accompanying documents and reproducing Ocaña's drawings and watercolors. A later edition in 1987 has Ocaña's text only. See Kenneth Mills, "Diego de Ocaña e l'organizzazione del miraculoso a Potosí (1600–1601)," in *Il santo patrono e la città. San Benedetto il Moro: culti, devozioni, strategie di età moderna*, ed. Giovanna Fiume (Venice, 2000), 372–90; Mills, "La memoria viva de Diego de Ocaña en Potosí," *Anuario: Archivo y Biblioteca Nacionales de Bolivia* (Sucre, 1999), 197–241.

6. On the Virgin Mary as conqueror in Spain, see José Antonio Ramos Rubio, *Historia del culto a Ntra: Sra. de la Victoria y so coronación canónica* (Trujillo, 1994), and the penetrating review of sources and ideas by Amy Remensnyder, "The Colonization of Sacred Architecture: The Virgin Mary, Mosques, and Temples in Medieval Spain and Early Sixteenth-Century Mexico," in *Monks and Nuns, Saints and Outcasts: Religion in Medieval Society. Essays in Honor of Lester K. Little*, ed. S. Farmer and B.H. Rosenwein (Ithaca, 2000), 189–210. For the Virgin in the conquest of Peru, see Ruben Vargas Ugarte, *Historia del Culto de Maria en Iberoamérica y de sus Imágenes y Santuarios* (Madrid, 1956), 21 ff. On the medieval literary development of the image of Santiago as conqueror of Muslims, see M. J. Lacarra, "El camino de Santiago y la literatura castellana medieval," in *El Camino de Santiago y la Articulación del Espacio Hispánico. XX Semana de Estudios Medievales. Estella, 26 a 30 de julio de 1993* (Pamplona, 1994), 315–35. On Santiago in Mexico, see Max Harris, *Aztecs, Moors and Christians in Mexico and Spain* (Austin, 2000).

7. Miguel León Portilla, *Visión de los vencidos* (Madrid, 1985), 161, from informantes anónimos de Tlatelolco.

8. Titu Cusi Yupanqui, *Instrucción al licenciado Don Lope García de Castro 1570)*, ed. Liliana Regalado de Hurtado (Lima, 1992), 47 (fol. 40r).

9. On Peninsular precedents to the conversion of entire communities in the Americas, rather than just individuals, cf. Antonio Garrido Aranda, *Organización de la Iglesia en el Reino de Granada y su proyección en Indias. Siglo XVI* (Seville, 1979).

10. Bernabé Cobo, *Fundación de Lima,* in his *Obras,* vol. 92, ed. Francisco Mateos (Madrid, 1964), chap. 3, 290a, the square, church, and solares; chap. 5, 293b, the cabildo. See also Maria Rostworowski de Diez Canseco, *Senoríos indígenas de Lima y Canta* (Lima, 1978), 67–88, esp. 75 ff. for the taking of the land.

11. Cobo, *Fundación,* chap. 8; see also Calancha, *Corónica moralizada del orden de san Agustín en el Perú,* ed. I. Prado Pastor (Lima, 1974–81), book I, chap. 21, 309–13), for the location of the first Augustinian convent, which was a private donation and thus not part of the original distribution of civic space; Juan Melendez, *Tesoros verdaderos de las Indias,* 3 vols. (Rome, 1681–82), vol. 1, book 1, chap. 7, for the Dominican convent, the land being granted to the Order by Francisco Pizarro in the original foundation of Lima.

12. Cobo, *Fundación,* chap. 3, 289b: "porque el principio de cualquier pueblo o ciudad ha de ser en Dios y por Dios y en su nombre." These words are quoted by Cobo from the original foundation document of which he had a copy.

13. Cobo, *Fundación,* chap. 5, 293b: "como el pueblo sin justicia, gobierno y leyes justas y buenas, aun no merezca el nombre de república y cuerpo político, ni sea más que como un tronco sin vida ni alma." The interdependence of civic and ecclesiastical government and institutions that is so dominant a feature in colonial Latin America goes back to the later Roman Empire. See Karl Leo Noethlichs, "Kirche, Recht und Gesellschaft in der Jahrhundertmitte," in *L'église au IVe siècle. Fondation Hardt pour l'étude de l'antiquité classique, Entretiens Tome XXXIV* (Geneva, 1987), 251–99.

14. Horacio Urteaga and Carlos Romero, *Fundación española del Cuzco y Ordenanzas para su Gobierno* (Lima, 1926), 37.

15. See Valerie Fraser, *The Architecture of Conquest: Building in the Viceroyalty of Peru, 1535–1635* (Cambridge, 1990).

16. Richard Morse, "Introducción a la historia urbana de Hispanoamérica," *Revista de Indias* 32 (1972): 9–53, is a brilliant introduction into this complex topic.

17. See Diego de Esquivel y Navia, *Noticias cronológicas de la gran ciudad del Cuzco* (Lima, 1980), chap. 13, 185–90.

18. Gaspar de Villarroel, *Govierno Eclesiastico Pacifico* (Madrid, 1656), part II, question 19, art. 1, 11–12.

19. For one of the parishes of Mexico City, see Juan Javier Pescador, *De bautizados a fieles difuntos. Familia y mentalidades en una parroquia urbana: Santa Catarina de México, 1568–1820* (Mexico City, 1992).

20. Villarroel, *Govierno,* II, 19, 1, 7.

21. See the telling description of the ceremonial advent of the Viceroy Blasco Nuñez Vela in Lima by Diego Fernández (el Palentino), *Historia del Perú* (Madrid, 1963, first published Seville, 1571), part I, book 1, chap. 9, 15–16.

22. Villarroel, *Govierno,* II, 12, 2, 14 ff.

23. Joan de Santa Cruz Pachacuti Yamqui Salcamaygua, *Relación de antiguedades deste reyno del Pirú*, ed. Pierre Duviols and César Itier (Cuzco, 1993), 268 (fol. 43v of the original manuscript).

24. Ibid.: "Al fin vinieron los españoles y curacas con mucha horden. . . ."

25. Bernal Diaz del Castillo, *The Discovery and Conquest of Mexico*, trans. A. P. Maudslay (New York, 1965), book II, chap. 35, 101–6; Richard Trexler, "Aztec Priests for Christian Altars: The Theory and Practice of Reverence in New Spain," in *Scienze, credenze occulte. Livelli di cultura. Convegno Internazionale di Studi. Firenze 26–30 giugno 1980* (Florence, 1982), 189 ff.; Hugh Thomas, *Conquest: Montezuma, Cortés, and the Fall of Old Mexico* (New York, 1993), 213–14.

26. Bernal Diaz del Castillo, *Discovery*, II, 52, 155–56.

27. Bartolomé de las Casas, *Apologética historia sumaria*, ed. Edmundo O'Gorman (Mexico City, 1967), chap. 63, 328.

28. Ibid., chap. 64, 333. For a fuller story of conversion in Tlaxcala, see Charles Gibson, *Tlaxcala in the Sixteenth Century* (Stanford, 1967), chap. 2.

29. For the church and square of Tlaxcala, see Barbara E. Mundy, *The Mapping of New Spain: Indigenous Cartography and the Maps of the Relaciones Geográficas* (Chicago, 1996), fig. 83 (Glasgow University Library Special Collections, MS Hunter 242, fol. 245v). On the government of Tlaxcala, Las Casas, *Apologética*, chap. 225, 450.

30. See Sabine MacCormack, "Ubi Ecclesia? Perceptions of Medieval Europe in Spanish America," *Speculum* 69 (1994): 74–99; MacCormack, *Religion in the Andes: Vision and Imagination in Early Colonial Peru* (Princeton, 1991), 406 ff.

31. José de Acosta, letter from Lima of 11 April 1579, in Antonio de Egaña, ed., *Monumenta Peruana II, 1576–1580* (Rome, 1958), 618–19.

32. José Maria Arguedas, *Yawar Fiesta* (Buenos Aires, 1974). The English edition is translated by Frances Horning Barraclough (Austin, 1985), chap. 7.

33. For the Colca valley, see A. Tibesar, *Franciscan Beginnings in Colonial Peru* (Washington, D.C., 1953), a pioneering work, remains useful; Ramón Gutierrez, Carlos Pernaud, et al., *Arquitectura del Altiplano Peruano* (Departamento de la Historia de la Arquitectura, Universidad Nacional del Nordeste, Argentina, 1978); Teresa Gisbert and José de Mesa, *Arquitectura Andina* (La Paz, 1997).

34. Jeanette Favrot Peterson, *The Paradise Garden Murals of Malinalco: Utopia and Empire in Sixteenth-Century Mexico* (Austin, 1993).

35. Emily Edwards, *Painted Walls of Mexico: From Prehistoric Times until Today* (Austin, 1966), esp. 105–8, about San Miguel Arcángel, Ixmiquilpan, Hidalgo.

36. The charango is a ten-stringed Andean instrument, often shaped like a guitar, but smaller.

37. See Teresa Gisbert, *Iconografía y mitos indígenas en el arte*, 2d ed. (La Paz, 1994), 46 ff. on sirenas; 60 ff. on birds and animals; Sabine MacCormack, Milagros, profecía y lugares santos: peregrinación en España y Perú durante la modernidad temprana, *Iacobus. Revista de Estudios Jacobeos y Medievales* 11–12 (Sahagum 2001), pp. 31–70,

on the Virgin Mary as a mountain. See also Manuel M. Marzal, Eugenio Maurer, Xavier Albó, and Batolomeu Melià, *The Indian Face of God in Latin America* (Maryknoll, N.Y., 1996).

38. Sabine MacCormack, "Art in a Missionary Context: Images from Europe and the Andes in the Church of Andahuaylillas Near Cuzco," in *The Word Made Image* (Boston, 1998), 103–26.

39. Osvaldo Pardo, *Nueva teología es menester: cultura cristiana y evangelisación in Mexico, siglo XVI* (Ph.D. diss., University of Michigan, 1993), 88–107.

40. Galatians 3:28.

41. The circumstance is mentioned in the acts of the Council of Elvira (*ca.* 300–306), text in José Vives, ed., *Concilios visigoticos e hispano-romanos* (Barcelona, 1963), chap. 2; see also chaps. 3–4, 55–57, 59.

42. On observing the Sabbath and related matters as viewed by the Inquisition, see Carlos Carrete Parrondo, *Fontes Iudaeorum Regni Castellae II. El Tribunal de la Inquisición en el Obispado de Sora (1486–1502)* (Salamanca, 1985), *passim*. See also Gretchen Starr LeBeau, Mari Sánchez, and Inés Gonzalez, "Conflict and Cooperation among Crypto-Jews," in *Women in the Inquisition: Spain and the New World,* ed. Mary E. Miles (Baltimore, 1999), 19–34. On matters of dress among those converting from Islam, see Francisco J. Florez Arroyuelo, *Los ultimos moriscos (Valle de Ricote 1614)* (Murcia, 1989), 111 ff.; Kathryn Camp, "A Divided Republic: Moriscos and Old Christians in Sixteenth-Century Granada" (Ph.D. diss., University of Michigan, 2001), chap. 3, sec. 2. On the cultural obstacles to the process of evangelization in Granada, see Darío Cabanelas Rodríguez, "Los moriscos. Vida religiosa y evangelización," in *La incorporación de Granada a la Corona de Castilla,* ed. Miguel Ángel Ladero Quesada (Grananda, 1993), 497–511. See also Francisco Antonio Garrido Aranda, *Organización de la Iglesia en el Reino de Granada y su proyección in Indias. Siglo XVI,* Publicaciones de la Escuela de estudios hispano-americanos no. 261 (Sevilla, 1979).

43. The treatise by Hernando Ruiz de Alarcón, *Tratado de las supersticiones y costumbres gentílicas que hoy viven entre los indios naturales desta Nueva España,* ed. Ma. Elena de la Garza Sánchez (Mexico City, 1988), completed in 1629, was designed to assist priests in Indian parishes to discover and eradicate non-Christian observances. It is eloquent evidence of the continuing importance of indigenous religious practices despite a century of missionary effort. Cf. Serge Gruzinski, *La colonisation de l'imaginaire. Sociétés indigènes et occidentalisation dans le Mexique espagnol. XVIe-XVIII siècle* (Paris, 1988). For a description of the more peaceful and harmonious aspect of life in indigenous parishes, see James Lockhart, *The Nahuas after the Conquest: A Social and Cultural History of the Indians of Central Mexico, Sixteenth through Eighteenth Centuries* (Stanford, 1992), chap. 6.

44. For two distinct approaches to this topic, see Kenneth Mills, *Idolatry and Its Enemies: Colonial Andean Religion and Extirpation* (Princeton, 1997); Nicholas Griffiths, *The Cross and the Serpent: Religious Repression and Resurgence in Colonial Peru* (Norman, Okla., 1995). At times, Christian missionizing generated explicit response and op-

position, see Rafael Vargas-Hidalgo, "El Perú de 1590 visto por el provincial de los Jesuitas," *Revista Andina* 27 (1996): 107–17, esp. 112: Indians are saying that "el Dios suyo y el de los españoles no era el mismo y que volviendo a sacrificar al proprio Dios antiguo, dejando el de los españoles, tratarían de aplacarlo" (at a time of pestilence). For the slow pace of conversion in Mexico, or, at any rate, much slower than missionaries desired, see William L. Merrill, "Conversion and Colonialism in Northern Mexico: The Tarahumara Response to the Jesuit Mission Program, 1601–1767," in *Conversion to Christianity: Historical and Anthropological Perspectives on a Great Transformation,* ed. Robert W. Hefner (Berkeley, 1993), 129–63.

45. Pedro Cieza de León, *Crónica del Perú. Primera parte,* ed. Franklin Pease (Lima, 1986), chap. 116, 307.

46. Archivo Nacional, Bolivia, CACH 472, 483, 488, 491–95, 498.

47. The collection of *waynus* by Gloria and Gabriel Escobar, *Huaynos del Cusco* (Cusco, 1981), containing numerous examples of love poems about loss and sorrow, is representative of the genre. For the hymn to Mary, see Bruce Mannheim, "A Nation Surrounded," in *Native Traditions in the Postconquest World,* ed. Elizabeth Hill Boone and Tom Cummins (Washington, D.C., 1992), 283–420, at 393.

48. For the early modern liturgical place of this prayer, see, e.g., *Officium Beatae Mariae Virginis Nuper reformatum . . . ad instar Breviarii Romani sub Urbano VIII recogniti* (Antwerp, 1680), Officium B. Mariae per annum ad Laudes (204–5 in this edition).

49. See Bruce Mannheim, "'Time, Not the Syllables, Must Be Counted': Quechua Parallelism, Word Meaning and Cultural Analysis," *Michigan Discussions in Anthropology* 13 (1998): 245–87, esp. 251: "Not all Quechua songs concern sorrow and loss, but most waynus do, and waynus are the most popular song style."

50. See the index to T. Hampe Martínez, *Cultura barroca y extirpación de idolatrías. La Biblioteca de Francisco de Avila—1648* (Cuzco, 1996).

51. John of the Cross, *Poems,* text and trans. John Frederick Nims (Chicago, 1979), 20 (the present translation is my own):

O noche que guiaste
O noche amable mas que el alvorada
O noche que juntaste
Amado con amada
Amada en el amado transformada.

52. The translation is mine:

Las doce han dado
Mi Jesús no viene
Quien sera la dichosa,
Que lo detiene?

See Ramón Mujica Pinilla, "El ancla de Rosa de Lima: Mística y Política en torno a la Patrona de América," in *Santa Rosa de Lima y su tiempo,* José Flores Araos et al. (Lima, 1995),

53–211, at 101, suggesting that the verses are derived from the novel *Calixto y Melibea*, "La medianoche es pasada, y no viene, sabedme si hay otra amada que lo detiene?"

53. For Mariana de Jesús, see C. E. Fernández de Cordoba, "Cuerpo, visión e imagen en el barroco," *Nariz del Diablo* 20 (Quito, [1994?]), 47–63; Sor Juana Inés de la Cruz, *Obras completas*, ed. F. Monterde (Mexico City, 1981), 318 (Letras sagradas en la solemnidad de la profesión de una religiosa, letra II): "Vengan a la fiesta, / vengan señores, Que hoy se casa una niña, y es por amores!"

54. See Kathryn Burns, *Colonial Habits: Convents and the Spiritual Economy of Cuzco, Peru* (Durham, 1999).

55. See Juan de Meléndez, *Tesoros verdaderos de las Indias* (Rome, 1681–82), vol. III, book 2, chaps. 1–25 on San Martín, who died in 1639.

56. See the Nahua foundation story by Luis Lasso de la Vega, in *Testimonios históricos Guadalupanos*, ed. Ernesto de la Torre Villar and Ramiro Navarro de Anda (Mexico City, 1982), 282–308; see also Stafford Poole, *Our Lady of Guadalupe: The Origins and Sources of a Mexican National Symbol 1531–1797* (Tucson, 1995), 110–26, for a discussion of this text (for words here quoted, see *Testimonios*, at 296). Beatriz Barba de Piña Chán ed., *Caminos terrestres al cielo. Contribución al estudio del fenómeno romero* (Mexico City, 1998), is a collection of contemporary accounts of pilgrimages in Mexico, preceded by an essay on precolumbian pilgrimages by the editor.

57. Translated freely, see Bartolomé de las Casas, *Historia de las Indias*, ed. Agustín Millares Carlo and Lewis Hanke (Mexico City, 1951), book III, chap. 4, 441–442: "[T]odos estáis en pecado mortal y en él vivís y morís, por la crueldad y tiranía que usáis con estas inocentes gentes. Decid, con qué derecho, y con qué justicia tenéis en tan cruel y horrible servidumbre aquestos indios? Con qué autoridad habéis hecho tan detestables guerras a estas gentes que estaban en sus tierras mansas y pacíficas? ... No tienen animas racionales? No sois obligados a amallos como a vosotros mismos? Esto no entendéis? Esto no sentís? Como estáis en tanta profundidad de sueño tan letárgico dormidos?"

58. For a biography of Las Casas that stresses the contemporary importance of his message, see Gustavo Gutiérrez, *Las Casas: In Search of the Poor of Jesus Christ* (New York, 1992).

59. Bartolomé de Las Casas, *De unico vocationis modo*, ed. P. Castañeda Delgado and Antonio García del Moral (Madrid, 1990), 404 ff. (fol. 160v. ff.), with quotations from Scripture and from Augustine, which, in his customary manner, Las Casas inserted to stress the canonical authority of his message.

60. Ibid., 380 (fol. 150v.).

61. Ibid., 350 (fol. 137r.).

62. See John Leddy Phelan, *The Millennial Kingdom of the Franciscans in the New World: A Study of the Writings of Gerónimo de Mendieta (1525–1604)*, University of California Publications in History, vol. 52 (Berkeley, 1956), chap. 7, and Phelan's subsequent book, with an expanded focus, *The Millennial Kingdom of the Franciscans in the New World* (Berkeley, 1970). See also Frank Graziano, *The Millennial New World* (New York, 1999).

63. For Quetzalcóatl as Saint Thomas, see Jacques Lafaye, *Quetzalcóatl and Guadalupe: The Formation of Mexican National Consciousness 1531–1813* (Chicago, 1974), part II. For the Andes, see Guaman Poma de Ayala, *Nueva Crónica y Buen gobierno,* ed. J.V. Murra, R. Adorno, and J. Urioste (Madrid, 1987), 92–94; Pachacuti Yamqui, *Relación,* 188–89 (fols. 3v–4r of the original manuscript).

64. Juan Pedro Viqueira, "Las causas de una rebelión india: Chiapas 1712," in *Chiapas. Los rumbos de otra historia,* ed. Juan Pedro Viqueira and Mario Humberto Ruz (Mexico City, 1998), 124–25 (my translation); for an English translation of extracts from this article, see John Womack Jr., *Rebellion in Chiapas: An Historical Reader* (New York, 1999), 78–86.

65. See Edict of 18 March 1781, in *La rebelión de Túpac Amaru* vol. 2, ed., Carlos Daniel Valcarcel (Colección documental de la independencia del Perú, tomo II, Lima, 1971), 579. See also 83 ff., about the mita of Potosi; 303, edict addressed to Lampa, objecting to misrule; 354 edict to Carabaya, for the well being of all races, safeguarding the Catholic Church; 374–75; to Chichas, "vivamos como hermanos, congregados en un cuerpo."

66. Xóchitl Leyva Solano, "Catequistas, misioneros y tradiciones en Las Cañadas," in *Chiapas. Los rumbos de otra historia,* ed. Juan Pedro Viqueira and Mario Humberto Ruz (Mexico City, 1998), 392.

67. Gonzalo Castillo Cárdenas, *Liberation Theology from Below: The Life and Thought of Manuel Quintín Lame* (New York, 1987), 104–5; see also ibid., 11, 42; Joanne Rappaport, *The Politics of Memory: Native Historical Interpretation in the Columbian Andes* (Durham, 1998), chap. 5.

68. Gustavo Gutiérrez, *La Teologia de la Liberación* (Salamanca, 1972), 30, quoting from the Second Vatican Council, *Gaudium et spes* 44; see also ibid., 4, urging Christians to watch for the "signs of the times," just as the missionaries of an earlier period had done: "per omne tempus Ecclesiae officium incumbit signa temporum perscrutandi et sub Evangelii luce interpretandi; ita ut, modo unicuique generationi accomodato, ad perennes hominum interrogationes de sensu vitae praesentis et futurae deque earum mutua relatione respondere possit" (*Concilio Vaticano II, Constitución Pastoral Gaudium et Spes. Sobre la iglesia en el mundo de nuestro tiempo*) (Salamanca, 1966).

69. I owe this point to a conversation with my colleague Thomas Tentler.

70. The concern for social and economic justice that forms so important a dimension in the writings of theologians of liberation was also expressed, repeatedly and insistently, by Martin Luther King Jr. See Clayborne Carson, ed., *The Autobiography of Martin Luther King, Jr.* (New York, 1998), 261, from his lecture at the University of Oslo in 1964: "Deeply etched in the fiber of our religious tradition is the conviction that men are made in the image of God and that they are souls of infinite metaphysical value, the heirs of a legacy of dignity and worth. If we feel this as a profound moral fact, we cannot be content to see men hungry, to see men victimized with starvation and ill health when we have the means to help them." Note also (ibid., 339) his concern for the poorer countries, including those of Latin America, articulated in the course of his opposition

to the Vietnam war. See also Dom Helder Camara, *The Conversions of a Bishop: An Interview with José de Broucker* (London, 1979).

71. See Enrique Dussel, *A History of the Church in Latin America: Colonialism to Liberation* (Grand Rapids, 1981); James R. Brockmann, *Romero: A Life* (New York, 1989). As a result of this breakdown of harmony, the Latin American church has become a church with martyrs at the hands of the state, not, as in colonial times, at the hands of Indians resisting evangelization. For the current position, cf. Adolfo Galeano, "Desafíos de la postmodernidad a la teología en América Latina," *Cristianismo y Sociedad* 137 (1998): 67–85; Walter Altmann, Oneide Bobsin, and Roberto Zwetsch, "Perspectivas de la teología de la liberación. Dificultades y nuevos rumbos en un contexto de globalización," *Cristianismo y Sociedad* 139 (1999): 49–57.

CHAPTER FOUR

What's in a Name?

"Fundamentalism" and the Discourse about Religion

R. Scott Appleby

Central to any effort to talk about religion, especially the religion of others, is the question of the adequacy of our language. Can our terms do justice to the experience of others, to the particular quality and meaning of their practices, to their modes of reading sacred texts or preserving sacred customs? In the fullest sense of course we cannot, but can we nonetheless manage to make sensible statements, to engage in useful conversations, in the terms available to us?

Drawing on his experience with the Fundamentalism Project, Scott Appleby here addresses these issues with particular attention given to our use of the term "fundamentalism": to what extent does it make sense to speak of fundamentalism in Hindu, Muslim, Jewish, and Christian contexts, as though each of these religions, and others, exhibited the same phenomenon? Appleby frankly traces out many of the difficulties involved in our effort to use this term, but concludes that despite them, if we proceed with appropriate awareness of the limits of our minds and languages, we can indeed use it fruitfully in the analysis both of certain religious phenomena and of the larger cultures against which they struggle.

The discourse *of* religion informs, shapes, legitimates—and occasionally corrupts—the discourse *about* religion. Nowhere is this more apparent than in the use of the term "fundamentalism" to comprehend the varieties of antisecular, antipluralist, antimodernist religiopolitical movements that have arisen or reemerged worldwide since the 1970s.

Scholars have developed their own lexicon, of course, ever since the German theologian and philosopher of religion Rudolph Otto inaugurated the modern study of religion with his classic text *Das Heilige* (1917).[1] Few believers, however, refer to their god as "the numinous," or describe their encounter with the sacred as "mysterium tremendum et fascinans." Nor do they construe their world according to the analytical categories of sociology (Emile Durkheim), phenomenology (Edmund Husserl, Mircea Eliade), or ritual performance (Victor Turner). Essentialist and functionalist definitions of believers' "symbol systems" and ritual and ethical behaviors are virtually unknown beyond the arena of religionists and cultural anthropologists. Believers and practitioners may not object to the theories of Clifford Geertz regarding religion as a cultural system, say, or Erik Erikson's correlation between the life cycle and stages of religious growth; they may even recognize elements of their own experience. But academic discourse, most believers would argue, does not adequately reproduce their perceptual horizon.[2]

The problem of representation becomes particularly acute whenever scholars, journalists, and other "outsiders"—those observers who do not practice the tradition in question and thus do not inhabit its mental universe—appropriate for their own purposes the language and self-descriptions of believers. In such cases the discourse of religion enters a discursive field beyond the range of its authority, where it is inevitably transformed. Outsiders do not necessarily distort the discourse of religion when they speak or write about it. But the risk of distortion is high whenever (and this is usually the case) the believers' self-understanding and self-descriptions are merely one of several criteria considered in the course of an outsider's analysis and evaluation.

"FUNDAMENTALISM": A BRIEF HISTORY

The term "fundamentalism," to take a case in point, was first coined by militant North American Christian evangelicals of the 1910s and 1920s who proclaimed themselves willing to wage "battle royal" for "the fundamentals of the faith" against their compromising liberal or modernist co-religionists. From the 1920s to the 1970s, journalists and scholars applied the term, with few exceptions, to that group of conservative Protestant Christians derided by H. L. Mencken as cultural barbarians and know-nothing rednecks.[3] During those decades, the so-called Christian fundamentalists did not reject the term, despite the fact that their secular (and religious) critics turned it into an instrument of mockery; indeed, they wore "fundamentalism" as a badge of honor precisely because the world scorned them for their literalist faith.

Their attitude changed in the 1980s, however, when journalists, academics, and other shapers of popular opinion extended the term well beyond its original North American context. By then, the world was apparently crawling with "fundamentalists." The trend was confirmed by the Shi'ite revolutionaries who led the overthrow of the Shah of Iran in 1978–79 and established an "Islamic republic" in that oil-rich, erstwhile client state of the United States. The Jewish extremists who spearheaded illegal settlements in the Israeli-occupied territories of the West Bank and Gaza (the biblical Judea and Samaria) were adopted into the fundamentalist "family," as were the Sunni Muslim assassins of Egyptian president Anwar Sadat (1981). Hindu militants, meanwhile, were agitating for a new desecularized India, a "Hindu nation" built on *Hindutva* (Hinduness), a concept devoid of unambiguous positive content, but firm in its opposition to affirmative action for lower castes and in its commitment to redefining Muslim and other "minority" religious communities around a notion of Hindu superiority. In 1981 the World Hindu Party (Vishva Hindu Parishad, or VHP), a militant wing of the Hindutva movement, emerged in reaction to the conversion to Islam of a small group of low-caste Indians in the south. In northern India, in the Punjab, Sikh radicalism gained startling momentum in 1984, after the Indian army stormed the holiest Sikh shrine, the Golden Temple at Amritsar, in pursuit of the Sikh militant Jarnail Singh Bhindranwale and his supporters. As these events were unfolding around the world, the New Christian Right was flexing its newfound political muscle in Ronald Reagan's America.

Observing and reporting on these disparate events, U.S. journalists ransacked their own cultural repertoire to retrieve a cognate for what they saw as militant, menacing, antimodern religion, and in their reportage "fundamentalism" took on a new and sensational connotation. The Southern Baptist Convention, not surprisingly, took to referring to itself as "conservative" rather than "fundamentalist." "How can you compare us to Middle East terrorists?" an outraged evangelical colleague asked me during an academic conference devoted to the topic. "We do not stockpile weapons in the basement of Moody Bible School!"

Studies of "global fundamentalism" proliferated. In 1986 the executive council of the American Academy of Arts and Sciences (AAAS)—an elite fellowship of distinguished U.S. and European scientists, social scientists, and humanists—voted to devote the greater portion of a major public policy grant from the

MacArthur Foundation to a comprehensive, interdisciplinary project examining worldwide religious resurgence. (Other global phenomena considered by the council included the then-unexamined specter of AIDS, and the growing crisis of teen pregnancy.) Martin E. Marty, the prominent historian of Christianity at the University of Chicago, participated in the deliberations and was named director of the multiyear undertaking; subsequently, he hired me to coordinate the day-to-day operations and to assist in recruiting the scholars and conceptualizing the scholarly results expected from the project.

From 1988 to 1995 the Fundamentalism Project, operating out of an office in the Divinity School of the University of Chicago, held approximately twenty scholarly meetings, consultations, or conferences in Chicago, London, and Cambridge, Massachusetts (at the headquarters of the AAAS); published five encyclopedic volumes containing seventy-five essays or case studies describing and analyzing dozens of religiopolitical movements on five continents; and collaborated with WETA, the BBC, and National Public Radio to produce five radio and three television documentaries based on the encyclopedic volumes described above. In addition, the co-directors of the project authored a companion book to the television and radio series. Several spin-off books and essays also appeared, including *Islamic Fundamentalisms and the Gulf Crisis*, published in several foreign-language editions, and *Spokesmen for the Despised*, a collection of biographical profiles of "fundamentalist leaders of the Middle East."[4] Today, fifteen years after the initial publication of *Fundamentalisms Observed*, the first volume in the Chicago series, spin-off volumes continue to appear, and the cottage industry of "fundamentalism studies" is still going strong.[5]

DIFFICULTIES WITH THE TERM

What have we wrought? The problems with the term "fundamentalism" are legion. To begin with, one risks replicating neocolonial patterns of cultural imperialism by imposing a term of Western Christian origin on a dizzying variety of disparate movements, including several in the developing world, that emerged from different host religions and thus have different ideological concerns, beliefs, rituals, allies, and enemies.

Indeed, Protestant Christian fundamentalism is the *only* movement to which the term ought to be applied by scholars concerned with historical and descriptive accuracy. Biblical inerrancy, for example, a distinctive and central identifying feature of Protestant Christian fundamentalism, cannot be stipulated as a universal trait of "fundamentalists" worldwide without inviting gross distortions and misunderstandings of the global rise of "inerrantist" and absolutist religious tendencies within most religions. Insistence on the historical, scientific, and theological inerrancy of the Christian Bible was a striking historical development within Protestantism of the late nineteenth and early twentieth centuries. It cannot be equated with Muslims' traditional belief that the Qur'an is the literal word of God, recited in Arabic to the Prophet Muhammad. Muslims believe in the inerrancy of the Qur'an, that is, but this is not a central identifying trait of the much smaller and historically restricted phenomenon known broadly as "political Islam," "Islamism," or "Islamic fundamentalism." Nor does scriptural inerrancy make much sense in the Hindu or Buddhist cases.

The perception that outsiders are clustering or clumping disparate phenomena under one term may lead believers in each of these communities to the reasonable conclusion that "fundamentalism" is little more than an empty but destructive label. Far from capturing the reality to which they are applied, such labels serve the ideological purpose of demonizing one's enemy. "Fundamentalism," in this view, is entirely in the eye of the beholder: one man's terrorist is another man's freedom fighter. "Why call me a fundamentalist rather than a liberationist?" asked Shaykh Husayn Fadlallah, the spiritual leader of Hizbullah, the militant Shi'ite movement in Lebanon. "I am fighting to free Lebanon of illegal foreign occupation."[6]

Scholars of comparative fundamentalism are therefore vulnerable to accusations that they are politically motivated. Believers and others acting in good faith certainly have a right and an obligation to demand that each group or movement be treated fairly and accurately. Yet such accusations, it must also be acknowledged, are all too convenient for those who seek to gain political advantage for their own cause. The tactic of playing the cultural imperialism card has been employed repeatedly by propagandists who seek to deny or obscure the sociopolitical reality to which the term "fundamentalism," however clumsily, points. In 1988, for example, a prominent Arab human rights lawyer, who was then president of the Mid-American Arab Chamber of Commerce in Chicago, accused the Fundamentalism Project of fabricating the phenomenon of "Islamic fundamentalism" as part of the project's "Zionist enterprise." From the opposite point of view, some of the reviewers of the project charged that the authors and editors were too soft on the fundamentalists because we did not expose them as intolerant zealots bent on destroying the freedoms, including freedom of speech, on which the Fundamentalism Project—and, indeed, all academic inquiry—is based.[7]

A second, and closely related, disadvantage of "global fundamentalism" is the impression the term creates in the popular mind of a worldwide conspiracy or movement dedicated to violence against the "heretic" or "infidel." Although the careful scholar employs "fundamentalism" as a construct or ideal type, to be used only for comparative purposes, the general and certainly the casual reader will likely not appreciate such fine distinctions. The very term "global fundamentalism" suggests that these movements and groups, whatever their individual particularities of belief and practice, are in the final analysis a homogeneous threat. The imagination conjures a coterie of reactionary obstructionists who seek to dismantle the rule of law and destroy individual freedoms. Such is the danger of employing one term to describe even a subset of the world's politicized, militant, and sometimes violent religious groups.

Fundamentalism in this way of understanding threatens to give religion a bad name. The reification of fundamentalism—the construction of a generic fundamentalist "type," personified by a variety of believers around the world—was and remains a temptation to outsiders who speak about religion, especially, perhaps, to those whose affinities lie with moderate or liberal religion, or with secularism or atheism. We who participated in the Fundamentalism Project were not immune to this temptation. Whenever Martin Marty put forth certain "family resemblances" (a concept developed in another context by Wittgenstein) that might be shared by otherwise disparate antimodernist religious movements, he also explained to our colleagues that these were indeed *hypotheses to be tested* and refined—or discarded altogether. Tell us about the religiopolitical groups and organizations you know best, measure them according to these hypothetical traits—but do not fit them into a procrustean bed called "fundamentalism." Nonetheless, a few scholars did exactly that, claiming to discover fundamentalism in the most unlikely places and among the most unlikely groups.

Furthermore, despite our repeated caution that scholars should use the term only as a comparative construct and never in lieu of tradition-specific terms (e.g., "Islamist" for "Islamic fundamentalists," or "haredim" for one type of "Jewish fundamentalist"), the larger world of scholarship and journalism continued to refer to Hindu fundamentalists, Buddhist fundamentalists, Muslim and Jewish fundamentalists.

From this elasticity of terminology it is a short distance to a third major weakness, namely, employing "fundamentalism" as a term of opprobrium hurled at all believers. Cultured despisers of religion love to extend the term to all manifestations of a religion, or to religion itself. The reaction of a group of distinguished scientists to an early outline of the Fundamentalism Project typified this mindset. "If you are devoting this much time, energy and money to the study of fundamentalism," one physicist instructed, "you must expose *religion* for what it is—the last bastion of rebarbarative, reactionary primitivism!" Some outsiders prefer to demonize a particular religion, such as Islam, by conflating all expressions of religious commitment under the category "fundamentalism," which is then construed as extremism and bigotry in its purest form. According to this dismal display of commutative reasoning, all practicing Muslims (for example) are fundamentalists, all fundamentalists are potential or actual terrorists, hence all Muslims are potential or actual terrorists.

The indictment of religion, and the clumping of all expressions of fundamentalism under the category "terrorism," is thus among the unintended consequences of studying religious extremism under the rubric "fundamentalism." This situation is painfully ironic to those of us who prefer to celebrate or at least respect most expressions of religious belief and practice, be they Muslim, Christian, Jewish, Hindu, Buddhist, or Sikh (the religious traditions centrally included in the Fundamentalism Project).[8]

A closely related tendency is the ideological use of the term "fundamentalist" by secular or nominally religious regimes to discredit dissenters and political opponents by tarring them with that label. The sociologist of religion Mark Juergensmeyer contributed an essay on this phenomenon to *Fundamentalisms Comprehended*, the final volume published by the Fundamentalism Project. Among the instances Juergensmeyer provides of "anti-fundamentalism" are the persecution of Muslim activists in central Asia by supposedly post-Communist governments, and the indiscriminate targeting of Sikhs by Indian security forces.

In Tajikistan, for example, Communists used the accusation of fundamentalism—"Islamic fundamentalism is a plague that spreads easily," as one Communist leader put it—as a reason for destroying the country's democratically elected Islamic government, leading to what one Tajik journalist described as a "genocide" of Islamic opponents in 1993.[9] In Bosnia during the early 1990s, to give another example, Serbian nationalists justified their policy of "ethnic cleansing" in part by citing their fear that the Bosnian Muslims would establish "a fundamentalist Islamic state" and use Bosnia as a base for Islamic expansion across Europe.[10]

In addition to the atrocities committed in the name of countering fundamentalism in such places as Bosnia, Tajikistan, and Punjab, Juergensmeyer notes, secular governments have also taken liberties with the democratic process as a way of countering what they perceive to be a fundamentalist threat. The governing National Liberation Party of Algeria annulled elections won by Islamic nationalists in 1990; Israel routinely arrested or exiled Palestinians suspected of belonging to Hamas and other radical Islamist organizations; the Congress Party, while still in power in India, banned Hindu nationalist organizations on the slightest pretense. Each of these cases, he argues, "has created a crisis of conscience for democratically minded citizens within these countries and around the world, and they raise critical issues regarding how one deals with the threat of religious activism within the context of democratic institutions."[11]

Anti-fundamentalism is also born of the discomfort or outright embarrassment felt by religious or nominally religious regimes that are pressured by ultra-orthodox forces on their Right. A high-ranking member of the government of Saudi Arabia told me that he preferred that scholars abandon the term "fundamentalism" because the Islamist opponents of the Saudi monarchy wear it as a badge of honor. "They claim to be upholding the *usuliyya,* or fundamentals, of Islam," he complained, "as their excuse for terrorist acts against the kingdom."

FLUIDITY OF THE CATEGORIES

The term "fundamentalism" in most contexts carries strong negative connotations. To label certain people or groups "fundamentalist," Marty often acknowledged, was in effect to banish them to the threatening, uncharted territories on ancient maps inscribed with the warning: "Here Be Monsters!" Thus, in an attempt to avoid demonizing or condescending to the subjects of our study, we described fundamentalism as a behavioral-attitudinal mode rather than as an anomalous or dysfunctional personality type (as if certain people were inherently, inevitably intolerant, absolutist, antipluralist, and so on). The fundamentalist mode was reactive, selective, absolutist, inerrant, authoritarian, separatist, and given to the apocalyptic or millennial in religious imagination. But believers were quite capable of moving, and often did move, in and out of this mode. Indeed, the fourth volume of the Fundamentalism Project was devoted to "accounting for" the shift in modes over time. How does the relationship between ideology and patterns in organization and behavior change over time? Under what circumstances do religious actors or groups become militant? Under what conditions do they adopt a "fundamentalist" mode? Under which conditions do they abandon this mode?

Fundamentalism in this understanding does not connote an unchanging identity predicated on personality type, level of education, or other specific personal or group characteristics. It refers, rather, to specifiable patterns of behavior and habits of mind that could be adopted by any modern believer, theoretically at least, from the middle-class, MIT-trained engineer to the poor denizen of Gaza, from the Brahmin elite of northern India to the underemployed university graduate in Algeria.

Lest the term lose its descriptive value, however, it remained necessary to distinguish the fundamentalist mode from other patterns and habits. "Revivalism" thus became an important category of contrast. By our mid-project reckoning, the revivalist was distinguished from the fundamentalist, decisively, by the former's apolitical behavior. The revivalist's strong reassertion of religious practice and identity in the public realm was not to be confused with the fundamentalist's aggressive, hegemonic, inherently political behavior.

In the real world, these theoretical categories proved at times disconcertingly elastic, leading me to the threshold of conceptual paralysis, a terminal disease for ivory-tower comparativists. While touring the Philippines during the mid-1990s, for example, when Christian–Muslim relations in Mindanao, Sulu, and other southern islands were deteriorating, I experienced something of the complexity of the relationship between revivalist and fundamentalist modes of behavior. During a series of "cultural immersion" meetings throughout the region, I asked Christian and Muslim civic leaders to pinpoint the moment when cooperative relationships had begun to unravel. Informed by my textbook distinction between supposedly civil revivalists and militant fundamentalists, I fully expected them to trace the troubles back to when the Abu Sayyaf had first formed in the jungles and began its terrorist operations against local Christians and "compromising" Muslims. Instead, in town after town, my local leaders pointed not to the "fundamentalists" of Abu Sayyaf, but to the region's (and perhaps the world's) largest "revivalist" movement, the Tablighi Jamaat (Association for the Propagation of Islam). Relations between local Christians and Muslim communities had soured, they recalled, when the Jamaat had come to town. "Why do you celebrate Christmas with the Christians and invite them to your homes to break the Ramadan fast?" the Muslim revivalists had pressed their co-religionists. Pressured into religiocultural conformity to a strict separatist and exclusivist standard, local Muslims felt compelled to choose between their loyalty to Islam and their friendships with non-Muslims. In most cases, the unconditional claims of absolutist religion prevailed.

These accounts destabilized my comfortable definitional boundaries. The Tablighi Jamaat, founded in India in 1926, is a *da'wa* movement composed of itinerant preachers with local branches present in more than one hundred countries. In Pakistan, the epicenter of the movement, the Jamaat has become a training ground for thousands of aspiring laymen among small-town schoolteachers, shopkeepers, government clerks, and artisans in the private sector. Its annual conference in Raiwind near Lahore attracts a million Muslims. The Tablighi Jamaat fits the standard academic definition of a revivalist movement, in that it has reportedly "remained aloof from political controversies and has focused on preaching the moral and religious precepts of Islam and reforming the socio-religious customs of South Asian Muslims in accordance with orthodox Islam."[12] The Abu Sayyaf, by contrast, is a secessionist movement that seeks, by violent means, to transform the predominantly Muslim islands of the southern Philippines into an Islamic state. Its exclusivist, absolutist, antisecular religious orientation, coupled with its bid for raw political power sought for the purpose of imposing religious law, qualifies the Abu Sayyaf for inclusion in the putative family of "fundamentalisms."

Yet the experience in the southern Philippines suggested that fundamentalism and revivalism are, or can be, overlapping, reinforcing, and somewhat indistinct phenomena. Do the categories, however brittle, hold up?

IN DEFENSE OF "FUNDAMENTALISM"

Having made a case for abandoning the term "fundamentalism," even as a comparative construct, I nonetheless argue that there is indeed a set of militant, antimodernist religious movements that exhibit a sufficient range of behavioral-attitudinal traits to warrant their being described as belonging to an identifiable "family." Allowing for the several qualifications already noted, that is, the definitions and descriptions of "fundamentalism" that evolved through the course of dozens of case studies proved sufficiently accurate to comprehend the ten movement clusters that we identified as sharing the family traits of fundamentalism.[13] We also despaired of selecting or coining an apt synonym for "fundamentalism" that would avoid further confusion and avoid replication of many of the problems associated with the term.

The Fundamentalism Project, along with several other studies, took seriously the intent, appeal, and modern sensibilities of fundamentalists. The cultural projects of Christian fundamentalists, militant Islamists, Jewish radicals, Sikh extremists, and Hindu nationalists are not trivial; indeed, "fundamentalism" in these cases amounts to nothing less than the attempt to establish and propagate an alternative order to secularism, a comprehensive political, economic, and cultural system rooted in and giving new life to antimodernist religion.

There were several moments of truth during the course of the project— occasions when I met and interviewed or overheard Muslim or Christian, Jewish or Sikh leaders we had included in the "fundamentalist" family. During my trip to the southern Philippines, our distinction between revivalism and fundamentalism did not hold up. More often, however, the best literature on fundamentalism proved not only responsible but strikingly appropriate.

In 1992, for example, I was invited to a presentation by Hasan al-Turabi, the leader of the National Islamic Front and the court theologian, so to speak, of the Sudanese government. Turabi was scheduled to defend his view of Islamism before a gathering of journalists, scholars, and U.S. government officials in Washington, D.C. I looked forward to the event with a mixture of anticipation and concern. If anyone qualified as an "Islamic fundamentalist," surely Turabi did. I worried, however, that he might prove our construction of fundamentalism a hollow stereotype.

Thus it was with both relief and dismay that I listened to Turabi articulate his worldview and political philosophy, including a scathing cultural critique of "the decadent West." My reactions stemmed from the close correspondence between Turabi's "attitudinal and behavioral mode" as an Islamist and the Fundamentalism Project's portrayal of Islamic fundamentalism in Sudan—and, indeed, of political Islam more generally.

Turabi described himself, immodestly, as the perfect leader of the "Islamic Awakening." Educated at the Sorbonne and at the University of London, he knew "from the inside," he said, Western law, economics, and political philosophy; yet he also had enjoyed the leisure, while imprisoned in the Sudan under Numieri's regime, of reading and studying the Qur'an and the schools of Islamic law at great length. His expertise in the Shari'a, Turabi claimed, rivaled that of any Mullah. Thus possessed of intimate knowledge of two cultures, he pronounced himself prepared to lead Islam into the twenty-first century, when Islamic civilization will emerge in its mature form across the Islamic arc from West Africa to Southeast Asia. "We will be governed not by Western epistemology and cultural presuppositions," he promised, but by the worldview and principles of the Qur'an and the Hadith of the Prophet, updated to meet the exigencies of the modern world.

The so-called Universal Declaration of Human Rights, Turabi added, is hardly universal; it is rooted transparently in the same secular-atheistic Western philosophy that marginalized God and thereby led the West to its current moral and spiritual malaise, characterized by rampant drug abuse and addiction, skyrocketing divorce, a pornographic popular culture, and so on. Those in the new Islamic order need not enter a state of war with the West, Turabi said; they will seek trade, economic cooperation, and the like. They will also speak of "human rights," of "women's liberation," and "freedom"; but the content of these terms, Turabi warned his audience, will not correspond perfectly to the Western understanding. Genuine women's liberation does not mean, as in the West, license for women to treat their bodies as their own private possessions apart from what God has willed for them, Turabi lectured; their freedom comes from doing God's will.

Although I am not an advocate of Samuel Huntington's seriously flawed but widely heralded "clash of civilizations" thesis, it is worth noting that Turabi's descriptions of himself and of the "Islamic Awakening" sounded as if they had been scripted by Huntington—or vice versa. Huntington's essay, which appeared shortly after the Turabi speech, provocatively declared that the twenty-first century would be an era defined not by confrontations between superpowers, but by competition and conflict between "civilizational blocs"—clusters of societies defined and set apart from one another not by their economic interests or military alliances or political systems as much as by their underlying worldviews and cultural systems, many of which are based in part or in whole on religious traditions. Hence, Huntington foresaw an Islamic bloc, a Western Judaeo-Christian bloc, a Russian-Eastern Orthodox bloc, a Chinese-Confucian bloc, and so on.[14]

During his speech, Turabi selectively retrieved and reshaped ideas or developments from modern Islam, such as the emergence of lay political leadership. He was bracingly open in describing the need to adapt Islamic law and practice to the exigencies of the present, for the sake of preserving and extending Islam as an orthodox community. The Islamic Awakening, he vowed, would build a social order that would succeed as an alternative to Islamic modernism, which his program strongly resembles, and to the secularism that Turabi believes has suffocated the Christian spirit and civilization of the West.

Turabi's presentation was not a textbook version of "Islamic fundamentalism," however. Enfolded within his characterizations of Islamic law as "inerrant" and the Islamist worldview as "absolute" in its truth was a subtle acknowledgment that the world is not and probably never will be governed by one cultural system and way of knowing. Whether one judges this concession to functional relativism to be tactical or substantive, it reflects a pragmatic bent to the fundamentalist mind.

Yet this aspect of the fundamentalist mode of thought, no less than inerrancy and absolutism, had also been anticipated by the most insightful scholars of fundamentalism. They recognize that the late modern, globalized world makes it virtually impossible for fundamentalists to maintain the strict separatist mode into which they often retreated in the late nineteenth and early twentieth centuries. In today's increasingly interdependent world, instantaneous communication by way of cyberspace and mass media, driven by the dynamics of proliferating markets and global economies, makes a mockery of attempts to construct the borders of a cultural enclave. Fundamentalists, drawn inexorably into interaction with outsiders, cannot escape the transformative effects of historical consciousness: they are aware of themselves as players in a much larger, evolving game.

Contemporary fundamentalists live at a time when the seamless coat of orthodoxy that once protected traditional religious communities has unraveled. A relativizing awareness of oneself as an historically conditioned actor living at a particular time and place is inevitable. Moreover, the range of choices available to individuals today—choices of everything, from brands of breakfast cereal to schools of self-help philosophy—has created a transnational culture of radical choice that has accelerated the fragmentation of once-orthodox communities. In this milieu, heresy (the preference for one's own interpretations and "truths" rather than those promulgated by an orthodox authority) becomes virtually unavoidable.[15] Those who attempt to hold fast to old ways find themselves pursued by the increasingly long arm of the law (as in the prosecution of a Mormon polygamist in Utah, by Mormon co-religionists working in the state attorney general's office), or drawn into power politics for their own preservation (as in the case of the haredim in Israel). A shared faith and practices that once bound the community together, often in defiance of outsiders, is no longer taken for granted.

In order to maintain that faith at a time when science, commerce, and cultural pluralism seemingly have eroded much of its plausibility, the anthropologist Clifford Geertz has noted, one must consciously choose it as a countercultural option. What once held the community together must now be grasped in an act of desperate, self-conscious affirmation; in such circumstances, orthodoxy becomes a weapon wielded against the heretic, or an instrument of enforcement deployed against the lukewarm, rather than a naturally held, organic way of life. In *Accounting for Fundamentalisms,* the third volume of the Fundamentalism Project, Haym Soloveitchik writes movingly of the loss of a natural fear of God among orthodox Jews of the post-Holocaust twentieth century. A culture of text and law has overtaken a culture of mimesis in the Jewish world, he laments; the Jewish mother's kosher kitchen and the practical but profound orthopraxis absorbed there by the family, has given way to a proliferating company of ratiolegal "experts" in religiosity. "Fundamentalist" manuals and pamphlets mass-produced by the new elite class of rabbis and rebbes instruct the modern Jew how to observe the faith in punctilious detail. What was once organic and familial and naturally "true" has become codified in text and legal prescription, weakening its life-giving wisdom.[16]

Considerations of this type constitute perhaps the most important contribution of fundamentalism studies for those who understand and take account of the ways that the term "fundamentalism" can distort the phenomena to which it refers, and who nonetheless continue to take the subject seriously. The study of the related phenomena described as "fundamentalist," that is, reveals a great deal more about the modern secularized world than its does about the pockets of resistance found within the world's major religious traditions. By examining the epistemological and material conditions within which belief in the sacred must occur in the late modern milieu, studies of comparative fundamentalism alert us to the distortions of the human experience introduced by secular attitudes and modes of belief, and expose the indignities and false choices imposed on believing communities by secular modes of behavior. In the best of such studies, as in the best academic discourse about religion, the discourse of religion is accorded a privileged place. In this way the humanity, insight, and integrity of the subjects of study—of the fundamentalists—is not only preserved but rightly privileged. For a critical but unprejudiced encounter with fundamentalists, those modern antimodernist believers who inhabit the "Here Be Monsters!" margins of our cultural maps, is absolutely essential to a sympathetic understanding of our shared humanity in the current age of disbelief.

NOTES

1. *The Idea of the Holy: An Inquiry into the Non-Rational Factor in the Idea of the Divine and Its Relation to the Rational,* trans. John W. Harvey (Oxford: Oxford University Press, 1971 [1923]).

2. By contrast, theologians who write from within a particular religious tradition tend to develop language that resonates with the confessional community; Karl Barth, for example, objected famously that "Rudolph Otto's 'Idea of the Holy,' whatever it may be, is at all events not to be regarded as the Word of God." Quoted in Walter H. Capps, *Religious Studies: The Making of a Discipline* (Minneapolis: Fortress, 1995), 132.

3. H. L. Mencken, *Prejudices: Fifth Series* (New York: Knopf, 1926), quoted in Henry May, ed., *The Discontent of the Intellectuals: A Problem of the Twenties* (Boston: Houghton Mifflin, 1963), 25–30.

4. The publications of the Fundamentalism Project include Martin E. Marty and R. Scott Appleby, eds., *Fundamentalisms Observed* (Chicago: University of Chicago Press, 1991); *Fundamentalisms and the State: Remaking Polities, Economies and Militance* (Chicago: University of Chicago Press, 1993); *Fundamentalisms and Society: Reclaiming the Sciences, the Family and Education* (Chicago: University of Chicago Press, 1993); *Accounting for Fundamentalisms: The Dynamic Character of Movements* (Chicago: University of Chicago Press, 1994); *Fundamentalisms Comprehended* (Chicago: University of Chicago Press, 1995). See also Martin E. Marty and R. Scott Appleby, *The Glory and the Power: The Fundamentalist Challenge to the Modern World* (Boston: Beacon Press, 1993); James Piscatori, ed., *Islamic Fundamentalisms and the Gulf Crisis* (Chicago: American Academy of Arts and Sciences, 1991); R. Scott Appleby, ed., *Spokesmen for the Despised: Fundamentalist Leaders of the Middle East* (Chicago: University of Chicago Press, 1997); and, Gabriel A. Almond, R. Scott Appleby and Emmanuel Sivan, *Strong Religion: The Rise of Fundamentalisms around the World* (Chicago: University of Chicago Press, 2003).

5. These studies include volumes devoted in part to analyses by the Fundamentalism Project, as well as a greater number of studies unrelated to the project. In the former category, see, e.g., Niels C. Nielsen Jr., *Fundamentalism, Mythos and World Religions* (Albany: State University of New York Press, 1993). An early entry in the latter category is Lionel Caplan, ed., *Studies in Religious Fundamentalism* (Albany: State University of New York Press, 1987). For titles and publication data of hundreds of works devoted in whole or in part to analyses and case studies of religious fundamentalisms, religious nationalisms, and related phenomena, see the bibliography in R. Scott Appleby, *The Ambivalence of the Sacred: Religion, Violence and Reconciliation* (Lanham, Md.: Rowman and Littlefield, 2000), 389–406.

6. Quoted in Martin Kramer, "Hizbullah: The Calculus of Jihad," in Marty and Appleby, eds., *Fundamentalisms and the State.*

7. Rosemary Radford Ruether, "A World on Fire with Fundamentalism," *New York Times Book Review,* February 1992.

8. A related, and personally uncomfortable, aspect of lecturing and writing on comparative fundamentalism was the necessity of explaining the exception that proves the rule: the virtual absence of "fundamentalism" within Roman Catholicism, my own religious tradition. There are antimodernist Roman Catholics who can be just as exclusive, absolutist, apocalyptically judgmental, and crisis-oriented as Protestant Christian fundamentalists, Muslim "fundamentalists," Jewish "fundamentalists," and so on. But the Catholic antimodernists lack an essential ingredient of bona fide fundamentalism: a creative and original plan for the future—a vision of renewed religion that is more than merely an attempted (and inevitably quixotic) restoration of the premodern past. Whereas Protestant, Muslim, and Jewish "fundamentalists" tend to be quite innovative, borrowing from modernity as well as tradition in order to create a fresh alternative to tired or compromising orthodoxy, their Catholic counterparts, such as the Lefebvrists (followers of the late Archbishop Marcel Lefebvre, who was excommunicated from the Roman Catholic Church after illicitly ordaining four bishops into the ranks of his movement), tend to be dour revanchists, praying for the return of the golden age (in this case, the Tridentine Catholicism of the sixteenth through the nineteenth centuries, which preserved and extended the achievements of the Roman Catholicism, or "Christendom," of the High Middle Ages). Roman Catholic antimodernists thus tend to act and think in the mode of "traditionalism" rather than "fundamentalism." They are restorationists rather than "progressives." Renegade Catholics encounter difficulty differentiating themselves from the host religion while simultaneously claiming to revitalize it from within—a maneuver that most self-respecting fundamentalists can perform in their sleep. Would-be Catholic fundamentalists are constrained by the fact that a central, perhaps *the* central, "fundamental" of Roman Catholicism is the doctrine of the church as the means of salvation. Archbishop Lefebvre, in order to justify his disobedience to the pope and his break with the church, claimed that the church has been in a state of apostasy since the pontificate of Pope John XXIII (1958–63). Most Catholic conservatives and antimodernists—the pool from which the would-be Catholic fundamentalists attempted to recruit adherents—are unprepared to accept this diagnosis, contravening as it does Christ's promise, recorded in the New Testament, that his church will prevail against serious errors and withstand even the gates of hell. Catholic antimodernists, unable to craft a compelling ideology from their critique of post-Vatican II Catholicism, fall back on a politically and ecclesially empty apocalypticism, ranting against the moral failures of the papacy and hierarchy but devoid of ideas for an alternative system.

However accurate this explanation of the absence of case studies of "Catholic fundamentalism" in the Fundamentalism Project, it remained odd, to say the least, for me to point to fundamentalisms in virtually every major religious tradition except my own. For the project's analyses of the Roman Catholic cases of radical antimodernism, see

William D. Dinges and James Hitchcock, "Roman Catholic Traditionalism and Activist Conservatism in the United States," in Marty and Appleby, eds., *Fundamentalisms Observed*, 66–141.

9. Timur Kchev, Tajik journalist in exile in Moscow, Tahir Akhmedov, a Tajikistan Foreign Ministry official, quoted in Cary Goldberg, "A Grim Prophecy Fulfilled," *Los Angeles Times*, 30 January 1993, A1. In many cases, the fear of "fundamentalism" is grounded in legitimate concerns. Often the animosities against militant, antimodern religious movements have been brought on by themselves, when they have employed what are often strident slogans, violent tactics, and dictatorial leadership styles.

10. Quoted in John F. Burns, "Serbs Would Deny Muslims a State," *New York Times*, international ed., 18 July 1993, 7.

11. In many parts of the world, not only fundamentalism but the fear of it has become a problem; in some cases it has led to a violation of human rights. A resident of Punjab told Juergensmeyer that the Indian government's brutal campaign that effectively quelled the Sikh rebellion in 1992 was often indiscriminate in its targets: "[A]nyone could be killed," he explained, if he or she was "accused of being a fundamentalist." Interviews in Amritsar, India, 5 June 1993.

12. Mumtaz Ahmad, "The Politics of War: Islamic Fundamentalisms in Pakistan," in Piscatori, ed., *Islamic Fundamentalisms and the Gulf Crisis*, 160–61.

13. The movements designated "fundamentalist" in the AAAS project included: (1) multigenerational Protestant fundamentalism in North America; (2) Comunione e Liberazione, the Roman Catholic movement active in Italy and other parts of Europe; (3) international branches or offshoots of the original Egyptian Muslim Brotherhood, including Hamas and Hassan Turabi's National Islamic Front of Sudan; (4) the Sunni jama'at extremist cells influenced by the ideology of Maududi and Qutb, and led by charismatic figures such as Omar Abdel Rahman of Egypt and Marwan Hadid of Syria (also influencing Algeria's Islamist movement, as it developed in the 1970s and 1980s, and the global terrorist networks of Osama Bin Laden); (5) Shi'ite movements in Iran (led by the Ayatollah Khomeini and his successors) and Lebanon (Hizbullah); (6) Maududi's Jamaat-i-Islami organization in South Asia, which remains strongest in Pakistan; (7) the haredi or ultra-orthodox Jewish enclaves in Israel and North America; (8) Habad, the movement of Lubavitcher Hasidim, another Jewish messianist enclave but with missionary outreach toward the larger Jewish community; (9) Gush Emunim, the extremist backbone of the Israeli settler movement; and (10) the Sikh extremists agitating for a separate state (Khalistan) in the Punjab.

14. Samuel P. Huntington, "The Clash of Civilizations? *Foreign Affairs* 72(3) (Summer, 1993): 22–49; also see Huntington, *The Clash of Civilizations and the Remaking of World Order* (New York: Simon and Schuster, 1996).

15. Peter Berger, *The Heretical Imperative* (Chicago: University of Chicago Press, 1979).

16. Haym Soloveitchik, "Migration, Acculturation, and the New Role of Texts in the Haredi World," in Marty and Appleby, eds., *Accounting for Fundamentalisms*, 197–235.

CHAPTER FIVE

A World-Creating Approach to Belief

Bilinda Straight

As Bilinda Straight shows in this essay, the question "How should we talk about religion?" can be presented with particular force and clarity in the life of an anthropologist. The anthropologist is often studying people whose religion—if that is even the right word—is to her novel, odd, strange, and in the usual sense plainly unbelievable. Yet she is committed to the reality and value of different cultures. How is this tension to be resolved? By a kind of scientific distance, under which the anthropologist describes what she cannot believe—that the god whom the Samburu of northern Kenya call "Nkai," for example, is visibly and actively involved in the natural and human world? But then one is likely to miss everything of real significance in the lives of the people one is studying, and simply not understand what their religion means. By somehow becoming a participant in the religion oneself, "going native," as it were? But then one no longer has the kind of distance necessary for reporting what one learns to the larger world.

Bilinda Straight addresses these questions in part theoretically, by a consideration especially of Durkheim, Douglas, and Peirce, in part experientially, by focusing on a particular set of interactions she had with an important informant among the Samburu. For her there is no easy answer at the levels of theory or practice; instead she works out a complex sense of cross-cultural work as a kind of mutual world-creation in which both parties participate.

The question whether the genus homo has any existence except as individuals, is the question whether there is anything of any more dignity, worth, and importance than individual happiness, individual aspirations, and individual life. Whether men really have anything in common, so that the community is to be considered as an end in itself, *and if so, what the relative value of the two factors is, is the most fundamental practical question in regard to every public institution the constitution of which we have it in our power to influence [emphasis added].*
—Charles Sanders Peirce

In this essay I bring the philosophy of Charles Sanders Peirce[1] to bear on an approach I call "world-creating"—an approach in which ethics and scholarship are inescapably entangled and, moreover, a stance that encourages us to be self-conscious as we create shared understandings out of seemingly incommensurate differences.[2] This stance relies on a vision of lifeworld and world-making similar to that described by Michael Jackson (1996), who brings together the phenomenologies of Edmund Husserl and Martin Heidegger and the pragmatism of John Dewey. It crucially differs, however, in that—following Mannheim and Tedlock 1995—it focuses on the cultural worlds that emerge out of encounters between ethnographers and their interlocutors, as well as between individuals representing what we commonly refer to as the same "culture."[3] The approach I am suggesting crucially hinges on the claim that *all* human interactions are mutually transforming and productive: they bring new possibilities and new, shared worlds into being.

SNAKES AND BITTER WORDS

The Samburu, with whom I have lived and worked since 1992 (thirty-six months spanning 1992–94 and 2001–2), are cattle, camel, and small stock herders inhabiting northern Kenya's semi-arid lands. Although less well known than their cultural "cousins" the Maasai, the Samburu are the quintessential example of "traditional Africa" as featured in travel brochures, postcards, and coffee table books. By no means isolated or "timeless," however, the Samburu of the twenty-first century subsist on a mixed economy of herding, livestock trading, hawking, and both skilled and unskilled wage labor. Although a 1995 *Newsweek* article[4] depicting a Samburu wearing "traditional dress" with cell phone in hand was premature, an increasing number of Samburu may be characterized as "cosmopolitan." Those living in towns typically send their children to school, while those in rural areas demonstrate savvy in selectively partaking of things "Western" (Straight 1997a, 1997b; Holtzman 2004). It is not uncommon for a rural household to send a couple of children to school so that they can gain the skills necessary to broker with Kenya's political elite and gain good employment, while keeping the others home to herd livestock.

Research on the Samburu has focused largely on social change and the grim realities of drought, poverty, and famine. While I have long been interested in religion and belief, my doctoral dissertation (Straight 1997b) considered the role of religious belief among the Samburu merely in term of its use for understanding and describing gender and social change. Yet, in spite of my rather single-minded devotion to quantitative surveys and structured interviews, my field site choices forced me to engage with the Samburu more intimately than my research methodology would have suggested. One field site in particular was too remote to reach by car alone. So, after driving over a rough, seldom-used track for three hours, my seven- and eight-year-old sons and I, along with my Samburu field assistant, walked another four hours carrying our supplies on our backs. Sleeping anywhere but inside the mud houses of my Samburu hosts was impractical, if not rude, and through the intimate contact that resulted, my sons and I came to be regarded as members of several families.

Such fieldwork is not unusual in anthropology, although anthropology's focus on out-of-the-way places and even single-site (or single ethnic group) fieldwork has been challenged in the past decade or so. While critiques of anthropology's long-standing emphasis on "isolated cultures" and exoticism are well placed, long-term relationships with people apparently quite different from ourselves is crucially important for the sort of "world-creating" process explored in this essay. As I have suggested elsewhere (Straight 2002), it is not only necessary to bridge misunderstanding; it is necessary to learn how to interact peacefully when people advance competing, even conflicting, claims as true. I think anthropologists have much to offer in this regard insofar as they have been forced to adopt this approach in the field for quite some time—even if their eventual findings undermine the truths of those they study in favor of their own.

When anthropologists venture into the field, it is not always with the intention to reconcile the seemingly incommensurable cultural differences found there. Often we go with a somewhat fuzzy version of cultural relativism in mind, which leaves us not quite certain how to go about making sense of others. Yet the training we do have—in many ways excellent—serves well enough to occasionally bring us to the brink of a radical understanding that might appear to others as untranslatable difference. Thus, though dutifully recording what I thought I came to record, I left Samburu District in 1994 with the audacious intent to plaintively utter the name "Nkai"—Samburu divinity—and mean it. Along the way, some of those who would become my dearest Samburu friends demonstrated a respect for the words of an American woman that they would have rarely if ever done for a Samburu woman. This last was, in fact, no small thing. I do not want to suggest that Samburu women are powerless—

which I do not believe in the least—but I do concede that in some respects they are at a powerful disadvantage (Straight 2005; Holtzman 2002). All of these things—Nkai and the status of women, along with my hybridity— coalesced in 2002.

When the wife of my dearest Samburu friend, Lerafiki (a pseudonym), ran away from him, he enlisted my aid in tracking her down and returning her. Especially because I thought it best for Meidimultim (a pseudonym) to be re- united with her children (who are always thought by the Samburu to belong to the father), I agreed. The task proved to be both difficult and expensive; the cost of gasoline is quite high in Kenya, and to traverse the roads in Samburu Dis- trict requires a gas-guzzling, four-wheel-drive vehicle. My husband, Jon Holtz- man, and I followed various leads, and after several failed attempts finally lo- cated her at a fairly great distance from her home. Meidimultim is also a very close friend, and she agreed to return to her home with me because, as she said, she trusted me to return her via a "good" way, by which she meant her father's home, where she would have the right to air the grievances that led her to run away in the first place.

Jon and I had to travel to Nairobi, and we left Meidimultim in our home for a couple of weeks, hoping that Lerafiki would not come looking for her until we were back. But when we returned, we found both of them there, and heard from our neighbors and research assistants how they had struggled to prevent Lerafiki from leaving with his wife. In the end, it was this respect for our friendship that kept him from leaving. Unfortunately, our friend- ship was further tested by my declaration of the promise given to Meidimul- tim that she would go to her father's home first. This is a bit like asking an abusive husband to willingly confess his deeds to the police and a judge, and to serve a little jail time in the meantime. Yet I could not break my word, and my various Samburu friends and acquaintances agreed that this was appro- priate because she would never have left her distant refuge were it not for my promise.

That night, Lerafiki and I quarreled as we had never done, reaching a tense climax when he told me emphatically that I should not listen to the word of a mere woman—meaning his wife and her plea to go to her father's home. With a shaking voice I told him that it was *my* word—the word of a woman—that we were discussing. "The word of a woman, the word of a woman," I repeated with emotion. After a pause, Lerafiki said that going to Meidimultim's father's home was a reasonable plan, and we would follow it. This came as a joyous

relief to me, but it is by no means the end of the story: the following morning something remarkable happened.

Lerafiki was enjoying his morning tea with Meidimultim in my living room
while Jon and I played a bit with our youngest child in our bed (William was
three at the time). Getting out of the bed, I noticed, out of the corner of my eye,
a black snake slithering across the headboard behind my son's head. I immediately called out to the other houses in the settlement, which brought Musa,
my fearless and long-time research assistant and friend, on the run. After carefully turning the room upside down, he found and killed the very poisonous
mamba, which had by then attached itself to the back of the bed. "But," you
might ask, "what did this encounter with a snake have to do with anything?"
For me, Jon, Musa, and others it had everything to do with everything. Nkai
is known to echo the words and intentions of people, rendering them powerful. As the Samburu understand it, people interact in such powerful ways that
their thoughts and feelings are capable—with Nkai's mimetic assistance—
of animating the inanimate and affecting the movements of the animate. In
short, the expressions of anger between Lerafiki and me called a mamba into
the house and into my very bed. Having spent a great deal of time immersed in
the culture of the Samburu, I cannot help believing that, somehow, this was indeed the case. You may disagree, but you have not made worlds with us. And it
is interesting to note that just as the snake harmed no one, our quarrel was in
the end harmless, for Lerafiki and I remain very close friends to this day.

VARIETIES OF RELATIVISM: DURKHEIM AND DOUGLAS

While anthropology has a reputation as a "relativist" discipline, what is meant
by that term, particularly as it relates to the vexing problem of belief, is far
from clear. Nineteenth-century anthropologists like Sir Edward B. Tylor and
Herbert Spencer created a hierarchical, evolutionary schema in which could
be placed the societies of "Others." Not surprisingly, Euro-American societies
(and forms of knowledge production) were placed at the apex. By the early
years of the twentieth century, however, scholars like Emile Durkheim had
begun to transform principles of tolerance—which, like religious persecution,
have ancient roots—into an anthropological version of cultural relativism
that offered a way of understanding "other" beliefs as possessing a rationality
equal to our own.[5] Mary Douglas, a Durkheimian structuralist, has been ad-

vocating cultural relativism since the 1950s and continues to offer what is possibly its most incisive defense. Douglas (1999) has praised Durkheim's contribution to cultural relativism, but has chided him for stopping short of a more radical relativism that might have brought about an intellectual revolution as powerful as that sparked by the work of Marx and Freud.

Her starting point is the fact that Durkheim's ideas are so fundamental to contemporary anthropological thought that much of his thinking has become as implicit as the meanings that anthropologists attempt to glean in the process of doing fieldwork. Durkheim posited that individuals necessarily, but in different ways, participate in the life of a community, together comprising it as a meaning-filled whole. As individuals internalize the norms of their community, something "sacred" is created—a belief too dangerously powerful to be questioned: sacredness inheres in the group's moral law formed by consensus, to which each individual herself or himself subscribes. Put another way, the sacred emerges out of the efforts of individuals to live together in society and to bind themselves to their agreed-upon rules. It is characterized by the dangers that are alleged to follow upon breach of the rules (Douglas 1999, xiv). The sacred—which is too dangerous to be questioned and is affirmed in ritual—dynamically binds communities together.

Three aspects of Durkheim's model of societies have held particular significance for anthropological scholarship: (1) all human communities have a recognizable structure; (2) that structure is rational, logical; (3) belief plays a specific role in sustaining the structure. It follows that humans equally possess the rationality that gives rise to structure—regardless of how different from one another individual societies might be. In this anthropologists have widely acknowledged (and variously attempted to navigate) a tension between the universal and the particular.

Durkheim's understanding of society has been echoed in different ways in the work of anthropologists who have come after him, whether their approaches have been explicitly structuralist or not. To mention just a few prominent anthropological theorists, E. E. Evans-Pritchard's version of functionalism—most pertinently here his (1937) analysis of Azande witchcraft belief—describes societies as rational, interdependent wholes. Claude Levi-Strauss's (1969, 1970) structuralist understandings of myth and gift exchange offer a different rendering of Durkheim's ideas, as does Mary Douglas's (1966) exegesis of Jewish food prohibitions. Some of Durkheim's most fundamental assumptions are implicit in the work of cultural materialists like Marvin Harris (1979), who interpret core beliefs as fitting logically into the particular ecological environments in which communities are located.[6] Here, society is still composed of interdependent parts, but the emphasis is on environmental limitations. Roy Rappaport's work (1979) is also largely supportive of this position, though he offered an important corrective in his suggestion that societies could, in fact, "behave" irrationally, and dangerously so.

More recent scholarship in anthropology continues to rely on a Durkheimian framework. Pierre Bourdieu's (1977) theory of the habitus, clearly influenced by Heidegger, complicates our understanding of social structure by positing that a society's structure is reproduced through individuals' unreflecting (bodily) performance of its rituals. Bourdieu's analyses imply equal rationality for the Kabyle social structure that he studies,[7] and moreover, he seems to locate, in the body-in-action, a notion of universality at the level of the individual as well (here, a mind and body that are mutually irreducible). In Foucaultian theory, "power" is a ubiquitous dimension of human sociality, and more recently, "embodiment" in a variety of approaches provides the grounding framework for a shared, while paradoxically diverse and antidualist, rationality (see Csordas et al. 1994 in particular).

Notably, postmodern theories, particularly as influenced by Derridean deconstructionism, have also surfaced and multiplied in anthropological discourse, with the effect in some instances of bringing relativism to its most radical point. We see this seeming groundlessness invoked by Mary Douglas as well. Proceeding from the assertion that all human societies are equally rational, she moves increasingly to the particular, eventually suggesting not only that the organization of experience differs across societies, but that there is not "one kind of truth more true" than another, including our own as anthropologists. This is the result of her critical reading of Durkheim.

As Douglas has rightly pointed out, Durkheim explained the beliefs of others as instrumental to sustaining community. At the same time, however, he did not subject his own beliefs (including his belief in the scientific method) to the same scrutiny. In similar fashion, Evans-Pritchard was willing to explain, for example, how Azande belief in witchcraft made sense for Azande society. He quite explicitly did not allow for the possibility that Azande witchcraft was "real."[8] Evans-Pritchard, and the majority of anthropologists after him, while acting on their own assumption that there *is* something universally shared among humans, did not regard this assumption as a belief. On the contrary, while the beliefs of "Others" have been objectified and explained by an instrumental analysis, one's own belief in something—whether universal human rationality exemplified in human societies, or a "ground" possibly transcending humans, or positivism, or the scientific method, or Western monotheism—is implicit or silent. These silent assertions on the part of anthropologists run counter to the claims of pluralism (and even relativism) that Mary Douglas advances; they indicate anthropologists' unexamined assumptions and confusion over what relativism does, or ought to, entail.

Pushing Durkheim's thought to its logical conclusion, Mary Douglas describes her own relativism in the following way:

> It is part of our culture to recognise at last our cognitive precariousness. It is part of our culture to be sophisticated about fundamentalist claims to secure knowledge. It is part of our culture to be forced to take aboard the idea that other cultures are rational in the same way as ours. Their organization of experience is different, their objectives different, their successes and weak points different too. The refusal to privilege one bit of reality as more absolutely real, one kind of truth more true, one intellectual process more valid, allows the original comparative project dear to Durkheim to go forward at last. (Douglas 1999, xvii)

Douglas's assertion that other truths are just as true as ours is promising, and I want to pursue it further—ultimately using it as a corrective to the sort of relativism espoused by Richard Rorty. First, though, it is important to further explore Douglas's claim in order to lay bare her underlying intention. One possibility is that she is espousing a relativism within which truth is context-specific—all truths are thus equally true within their proper contexts. This position was suggested by anthropologist Peter Winch (1964), adapting Wittgenstein's notion of "language games" (see Ulin 1984). Another reading of Douglas's statement, however, and the one I think that better reflects her thinking, understands her to be proposing a relativism under which even her own approach, based on the scientific method, is merely one possible truth among others. Yet if Douglas is indeed claiming that there are a number of possible "truths," how can she account for the interest in universality that undergirds her own approach? Douglas seems to posit some form of reason shared by humans—but what exactly is *shared* in reason if all truths are equally true? What can "reason" or "rationality" mean in this context? Let us examine some of the possibilities.

From a radically relativist perspective, questions of truth regarding human experience are grounded in nothing outside that experience itself; context-specific truth is all we have. This is Rorty's (1982) position, and it can be found throughout the writings of many anthropologists.[9] In this light, Mary Douglas may be better understood to advocate a "pluralism," rather than a "relativism" of the sort just described, insofar as she is able to acknowledge a "ground" underlying human experience and reason, but that we *perceive* and therefore describe that "ground" differently, quite differently, in different places. The problem with the radically relativist position is that, while it allows for different and perhaps even equally valid truths, their groundlessness suggests they are fundamentally separate. In this case, cultural translation is all but impossible. Moreover, while it may be strategic, this form of relativism is unsupportable in my view. It presupposes a Western mind-body dualism according to which shared human physiology and its role in human experience can be bracketed and laid aside in the process of examining people unable to touch world or one another.

It is important, I think, to counter this untranslatability. Yet pluralism, too, can bear within it a tension of its own, depending on how a perceived grounding is specified. If it is conceded, for example, that there is metaphysical ground underlying reason and experience, it is possible (if not inevitable) for someone to claim that they have the best translation of that metaphysical "it," whether that means privileging the scientific method or a particular view of divinity. And indeed, such truth claims surface in the seemingly best of circumstances. Thus, despite their insistence that they treat opposing beliefs seriously, even scholars following the hermeneutic approaches of Paul Ricoeur and Hans-Georg Gadamer, with their assumption of context-specific truths, leave cultural "texts" to be read by those external to them, or by those who have navigated the "distance" necessary to accomplish the hermeneutic method. Moreover, I think that Richard Rorty mistakenly assumes one truth to be the more true, one position the correct one—despite his assertion of the groundlessness of radical relativism. Rorty reduces, for example, all claims to numinousness to "expressions of our awareness that we are members of a moral community, phrased in one or another pseudo-explanatory jargon. This awareness is something which cannot be further 'grounded'—it is simply taking a certain point of view on our fellow humans" (Rorty 1982, 202). This is quite a bold truth claim for a groundless relativist. Indeed, aside from the obvious difficulty of how to make ethical evaluations across very different human communities, Rorty's argument precludes acceptance of any truth, any cosmology, even any ontology other than his own Western, atheist, pragmatic one. From a cross-cultural point of view, this is a conversation stopper.

In the next section, I suggest an approach that, while more expansive, has much in common with Rorty's from the perspective of shared human experience, but that pushes the Durkheimian limits of "truth" as Douglas has called for.

PEIRCE: BACKGROUND TO A WORLD-CREATING APPROACH

Reminding us that "in most human communities the measure of the worth of any knowledge is its social value," Michael Jackson (1996) suggests that anthropologists "revalidate the everyday life of ordinary people" (36). As Jackson makes clear, this task speaks to the ethics necessarily embedded in knowledge production. How do we recover this "everyday life," however—particularly if we begin the project firmly rooted in our own epistemological and ontological traditions? As an answer, I suggest that we choose a theory of perception that *irreducibly* encompasses an ethics of knowledge production and an ethics of human interaction in such a way that radically different truths can be given voice. That is, while we may or may not solve the ultimate metaphysical conundrums, we may expand the scope of Rorty's context (and Wittgenstein's language games) to encompass human experience broadly. Charles Sanders Peirce offers such a fundamentally ethical philosophy of human being in the world, which those of us grounded in the traditions and values of the West can use in navigating diverse worlds.

A key component of Peirce's thought is his triads, most notably his triadic "sign" composed of representamen, object, and interpretant, which in turn, is central to an overall philosophy organized around the experiential elements of "firstness," "secondness," and "thirdness." Firstness is the most ephemeral of the three and points to a potential theory of human experience[10] that encompasses linguistic signs without being exhausted by them. Peirce describes experiential firstness thus:

> All that is immediately present to a man is what is in his mind in the present instant. His whole life is in the present. But when he asks what is the content of the present instant, his question always comes too late. The present is gone by, and what remains of it is greatly metamorphosized. (Peirce 1958, 1)

Importantly, Peirce allows for the possibility of experiential immediacy yet supposes that we do not necessarily have access to it. Whatever we do know of the world is all that humans *can* know of it: "It is perfectly true that we can never attain a knowledge of things as they are. We can only know their human aspect. But that is all the universe is for us" (Peirce 1958, 426). It is to this human aspect that Peirce's pragmaticist philosophy seeks to attend.

While Peirce's firstness is the immediacy of a feeling, an immediacy that cannot be reduced, secondness is a brute force impinging on that feeling. Peirce gives the example of your enjoying a moment of calm and stillness, when suddenly a steam whistle pierces that calm. While the experience of calm is firstness, breaking that calm with the whistle is secondness, a "consciousness of the action of a new feeling in destroying the old feeling" (Peirce 1958, 385).[11] Secondness is a "brute" awareness that the mind has not yet synthesized into thought. Peirce then refers to the synthesizing, interpretative dimension of the experiential (and signifying) process as "thirdness." While the triad of firstness, secondness, and thirdness describes the process of human experiencing and being in the world, the triadic sign (always a form of thirdness) describes understanding and communicating as a single process with transformative effects.

Put succinctly, signs (the representamen, or first) are always signs of something (an idea or object, or second) *to* something or someone (the intepretant, or third). In this way, Peirce's triadic, relational sign makes interpretation an *irreducible* aspect of it: "Thirdness is the triadic relation existing between a sign, its object, and the interpreting thought, itself a sign, considered as constituting the mode of being a sign" (Peirce 1958, 388). By way of this notion of thirdness, Peirce suggests that what we know of the world is fundamentally mediated *in community*, whether the community comprises the various voices within ourselves, our dialogues with others, or texts (or even the universe generally).[12] That is, *shared* meaning inescapably belongs to the process of experience and perception itself. Moreover, and crucially, shared meaning inescapably entails an ethical dimension because human communion is powerful: "To develop its meaning, we have therefore, simply to determine what habits it produces, for what a thing means is simply what habits it involves" (Peirce 1958, 123). In Peirce's system, interpretation and meaning are not only irreducibly a part of a signifying perception, but are that very process of perception, of thought, and of communication that entails *action upon the world.* Following Peirce's triadic approach to human experience and signification, every human encounter enacts a moment of world-creating communion with transformative consequences.

A WORLD-CREATING APPROACH TO BELIEF

We are world-makers; we are constantly making "new worlds out of old ones." What we see, perceive, touch is all in flux—a flux of our own creation. The real psychological question is how we shape this flux and how we maneuver in it. (Putnam 1990, 308)[13]

What implications does my pluralistic approach have for the effort to understand cultural beliefs different from my own? To answer that question, I start by identifying three general but different ways to carry out fieldwork, writing, and human interactions more broadly; these ways can be characterized as "distanced," "empathetic," and "world-creating." While I do not suggest that a distanced approach, ultimately rooted in the scientific method, is fundamentally unethical or useless, I do suggest that it imposes a preconceived barrier between anthropologists and those whom they study. It implies a peculiarly Western (and typically, though not necessarily, atheist or agnostic) view of the world that precludes the possibility for truths that are different from the ones we hold, but are nonetheless true. James Clifford and others have attempted to ameliorate the problem by pointing out the limits of every human perspective. Yet, while promising, the seemingly ubiquitous tendency within anthropology to admit to offering "partial truths"[14] does not, by itself, widen the public's consciousness of other possible ways to understand the world. It does not, by itself, throw into question the sanctity of the scientific method, for example, and thus, like Durkheim, stops short of expanding our view of human experience and creating new shared worlds.

A more promising approach has been attempted by a number of anthropologists who have brought self-conscious, *empathetic* experience to bear on their analyses (e.g., Briggs 1970; Rabinow 1977; Rosaldo 1989). In studies using this approach, anthropologists have written openly about their fieldwork-related failures. Some, like Renato Rosaldo, have gone on to describe the painful process of identifying forcefully enough with those one studies that a powerful, empathetic shared understanding takes place (Abu-Lughod 1986; Kondo 1990).

In other cases, the anthropologists' empathic experiences of other belief patterns and lifeworlds have gone so far as to achieve what I call "world-creating." Edith Turner's experience offers a good example of this approach.[15] In her book *Experiencing Ritual* (1992), she describes her experience of participating in a healing ritual involving the removal of a deceased hunter's tooth that flowed through the victim's veins, causing ill health, depression, and malaise. The ritual is complex, involving the airing of grievances, the removal of the hunter's tooth itself, and later giving food to the removed tooth to pacify the deceased hunter and thereby cure the patient as well. Turner writes:

> Quite an interval of struggle elapsed while I clapped like one possessed, crouching beside Bill amid a lot of urgent talk, while Singleton pressed Meru's back, guiding and leading out the tooth—Meru's face in a grin of tranced passion, her back quivering rapidly. Suddenly Meru raised her arm, stretched it in liberation, and I *saw* with my own eyes a giant thing emerging out of the flesh of her back. This thing was a large gray blob about six inches across, a deep gray opaque thing emerging as a sphere. I was amazed—delighted. I still laugh with glee at the realization of having seen it, the ihamba, and so big! (Turner 1992, 149)

In this and other writings, Edith Turner points toward the possibility of a *new world* mutually created jointly by her and the Ndembu with whom she has done fieldwork, a world that has transformed them all.

Such an acute and intentional awareness of a new world being created through interaction, particularly between those already attempting to bridge significant cultural differences, is at the core of what I mean by "world-creating." Moreover, while anthropologists should be certain to avoid, as Rorty does, asserting absolute truths, we need not be content to only serve as "interpreters for those with whom we are not sure how to talk" (Rorty 1982, 202). It is not sufficient, that is, to translate the world of others, except insofar as a radical form of translation renders new, shared worlds possible. World-creating presupposes that human encounters are inherently powerful. Like the signifying acts of which those encounters are composed, their meaning can be discerned, as Peirce suggests, in the *habits they produce.* If those habits continue to reflect a single, dominant version of reality and human experience, then genuine sharing of cross-cultural experience will be impossible.

Whether speaking of anthropologists and their interlocutors, or about those who encounter other persons or groups who have not previously shared a life-world, a world-creating approach redirects our focus from an emphasis on incommensurability to the recognition that "new worlds" (both desirable and undesirable for some participants) are constantly and inevitably being created through cultural and personal interactions. In making this point, I have relied on the ethical dimensions of Peirce's theory of perception, have taken account of Jackson's (1996) emplotment of experience and lifeworlds, and have broadened Mannheim and Tedlock's (1995) notion of culture as emergent from dialogue. I have suggested that it is necessary to recognize that multiple lifeworlds are implicated in any individual or collective understandings—something that anthropologists are increasingly doing. It is likewise important to recognize that when different lifeworlds meet, new shared understandings—that is, new worlds—are created.

Acknowledging that every interaction of the sort we have been exploring brings a new world into being is not sufficient, however; we must go on to examine what sorts of habits each new world entails. Thus, a world-creating approach combines a critical praxis[16] with an ethical *attitude*, or stance. It requires the brute force of Peircean secondness to give way to the world-creating understanding of thirdness, to let Other beliefs find a place in our thinking and partake of new, shared worlds that transform all involved. In anthropological terms, we and our interlocutors can produce a more politically relevant, as well as ethnographically richer, dialogue if we are willing to destabilize our own conventional understandings. And this is quite possible insofar as a genuine meeting *is* taking place: interactions always entail consequences.

EMBRACING PARADOX: SHARING TRUTHS IN A POTENTIALLY GROUNDLESS UNIVERSE

During the late 1950s and early 1960s, Nkai brought both fire and water at once to descend upon and destroy the home of a selfish Samburu family. Once a woman's house had sheltered a fire; once a thorn enclosure had protected the family's cows; and once a well had provided water that neither the husband nor the wife would share with their neighbors. Now, almost nothing remains— nothing that is, except the horns of a cow poking up from the ground to confirm that this was indeed the place. Several friends I made during fieldwork among the Samburu independently told me about this family—their name and the place they had formerly lived. Am I to take this event—and the idea that Nkai echoes back our behavior to us in some way—as "myths," regardless of how the Samburu experience them? Shall we likewise contend that Noah's flood, Moses' transfiguration, and Mohammed's reception of the Qu'ran are myth, regardless of how millions of people experience these accounts? Are scientists' claims of detecting sounds produced "soon" (in astronomic time) after the birth of the universe, or of witnessing the birth and death of stars myths as well? How do our understandings change when we answer "Maybe not"? How many ways do we limit our understanding of and respect for other cultural universes when we answer "Yes"?

If I were to write as part of my fieldwork findings that belief in Nkai is the belief of an animist pastoralist group, then go on to examine how the characteristics of Nkai are "true in context," I will have explained much about Samburu daily lives. But, if two Samburu and I ponder together what Nkai is and why Nkai exists, in connection perhaps with what I might believe to be true of humankind and divinity, then we may have created something—a world—that could not have existed otherwise. These worlds, created in the encounter with others, move us closer toward enacting Peirce's desire that the human community—and the needs of its diverse members—would be an end in itself, without foreclosing the possibility that Nkai likewise exists, for ends we may not recognize.

NOTES

The research from which this essay draws was generously supported by Fulbright IIE, Ford Foundation/University of Michigan Center for Afro-American and African Studies, a University of Michigan Rackham Thesis Grant, a National Science Foundation Grant, and the Department of Anthropology at Western Michigan University. I would like to thank the University of Nairobi Institute of African Studies for affiliation, the Ministry of Education for permission to conduct field research, and the Samburu people for their continuing friendship. I would also like to express my heartfelt gratitude to Jim White, Ruth Abbey, and Jon Holtzman for their generous and incisive comments on earlier versions of this essay. I owe thanks as well to Jim and my fellow participants in the Erasmus Institute Faculty Summer Seminar (2000) for their inspiration.

1. Within cultural anthropology, Peirce has not received the attention he deserves. The work of E. Valentine Daniel (1984, 1996) is the most notable exception. In his most recent work, Daniel draws upon Peirce to develop a critical view of representation—that is, the relationship between "word" and "thing". While the approach to fieldwork and writing I outline here is consistent with his in many respects, my focus is on recognizing, critically evaluating, and approaching intentionally the "worlds created" through human encounter. My approach, influenced by Peirce, the founder of pragmaticism, is pragmatic. Taking up a slightly different aspect of the debate, Daniel cautions us to be wary of the very moments of consensus Peirce told us were inevitable. If Daniel rightly

cautions us, I seek to move us toward an active, though ever questioning and cautious, doing. See also Jackson 1998, where Peirce is used to understand the construction of individual and collective identities.

2. My approach is consistent in important respects with Nelson Goodman's "world-making," but since I have developed it for a cross-cultural context prior to reading about Goodman's work, out of my reading of Charles Sanders Peirce and a combination of anthropological method and theory, I am calling it "world-creating."

3. See also the inspirational discussion in White 1990 on justice as translation, where he similarly argues that something "new" is created in the process of translating texts (241), and suggests that translation "has an ethical as well as an intellectual dimension" (257). White is eloquent in arguing why our interpretations of texts are or should be ethical acts—that indeed, "our every utterance is a way of being and acting in the world" (xi). I hope to connect Peirce's claim that ethics are tied into the very act of perceiving with a way of approaching religious belief.

4. In an article about how rebels use satellite and internet communication to undermine dictatorships (starting with Zapatista rebels), *Newsweek* included a photo of a Samburu elder (incorrectly labeled a "warrior") wearing a tartan blanket and a shoulder bag, holding a spear in one hand and a cell phone in the other. The caption read, "In a remote and desolate region of northern Kenya, a Samburu warrior makes a call on a cellular phone" (*Newsweek* 1995, 37). As of 2003, cellular phones remained out of range of Samburu District. Even satellite phones were prohibitively expensive for most political elite, who would not in any case wear a blanket and carry a spear.

5. Durkheim was not the only early champion of such a view. In the United States, for example, Franz Boas's anthropology was similarly inspired by a relativism that accorded equal rationality to all human cultures; Boas would train an entire generation of anthropologists, including Alfred Kroeber, Margaret Mead, and Ruth Benedict.

6. To cite two other prominent examples, Marshall Sahlins (1976) has argued that all humans lived in cultures operating according to a definite symbolic scheme; Clifford Geertz (1973) has suggested that all human cultures are interconnected webs of (symbolic) meaning, with religion being one system of meaning.

7. The Kabyle are a Berber community in Algeria.

8. The problems entailed by analyzing witchcraft while not believing that witches are "real" are pointed out in Winch 1964 in the context of what has been called the "rationality debates." See Ulin 1984 for a useful summary and analysis of these debates. Peter Winch's arguments notwithstanding, however, Ulin points out (and I agree) that the majority of anthropologists have continued to operate in Evans-Pritchard's terms—as if things like witches did not exist, even if they made sense culturally.

9. This is also Derrida's strategic contention, and the basis for one of his critiques of Heidegger, who he suggests uses "Being" as a sort of ultimate "ground."

10. It could also refer to a theory of reality, though this is a more controversial aspect of Peirce's thought.

11. Peirce links his idea of firstness, secondness, and thirdness to Hegel's three stages of thought and to the three categories of Kant's four triads (Peirce 1958, 384). I find his notion of secondness to be similar in some respects to Freud's *unheimlich,* as an experience of one world pushing brutely into another.

12. The hermeneutics of Gadamer and Ricoeur point to intertextuality, but they do not, of *necessity,* point to a critically transformative dimension within and beyond texts. Ethics are not an irreducible component of their approaches. Robert Ulin (1984) has also made this point specifically in terms of the inadequacy of hermeneutics to deal with inequality, but he formulated a response different from mine. He suggested absorbing Gadamer's and Ricoeur's hermeneutics within a materialist dialectic informed by both structuralist and historical culturalist strands of Marxism. My concern is both more specific and more general: I have chosen to focus on Peirce because I think his work can be interpreted to overcome the deficiencies of a Gadamer- and Ricoeur-styled hermeneutics without recourse to Marx or any other thinker. At the same time, I think Marx is one possible choice among many for an ethical approach to interpretation. Besides hermeneutics, we can also look to recent work coming out of linguistic anthropology building on the works of Julia Kristeva and Mikhail Bakhtin, which proceeds in light of the notion that culture emerges dynamically from dialogic encounters, and that those dialogues (including textual ones) are "already replete with echoes, allusions, paraphrases, and outright quotations of prior discourse" (Mannheim and Tedlock 1995). Again, however, although Mannheim and Tedlock are deeply concerned with issues of power and inequality, I am not convinced that ethics are *irreducibly* bound to their approach.

13. This excerpt is part of Hilary Putnam's favorable review of the work of philosopher Nelson Goodman.

14. James Clifford (1986) popularized the notion of "partial truths"—that anthropologists can never offer a complete description of the societies they study, but only partial truths from the perspective that their own social-cultural-economic-ethnic-gendered-etc. position affords them. It is less widely known that he was preceded in this notion of partial truths by Margaret Mead (1949).

15. Others include Stoller 1989; Desjarlais 1992; and Brown 1991. Edith Turner (1996) offers a more exhaustive list.

16. By "praxis," I mean theory and methods combined.

WORKS CITED

Abu-Lughod, Lila. 1986. *Veiled Sentiments: Honor and Poetry in a Bedouin Society.* Berkeley: University of California Press.

Bourdieu, Pierre. 1977. *Outline of a Theory of Practice.* Translated by R. Nice. Cambridge: Cambridge University Press.

Briggs, Jean. 1970. *Never in Anger: Portrait of an Eskimo Family.* Cambridge: Harvard University Press.

Brown, Karen McCarthy. 1991. *Mama Lola: A Vodou Priestess in Brooklyn*. Berkeley: University of California Press.

Clifford, James. 1986. "Introduction: Partial Truths." In *Writing Culture: The Poetics and Politics of Ethnography*, ed. James Clifford and George E. Marcus, 1–26. Berkeley: University of California Press.

Csordas, Thomas J., et al. 1994. *Embodiment and Experience: The Existential Ground of Culture and Self*. Edited by Thomas J. Csordas. Cambridge: Cambridge University Press.

Daniel, E. Valentine. 1984. *Fluid Signs: Being a Person the Tamil Way*. Berkeley: University of California Press.

———. 1996. *Charred Lullabies: Chapters in an Ethnography of Violence*. Princeton: Princeton University Press.

Desjarlais, Robert. 1992. *Body and Emotion: The Aesthetics of Illness and Healing in the Nepal Himalayas*. Philadelphia: University of Pennsylvania Press.

Douglas, Mary. 1966. *Purity and Danger*. London: Routledge.

———. 1999. *Implicit Meanings: Selected Essays in Anthropology*. London: Routledge.

Evans-Pritchard, E. E. 1937. *Witchcraft, Magic, and Oracles among the Azande*. Oxford: Clarendon Press.

Geertz, Clifford. 1973. *The Interpretation of Cultures: Selected Essays*. New York: Basic Books.

Harris, Marvin. 1979. *Cultural Materialism: The Struggle for a Science of Culture*. New York: Random House.

Holtzman, Jon. 2002. "Politics and Gastropolitics: Gender and the Power of Food in Two African Pastoralist Societies." *Journal of the Royal Anthropological Institute* 8(2):259–78.

———. 2004. "The Local in the Local: Models of Time and Space in Samburu District, Northern Kenya." *Current Anthropology* 45(1):61–84.

Jackson, Deborah Davis. 1998. "Our Elders Lived It": American Indian Identity and Community in a Deindustrializing City (Urban Communities, Michigan). Ph.D. diss., University of Michigan.

Jackson, Michael. 1996. "Introduction: Phenomenology, Radical Empiricism, and Anthropological Critique." In *Things As They Are: New Directions in Phenomenological Anthropology*, ed. Michael Jackson. Bloomington: Indiana University Press.

Kondo, Dorinne. 1990. *Crafting Selves: Power, Gender, and Discourses of Identity in a Japanese Workplace*. Chicago: University of Chicago Press.

Levi-Strauss, Claude. 1969. *The Elementary Structures of Kinship*. Translated by James Harle Bell, John Richard von Sturmer, and Rodney Needham. Boston: Beacon Press.

———1970. *The Raw and the Cooked: Introduction to a Science of Mythology*. London: Cape.

Mannheim, Bruce, and Dennis Tedlock. 1995. "Introduction." In *The Dialogic Emergence of Culture*, ed. Dennis Tedlock and Bruce Mannheim, 1–32. Urbana: University of Illinois Press.

Mead, Margaret. 1949. *Male and Female: A Study of the Sexes in a Changing World.* New York: Morrow.

Newsweek. 1995. "When Words Are the Best Weapon." 27 February 1995. International ed., 36–40.

Peirce, Charles Sanders. 1958. *The Collected Papers of Charles Sanders Peirce.* Edited by Charles Hartshorne and Paul Weiss (vols. 1–6); A.W. Burke (vols. 7–8.). Cambridge: Harvard University Press.

Putnam, Hilary. 1990. *Realism with a Human Face.* Edited by James Conant. Cambridge: Harvard University Press.

Rabinow, Paul. 1977. *Reflections on Fieldwork in Morocco.* Berkeley: University of California Press.

Rappaport, Roy. 1979. *Ecology, Meaning, and Religion.* Richmond, Calif.: North Atlantic Books.

Rorty, Richard. 1982. *Consequences of Pragmatism.* Minneapolis: University of Minnesota Press.

Rosaldo, Renato. 1988. *Culture and Truth: The Remaking of Social Analysis.* Boston: Beacon Press.

Sahlins, Marshall. 1976. *Culture and Practical Reason.* Chicago: University of Chicago Press.

Straight, Bilinda. 1997a. "Gender, Work, and Change among Samburu Pastoralists of Northern Kenya." *Research in Economic Anthropology* 18:65–91.

———. 1997b. Altered Landscapes, Shifting Strategies: The Politics of Location in the Constitution of Gender, Belief, and Identity among Samburu Pastoralists in Northern Kenya. Ph.D. diss., University of Michigan.

———. 2000. "Development Ideologies and Local Knowledge among Samburu Women in Northern Kenya." In *Rethinking Pastoralism in Africa,* ed. Dorothy Hodgson, 227–48. Oxford: James Currey.

———. 2002. Introduction to "Conflict at the Center of Ethnography," special issue edited by Bilinda Straight. *Anthropology and Humanism* 27(1):3–9.

———. 2005. "In the Belly of History: Memory, Forgetting, and the Hazards of Reproduction among Samburu in Northern Kenya." *Africa* 75(1): 83–104.

Turner, Edith. 1992. *Experiencing Ritual: A New Interpretation of African Healing.* Philadelphia: University of Pennsylvania Press.

———. 1996. *The Hands Feel It: Healing and Spirit Presence among a Northern Alaskan People.* DeKalb, Ill.: Northern Illinois University Press.

Ulin, Robert. 1984. *Understanding Cultures: Perspectives in Anthropology and Social Theory.* Austin: University of Texas Press.

White, James Boyd. 1990. *Justice as Translation: An Essay in Cultural and Legal Criticism.* Chicago: University of Chicago Press.

Winch, Peter. 1964. "Understanding a Primitive Society." In *Rationality,* ed. Bryan R. Wilson, 78–112. Oxford: Basil Blackwell.

CHAPTER SIX

The Only Permanent State

Tocqueville on Religion in Democracy

Patrick J. Deneen

How is one to talk about religion in the language of politics, especially democratic politics? Patrick Deneen addresses this question, which has of course great contemporary significance, by analyzing the work of Alexis de Tocqueville, who saw over a hundred and fifty years ago that a most complex relation existed between religion and democracy. Democracy is based on the primacy of the human will, especially the will of the majority; it leads naturally to a kind of restless materialism, to an excessive individualism, and to the loss of shared substantive standards of judgment. For Tocqueville religion was a potential counterforce resisting these tendencies. In this essay, Deneen elaborates Tocqueville's complex and somewhat paradoxical argument, suggesting that it is still cogent in our time.

> *When the old God leaves the world, what happens to all the unexpended faith?*
> —Don Delillo, *Mao II*

Those caught up in contemporary debates about the presence and role of religion in the liberal-democratic polity tend to take extreme sides on the ancient controversy about the proper place and role of religion in political life. Some claim that religion poses too great a danger to the liberal polity to be allowed entrance into the public sphere; others insist that democracy cannot survive without a religious basis, that the continued civic health of the polity requires the moral underpinnings and ethic of self-sacrifice that religion alone provides. It is a truism, perhaps, to acknowledge that both positions have certain merits: religion is indeed not altogether without its dangers to a liberal-democratic polity (as we see in its most extreme forms by some contemporary expressions of religious fundamentalism); yet, corrosive individualism, crass material hedonism, high levels of lawlessness, and widespread loss of civic responsibility suggest to many that only the broader inculcation of religious values can forestall these perceived threats to the polity. While this debate has brought forth many persuasive and valuable observations, it is perhaps time to acknowledge that proponents of both of these positions have staked claims that makes them unlikely to hear the persuasive claims of their opponents.

This acknowledgment would force us to consider anew the potential benefits and threats of religion for a *democratic* polity. Democracy places special demands on the governing capacities and moral decencies of each citizen; absent those decencies, even virtues, democracy has the potential to devolve into the most vicious of regimes if the citizenry is itself vicious and entirely lacking self-rule and respect for the claims of the minority. While Plato first argued that democratic regimes have the greatest tendency to become tyrannical, the most powerful articulation of modern democracy's tendencies toward a peculiarly democratic despotism is that of Alexis de Tocqueville. In describing the potential of "tyranny of the majority" and "democratic tyranny," as well as the different but related threats posed by excessive individualism and materialism, Tocqueville analyzed the internal logic of democratic equality and individualism to its theoretical denouement. At the same time, however, he believed that democracies should, and America did, avail themselves of the moral resources of religion as a counterweight to those more virulent tyrannical tendencies that inhere "in the rule of the people." Most of all, unlike many of today's academic theorists, Tocqueville believed that religion was not only compatible with democratic polities, but indeed that religion of a certain kind was *necessary* for the continued flourishing of a democratic regime. This position was based not only on his experience in America, but on certain theoretical insights into the religious underpinnings of contemporary belief in equality and human dignity, and on the implications of his analysis of the internal dynamics of democracy itself.

Much of today's (largely, but not exclusively academic) hostility toward religion in the public sphere is based on assumptions remarkably similar to Tocqueville's own assessment of the hostility of European liberals toward the Catholic Church, in particular.[1] By demonstrating the deficiencies of this understanding—both by pointing to the example in America, but more importantly by pointing out the dangers of this hostility and the necessary influence of religion to the flourishing of a democratic regime in a more philosophical register—Tocqueville hoped that he might disabuse his contemporary antireligious liberals of their prejudice.

Yet, as important as the recognition of the beneficial aspects of religion for democracy, equally essential is the recognition that Tocqueville himself was troubled by the implausibility of his own suggestions, a form of chastened analysis that even the most ardent enthusiast of his views must heed. While acknowledging that modern democracy needed the countervailing force of religion, he was not sanguine about the possibility of religion's continued influence in a democratic age. He even seemed, at times, to succumb to the temptation of recommending a kind of "civil religion," which by his own analysis would be insufficient to the task he sets for religion in democracy. His analysis, then, should be the cause of reflection for those concerned with democracy's future, but at the same time hardly reason for celebration by those who would find there an ardent recommendation of school prayer and biblically themed wall decorations. Religion was most useful to democracy when it was viewed as least useful; and in times when democracy was most imperiled, Tocqueville suggested that perhaps the most dangerous impulse would be to try to recommend the inculcation of religion as a necessary support for democracy. Nevertheless, Tocqueville did not despair of religion's playing a possibly significant role in democratic life, although his chastened hopes suggest that religion's greatest apparent friends may in fact be democracy's—and, curiously enough, even religion's—potential foes.

TOCQUEVILLE'S "RELIGIOUS DREAD":
THE PROBLEM OF EQUALITY

As he explains in the introduction to the first volume of *Democracy in America*, Tocqueville was inspired to write about the promise and dangers of modern democracy, and particularly about what he regarded as the inevitable spread of equality of conditions, due to "a kind of religious dread (*d'une sorte de terreur religieuse*) inspired by contemplation of this irresistible revolution [of democratic equality] advancing century by century over every obstacle and even now going forward amid the ruins it has itself created" (12).[2] His sense of "religious dread" is at least curious, since in the following paragraph Tocqueville asserts that it is the will of divine providence that this universal spread of equality occurs: "God does not Himself need to speak for us to find sure signs of His will; it is enough to observe the customary progress of nature and the continuous tendency of events" (12). Tocqueville concludes "in that case effort to halt democracy appears as a fight against God Himself, and nations have no alternative but to acquiesce in the social state imposed by Providence" (12). In Tocqueville's view, the spread of democracy is a result of the irresistible divine plan of God.

Why, then, does he express "religious dread" at the prospect of God's divine will coming to pass? For Tocqueville, it is one of the eternal paradoxes of human existence that the greatest legacy of the Christian tradition—the universal belief in human equality and equal human dignity—simultaneously represents one of the greatest threats to that tradition at the moment of its fruition in the world of politics. Tocqueville held that one of the most pernicious effects of democracy would be to turn humanity away from considerations of the divine, and hence an appreciation of the ultimate source of human equality, and instead credit human efforts alone for equality's triumph. If equality was in the first instance the result of God's divine plan—the inheritance of the belief that all humans are created from the same divine source—the paradoxical result would be to create the possibility of a tyrannical form of democracy based precisely on the widespread acceptance of human equality. Thus, equality ultimately threatened to undermine the capacity of humanity to acknowledge the divine source of equality, and thereby unleash a range of pernicious effects resulting from disbelief, including materialism, individualism, selfishness, and political lassitude.

For Tocqueville, "equality of conditions" did not mean the literal equality of material resources—although he recognized that material conditions had become more equal in the democratic America of the 1830s—but primarily a psychological condition under which no person is recognized as having any claims to superiority over or deference toward to any other person. This view was a direct inheritance of the Christian tradition, in which all human beings are equal in the eyes of God, regardless of their social situation, wealth, accomplishments, even claims to moral worth. It is an equality deriving in part from an implicit recognition of the insufficiency of all humans in relation to the divine; at the same time, in Tocqueville's view, it is simultaneously ennobling inasmuch as each person is equally part of God's creation. As Tocqueville observes, this religious conception of equality inevitably leads to a political conception: "Christianity, which has declared all men equal in the sight of God, cannot hesitate to acknowledge all citizens equal before the law" (16).

This form of equality, however, is threatened by another, more debased, form. If every system of government operates on certain unquestioned assumptions (lest its legitimacy be constantly called into question), in democracy that assumption of equality was transformed into "the dogma of the sovereignty of the people" (58). A legitimate government must respect the sustained will of the people, Tocqueville suggests; however, in democracies this principle is raised to a dogma, meaning that the sovereignty of human opinion goes all but unquestioned, and thereby threatens to become a potentially tyrannical force. Tocqueville maintains that it is "an impious and detestable maxim that in matters of government the majority of people has the right to do everything, and nevertheless I place the origin of all powers in the will of the majority" (250). A government based on decisions of the majority is animated by fundamental *egalitarian* assumptions, since each person's vote, and by extension each person's view and opinion, is deemed to be absolutely equal to any other person's. But Tocqueville distinguishes two forms of majority rule that mirror the two forms of equality he has identified. In its debased form, majority rule is a reflection of a leveling democratic equality in which the majority is comparable to "an individual with opinions, and usually with interests" (251), a collective body of interests against which a minority has no recourse or appeal (252). Tocqueville contrasts this limited sense of democratic majority with "the majority of all men," whose single law is justice, and which "forms the boundary to each people's right" (250).

"Equality of conditions" produces an unwillingness to defer to the view of any other person, a condition of complete but misguided self-reliance arising from an assumption of equal worth in its most debased sense: "There is a general distaste for accepting any man's word for anything" (431). This unwillingness to submit to another's judgment, however, does not result in a strong sense of self-regard and a confidence of the validity of one's own position. Rather, it is accompanied by the unwillingness to judge anyone or anything in turn, which validates majority opinion on the ground that one simply cannot judge based on other standards. This leads to the creation of a "tyranny of the majority," one of Tocqueville's original and counterintuitive analyses of the potential perniciousness of democratic equality.

Tocqueville believes that all regimes have an inclination toward tyranny when that regime's guiding principle ceases to have any check to restrain that principle. He explicitly rejects the classical conception of mixed government as a "chimera," since all governments must place "somewhere one social power superior to all others" (251). In a democracy, then, "freedom is in danger when that power [of the majority] finds no obstacle that can restrain its course and give it time to moderate itself" (251–53). Tocqueville worries that there will be no political recourse or remedy when a democracy has committed an injustice, since all of the levers of government are inevitably subject to majority control (251).

This is only the most obvious form of democratic tyranny, and its structural form says little about the psychological features that Tocqueville described as emanating from a combination of majority rule and "equality of conditions." The more powerful critique that Tocqueville levels at the "tyranny of the majority" concerns the power that the majority exerts over the freedom of thought itself: people will avoid even the possibility of thinking in contradiction to a perceived widespread majority consensus out of fear of social ostracism. Ironically, despite the social controls that exist in aristocratic Europe, Tocqueville sees more allowance for widely disparate views on, among other things, religious and political theories in Europe than in democratic America: "I know of no country in which, generally speaking, there is less independence of mind and true freedom of discussion than in America" (254–55). In Tocqueville's view, Americans effectively internalize the fear of social rejection and avoid even the possibility of nonconformity to the perceived agreements of the democratic majority. He expresses deep reservations concerning the view that democratic freedom is to be preferred to aristocratic constraints if the price of that "freedom" is an even more insidious form of enslavement:

> Formerly tyranny used the clumsy weapons of chains and hangmen; nowadays, even despotism, though it seemed to have nothing more to learn, has been perfected by civilization. Princes made violence a physical thing, but our contemporary democratic republics have turned it into something as intellectual as the human will is intended to constrain. Under the absolute government of a single man, despotism, to reach the soul, clumsily struck at the body, and the soul, escaping from such blows, rose gloriously above it; but in democratic republics that is not at all how tyranny behaves; it leaves the body alone and goes straight for the soul. (255)

The individual, without recourse against the majority and bereft of intellectual resources external to the "dogma of the sovereignty of the people," is in the gravest peril of a thoroughgoing enervation as he retreats from the seeming omnipotence of the faceless and nameless democratic majority. The ironic result of the conformity that is engendered by the tyranny of the majority is not so much the creation of a collectivist majoritarian nightmare as it is an exacerbation of the other effect of equality—namely, individualism.

Thus, Tocqueville concluded that "equality of conditions" led not to mass conformity *per se*, but rather, in response to the perception of individual weakness in the face of a perceived "tyranny of the majority," to a kind of virulent individualism. "Individualism is a calm and considered feeling which disposes each citizen to isolate himself from the mass of his fellows and withdraw into the circle of his family and friends. . . . Individualism is of democratic origin, and threatens to grow as conditions grow more equal" (506–7). In response to perceptions of his individual weakness, democratic man retreats further from the public sphere that might otherwise sustain his sense of individual strength. While people in democracies are individually weak amid a large and faceless majority, they sense a potency when left to themselves and a small private circle: "They form the habit of thinking of themselves in isolation and imagine that their whole destiny is in their own hands" (508). This perceived potency, born of withdrawal from conditions that otherwise confirm their individual weakness, in fact leaves them weaker than before as they have no influence on public affairs and each person's voice—made more singular in the absence of a wider circle of associates—is altogether drowned out. The response, ironically in Tocqueville's view, is not to seek out fellowship that would strengthen the individual, but to retreat further from the perceived indignity of public life: "Thus, not only does democracy make men forget their own ancestors, but also clouds their view of their descendants and isolates them from their contemporaries. Each man is forever thrown back on himself alone, and there is danger that he may be shut up in the solitude of his own heart" (508).

This withdrawal in the face of perceived insignificance, combined with the "equality of conditions" that led to it, creates a kind of thoroughgoing materialism that is singular to the democratic age. The same unwillingness to judge or to be judged that results in the "tyranny of the majority" also leads surprisingly to a form of willful self-reliance. From this simple effect of equality, Tocqueville deduces an iron law of materialism and of a democratic optimism that borders on overconfidence. When equality of conditions becomes widespread,

each man is narrowly shut up in himself, and from that basis makes the pretension to judge the world. This American way of relying on themselves alone to control their judgment leads to other mental habits. Seeing that they are successful in resolving unaided all the little difficulties they encounter in practical affairs, they are easily led to the conclusion that everything in the world can be explained and that nothing passes beyond the limits of intelligence. Thus they are ready to deny anything which they cannot understand. Hence they have little faith in anything extraordinary and an almost invincible distaste for the supernatural. (430)

Through the internal logic of equality's implications, Tocqueville wryly observes that "of all the countries of the world, America is the one in which the precepts of Descartes are the least studied and best followed" (429). The tendency of equality—itself born of the Christian tradition, in Tocqueville's view—is to undermine all religions, and put in its place the radical skepticism of Descartes, derived not from study, but from democratic practice.

Tocqueville's "religious dread" thus points to the likely decline of religion that is ironically the legacy of Western Christianity. Christianity's insistence that all men are created equal in the eyes of God moves humankind providentially toward the ascendance of democracy and the accompanying "equality of conditions." This very equality, however, in its most virulent manifestation, undermines the religious basis from which it derived, which in fact offered the best obstacle to equality's tendencies toward skepticism, individualism, and materialism. At some level, one can understand Tocqueville's *terreur religieuse* to be both a dread for religion and, at the same time, a dread of what religion has wrought.

TOCQUEVILLE'S CRITIQUE OF MATERIALISM AND THE DEMOCRATIC FAITH

There is, in Tocqueville's view, a nearly unavoidable inclination in egalitarian societies toward doctrines of materialism. He understood such doctrines to release human ambitions in directions hitherto restrained by religious admonitions of humility. Addressing directly the need for religion to serve as a corrective for this materialist tendency, Tocqueville writes that "when [materialists] think they have sufficiently established that they are no better than brutes, they seem as proud as if they had proved that they were gods" (544). If "faith is the only permanent state of mankind" (297), Tocqueville feared that in a materialistic, egalitarian democracy, faith would manifest itself as a belief in human perfectibility resulting in an unbounded human restlessness.

It is not in spite of the materialist bent of democratic man that he is restless; it is because of his materialism. At its most mundane level, this materialism is expressed by the hedonistic pursuit of worldly success. Despite their comparative wealth and success, Tocqueville finds it curious "with what feverish ardor the Americans pursue prosperity and how they are ever tormented by the shadowy suspicion that they may not have chosen the shortest route to get it" (536). He wonders at the drivenness of Americans, their constant desire for more abundance, more security, more possessions. Tocqueville accounts for their restless anxiety by pointing to a more fundamental kind of materialism, a submerged but evident desire to outrun death through accumulation.[3] This leads to a rushing from thing to thing, from sensation to sensation, and results in a loss of any sense of true human permanence, but instead exacerbates the sense of impermanence that pervades the material age:

> Americans cleave to the things of this world as if assured that they will never die, and yet are in such a rush to snatch any that come within their reach, as if expecting to stop living before they have relished them. They clutch everything, but hold nothing fast, and so lose grip as they hurry after some new delight. . . . A man who has set his heart on nothing but the good things of the world is always in a hurry, for he has only a limited time in which to find them, get them, and enjoy them. Remembrance of the shortness of life continually goads him on. Apart from the goods that he has, he thinks of a thousand others which death will prevent him from tasting if he does not hurry. This thought fills him with distress, fear, and regret and keeps his mind continually in agitation, so that he is always changing his plans and his abode. (536–37)

In contrast to aristocratic ages, when man was neither materialist—believing in a good beyond the material world—nor endowed with the freedom to make oneself wholly new in whatever direction one wished, the democratic age is marked by a kind of endless motion that ceases only in death. These two new conditions—democratic materialism and the decline of social restraints that hold one in a particular status—thus combine to create a universally restless nation (537): "At first there is something astonishing in this spectacle of so many lucky men restless in the midst of their abundance. But it is a spectacle as old as the world; all that is new is to see a whole people performing in it" (536).

Yet, rather than leading to a strengthening of the individual's confidence in the unlimited freedom to remake oneself, Tocqueville concludes that the democratic citizen's restlessness in fact leads to a peculiar condition of enervation. "The same equality which allows each man to entertain vast hopes makes each man by himself weak. His power is limited on every side, though his longings may wander where they will" (537). This is a noteworthy paradox that one finds repeated in different permutations in Tocqueville's analysis: the appearance of individual puissance in fact reveals a more subtle form of individual weakness. Thus, as previously discussed, whereas the "equality of conditions" leads to the appearance of individual political strength, Tocqueville's analysis shows that the result of the democratic dogma is an individual weakness arising from the "tyranny of the majority." So too, in analyzing the consequences of materialism and the unleashing of human potential from restraints of the aristocratic past, Tocqueville concludes that this apparent confidence— located in an increasingly weakened and solitary individual—in fact ironically also results in a condition of individual enervation.

Even as this form of restlessness—the perception of a fluid new world shorn of traditional limits—contributes to a sense of individual weakness, it also encourages a new form of the belief in human perfectibility. Such an idea, Tocqueville notes, is not new to democratic times; perfectibility, like the restless pursuit of material abundance, is likely "as old as the world" (452). However, under aristocracies "citizens are classified by rank, profession, or birth . . . and everyone thinks he can see the ultimate limits of human endeavor quite close in front of him, and no one attempts to fight against an inevitable fate" (452–53). Democratic ages, by contrast, present new social arrangements that encourage perfectibility not as a distant ideal, but as more immediately realizable through striving and achievement. While aristocratic ages did not deny the possibility of improvement, in democratic ages that legitimate pursuit is thought to be "unlimited" (453).

As majority rule simultaneously empowers and weakens, and as restlessness offers simultaneous opportunity and enervation, so the belief in human perfectibility engendered by democratic equality produces a concomitant resulting disappointment. Democratic man "concludes that man in general is endowed with an indefinite capacity for improvement. . . . Thus, searching always, falling, picking himself up again, often disappointed, never discouraged, he is ever striving toward that immense grandeur glimpsed indistinctly at the end of the long track that humanity must follow" (453). What was once a goal thought to be achievable only in the afterlife is now, in a materialist age, thought to be realizable within one's lifetime. Yet, Tocqueville also notes that this belief is no less a form of faith than the faith that it displaced: the constant and inevitable setbacks to human perfection present a cause for "disappointment" but not "discouragement," and this is solely due to the secular faith in perfectibility that results from the new and wholly open social conditions. In Tocqueville's view, the conditions neither of aristocratic limitation nor of democratic openness are ultimately desirable; both represent extremes that seem to abandon a form of moderate and chastened striving toward material and moral improvement. So, Tocqueville concludes, "aristocratic nations are by their nature too much inclined to restrict the scope of human perfectibility; democratic nations sometimes stretch it beyond reason" (454).

All this gives us some insight into Tocqueville's view of democratic faith. Faith in the "dogma" of democracy, unmediated by those institutions that Tocqueville saw as affording some corrective to the worst ravages of this democratic faith—family, associations, newspapers, and above all, religion—which resulted in a curious and novel condition, in which democratic man at once imagined himself to be thoroughly omnipotent and yet found himself to be utterly impotent. Democratic faith transfers faith from divine objects to human endeavors, a result of the materialism that Tocqueville thought was the consequence of democratic equality. If democratic faith called for belief in the "unseen" and "unproven," just as did the faith in divinity that it displaced, its results were widely divergent, in large part due to the *object* of the faith itself—not now a divine Creator whose very perfection required the recognition of human fallibility—but instead a belief in democratic capacities and human perfectibility. If a religious faith necessitated the admission of human imperfection, leading citizens to acknowledge a condition of mutual insufficiency that favored endeavors undertaken in common, that recognition also involved a concomitant acknowledgment of human *dignity* that resulted from humanity's participation in, and guidance from the divine, thereby serving as a potential source of moral strength for each individual in a democratic setting. By contrast, the "democratic faith," premised on human perfectibility, ironically resulted in a condition of radical *indignity* as it placed human life on an ultimately unsatisfying material basis, contributed to the shattering of human associations, and thereby rendered individuals politically and socially ineffectual.

As Tocqueville pointed out when speaking of perfectibility, there is no more cause for regarding perfection as realizable on the earth than for believing in our likely acceptance into heaven, but the fact that human beings are now regarded as thoroughly responsible for its realization alters our view of perfection. Democratic man becomes more optimistic, thinking that human efforts alone will suffice; yet, the almost inevitable frustration of those efforts leaves him dissatisfied, restless, and impatient. Democratic faith increasingly sees democracy itself as the source of its own correction, thus exacerbating those worst aspects that derive from that faith in the first place. For the more completely people believe in democratic equality and "the dogma of the sovereignty of the people," the more the tyranny of the majority becomes firmly entrenched; the materialism resulting from this thoroughgoing belief in equality deepens and magnifies democratic restlessness and the idea of perfectibility; and, as these ambitions are frustrated, more emphasis is placed on *democratic* correctives, further deepening the simultaneous senses of democratic omnipotence and weakness. The democratic citizen is simultaneously overconfident and overwhelmed:

> Since in times of equality no man is obliged to put his powers at the disposal of another, and no one has any claim on the right to substantial support from his fellow man, each is both independent and weak. These two conditions, *which must be neither seen quite separately or confused,* give the citizen of a democracy extremely contradictory instincts. He is *full of confidence and pride* in his independence among equals, but from time to time his *weakness* makes him feel the need for some outside help which he cannot expect from any of his fellows, for they are both impotent and cold. (672 [emphasis added])

Tocqueville thus suggests two apparently contradictory conditions arising from democratic equality. On the one hand, "tyranny of the majority" leaves democratic man individually weak, unable to render judgments or to resist the perceived tide of majority consensus, and drives him further into "the solitude of his own heart." On the other hand, his unwillingness to render judgment, or to view any other person's judgment as potentially superior (or inferior) to his own, creates a form of individualism that devolves into a form of materialism, a thoroughgoing restlessness, an unwarranted belief in human capacities, even a faith in the possibility of human perfectibility. The logic of "equality of conditions" places democratic man simultaneously in the position of enervated isolation and overweening self-confidence. Tocqueville, quite startlingly, sees these conditions as compatible, not contradictory, and moreover as extremes that democratic humanity is likely to manifest both simultaneously and perpetually. From the dynamics of democratic equality Tocqueville thus perceives a resulting democratic man who exists simultaneously as a version of both Aristotelian extremes and increasingly lacks the resources to reach, by moving simultaneously in opposite directions, a form of the virtuous Aristotelian mean.

This seemingly contradictory condition of individual weakness and overconfidence is a result of consequences that Tocqueville adduces from the "equality of conditions" that marks the new democratic age. Yet this belief in equality is a result of the divine plan that now brings the world toward this democratic age. The selfsame religion that made equality the accepted order now stands threatened by the logic of that equality. Moreover, in Tocqueville's view, the paramount way of combating what he regarded as these most corrosive effects of equality is religion itself. He effectively describes a vicious circle: the Christian religion bequeaths to the modern age a belief in equality and a new democratic form that manifests this belief most fully; the "equality of conditions," placed now in this democratic context, results in forms of subtle tyranny, materialism, restlessness, and a belief in perfectibility that were formerly precluded by older aristocratic forms and religious belief. Now what is most needed to combat these tendencies is not a return to aristocratic forms— our age of equality precludes this possibility[4]—but a strengthening of the religious beliefs that stand to mitigate these vicious outcomes of the belief in equality that arose in the first place, from the same religious tradition. Religion, indirectly the cause of the democratic faith, is needed for its moderation.

THE UTILITY OF RELIGION

Tocqueville believed he had described the unperceived weakness that would undermine his highest hope for the democratic age: equality is both the greatest boon and the insoluble problem of modernity. In a chapter entitled "Why in Ages of Equality and Skepticism it is Important to set Distant Goals for Human Endeavors" (II.i.17), Tocqueville explained why religion was most needed for a democratic age marked especially by materialism, restlessness, and a belief in human perfectibility:

> In ages of FAITH the final aim is placed beyond life.... Religions instill a general habit of behaving with the future in view. In this respect they work as much in favor of happiness in this world as of felicity in the next. That is one of their most salient political characteristics.

But as the light of faith grows dim, man's range of vision grows more circumscribed, and it would seem as if the object of human endeavors came daily closer. When once they have grown accustomed not to think about what will happen after their life, they easily fall back into a complete and brutish indifference about the future, an attitude all too well suited to certain propensities of human nature. As soon as they have lost the way of relying chiefly on distant hopes, they are naturally led to want to satisfy their least desires at once; and it would seem that as soon as they despair of living forever, they are inclined to act as if they could not live for more than a day. (547–48)

In order to combat this tendency, one "suited to certain propensities in human nature," Tocqueville argued that another propensity, one possibly stronger than unbelief, but less supported in a democratic age, should be encouraged as a counterforce to excessively short-term, materialistic thinking. This "propensity" was the wellspring of religion itself, the longing for a continuation of one's existence beyond the short time allotted to humans to traverse this planet:

The short span of sixty years can never shut in the whole of man's imagination; the incomplete joys of this world will never satisfy his heart. Alone among all created beings, man shows a natural disgust for existence and an immense longing to exist; he scorns life and fears annihilation. These different instincts constantly drive his soul toward contemplation of the next world, and it is religion that leads him thither. Religion, therefore, is only one particular form of hope, and it is as natural to the human heart as hope itself. (296–97)

It seems contradictory that Tocqueville should declare that humans have as much a propensity for *disbelief* in religion, and a concentration on things of this life, as they have a propensity for *belief* in religion, as he reveals when he writes "incredulity is an accident: faith is the only permanent state of mankind" (297). Yet Tocqueville believed that in a democratic age the propensity for belief could be redirected, if not altogether thwarted, but only at the cost of tremendous psychological and social damage. In a skeptical and materialist age, faith could too easily resurface not as supportive of democracies, or in Tocqueville's view more importantly, as a necessary response to the human confrontation with finitude, but in a perverse and fanatical form:

If ever the thoughts of the great majority came to be concentrated solely on the search for material blessings, one can anticipate that there would be a colossal reaction in the souls of men. They would distractedly launch out into the world of spirits for fear of being held too tightly bound by the body's fetters.... If their social condition, circumstances, and laws did not so closely confine the American mind to the search for physical comfort, it may well be that when they came to consider immaterial things they would show more experience and reserve and be able to keep themselves in check without difficulty. But they feel imprisoned within limits from which they are apparently not allowed to escape. Once they have broken through these limits, their minds do not know where to settle down, and they often rush without stopping far beyond the bounds of common sense. (535)

In another of Tocqueville's paradoxes, skeptical and material ages are wont to exhibit the most "enthusiastic" and even fanatic forms of spirituality, precisely because the widespread materialism of the age does not give expression to any of the most fundamental human desires, including the desire for eternity. Democratic materialism coincides comfortably, even necessarily, with religious fanaticism in Tocqueville's view, not as contradictory but as the necessary consequence of humanity's two "propensities"—the desire for material satiation and longing for life after life. Yet, this form of unleashed spirituality, rather than tending to correct or balance the excesses of democratic materialism, in fact only further supports the kind of restlessness and boundlessness that is its inheritance.

Thus, it was not simply that religion could serve to combat democracy's self-destructive dynamics; Tocqueville suggested that religion itself might simply become one more expression of, and response to, democratic materialism. In his view, religion could best support democracy if it took a form that resisted democracy's prevailing tendencies. Religion could do this in two ways: first, by taking democratic man beyond the confinement of narrow self-interest and solitude; and second, by lifting the democratic purview beyond its own horizons, toward a contemplation of the transcendent and final things beyond fleeting opinion. By resisting democracy's claim to universal rule, religion actually served the cause of democracy. It was most supportive of democracy, according to Tocqueville, when it moderated democracy's claims while strengthening the resolve of individual democratic citizens to seek a standard outside the democratic will. Where democracy simultaneously contributed to illusions of perfectibility and undermined the individual's sense of dignity, religion could offer antidotes for each condition, at once chastening and strengthening.

In the first instance, religion is the primary source of resistance to the specter of "tyranny of majority." Tocqueville begins his discussion of that new tyranny by noting that no form of rule, not even majority rule, can make exclusive claim to justice. While an informed and judicious majority might arrive at conclusions that would ensure greater justice for all its participants, thereby following the theories of Rousseau, Tocqueville held that majority rule was ultimately as subject to human failing and limiting interests as any other form of rule. He contrasted the rule of the majority to a universal rule of justice: "There is one law which has been made, or at least adopted, not by the majority of this or that people, but by the majority of all men. That law is justice. Justice therefore forms the boundary to each people's right" (250).

While all human forms of rule can aspire to justice, no form can claim to attain it: "[O]nly God can be omnipotent without danger because His wisdom and justice are always equal to his power" (252). Human rule that does not recognize its insufficiency tends toward omnipotence that is not its due, and leads inevitably toward tyranny. "There is no power on earth in itself so worthy of respect or vested with such a sacred right that I would wish to let it act without control and dominate without obstacles" (252). Tocqueville regards religious belief as affording a transcendent law, a standard outside the shifting and temporary opinion of majorities, "beyond the ebb and flow of human opinion" (298), an alternative code of morality to which a citizen can appeal even when a vast majority opposes him or her. Tocqueville concludes:

> When I see the right and capacity to do all given to any authority whatsoever, whether it be called people or king, democracy or aristocracy, and whether the scene of action is a monarchy or a republic, I say: the germ of tyranny is there, and I will go look for other laws under which to live. (252)

Democracy stands to be corrected and guided by such laws, and perhaps, if those laws are willfully ignored, knowledge of them outside the majority opinion can shore up the individual soul as in the case of the believer whose soul was impervious to the inquisitor. In a democracy informed by such a religious view, both the body and the soul have the potential to be free, rather than one or the other enslaved by the omnipotent claims of a particular regime.

Religion conditions democratic man's inclination toward self-interest by restraining the tendency to draw within his own private circle and to regard all decisions, personal and political, purely as expressions of utility or economic calculation. Elaborating on the American's praise of the concept of "self-interest properly understood," Tocqueville observes that Americans often claim to be acting in accordance with liberal assumptions of self-interest, but in fact "in this they often do themselves less than justice, for sometimes in the United States, as elsewhere, one sees people carried away by the disinterested, spontaneous impulses natural to man" (526). Despite having earlier asserted that Americans tend to be Cartesians without ever having read Descartes (429), here he implies that Americans claim to be Lockeans but in fact act in accordance with an entirely different motivation of benevolence. He wryly comments, "They prefer to give the credit to their philosophy rather to themselves" (526). "Self-interest properly understood," in Tocqueville's view, has as its wellspring a religious sentiment deriving from the inescapable concern with the afterlife: "[H]owever hard one may try to prove that virtue is useful, it will always be difficult to make a man live well if he will not face death" (528). Even the "official" liberal doctrine of America, an Enlightenment liberal philosophy that posits self-interest as the animating feature of human action, needs and receives moderation by the more long-term and benevolent influence of religious thought.

Stating most explicitly how religion moderates the harmful dynamics of democratic equality and individualism, Tocqueville points to the aspect of religion that draws men outside of themselves, outside of their times, and points them toward a concern for the eternal and the place of all human beings in that order:

The usefulness of religion is even more apparent among egalitarian peoples than elsewhere. One must admit that equality, while it brings great benefits to mankind, opens the door ... to very dangerous instincts. It tends to isolate men from each other so that each thinks only of himself. It lays the soul open to the inordinate love of material pleasure.

The greatest advantage of religions is to inspire diametrically opposed contrary urges. Every religion places the object of man's desires outside and beyond worldly goods and naturally lifts the soul into regions far above the realm of the senses. Every religion also imposes on each man some obligations toward mankind, to be performed in common with the rest of mankind, and so draws him away, from time to time from think-ing about himself. (444–45)

This is the kernel of Tocqueville's thoughts on the usefulness of religion. Nei-ther contradicting nor damning human equality or liberty—both of which are endorsed and perfected by religion, in Tocqueville's view—by exerting a contrary force against extreme expressions of each, religion protects democ-racy from itself. Without *being* democratic, religion supports democracy more thoroughly and better than could any expressly "democratic" doctrine. For Tocqueville, the cure for the ills of democracy is not more democracy; such a "cure" only worsens the underlying disease. Instead, democracy requires the support and chiding of religion if democracy is to thrive. Chastening humans when they become too prideful, and giving them support when they become too enervated, religion pulls democratic man away from the extremes toward which "equality of condition" thrusts him, back toward a version of the "Aris-totelian mean," neither immobile from fear of the majority's tyranny nor rest-less amid discontent; neither fearful of democracy's omnipotence nor hubris-tically holding to the view of human perfectibility. Religion is most useful for democracy, Tocqueville concludes, when it points us away from doctrines of utility and toward a conception of the self and humanity as part of a greater and comprehensive order.

THE UTILITY OF RELIGION?

Tocqueville expressly saw the utility of religion in democracies as a promis-ing means of correcting democracy's self-destructive tendencies. In the view of many scholars, Tocqueville actively sought to promote a form of beneficent religion for a democratic age, effectively engaging in a project similar to that of Montesquieu and Rousseau, the creation of a "civil religion." Indeed at sev-eral points in *Democracy in America*, Tocqueville appears to recommend that democratic governments should actively seek to promote a salutary form of religion to support the continued survival of democracy. In one of his baldest statements to this end, Tocqueville writes:

I think that the only effective means which governments can use to make the doctrine of immortality of the soul respected is daily to act as if they believed it themselves. I think that it is only by conforming scrupulously to religious morality in great affairs that they can flatter themselves that they are teaching the citizens to understand it and to love and respect it in little matters. (546)

These comments in the second volume of *Democracy in America* are in stark contrast to Tocqueville's observations in the first volume, where he argues that religion can best serve democracy primarily through its "indirect effects": "[I]ndirect action seems to me much greater still, and it is just when it is not speaking of freedom at all that it best teaches the Americans the art of being free" (290). Following the spirit of this observation, Tocqueville asserts that religion is best kept separate from the apparatus of the State. This is not primarily out of a liberal concern about religious repression; rather, it is due to his desire that religion should maintain its legitimacy and force. In this context Tocqueville expressly rejects the concept of a "civil religion," inasmuch as a religion that adopts itself to the requirements of a specific regime "sacrifices the future for the present," and adopts "maxims which apply only to certain nations" (297). By allying itself with a particular nation, it ceases to appeal to the universal and calls on itself all the support and detraction associated with a particular regime. Moreover, given the fluctuating fortunes of political life, a religion endangers its long-term appeal by aligning itself with the inherently changeable status of regimes and its leaders: "[W]hen a religion chooses to rely on the interests of this world, it becomes almost as fragile as all earthly powers. Alone, it may hope for immortality; linked to ephemeral powers, it follows their fortunes and often falls together with the passions of a day sustaining them" (298).

To be the greatest support to democracy, religion must reject the endorsement of the government; at the same time, however, it must point democratic man beyond the earthly and in some regards challenge the foundations of democratic government itself. It is difficult to deny that Tocqueville appears both to endorse a form of "civil religion" in some instances, and yet expressly rejects any identification of a religion with a specific State in others. Yet, as in many other instances in his thought, the paradox is only apparent.

Pierre Manent has suggested that one must distinguish the perspective of Tocqueville *qua* observer from the beliefs of the democratic citizens he observes. Manent notes that religion's force as a corrective to democracy's excessive claims to rule rely on the authentic and purely religious attachment of each man to his religion. This utilitarian assessment is brought by an outside observer who takes into consideration the natural and universal characteristics of men and the needs of society—in particular democratic society. When this utilitarianism becomes that of the citizens themselves, the argument of the observer, far from being strengthened is to such an extent undermined. For religion to have its proper force, it is necessary for men to be devoted to it for itself and not for social utility or by love of the political institutions to which it can be fused.[5]

This would seem to be the only view that can be maintained through a full appreciation of the source of religion's force, in Tocqueville's own view, as a corrective for democracy's inclinations. He notes that "the unbeliever, no longer thinking religion true, still considers it useful. Paying attention to the human side of religious beliefs, he recognizes their sway over mores and their influence over laws" (299).

In short, the unbeliever recognizes what Tocqueville himself observed, often prefacing his observations with variations of the very phrase "looking at the human side of religion." However, while a few unbelievers, or an observer like Tocqueville, might make such an observation without undermining the belief of the broader citizenry, once democracy's materialist tendency has itself undermined belief, and all or most people begin to view religion as useful to democracy, at that point it altogether loses its effectiveness. Religion no longer governs democratic man's excessive impulses, because its precepts are no longer believed. Rather than offering a corrective to democracy, religion merely becomes one more weapon in the utilitarian arsenal.

Tocqueville's arguments in favor of the role in religion in democracy often afford encouragement to those who would like to see the reinvigoration of religious belief among a democratic citizenry. However, Tocqueville's stern warning against the temptation to "use" religion for the express purpose of supporting democracy by offering a counterforce to democracy's internally destructive logic—thereby further undermining religion's potential power as democratic antidote—is often studiously ignored by Tocqueville's most ardent admirers. Far from offering confirmation for putting religion back in the public square for the purpose of strengthening democracy, Tocqueville himself appears to advise a form of chastened faith in religion's capacity to act as a corrective to the dangers of democracy faith.

NOTES

I would like to thank Ruth Abbey, Aurelian Craiutu, and James T. Schleifer for generous and helpful responses to an early draft of this essay. Portions have appeared in my *Democratic Faith* (Princeton: Princeton University Press, 2005) and are used here by permission.

1. Alexis de Tocqueville, *Democracy in America,* trans. George Lawrence, ed. J. P. Mayer (New York: Harper and Row, 1969), 297–301. All subsequent references to *Democracy in America* are to this edition, and are cited parenthetically in the text.

2. Quotations in French are drawn from Tocqueville, *Oeuvres,* 2 Vols., ed. André Jardin (Paris: Éditions Gallimard, 1992). Tocqueville, *Oeuvres,* II.7.

3. Tocqueville would almost certainly have found the popular bumper sticker, "WHOEVER DIES WITH THE MOST TOYS WINS" to be revealing of this American tendency, and not entirely in jest.

4. "There is therefore no question of reconstructing an aristocratic society, but the need is to make freedom spring from that democratic society in which God has placed us" (695).

5. Pierre Manent, *Tocqueville and the Nature of Democracy,* trans. John Waggoner (Lanham, Md.: Rowman and Littlefield, 1996), 91.

CHAPTER SEVEN

Science versus Religion

Can Rhetorology Yield an Armistice?

Wayne C. Booth

In this essay Wayne Booth faces head-on one of the deepest and most difficult problems relating to religion—namely, how to imagine a connection between that side of life and what we call "science," which seems to many to be so deeply opposed to it. If one talks like a scientist, there seems to be no respectable and respectful way to talk about religion; yet if one talks as some religious people do—as though a particular narrative or set of sacred texts or ritual practices state or embody the only real truth—it is impossible to talk respectably and respectfully about science. Booth finds the beginning of an answer in what he calls a "rhetorological" approach, one that tries to uncover the deepest commitments of contrasting ways of thinking and speaking, which in this case, he argues, demonstrates that true science and genuine religion share several deep and crucial understandings. On this basis it is possible to imagine a far more constructive conversation about the tensions and overlaps between science and religion than any we have yet enjoyed.

Like anyone who has thought about the relation between science and religion, the topic has led me to dozens of approaches and scores of titles. The title of this essay is absurdly hopeful. A better one might read "Why many self-proclaimed atheistic philosophers, like Richard Rorty, and scientists, like Bernard Weinberg, are religious without knowing it."

Every effort to relate science and religion, whether rhetorically or metaphysically, can be described as overly ambitious. There has been an astonishing flood of books and articles in recent decades about diverse conflicts between religion and science. I have a shelf more than eight feet long containing books and articles on the topic, most of them published since Fritjof Capra's *The Tao of Physics,* in 1975.[1] The wealthy Temple Foundation is now giving huge cash awards for the best books relating science and religion, and I am told that the foundation is flooded with applicants and recommendations.

As everyone who has read any of those books knows, the war—or if you prefer, the controversy—is not likely to end soon. Whether the oppositions are cast in such terms as reason vs. superstition, blind dogmatic rationalism vs. genuine human values, secular humanism vs. religious fundamentalism, or atheism vs. theism, the conflict between hard thought about natural laws and hard thought about the source and grounds of nature and value will outlive you and me and our grandchildren. Even if some attempts like this one produce an armistice, the threat of further warfare will remain.

Approaches to the battles between various "sides" are overwhelmingly diverse. Some books continue to echo earlier portrayals of a flat-out war, with science the proud victor: the enemy of truth, which is religion, which is in turn superstition, will finally die. But recently there have been increasing attempts to arrive at something like a truce, or even full conciliation. Many still see science as obviously the final winner: we still have books like Michio Kaku's *Visions, How Science Will Revolutionize the Twenty-First Century,* books that without talking about religion directly predict science's solution to every "why" question and every religious need, including how to achieve a zany kind of immortality.[2] Other works have even attempted to prove that genuine science is compatible with some one particular religion. John Polkinghorne, a brilliant particle physicist and priest, claims to experience no conflict whatever between his version of hard science and his version of Christianity.[3] Some, like Ian Barbour, in books that deservedly won the Temple Foundation prize, dig somewhat more deeply into scientific method and theological arguments, claiming to find a meeting ground in the tradition of Alfred North Whitehead and Charles Hartshorne (process theology).[4] And of course many are more superficial than Barbour's, pursuing one or another of the three most tempting approaches: diplomacy, tolerance, or utter relativism.[5]

In effect the diplomat says, "If you'll grant us our territory, we won't impose on yours." In *Rocks of Ages,* Stephen Jay Gould, perhaps the best known of all biological rhetoricians, claimed total validity for both religion and science, but with absolutely no overlap: he coined the acronym NOMA, for Non-Overlapping MAgesteria. Gould's approach is analogous to what it would be like for two nations, long at war with one another, to quit fighting and say, "You go your way, legitimately, as I go mine, legitimately."[6]

Toleration is a bit different: "I know that my views are the only correct ones, but I'll not interfere with yours—provided you don't attack me too strongly." Most serious scientists spend little or no time attacking religion; most serious theologians don't waste their time attacking science, they just acknowledge its importance. Many religious "conservatives" do waste a lot of energy attacking science, especially evolutionary theory, but my hunch is, with no statistical evidence to back it, that when pressed most would take the tolerant line: let those folks pursue their narrow bits of truth, while we deal with the more important stuff. Let them work on the fossils and dinosaurs, while we work on the soul. And vice versa.

The extreme form of accommodation, *utter* relativism, is not just tolerance: it is indifference. There is no real truth in either direction, no ultimate reality in science or religion, so why not just stop arguing? If it's all mere guesswork, or cultural dogmatism, why argue about it?[7]

Whichever of these three approaches is taken, the results seem about the same: you freely go your way within the domain of your interest (science or religion), and I'll freely go my way within mine; if we encounter places of conflict where those domains overlap, all we can do is either bargain, tolerate, or just scoff. (Though Nietzsche is not for me a real intellectual hero—he is a genius but a dangerous one—I do like what he has to say, throughout his works, about the absurdities and destructiveness of bland tolerance: the failure to engage fully in the true significance and probable consequences of a given disagreement.)

RHETORICAL OVERLAPS

Diplomacy, toleration, and skeptical relativism at least diminish the open warfare, but they simply ignore the plain fact that when one carefully examines the *rhetoric* of scientists and religious thinkers one inevitably finds grand overlappings in their deepest convictions. Science and religion are not completely separable enterprises. Both rely on fundamental convictions about the nature of nature, including human nature. And whenever the deepest of human interests are engaged, and *seem* to clash, especially when the clashing is not merely a territorial dispute but concerns ideas and human values, deep rhetorical analysis is invited. Diplomacy, the most promising of the three standard methods identified above, gets us nowhere when the quarrel offers no bargaining chips, nothing to "give up" in exchange except the very ideas we care most about; it gets us nowhere if we are discussing whether Plato's Ideas really exist; or whether God is really dead; or whether pursuers of scientific truth and pursuers of religious truth can ever discover that they are on the same path; or whether, contrary to the relativists, truth of any kind really exists; or whether, as many like Steven Weinberg and Michio Kaku argue, hard science will ultimately arrive at a final theory that will explain everything, and may leave life itself pointless.

RHETOROLOGY
(OR IF YOU HATE NEOLOGISMS, DEEP RHETORIC)

What we obviously most need is a sharpening and deepening of a version of rhetorical study usually at best hinted at: not mere persuasion, and not merely the more responsible kinds of persuasion, and not the study of how this or that author has persuaded, but the probing of the deepest convictions underlying both sides in any conflict, to see where they might join. Do they stand on common ground? Do they have, as John Dewey put it, a "common faith"?[8] We need to push the pursuit of understanding, of genuine listening to the opponent, to its furthest possible limits: to the depths where our ultimate commitments, our "religions," or "faiths," or "ultimate passions" seem to clash, but perhaps do not. And because the usual terms in rhetorical studies carry narrower implications than that, I have proposed (from 1983 until now, so far unsuccessfully) that we label this kind of rhetorical inquiry with the ugly neologism "rhetorology." Maybe you can think of a better word, but I cannot: "dialogue" is too narrow, "dialogology" too unwieldy, "discourse analysis" totally uninformative and unchallenging. I'm told that someone recently proposed "rhetoristics," but that is even uglier than rhetorology. "Dialectics" or "dialecticalism" are perhaps the best rivals, but they seem to leave rhetoric behind. And so on through hermeneutics, or what Steven Mailloux has called "cultural hermeneutics," which is still misleading. So why not rhetorology: the deep study (-logy) of the shared grounds underlying any two rival rhetorics?

As is obvious by now, my rhetorological pursuit of grounds shared by scientists and religionists is already based on a prejudice: the assumption that after all there must be some ground that is shared. I have been a passionate lifetime believer in science—of the genuine kinds.[9] I have been also a lifetime pursuer of religious truth—of all genuine kinds. I still call myself "genuinely" religious, though I have to think in metaphorical, symbolic, or mythological terms when asked what I think about the world's being created in six days.

In previous discussions about how these two belief systems can jibe, I've learned that some science-minded atheists are furious at me, and many a religionist claims that I've sold out.[10]

THE FIVE "CAUSES," BORROWED FROM ARISTOTLE, RICHARD MCKEON, AND KENNETH BURKE

What are the rhetorological paths for making our way through this mess? I like to fall back on a very rough parallel with Aristotle's four causes, which too many dogmatic scientists—the kind I like to call "scientismists"—reduce to one or two, the efficient and material causes, leaving out final and formal causes, especially when those scientists are in the laboratory: it's all "bumps and grinds," with no attention given to "why" questions. But if we want to find out where the differences and similarities lie, we have to move beyond what Aristotle called "efficient" and "material" causes to ask about at least four others.

First, "What are the rival *goals* or *ends* of this or that project?" Then, "What are the rival *methods* for pursuing the goals?" Then, "What are the rival *definitions of the subject matter* that is being quarreled about?" And then, "What are the rival *general principles or deepest assumptions* underlying the arguments?"— the metaphysical and social commitments, or what some call the "thought modes." Finally, borrowing a word from Kenneth Burke's dramatistic pentad (which was actually based on Aristotle's four causes), we who are living in the time of cultural studies must add a fifth cause: the *scene* of any dispute is the range of cultural influences playing upon the disputants.[11]

No one could hope to cover in a short essay more than a fraction of all the ways in which the best scientific inquiry and the best religious inquiry overlap or genuinely conflict on each of these five causes.[12] For now I shall concentrate on only one of the "causes," the definition of the subject.[13]

PROBLEMS IN DEFINITION

Do scientists share with religionists, at the deepest definition of their subject, of their project, of their world, any common ground, any deep marks—what Aristotle called *topoi*, or "places"—that define the subject being pursued and their relation to it? In concentrating on this special kind of definition—not a simple verbal formula but a collection of agreed-upon "standing platforms"— the other four rhetorical categories will of course be implicit all along, most obviously the search for shared general principles. But for now, I simply ask whether, in any definition of a genuine religion, one can find that all religionists and at least some scientists—and rationalists, and secular humanists, and atheists—in some sense join it, even when they don't recognize the fact.

This search for common ground of definitions between entire belief systems is appallingly difficult. Even those who look only for the ground shared by explicit religions face a threatening task, as William James learned when preparing his Gifford Lectures, published as *The Varieties of Religious Experience.*[14] But his search was in a way simpler than ours, because he was looking for a definition that concentrated on religionists' feelings. For him religion is "the feelings, acts, and experiences of individual men [and women] in their solitude, so far as they apprehend themselves to stand in relation to whatever they may consider the divine" (31).

It is not hard to understand why James found the pursuit of that psychological definition almost overwhelming. But ours is even more difficult. It can sometimes feel like sheer madness. It has often made me wonder whether any reader anywhere will dare plunge with me into such roiling waters.

What has kept me going—to repeat—and what I hope will keep readers with me even when there are hurricane warnings, is the immense importance of reducing, if possible, the blind misunderstandings that flood our controversies between science and religion.

HOW TO DEFINE RELIGION

It is hard to think of any terms more slippery, more polymorphous, even perverse, than "religion," "religious," and "religiously," let alone "spiritual" or "devout" or "belief." "She practiced the violin religiously for five years, and then quit." Many scholars, in all fields, are described as pursuing truth with "religious fervor." "Hemingway was absolutely religious in his writing—every day standing at that desk, writing his four hundred words." "I watch *60 Minutes* religiously," said a recent letter to the *New Yorker*. "Spiritual" was the word that television star Rosanne thought best described how she felt when responding to the perceived sexism of *Saturday Night Live!* After three frustrating tries hosting the show, she said, she "got really spiritual" and wrote her protest letter. We could go on to crazy varieties of use of "faith," "devotion," "believer," and the like.

I have several friends who claim to be enemies of, or at least indifferent to, what they call "religion," but who clearly fall under or embrace the seven marks of genuine religion that I'm coming to here. Of course it usually annoys them when I call them religious, though sometimes they admit that my claim has challenged them to some thinking. On the other hand, we all know partisans of this or that official religion who claim that all other so-called religions don't really deserve the name. In my emerging definition, some of these self-proclaimed religionists don't even deserve the name "religion" that they grant themselves— not in the broad definition of religion and the religious that I am targeting in this essay. They reduce everything to the question of whether their church gives them moments of feeling high, whether it serves their private souls, which for me is at best only one of the seven marks to be found in all genuine religions. (I'll deal with the troublesome judgmental term "genuine" later.) For such reductionists we need some other label—perhaps "gee-ligion," with an exclamation point, or "dis-ligeon." Some of those that offer little more than a self-praising cheering up before Sunday brunch—"I'm OK!, you're OK!, the world's OK!"—we might call "me-ligions," or, in the extreme forms, "narcissism" or even "spiritual autism." Jacques Derrida uses the term "irresponsible orgiasts" for the me-ligionists, those who have no sense of responsibility to "the other."[15]

But there I go already, rejecting one belief system, me-ligions, as a non-religion, when the whole point of my project is to produce more and better rhetorology among rivals. My judgment dramatizes the fact that no matter what definition of religion we settle on, we ourselves will be committing, by the very act of defining, problematic evaluations of the kind I just committed. If our definition is accepted, that means that a new friend has earned our badge of approval: we join in the "religious community." If our definition is rejected, it will be because this "outsider" is sure that it was chosen in order to eliminate his or her absolutely religious religion.

THREE STANDARD APPROACHES TO DEFINITION PROBLEMS

The three standard ways for dealing with both overlapping and contradictory definitions are, first, to avoid definition entirely, since "religion" is nothing more than a catchall term—what I've even heard called a "garbage bag." Richard Rorty has claimed that whenever religion enters the discussion, any sensible person will just withdraw because real conversation has been blocked. Second, one can do what I would have done in my teens, as an officially devout Mormon, if asked to define religion: just proclaim the one true definition that best fits my one true church. Third, one can attempt an ecumenical definition like James's, one that uncovers the analogies among seemingly contrasting believers, without becoming so broad as to be meaningless.

Obviously whether or how one uses the label "religion" in referring to any or all of the movements that I'll touch on here will depend on which of these paths we choose.[16]

On the one hand are those who resemble the young Booth in believing that you have not in any real sense defined a religion as genuine until you have described it in its full particularity, including the precise details of its unique foundation story and its unique rituals. A genuinely religious believer under this definition, whom we might call a "uniquist," is one who is certain about the unique validity of his or her particular foundation story and about most or all of the details of doctrine that story is claimed to embody. Such uniquists take for granted that religious inquiry consists mainly in the pursuit of what some one true story has to say about our origins and how we should live our lives. Other religions can be tolerated, even respected, but you cannot fit them under any umbrella that covers you. The best they deserve is something like "misguided religions" or "partial religions." Religion for them is not to be found in any ecumenical or pluralistic definition of common characteristics, but in the full, intratextual, thick description of the details of one faith, one ritual, one communal practice, and one scriptural embeddedness. Can you imagine how shocked that young Mormon was when he learned that some of the benighted churches actually used wine instead of water in the Sacrament? I can remember feeling miserable when my favorite scout master on a tour with us boys sinfully ordered a cup of coffee!

Any one detail of that kind can seem enough to credit or discredit any religion as sinful: my religion bans pork, while your fake religion bans alcohol; mine offers a Sacrament consisting literally of the blood and flesh of Jesus Christ, while yours is so silly as to describe that offering as metaphorical only. And so on. Even when an ecumenicist like me attempts to do full justice to particularity, the result will always look a bit "thin" from the perspective of such uniquists, since it is still bound up with a project that puts aside superficial differences and stresses the common core.

Though ecumenicists who are explicitly religious will almost always at some point succumb to making judgments about relative worth, what is at their center is what is shared, not what makes the different religions peculiar. And if they make value judgments against some professions of religion, as I have already revealed that I do, they are still likely to leave not a single one clearly at the top of the hierarchy but rather a plurality of the "great religions," contrasted with the not so great or utterly defective.

The difficult search for shared ground always makes me think of an experience of my colleague David Tracy, Catholic theologian, as he met for several years with leaders of other "great religions" hoping to find common ground. Meeting annually with Buddhists, Muslims, Jews, Catholics, and Hindus—no Mormons, of course—Tracy would return looking discouraged. "We found little or nothing this year." But one year not long ago he came back much buoyed up, looking positively optimistic. When asked what they had agreed on, he said, as I remember it, "We all agreed that something is radically wrong with creation."[17]

No matter how we feel about this quest, our choice between the particularist and the shared-groundist definitional routes will determine how we treat any one religion, or secular rival or opponent to religion. If we follow James and Tracy and pursue ground shared, putting to one side the particularist differences, we follow what is to me not just an interesting intellectual route, but a moral command implicit throughout. Our task is to discover not whether all faiths or devotions or passions or commitments show, when lumped together, that they have somehow contributed to a grand common worldwide project. Obviously many have not. Rather we must ask whether any one of them— most particularly this or that "scientific" view—when probed to the core, exhibits the common elements we claim are shared by all *genuine* religions. And we have to recognize that the arrogant word "genuine" inevitably brings in moral judgments. Throughout what follows, readers will find implicit the assertion that many so-called religions are only *half* religions, or perhaps five- or six-seventh religions. Though their followers will of course continue to insist on using the name "religion," the fact will still remain that they lack what all the "great religions" share.

THE SEVEN MARKS

Throwing all caution to the wind, I now turn to seven absolutely essential marks shared by all of what are called the world's "great religions," and what I call "genuine religions." Here we move beyond William James's common emotional experiences to the unshakable convictions underlying those experiences. My list is sure to leave out something you consider essential to your religion. But remember, we're not here defining "complete" or "best" religion: it's just genuine religion. As soon as one adds any of the various "blessings" that this or that denomination claims to grant, you move closer to uniquism, and then Wittgensteinean "family resemblances" must take over. This handful overlaps with that handful, which in turn overlaps with a further handful, but none share all qualities with all the others.

Mark One: insistence that the world as we experience it is somehow flawed, as compared with what would be better. Something is wrong, deficient, broken, inadequate, lacking. Something is rotten not only in the state of Denmark, but everywhere. As the popular bumper sticker puts it, "Shit Happens." (I recently saw a sticker that read "Defecatory Disasters Inevitable.")

I don't have to tell you that in one form or another everybody in the world believes in, and actually experiences, this mark, except perhaps in moments of ecstatic oblivion. As David Tracy and his fellow religionists from four other "great religions" agreed, something is wrong, or something went wrong, with creation.

There is obviously implicit in the notion of wrongness a value judgment: if something is judged to be wrong, there has to be a notion of something righter, which leads to . . .

Mark Two: flaws must be seen in the light of the Unflawed, some truth, some notion of justice, or "goodness," or of some possible purging of ugliness. You can't say that something is wrong without implying that some standard for the judgment exists. Again, it is obvious that all or almost all scientists would join us here: they have the standard of scientific truth and personal integrity in the pursuit of science. As many of them have fulminated against various postmodernist questioning of "truth," they are implicitly confessing to their religion. Which leads us to . . .

Mark Three: insistence that there is some supreme order or cosmos or reality, something about the whole of things that provides the standard according to which I make the judgments of Marks One and Two. In other words, when Mark Two and Mark Three—the "rightness" and the cosmic source of that rightness—disappear, there is no genuine religion. Some me-ligionists fall off the boat here: it's all just personal feeling. But most scientists do not. Have you noticed how many books have been coming out about the quest for a final theory that will explain everything? Most scientists, even the most ardent atheists, believe in Mark Three: there *is* a cosmos, often thought of in terms that resemble astonishingly what many theologians have called "Being." As Matthew Arnold's truncated definition puts it, religion is belief in some power "greater than ourselves, making for righteousness." The word "righteous" will put some people off these days, meaning something like dogmatic or arrogant. But what Arnold meant was "something righter than wrongness," and every scientist has to believe in that or else give up the quest for truth. The scientist who claims to see no greater virtue or value or wonder in a rose or a child than in a fungus or streptococcus bug hasn't thought very hard about life.

These three marks, intertwined, are nicely revealed by the David Tracy anecdote: "Something is radically wrong with creation." His report of the discovery was not just that "something is wrong with the world I live in," or "there's a lot of stuff around me that I personally disapprove of or grieve over." Everybody believes that, not just devout Muslims and Catholics and Calvinists and Mormons, but also the me-ligionists and atheists and drug addicts and serial killers: everybody thinks that something could and should be better about the world—even if it is only that "I ought to have more drugs available" or "I don't have enough corpses yet buried in my cellar" or "Why can't I get every day the feelings I get in that new entertainment church on Sunday morning?" That is why M. Scott Peck made the mistake of concluding, in his best-selling book *The Road Less-Travelled,* that everyone in the world is religious, whether they know it or not. Peck is wrong in lumping everyone on the basis of only one mark—namely, passionate caring about *something.* But he is right about the universality: You don't have to talk with even the most Nobel-minded scientist very long to capture his or her lamentations about the state of the fallen world. And all of the me-ligionists will at least complain because so many in the world don't accept their celebration of this or that liberating feeling.

To reiterate the point, in order to qualify as a religion, a belief system has to relate the first mark to the second and third: it must at least imply a moral story, some sort of master narrative that says things like, "Something went wrong with creation," or "Something ought to have been righter," or at least "I can see what would have been better." It's not just "I don't like some things about it," but rather "Some things are wrong when judged by what would be right, by what a full rightness would demand, by what the whole of creation as I see it—my cosmos, my God, my view of nature—implies as the way things should be but are not."

In more traditional language, there was, and in some sense there still is, a fall, a brokenness, a decline from what would have been better to what is in fact at best a combination of the better—some ideal—and the worse. Some Buddhists, I gather, would reverse this temporal scheme: not a "fall" but a "rise." But to do that does not destroy the real meaning of "something went wrong": it either was or could have been better. My hints of a kind of temporality here—echoing the biblical account of the Fall—needn't be taken literally. As Kenneth Burke makes clear in *The Rhetoric of Religion,* stories about temporal rising and falling can always be translated into nontemporal, vertical ladders: temporally, we were up there and now we're down here trying to climb back up; nontemporally, we're standing on that ladder in a fixed, "eternal" moment.[18]

Religious believers in this sense experience a kind of double vision: on the one hand a vision of a possible past or present or future order or cosmos superior to the way things actually work now, and on the other hand an awareness that much of what we experience seems out of whack in that order, that the times are out of joint, dis-ordered. The cosmos has moved toward chaos—or has always been doing so and is threatening to be doing so now. The origins, or what might have been the origins, have gone askew, developing a vast collection of flaws. It is not, to repeat, just that I'd like it to be different, for personal reasons. It *ought* to be different, because there are real reasons for seeing "it" as flawed. What's more, I have at least a dim notion of what it might mean to be fixed, and I know that what's wrong about it is wrong, not just unpleasant.

Lamentation thus moves toward religion only when it is linked with the second and third marks—only when the lamenter realizes not just that shit happens but that shit's happening, and it's definition in relation to what is not shit but genuine nourishment is somehow built into the very structure of things. Shit has always happened from the beginning (or, for some, almost from the beginning), but there was/is a place from which the fall can be judged as fall. It is defined by an elusive notion of its opposite, an order or cosmos that in some sense judges the happening as wrong.

Mark Four, emerging from the first three: all who are genuinely religious (not just complaining) will somehow see themselves as in some inescapable sense a part of the brokenness.

It's not just other people—those terrorists out there, say—who are out of joint. *I* am. I'm not as good or kind or effective or smart or learned or organized or courteous or alert or wise as I ought to be. Even the best of us, even the strongest, the purest, the humblest, are inherently lacking, deficient, in need of further repair, or if you prefer the words, we are "sinful" or "guilty." I am an inseparable part of a cosmos that produced this flawed fraction of itself, me, including in that fraction a sense of regret about my flaws. I may or may not feel deep gratitude to my "creator" for creating me: that mark would have to be given under an entirely different list, labeled something like "blessings" or "rewards," some shared by some religions but not by others. But it is lacking in many genuine religions, none of which lack mark three. As we see in all honest scientists, this mark is revealed as lamentation about personal ignorance: what I don't know and ought to know![19]

Mark Five, following inescapably from the first four: the cosmos I believe in, the cosmos I may or may not feel gratitude toward for its gift of my very existence, the cosmos that is in its manifestations in my world in some degree broken—my cosmos calls on me to do something about the brokenness.

I must do what I can in the repair job, working to heal both my own deficiencies and to aid my fellow creatures in healing theirs. In some scientific religions that I would hope to discuss in any book emerging from this essay, this sometimes means no more than "I have a duty to work at removing my own ignorance." More often even for scientists it becomes a moral command to remove the world's ignorance. For some official religions, as in versions of Judaism and in the Mormonism still naggingly active in my soul, it produces floods of daily self-reproach: that which I have done I should not have done, and that which I have not done I should have done. In many denominations, perhaps especially Mormonism, it produces missionary work. But regardless of our various feelings, we are granted, by any genuine religion, a sense of at least this one indisputable meaning of life: a purpose that transcends our particular feelings of the moment.

Has anyone ever met a genuine scientist who does not share this sense of a passionate purpose for improvement—of something? Steven Weinberg has expressed the fear that the sense of purpose in life may well disappear, for him and other devout scientists, once they have obtained the full "final theory." Cosmologists have responded in contrasting ways to that fear. Weinberg's problem is that for him—in his public presentation of science—the only flaw we can do anything about is our ignorance.[20]

Mark Six, an inescapable corollary of the other five: whenever my notion of what my cosmos requires of me conflicts with my immediate wishes or impulses, I ought to surrender to its commandments. Rather than pursuing what is easiest or most pleasant or most reassuring to my present sensations or wishes, I obey or pursue *It*. Our impulses, our immediate wishes, ought to be overridden whenever they conflict with responsibility to cosmic commandments. We have obligations not just to others but to the Other. Religious talk dwells on this; for scientists it is often only implicit—but next time you meet a scientist who is furious about a colleague who has cheated, ask him or her why cheating is *really* wrong. If I am a scientist, for example, and am tempted to make a reputation or fortune by falsifying my results, I have an absolute command, not just from my conscience but from my cosmos, to combat the temptation.

Finally, *Mark Seven*, which everyone, not only William James, would make essential to all religions: the psychological or emotional feelings connected with all of this. Specifically, all genuine religions either openly or subtly offer spiritual "highs," moments of deep spiritual feeling, that result from contact with the ultimate, the cosmos, the whole of things, God, Being. I could fill the rest of this essay with quotations from scientists about how thrilled they are when they make full contact with what they consider reality or scientific truth or the challenge of the ultimate mysteries or beauty: both words, "mystery" and "beauty" fill Steven Weinberg's book *Dreams of a Final Theory*.[21]

Most religions have offered in their myths—unlike the truncated stories told by many sciences—explicit acknowledgment of finally irresolvable mystery, since the wholeness of the invisible cosmos is beyond total rational demonstration. The order was always some kind of numinous *mysterium tremendum*.[22] Some contemporary scientists have captured something of this mysterious wonder, admitting that no human being will ever grasp the "incomprehensible" whole. But many like Kaku aggressively claim that "in principle" our "religion" will capture it all. Even they usually reveal, however, a spiritual sense of awe or glory or gratitude for that "all."

THE NEGLECTED BLESSINGS

It's obvious that many a religionist will feel impatient because my seven marks leave out so many important matters: this or that reward or blessing that his or her religion considers essential. Even among common groundists who might happily accept the seven marks, there would be striking differences as soon as we turn to the relative value of various psychological or emotional rewards in addition to the spiritual highs. "Yes, I agree that a passionate, honest scientist's faith exhibits all those seven marks, but they completely overlook what are for me the essentials, such as my sense of gratitude for Jesus' love." Or: "You've left out the radical sense my religion provides of the sacredness of the holy shroud, or of the blessed Sacraments." In some religions this has led to protective, detailed rules, commandments dictating precisely how to live: what to touch and not to touch, what to eat and not to eat. To true believers these are at least as important as anything I've said, and they seem absurd to most scientists and to devotees of rival religions: "My rules makes sense; yours are silly." "You think not drinking coffee is an essential religious requirement? Oy vey!" "You think it's sinful to eat pork? That's crazy." "You think that cows are sacred and must not be killed, while people are starving? That's cruel." "You think that worshipping privately, without ever joining a congregation, is a holy act? You're just plain wrong." And so on.

Some religionists will think my marks deficient for not mentioning any sacred book, or even any sacred stories except that of the Fall. I could have included that mark, perhaps, noting how too many scientists these days treat the evolutionists narratives, the shattering story of what was in the beginning, almost as if it were a sacred text.

It may even seem that I've left out what for some theologians has been the supreme gift, the gift of character guidance. I've not mentioned courage, which is the one grand unifying gift of religion in Paul Tillich's *The Courage to Be*.[23] (He announced it as an effort to interrelate science and religion, but without really working on that project in any depth.) What's more, I've left out humility. Most of the genuine religions, in contrast to some of what I've called the "me-ligions," have provided a critique of unrestrained hubris: we are puny as compared with Supreme but Mysterious Reliability. The cardinal sin is pride; the cardinal virtue genuine humility, which at its best is not a crushing of self-esteem but a sense of release. I need not worry about competing: my precious ego, and its place on any competitive scale, is insignificant when compared with the wonders of my cosmos, including all the other creatures who are as important as I am. Now this one happens to be high on my list of blessings from my current "rhetorological" religion; one of my strongest criticisms of my Mormon upbringing is that it implanted in my arrogant young self the notion that if I kept my nose clean I would someday become God of another planet!

In my view, genuine science, especially by now when almost all of the most penetrating scientific thinkers admit to deep puzzlement about consciousness and the purpose of life, should teach humility to any arrogant scientist, Mormon, or atheist who has lacked it. But somehow many scientists, fortunately not all, do seem to learn from science the "religious" arrogance that I learned from my Mormon upbringing.

Hope is another blessing the seven marks don't mention. Similarly ignored is the wondrous comfort of joining a loving community or of finding ultimate truth; or the stabilizing effect of regularly experienced ritual; or the blessed daily reminders of the importance of learning to love your enemy or remembering to engage in charitable giving. These are a bit hard to find in scientific rhetoric, but they are also hard to find in this or that genuine religion.

But of all the religious blessings not included in the marks, no doubt the most striking—and crucial in the thinking of antireligious scientists—is the intervention by God, when appealed to, in human affairs: the hope, comfort, and sense of love provided by a God willing to violate natural law. A great majority in most countries believe that if and when we pray in the right way for intervention, God hears us and acts, and that he allocates good fortune to us according to what we deserve. For many this is not only *one* of the blessings, but is absolutely the number one definition of religious belief: if you believe in a Great Meddler, you're religious; if you don't, you're an atheist.

Most prophets of most traditional religions would agree. They have seen their foundational cosmos as not so tightly organized as to prevent divine intercession in the order of things: a powerful god or gods is/are both able and willing to perform unpredicted, or at least inexplicable, acts of grace or punishment that modify the original creation providentially, or even, as one reading of the story of Job has it, capriciously. Thus in most official religions the gods have been seen as manipulators of our lives, sometimes actually increasing the brokenness, day by day: I pray for rain and it rains here, while others around the world suffer drought; I pray to be saved from the hurricane and I'm saved, while you are killed.

In religions that put a providential lord at the center, our final hope rests only on what God or Allah or Jahveh has in mind, or has had in mind from the beginning, and on how close we can come to harmony with his or her will and power. While it remains true that we must do what we can to heal ourselves or the world, you do not have a genuine religion unless you fit whatever is the ultimate divine plan.

I have no interest here in refuting any one belief of this kind that many call "superstitions." Indeed, I think that many beliefs that rationalists like

Hume once considered superstitious would now be respected by even the hardest-nosed scientist. But the nasty fact is that disagreement about this blessing produces perhaps the most pointless battles in the destructive warfare between the religious and those who think they are not religious. To make this mark essential to religious belief rules out of religion many people whom my shared-groundist project wants to rule in. Fortunately many of the most serious theologians even within the Christian-Judaic tradition have condemned praying for providential, meddling gifts as a reduction to a kind of cheap bargaining or bribery: our reason for obedience to our God becomes, many have lamented, merely an attempt to get paid back at the end.[24]

Vigorous rejection of this mark has been a major goal of many scientists and philosophers for centuries now. Some have even defined the so-called warfare between science and religion precisely as a battle between what some would call true belief in providential intervention and others see as rank superstition.

To grapple with this conflict would require a whole book. I can only suggest, in concluding, that thinkers on both sides should probe, rhetorologically, the deep grounds of just what is meant by "providence" and "intervention." All of us in the long run will, I hope, give up the notion that if we pray to God as the hurricane approaches, he will save us while killing all of our neighbors. But must the true scientist give up the notion that some power, greater than ourselves, some Cosmos, Being Itself, *provided* the conditions of his or her research, and still *provides,* daily, the whole range of possibilities that life itself yields? If I'm saved in the hurricane, that God—the range of blessed possibilities—was providential: he/she/it provided the conditions that made me and saved me.[25] If I prayed not for meddling but for a condition of soul suitable for dealing with threatening disaster, that God provided the condition of my soul enabling me to utter that prayer. Of course that God also provided the conditions that led to the hurricane, which lands us back in the old tangled mess of theodicy: how to pardon God for creating evil. Not the subject for this essay.

I conclude only with two rough questions. First, is not the atheistic scientist who passionately pursues truth, supported by a faith in a cosmos that includes both truth and the moral command to pursue it, religious? And second, the question underlying this essay as a whole project: can we hope that by practicing rhetorology of some kind, pursued more skillfully than I've done here, we can diminish at least some of the pointless demonizing that diverse "sides" commit, as they attempt to destroy the other "sides"?

NOTES

This essay appeared in its original form as "Can Rheterology Yield a Truce between Science and Religion?" *Journal for the Study of Religion* 14, no. 1 (2001): 15–33, published by the Association for the Study of Religion in Southern Africa, and is published here, with some revisions, by permission.

1. Fritjof Capra, *The Tao of Physics: An Exploration of the Parallels between Modern Physics and Eastern Mysticism* (New York: Random House, 1975).

2. Michio Kaku, *Visions: How Science Will Revolutionize the Twenty-First Century* (New York: Anchor Books, 1997).

3. John Polkinghorne, *The Faith of a Physicist: Reflections of a Bottom-up Thinker* (Princeton: Princeton University Press, 1994); Polkinghorne, *Belief in God in an Age of Science* (New Haven: Yale University Press, 1998).

4. See Ian Barbour, *Religion and Science: Historical and Contemporary Issues,* rev. and expanded edition of the Gifford Lectures (San Francisco: Harper, 1997); Barbour, *Religion in an Age of Science,* the Gifford Lectures (San Francisco: Harper, 1990).

5. The word "relativism" is almost as ambiguous as "religion." What I here call "utter" relativism is a synonym for complete skepticism. But for some the term comes closer to the "pluralism" that I've been defending for decades: not "there is no truth," but "there are many genuine truths, truths that only *seem* to refute each other." See my *Critical Understanding: The Powers and Limits of Pluralism* (Chicago: University of Chicago Press, 1988).

6. Stephen Jay Gould, *Rocks of Ages: Science and Religion in the Fullness of Life* (New York: Ballantine, 1999).

7. For a splendid questioning of utter cultural relativism, probing the religious issues it raises, see Richard Shweder, "Post-Nietzschian Anthropology: The Idea of Multiple Objective Worlds," in *Relativism: Interpretation and Confrontation,* ed. Michael Krausz (Notre Dame, Ind.: University of Notre Dame Press, 1989), 99–139.

8. See John Dewey, *A Common Faith* (New Haven: Yale University Press, 1934).

9. The value judgments here are deliberate and inevitable—as scientists too often fail to confess about their own arguments in favor of science.

10. I don't like that word "religionist," but it's hard to find a better one. Call them the "believers"? Well, scientists are believers. The "faithful"? Well, scientists are pursuing their faith. The "devout"? Sounds pejorative. "Theologians"? Sounds too exclusive. So it will have to be "religionist"—even though one of my dictionaries defines the word to mean simply bigots. For those who want the term "religionist" to mean bigot, I would like to revive a term I invented decades ago, "scientismist," for bigoted scientists. Greg Wilson, in an address to the Rhetoric Society of America, referred to one current branch of statisticians as sometimes called "religious bigots."

11. See Kenneth Burke, *Language as Symbolic Action* (Berkeley: University of California Press, 1966), 52–56.

12. I've attempted, for some years, a book on the subject, more than five hundred pages lying inert in a drawer full of notes.

13. Readers interested in overlapping methods of scientists and religious thinkers should have a look at Michael Polanyi's wonderful *Personal Knowledge: Toward a Post-Critical Philosophy* (London: Routledge and Kegan Paul, 1958).

14. William James, *The Varieties of Religious Experience* (New York: Longmans, Green, 1902). Scholarly edition published in *The Works of William James,* ed. Frederick Burkhardt, vol. 13 (Cambridge: Harvard University Press, 1985).

15. Jacques Derrida, *The Gift of Death* (Chicago: University of Chicago Press, 1995).

16. One of the very best discussions of the ambiguities in all religious language—a kind of "deconstruction" and "reconstruction"—and a book well known to William James is Matthew Arnold's *Literature and Dogma: An Essay towards a Better Apprehension of the Bible* (London: Smith, Elder, 1873). For various phrasings of his definition of religion, see the Popular edition (1883), 184, 185, 190, 191. Arnold's reputation has suffered sadly through the postmodernist movements, with critics who hate his moralizing unable to recognize how many of their "radical" claims fit his ideas.

17. I wonder how Leibnitz would respond to that, as he worked out his theory of the best of all *possible* worlds. But of course his whole project was based on the acknowledgment that when judged from the human perspective, a very great deal "went wrong" in creation.

18. Kenneth Burke, *The Rhetoric of Religion* (Boston: Beacon Press, 1961).

19. Thomas Merton saw as the turning point in his life the moment when he realized he had been ignoring Mark Four: his "religion" before that had never acknowledged his own need for repair. See Robert Inchausti, *Thomas Merton's American Prophecy* (Albany: State University of New York Press, 1998), chap. 2. One reader of a draft complained strongly about this mark, because she knows an African tribe in which many of the leaders are taught, by their religion, to think of themselves as totally unflawed. To me that simply means that they have only a half-religion: they may behave "religiously," they no doubt think of themselves as "religious," but what they have is a version of "me-ligion."

20. See Alan Lightman and Roberta Brawer, *Origins: The Lives and Worlds of Modern Cosmologists* (Cambridge: Harvard University Press, 1990).

21. Steven Weinberg, *Dreams of a Final Theory* (New York: Pantheon, 1992).

22. Rudolf Otto, *The Idea of the Holy* (Oxford: Oxford University Press, 1950), 1–30.

23. Paul Tillich, *The Courage to Be* (New Haven: Yale University Press, 1952).

24. See the wonderful book by John T. Noonan Jr., *Bribes: The Intellectual History of a Moral Idea* (New York: Macmillan, 1984).

25. On this claim I always find pertinent the story of Thomas Merton's conversion from unbelief to belief. As Robert Inchausti describes it, when Merton stumbled upon Etienne Gilson's book, *The Spirit of Medieval Philosophy,* he "discovered for the first time in his life an intellectually respectable notion of God. God was not *a* Being; God was Being *itself.* If this was true . . . then all those sophomoric debates about God's existence couched in the narrow, epistemological terms of Enlightenment skepticism were

simply beside the point. One could read Medieval theology as food for self-making without abandoning logic, science, or common sense" (Inchausti, *Thomas Merton's American Prophecy*, 15).

SUGGESTIONS FOR FURTHER READING

Attfield, Robin. *God and the Secular: A Philosophical Assessment of Secular Reasoning from Bacon to Kant.* Cardiff: University College Cardiff Press, 1978.

Bonnor, William. *The Mystery of the Expanding Universe.* New York: Macmillan, 1964.

Brownowski, Jacob. *Science and Human Values.* Revised edition. New York: Harper and Row, 1965.

Davies, Paul. *God and the New Physics.* New York: Simon and Schuster, 1983.

Dewey, John. "Religion, Science, and Philosophy." In Dewey, *Problems of Men.* New York: Philosophical Library, 1946.

Draper, John William. *History of the Conflict between Religion and Science.* New York: Appleton, 1875.

Einstein, Albert. "Science and Religion." In *The World Treasure of Physics, Astronomy, and Mathematics.* Edited by Timothy Ferris, 828–35. Boston: Little, Brown, 1991.

Ferrarotti, Franco. *Faith without Dogma: The Place of Religion in Postmodern Societies.* London: Transaction Publishers, 1993.

Ferris, Timothy, ed. *The World Treasure of Physics, Astronomy, and Mathematics.* Boston: Little, Brown, 1991.

Funkenstein, Amos. *Theology and the Scientific Imagination, from the Middle Ages to the Seventeenth Century.* Princeton: Princeton University Press, 1986.

Gilkey, Langdon. *Naming the Whirlwind: The Renewal of God-Language.* Indianapolis: Bobbs Merrill, 1969.

Gross, Alan B. *The Rhetoric of Science.* Cambridge: Harvard University Press, 1996.

Jaki, Stanley L. *Science and Creation: From Eternal Cycles to an Oscillating Universe.* Revised ed. Edinburgh: Scottish Academic Press, 1986.

Matt, Daniel C. *God and the Big Bang: Discovering Harmony between Science and Spirituality.* Woodstock, Vt.: Jewish Lights, 1996.

Pratt, Vernon. *Religion and Secularisation.* New York: Macmillan, 1970.

Richardson, W. Mark, and Wesley J. Wildman, eds. *Religion and Science: History, Method, Dialogue.* Foreword by Ian G. Barbour. New York: Routledge, 1996.

Rorty, Richard. "Religion as Conversation Stopper." *Common Knowledge* 3(1) (Spring 1994): 1–6.

Weinberg, Steven. *The First Three Minutes: A Modern View of the Origin of the Universe.* New York: Basic Books, 1976.

CHAPTER EIGHT

How Can a Liberal Listen to a Religious Argument?

Religious Rhetoric as a Rhetorical Problem

Eugene Garver

A question that arises for all of us, particularly in the field of political discussion and debate, is how to respond to the religious claims of others. Obviously people should be free to express their religious views on matters of common concern, but it is not obvious what attitude others should take toward those claims. We have a right not to listen to what makes no sense to us. This freedom presents us as listeners with a question of ethics: should we in fact listen to the religious claims of others, and if so how, and why?

In this essay Eugene Garver explores this question, showing that this kind of conversation—on matters of public concern but across religious lines—presents both the speaker and the listener with special opportunities and special dangers. Learning to manage the tension between them requires hard work, of a kind that is both intellectual and ethical in character. It is Garver's object here to make this work the object of conscious attention and thought, so that we may engage in it with greater understanding and wisdom.

A few years ago the Judiciary Committee of the Minnesota House of Representatives held hearings on whether to reinstate capital punishment. One of the hearings was held on our campus at St. John's University, and I arranged for my students to attend. During the class session before the hearing, I asked the students to go and listen to the different arguments presented, and told them that we would in the next class meeting talk about which were useful, relevant, or otherwise worth listening to and which in their eyes were unsuccessful. One of the speakers, and in my mind one of the most impressive speakers, was the Roman Catholic bishop of St. Cloud, Minnesota. When we discussed the hearing the next day, none of my students mentioned his speech. I finally asked about it, and it turned out that not one member of the class had listened to the bishop's statement. They didn't want to hear anything a religious authority might have to say about political issues. Students who were as opposed to capital punishment as was the bishop were no more receptive to his arguments than the students who thought that capital punishment was a good idea. Eighty-five percent of my students are Roman Catholic, and not just nominally so. They are not hostile to religion, but apparently are hostile to religious authorities who take positions on political questions.[1]

Generalizing from this experience, I conclude that the religious speaker has a large presumption to overcome. There is, as the anecdote clearly suggests, a large difference between the commonly leveled charge that "liberalism" or contemporary American politics is hostile to religion, which seems to me false, and the charge that many citizens, including religious believers, are hostile to religious speech about political issues. Demonizing the forces of secularization seems to me to locate the problem wrongly.

Our experience at the hearings also points out that the difficulties in paying attention to a religious argument are not confined to atheists and Jews listening to Christians. The bishop couldn't get his co-religionists to listen to him. I may have been more receptive to the bishop's argument just because I am not a Christian. But I don't think this lack of receptiveness can be overcome by once again reciting the standard examples of William Lloyd Garrison, Martin Luther King Jr., and Desmond Tutu. Rather, we should take the resistance and suspicion seriously and grant that my students and other citizens might have good reason to mistrust the religiopolitical speaker. Then we can talk about how those good reasons can be overcome.

The anecdote about the bishop and my students indicates something about the current role of religious argument. There is a great deal of religious *language* in the public square, but little *argument*. The legal separation of church and state may be unique to the United States, but so are the obligatory public confessions of faith required of American politicians. There is a great deal of dishonesty when religiously motivated citizens and politicians seek to further specifically religious objectives while masking their designs with secular language and arguments to evade the law, as with claims that there is no religious purpose or meaning behind Christmas displays of nativity scenes or postings of the Ten Commandments in the schools.[2] It's easy to be optimistic about the prospects for reforming religiopolitical speech in the public sphere: we can't do much worse than we've done so far, so it should be possible to do better.

I want to re-orient the discussion about the place of religious argument in democratic deliberation away from a focus on the rights of the speaker and more toward the advantages for the listener. I take it as settled that you have a right to present religious arguments. Whether I should listen is a different issue. To address these issues in terms of rights is to illustrate the poverty of rights talk and of legal discourse more generally. Instead, I want to ask the all-American question: what's in it for me? Why should I listen?

Showing that you have a right to speak says nothing about whether I should listen. This is the fallacy Stephen Carter commits:

> What is needed is not a requirement that the religiously devout choose a form of dialogue that liberalism accepts, but that liberalism develop a politics that accepts whatever form of dialogue a member of the public offers. Epistemic diversity, like diversity of other kinds, should be cherished, not ignored, and certainly not abolished. What is needed, then, is a willingness to listen, not because the speaker has the right voice but because the speaker has the right to speak. Moreover, the willingness to listen must hold out that possibility that the speaker is saying something worth listening to; to do less is to trivialize the forces that shape the moral convictions of tens of millions of Americans.[3]

Carter has made the counterargument too easy. You have the right to all kinds of speech that I have no reason and no duty to listen to. Tens of millions of Americans believe all sorts of things that are not worth listening to, and not all diversity, of any kind, should be cherished. You have the right to engage in racist speech to which I have a duty *not* to listen. Your right to speak implies my obligation not to interrupt or heckle, but no duty to pay attention, to take your words seriously. Life is too short and there are too many voices jockeying for a privileged position. It's not that I should refuse to listen at all, for keeping an open mind is a condition of learning; but that is different from saying that I should listen *to you*, to any particular speaker or appeal.[4]

The difference between whether you should speak and whether I should listen is at the heart of religious freedom. Religious freedom includes your right to speak as you like. It includes my right to choose not to listen. The difference between whether you should speak and whether I should listen is not only the paradox of religious freedom. It is also a more general fact of life. Only in the most ideal and intimate friendship would there be no difference between the two issues of whether one should speak and another listen. In such friendship, there is, as Aristotle says, no distinction of mine and thine, and so no individuality, no difference between considerations that lead to your speaking and considerations that lead to my listening. In any realm of freedom, however, the desires and interests of speakers and hearers do not have to coincide.

Recognizing the gap between speaking and listening is the beginning of maturity. That there is a difference between what is a reason for you and what a reason for me has nothing to do with the coercive powers of a state and the need for consent. That might be the form the gap takes in liberal democracy, but the issue is deeper and more general.[5] Americans, especially American lawyers, might be tempted to see this difference as generated by a conflict between free exercise and non-establishment, but even if the First Amendment were not worded as it is, even if the First Amendment did not exist, the difference would still be there. Fidelity to the way I was brought up might be a reason for me to act in a certain way, but it is no reason at all for you to go along. Equally important, the fact that something is not a reason for you doesn't mean that it can't be a reason for me, that it is only a prejudice or preference on my part. To ignore the difference between speaking and listening is to assume that all reasons are reasons for everyone.

Why and how to listen are not questions of law. They are not "moral" issues of rights and duties. They are, instead, *ethical* questions about the sort of community we want to live in. They are ethical in the sense of involving character—the character of speakers, audiences, and communities.

If the ethical questions about whether, when, why, and to whom I should listen are not answered by settling questions about the right to speak, then a rhetorical space opens up in which hearers and not only speakers and the state exist. Both the free exercise and establishment sides of the First Amendment concern only speakers and the state, while my interest at present is in hearers. In this essay I explore how the ancient art of rhetoric can make visible and intelligible the important deliberative space that lies between rights and etiquette, between law and freedom. This is the space that Kent Greenawalt talks about as "desirable standards of public reason," Sanford Levinson as "propriety," Michael Perry as "political morality," and Nicholas Wolterstorff as "civility" and the "virtues of the conduct of the debate."[6] We live together through speech, and many of our most important ethical relations consist in how speakers and hearers treat each other.

The citizen may speak religiously, but the state cannot act on religious grounds. Between the speaking citizen and the coercing state lies the civic audience, midway between the speaker's voluble freedom and the state's deafness. The closer a given discussion is to official decisions or official speech, the more questions of religious argument become questions of establishment. The closer any given discussion is to community rather than state, the more the appropriate standards are those of free exercise.

Part of the difficulty of understanding alien voices—and my Catholic students certainly regarded their bishop as an alien voice—comes from an ambiguity in the hermeneutic principle of "charity." I have a duty to make the best I can of what you say. To understand you at all, even to disagree, even to come to the conclusion that you don't know what you're talking about, I have to assume that most of what you say is true and intelligible.[7] So much is built into the logical requirements of our understanding each other. One common strategy for charity is to assume that most of what you say is what I would say and what I agree with. After all, most of what I think is the measure of what I take to be true. So I understand you by hearing you say what I already think. But that useful strategy may be troublesome when it comes to listening to religious language. Sometimes I can make the best of what you say, measuring truth by my own opinions, only by ignoring or excising aspects of your discourse that are to me false or unintelligible or offensive. I take your elaborate argument about the nature of sin and redemption, bracket off the Christian elements that I can only hear as either false or unintelligible, and translate them into familiar ideas like "crime" and "punishment," which do not require as many metaphysical assumptions to be understood. I might charitably hear only public and readily accessible reasons although you are offering what you think is more than that. I am being charitable to you by ignoring part of what you say, since in that way we have the most in common. You might not think such charity a boon. At other times, the charitable approach leads not to consensus but, by understanding a greater part of what you say, to my hearing you as saying something wrong. I take you at your word, and therefore realize how alien you are to me. This exercise of charity, too, is not obviously welcome. For example, you argue against capital punishment by saying that such an ultimate sanction can only be pronounced by God. I can either ignore your theology and agree with you in a policy of skepticism about human reason, or I can acknowledge the integrity of your thought by paying attention to your claim about God, which I find without evidence and therefore objectionable. Either way, you may not like my interpretation. Thus my problems with how to listen.[8]

ARISTOTLE'S *RHETORIC* AND THE ETHICS OF ARGUMENT

The test for whether I should listen to a religious appeal is the same test for whether I should listen to any appeal. I want to listen to arguments that advance the discussion, and thus should listen to a religious argument when it says something useful that will not be heard otherwise. I should listen to a religious argument when I think it is more likely to lead to a good decision, and more likely to be part of a community of argument.[9]

Of course this assumes that I can recognize rationality when I see it, that there are criteria for what counts as rational. Aristotle's *Rhetoric* provides some surprising help at this juncture by way of three claims that are crucial for practical rationality. I elaborate them in greater detail elsewhere, but here can only state them in brief, though I fill in some of the details as we go.[10]

First, the heart of the art of persuasion is reasoning, *logos*. Reasoning is the "body" of persuasion, *pistis*, a word that can also fairly be translated as "proof," "belief," "trust," and "confidence." If I get you to do what I want by tainting your water supply, I haven't persuaded you of anything. And if my manipulations of your emotions make your assent as uninformed and involuntary as such pharmacological manipulations, then you aren't persuaded either. There is no community between us.

Second, while reasoning is the essence of persuasion, *êthos*, or character—and not *logos*—is the most authoritative source of belief. We trust in people more than we trust that some proposition is true. The more an issue is cloudy, contested, far in the future, the more being persuaded is a matter of trust, not propositional belief. And when Aristotle says that *êthos* is the most authoritative he means that it both is and ought to be the most persuasive. The more rational and ethical persuasion is, the more we should find the stronger appeals persuasive. A commitment to rationality is a commitment to trust and be persuaded by character.

Third, the *êthos* that is authoritative must itself be a function of reasoning. There is no reason to think that in general we should be persuaded by the external *êthos* of preexistent reputation. But an *êthos* created by the speech itself is a rationally constituted character. It is rational to trust and believe in such a character. It is this complex relation between *logos* and *êthos*, between thought and character, that I find fruitful in thinking about the place of religious argument in democratic deliberation.

The relation between *logos* and *êthos* in the *Rhetoric* has a counterpart in the *Ethics,* where Aristotle confronts the equally complex relation between justice and friendship:

> Friendship would seem to hold cities together, and legislators would seem to be more concerned about it than about justice. For concord would seem to be similar to friendship and they aim at concord above all, while they try above all to expel civil conflict, which is enmity. Further, if people are friends, they have no need of justice, but if they are just they need friendship in addition; and the justice that is most just seems to belong to friendship. (*Eudemian Ethics* VIII.1.1155a22–29; see *EE* VII.1.1234b23–32)

Friendship exceeds justice, especially legal justice, but it is never unjust. *Êthos* exceeds reason but is never irrational. The deeper the friendship, the more appeals count as rational. There is a circularity between trust and rationality. The more rational an appeal appears to be, the more it can be trusted. The more trustworthy the speaker, the more her appeals can and will be regarded as rational. This circular relation between trust and reason is precisely the mutually reinforcing relation between *êthos* and *logos* in Aristotle's *Rhetoric.*

Whether an appeal is rational, coercive, or merely assertive depends on trust. "How can I listen?" is a question of *êthos*—what attitude I should take toward religious language and argument? It is a matter of trust and charity. This question of attitude, like charity in hermeneutics generally, is not a question of rules, methods, or principles. It is an issue of *êthos* that cannot be reduced to *logos. Êthos* can be a force of coercion as well as rationality, for coercion can be effected through appeals to personal experience, to tradition, or to a position of authority. All these are external manifestations of character that are substitutes for argument. They serve as a bar to my hearing what the speaker has to say as an argument. When rationality is a contested concept, so too is coercion, and liberal democrats and religious advocates often differ on what counts as coercion, and consequently on what counts as rational. However much we might disagree about whether a particular case is coercive, the standard is clear. Anything I cannot talk back to is coercive and irrational.

Rationality and trustworthiness increase and decrease together. Therefore, the practical question for the place of religious argument in democratic deliberation is how rationally to increase trust, where trust is a function of argument. Religious appeals are or are not rational depending on who offers them to whom. From an enemy, a religious presentation can be coercive. From a stranger, it might be the expression of a preference. From a friend, it could be a rational concern for the common good.

Why should I trust a religious speaker? How does the religious speaker make himself or herself trustworthy? Aristotle says that, apart from knowing what he or she is talking about, there are three qualities in a speaker that produce trust (*Rhetoric* II.1.1378a6–9). The first two are virtue and practical wisdom. The third in Greek is *eunoia,* literally "being well-minded." It means having good will or being well disposed to the audience. We trust people when we think they are with us. The difficulty citizens have in listening to religious argument involve establishing such good will, difficulties that are partly problems for the speaker and partly for the democratic audience. The lesson of the *Rhetoric* is that, to the extent I trust you, I take you seriously as having something to say that is worth my consideration.

Establishing trust is partly a job for speakers, thinking about how their presentation can be trustworthy; partly a job for hearers, taking things at least temporarily on trust; and partly a job for the community, where it is a matter of institutional design. In all three dimensions, the issue is what Jonathan Shay in *Achilles in Vietnam* calls "safe struggle," the construction of a context for disputes in which the winner does not take all and in which we can dissent without total war. I cannot trust you if I think you aim at total victory. Speakers and hearers and the community as a whole can increase or decrease the perception of safe struggle. Anything that seems to transform situations of debate into one of total winners and total losers threatens democracy.[11]

None of this so far is unique to religion. My students, like most citizens, are at once both highly suspicious and highly gullible. When I raise the question of how to listen, I am asking how we can rationally distribute our innate credulousness and suspicion. But religion does pose some special problems, both for the individual speaker and hearer and for institutional design. Contemporary liberals such as John Rawls and Richard Rorty who want to bar, or restrain, religious argument have as their goal agreement, and see religious argument as standing in its way. Advocates who want to propose religious arguments posit truth as their goal, to which civility and agreement are necessarily subordinate. One can say, then, that agreement is the goal of a society of strangers, truth of a society of friends. Note that truth and agreement as goals of discourse differently interpret the principle of charity. If I aim at agreement, then I extend you hermeneutic charity by hearing you as agreeing with me as much as possible. If I aim at truth, then hermeneutic charity will result in increased possibilities for disagreement insofar as I see your approaches to truth diverging from mine. Of course, truth and agreement are the extremes of a continuum, but their difference sets the problem for religion in a democracy.

It is the eruption of truth into liberal discussion that causes the peculiar problems of the place of religious argument in democratic deliberation. When Aristotle said that states are held together by friendship, he could not imagine the success of liberalism at ignoring this advice and still creating stable and prosperous communities. Religious argument is a periodic reminder of the price we pay for the success of liberalism. Reducing belief to preferences, acting as though all our disagreements were differences about means to universally accepted ends—these are successful strategies for living together. But they exact a cost on the individual and the community.

The burden of proof is on the religious speaker, as it is on any other speaker, to show why I should allocate scarce time and attention to listen to what is being said. Yet the religious speaker must overcome unique presumptions that religious discourse is irrational and out of place in the broader sociopolitical context. Religious speakers have to face such presumptions simply because of the nature of the higher and larger claims religious speech purports to make.

The burden is on the listener as well, though. The listener has to overcome his or her own suspicions that the resistance to religion is itself a form of prejudice, or simply a resistance to what one fears might be someone giving unwelcome news. The burden of proof is on the listener who must overcome presumptions that everything alien is false and dangerous.

In each of the following four sections, I identify a practical problem with the intent to listen profitably to religious argument. None of these is unique to religion, but each presents acute rhetorical problems for the religious speaker and the democratic audience. Importantly, the four special challenges to religious speech in fact emerge out of religion's natural advantage—namely, its higher standard of truth rather than agreement. Each is therefore a "topos" in the classical rhetorical sense, a source of argument on both sides of a question that presents both an opportunity and a danger. Religious rhetoric has a higher cost and a higher benefit than other kinds of appeal. None of these four is a peculiar ontological or epistemological disability of religion. Attempts to prove that religion is undemocratic for being foundational, inaccessible, or comprehensive have been tried and failed. "We are tolerant; they're dogmatic!" has lost its appeal. But that does not imply that religion is no different from other sources of belief and argument. Neither proponents nor opponents of religion think that. The four places where religion creates suspicion in democratic deliberation are ethical and rhetorical, not metaphysical. They are sources of suspicion, and the challenge is to find in each place an opportunity to create trust and friendship.

RELIGIOUS RHETORIC AS COMPREHENSIVE

The first advantage religion has over secular sources of argument is that it is comprehensive. "Comprehensiveness" is ambiguous, and my four places, or *topoi*, could be seen as defining religious argument as comprehensive in four different ways. In each case comprehensiveness is not a logical property but an ethical one: it makes community harder to establish, and so the more comprehensive an appeal, the more an audience will mistrust and resist it. For the same reasons, though, the more comprehensive an appeal, the deeper the community that is established when the appeal is successful.

My initial exploration of comprehensiveness involves personal identity. The fact that I can be persuaded by your arguments about the useful consequences of some proposal does not make me a utilitarian. Likewise, the fact that I find your argument about the original meaning of the Constitution conclusive does not make me a legal fundamentalist. I can believe that original meaning is the best account of the right to bear arms, but not of the ban on cruel and unusual punishment. But there is more at stake when I accept or reject religious arguments. Once I am committed religiously, I am committed to a wider range of consequences, and with a higher degree of adhesion, than in my commitments to secular arguments that I have accepted.

Thus the first special rhetorical problem for listening to religious argument: when you present a religious argument, I naturally ask myself that, if I agree with you, what and how much am I agreeing to. If I agree with your conclusion—spend more money on job training for the poor—am I committed to accepting your premises, the religious source of your political argument? Have I converted without realizing it? "God is love, and whoever remains in love remains in God and God in him" (1 John 4:16). Does that mean that if I am "in love" I am "in God" whether I know it or not, whether I want to be or not?

Along the same lines, if I reject your conclusion, do I thereby reject its source? Since I oppose spending more money on job training for the poor, must I also reject the apostolic sources of your thought? "Whoever fails to love does not know God, because God is love" (1 John 4:8). If I do not want to do what for you counts as love, have I also rejected your God? I should be suspicious of an argument that seems to put my identity so much at stake, since the risks are so much larger than usual. If I regard the burden of proof as falling on the religious speaker, this isn't prejudice. It is a reasonable assessment of the high cost of assent. It used to be that people wondered whether an atheist could be a good citizen and a moral person. I don't mean to turn the tables and ask the same of a religious believer. That is not the reason to impose this high burden of proof.

Thus there arises a practical problem: how do I talk back to a religious argument? The more religious arguments seem rooted in personal identity, the harder they are to respond to. Your appeal seems coercive or emotive to me, not rational or argumentative, because I cannot figure out a way of talking back, even though it is not coercive but rational to others, and even though I impute nothing but good will to you. If I think I have no room to negotiate, religious rhetoric appears coercive, even when it has no sanctions. Without community and friendship, otherwise rational appeals are aggressive and coercive. How can I accept or reject your conclusion without accepting or attacking, respectively, its religious sources? How can you hear my criticism as disagreement with the conclusion and not with your religious faith?[12]

I want to be able to listen to a religiously based political argument without thinking that there is also a case concerning religious faith itself that I must somehow attend to. For you to persuade me about a political issue, I have to trust that you are not also trying to persuade me about a religious issue. In order to listen to you, I have to trust that you want to persuade me of a particular conclusion about what to do, without thinking that you also want to convert me. It is one thing for you to persuade me that any belief in divine creation implies a proper regard for the sanctity of all human life. It is quite another if I think you are arguing in the other direction, that I cannot really hold all human life sacred without also holding the religious commitments that you hold. That is the first reason why religious speech causes mistrust.

One of the great achievements of liberal democracy is allowing us to agree on what to do for different, even conflicting, reasons. For religious argument to participate in democratic deliberation, speakers and hearers have to develop a form of trust that allows the listener to assent to a conclusion without agreeing with the premises, or to disagree with a conclusion without making any judgment about the premises at all.

For example, Kent Greenawalt says that "the government of a liberal society knows no religious truth and a crucial premise about a liberal society is that citizens of extremely diverse religious views can build principles of political order and social justice that do not depend on particular religious beliefs."[13] I think that sentence can be meaningfully rewritten eliminating the three occurrences of the word "religious": The government of a liberal society knows no truth and a crucial premise about a liberal society is that citizens of extremely diverse views can build principles of political order and social justice that do not depend on particular beliefs. The crucial premise of liberal society is that agreement on what to do does not depend on agreement on any particular principles or beliefs. To be a good citizen does not say anything about one's identity, about the principles, beliefs, and values one holds most closely. The relation between principles and consequences is very loose in a functioning democracy: one principle, whether respect for persons or the commitment to antidiscrimination, can in deliberation yield competing practical proposals, and a single policy can be generated and justified from multiple starting points.[14]

Liberalism therefore is characterized not only by the absence of consensus on fundamentals, but also by a principle of practical reason that allows us to reason toward a particular policy decision, but not backward from a decision to its grounds. Democracy rejects the inference from particular opinions and actions to the kind of person one is. "Its refusal to look beyond what citizens affirm to how or why they affirm what they do is an essential part of political liberalism's neutrality."[15] So when I worry about my commitments, my concern is whether I can agree with you about a conclusion alone, or whether that agreement doesn't commit me further to its underlying premises. Religions often with good reason ask for tighter connections between one's religious beliefs and one's actions: a good Jew will do X, and doing X makes you a good Jew. To be trustworthy, the religious argument has to present democratically loose, contestable, and only probable connections between premises and conclusions.

RELIGIOUS RHETORIC AS PRINCIPLED

The second advantage of religious rhetoric is that it appeals to higher grounds and to a higher part of human nature. Its arguments are not only about human dignity, but they appeal to the dignity of the speaker and the hearer. I might think it practically appropriate to agree with your utilitarian appeal, but I am proud to assent to your religious argument. Just as I reinterpreted comprehensiveness as rhetorical and ethical rather than ontological or epistemological, the same holds here for the principled nature of religious discourse. Appeals to principle are persuasive because they are appeals to my better self. That advantage, however, carries with it peculiar burdens for the religious speaker and the listener to religious rhetoric.[16]

The principled nature of religious rhetoric poses a special problem not only for religion but for religion in a liberal democracy. Liberalism, in spite of its insistence on fundamental rights and equality, finds it hard to know what to do with appeals to something other than self-interest.[17] (I'm setting aside issues where personal interest is also involved, for example, tax aid to parochial schools.) Political disputes that involve allocation of resources, even when the recipients include religious organizations, are far less divisive than political disputes about religious symbolism. The more I see religious forces trying to capture the government's powers of symbolic speech, through public prayers and displays, the less I am inclined to listen to religious arguments about matters of common concern. Religious groups must choose between aiming at vindication, capturing the symbolic capacities of the state to proclaim the United States a Christian nation, and aiming at policies, abolishing capital punishment, abortion, or poverty. To listen to you, I must trust that you are not after total victory, that you distinguish between winning this issue and more comprehensive domination. That implies that I trust you to invest greater commitment in our community than in some other locus of loyalty. Therefore, an overlapping consensus presupposes fidelity to something citizens hold in common, even if it is argument rather than belief—a community joined by argument rather than by blood or creed.[18]

The person who sees all human problems as questions of the gratification of desire and a calculus of pleasure and pain is at least as narrow minded and as alien to me as the person who sees everything as the confirmation of biblical prophecy. Both exclude themselves from a community of argument and friendship. Still, I would rather try to cooperate with the former.[19] I'll take my chances with the materialist who reads evolutionary biology as confirming reductionist materialism rather than the creationist. At least the materialist and I can negotiate and compromise. We can bracket truth and aim at agreement. It is easier for me to talk with the reductionist economist than the Christian because I can take her as she presents herself, ready to debate the instrumental value of her argument, while to take a religious argument as instrumental is to take it other than as it is meant. The supposed priority of the right to the good is a metaphysical thesis about the nature of value. I recommend instead its rhetorical equivalent, the priority of agreement to truth. That essential strategy of liberalism, bracketing truth and aiming at agreement, seems unavailable for many religious thinkers.[20] The nature of religious argument not only makes compromise difficult, and makes it seem hypocritical, but rhetorically presents itself as the only possible course of action, while liberal rhetoric characteristically presents comparisons of costs and benefits. Principled rhetoric is thus "hotter" than the temperature appropriate to democracy.

But the picture for religious speakers is not all that bleak. There are other "conversation stoppers," to use Rorty's apt term, besides religion. Just as I would prefer to cooperate with the believer in the selfish gene rather than try to cooperate with the creationist, I would prefer to try to deliberate about the Defense of Marriage Act with the scriptural literalist than with someone who thinks that public opinion polls should settle the matter. Robert Bork, for example, claims that "moral outrage is a sufficient ground for prohibitory legislation."[21] That seems to me conclusory in a more fatal sense than those who would base their desire to ban homosexuality on the Bible. "Moral outrage" is as much a conversation stopper as the citation of Scripture. It is a more permanent conversation stopper, more irrational and harder to overcome. If "sufficient ground" means that a majority can pass coercive laws, of course Bork is right. But, although they can command obedience, such feelings of outrage command no respect or authority. Here is passion as irrational, as a substitute for argument. But might does not make right. Individuals may or may not be open to argument, but there is room within the Bible and within religious traditions for counterargument, while "moral outrage" purports simply to settle the matter. Thus religious advocates often complain that they are barred from appealing to comprehensive principles. I object to their doing anything else. To the extent that they appeal to power, to how popular or traditional their views are, they lose their character as religious arguments, and they lose my trust.

That contrast between religious and popular arguments against homosexuality shows that sometimes claims of truth are more irenic and dialogical than claims of agreement.[22] The challenge to religious rhetoric, both to speakers and hearers, is to take advantage of these connections between principles and respect.

Democracy has made it possible to regard appeals to interest as equally dignified and respectful as appeals to principles, and so has neutralized the advantage of being principled that religious argument once enjoyed. Religious argument ignores this revolution at its peril. Consider the famous lines of Adam Smith (*Wealth of Nations,* I.ii.2):

> It is not from the benevolence of the butcher, the brewer, or the baker, that we expect our dinner, but from their regard to their own interest. We address ourselves, not to their humanity but to their self-love. And never talk to them of our own necessities but of their advantages. Nobody but a beggar chuses to depend chiefly upon the benevolence of his fellow-citizens.

It is more dignified and respectful to negotiate on the basis of self-interest than of higher appeals. My relations with you can have greater equality, and hence greater moral depth, when we are negotiating self-interest than when I am asking, or begging, you to act on moral principles. When you take your stand on religious principles, on the other hand, I am in the position of having to defer to you, which is not a position of respect at all. Justice Warren stressed that the opinion in *Brown v. Board of Education* had to be "non-accusatory." For a white southerner to be told that segregation could no longer be legal because of the increased importance of education to citizenship is easier to accept than to be told that since all people are equal in the eyes of God, segregation is therefore not only unconstitutional but impious as well.

In talking about comprehensiveness, I earlier showed that listening to religious argument in a democracy required an ethical, rational virtue of drawing loose connections between principles and consequences, identity and action. Here we see the need for another virtue. Listening to a religious argument requires a fairly sophisticated repertoire—which doesn't necessarily mean an explicit or conscious repertoire—of propositional attitudes, which can be summed up by the familiar phrase "for the sake of argument." I have to know how to entertain premises hypothetically. That means that I have to take a premise in a spirit different from the one in which you enunciate it. You say that preference for the poor is justified by the teachings of the gospel. I take your biblical premises to fall somewhere between "true" and "true for you." Listening to religious arguments means finding such an intermediate place.

Saying that listening to religious argument takes sophistication, though, does not mean that it is an intellectual activity to be practiced only by an educated elite. It involves an ethical, not a logical, demand. To be able to have nuanced prepositional attitudes is a case in which common practice outruns theory. Theoretically, it looks as though we must choose between assertion and hypothesis, between holding something as true and taking it only as something that *you* believe, between assertions of fact and expressions of opinion. I either take your assertions as truth claims or as beliefs on a par with your desires and preferences, as I aim for either truth or agreement. In practice, though, people are able to find a continuity of intermediate positions. Thus in a contemporary political debate, I would give more attention to an argument from Christian premises, to which I give no personal credence, than to an argument from Roman gods. In other circumstances, either an academic discussion or a personal one, I might regard Christianity and Roman religion as equally implausible, or as equally interesting subjects for discussion; but in my political community I will listen to a Christian argument without agreement but with more attention than I give to a myth or a fiction. My attitude toward Christian arguments lies at a range of places between truth claims and expressions of belief. American Christians and Jews are having to learn how to listen to Muslim arguments, and could also do better at listening to nonreligious but comprehensive appeals. Such improvements in our listening ability would be acts of friendship.

RELIGIOUS RHETORIC AS MOTIVATED

I've claimed so far that religious argument differs from political argument in general because it rests on the character of the agents and on principle. Each makes it harder to establish a community between speaker and hearer, and each makes the community that *could* be established all the more powerful. Put those two together, and a third advantage (and also a problem) emerges for religious argument. One of the modern ways of dividing politics from both religion and morality is to say that while politics and law are concerned with the performance of actions, moral and religious assessments concern the motivations and purposes of the agents. As Michael Walzer puts it, "A democratic society cannot inquire into how or where the political views of its citizens are shaped, and it cannot censor the doctrinal or rhetorical forms in which they are expressed."[23] And as I quoted Stephen Gardbaum earlier, "Its refusal to look beyond what citizens affirm to how or why they affirm what they do is an essential part of political liberalism's neutrality."

Those bound in friendship in a liberal democracy might not need to think about one another's motives, but partners in a fuller moral friendship must do so. As moral and religious principles place higher demands on us, the standards relevant to assessing religious arguments are themselves higher than we apply to appeals to interest or consequences. These higher standards are both an advantage and a source of mistrust.

Religious arguments are therefore open to questions about purposes and motives in a way that need not trouble, for example, arguments that are purely about self-interest. If I present you, as I did in the quotation from Adam Smith, with an argument from my interest and about your interest, a hermeneutics of suspicion seems out of place. We don't need to uncover interest because it is already apparent. (And therefore the crafty speaker can use self-interest as a cover for principle! Diodotus in Thucydides is a classic example.) But a principled argument invites a hermeneutics of suspicion. Liberalism functions through a narrow attention to arguments and a rejection of *ad hominem* considerations of the speakers. Just as the ideal scientist is anonymous, since the truth of his or her claims have nothing personal about them, so the ideal political speaker is similarly anonymous, depending on the cogency of reasoning and not on the status or reputation of the speaker. But religious argument invites such consideration of motive and other personal factors.

Democratic deliberators are often confronted with practical arguments that are not explicitly religious in content but that are religiously "motivated." At issue is whether the religious content of arguments should be the concern of the democratic audience, or whether, if I decide to listen to you, I must also concern myself with your possibly religious motivation. It is generally poisonous to look for motivation. Such a suspicious inquiry destroys community and, by looking beyond an argument toward something else, discounts the argument and avoids true conversation. To the extent that religious arguments invite inquiry into motives, they destroy trust and friendship. To the extent that the audiences of religious arguments inquire into motives, they do the same. It doesn't matter whether speaker or hearer is "at fault" in such circumstances. What matters is the loss of trust. Moreover, this is an inquiry that cannot be satisfied. It isn't the hidden motive that the inquiry discovers that is destructive of community. It is the inquiry itself, regardless of what it finds.

The language of motivation seems inappropriate for any appeals worth considering. It also seems sometimes appropriate and inevitable when it comes to religious argument, invited, as I claimed, out of the properly religious concern for intentions. In cases such as the creationist's "equal time" laws, which are motivated by a desire to teach creationism and to avoid prior court rulings, or laws about moments of silence or "student-led prayer," the religious motivation seems a part of what I should think about in evaluating the policy proposal. The language of motivation fits the examples such as these, but they are weak arguments. Inquiry into motives seems appropriate only for weak arguments, so maybe the problem isn't with the motivations but with the quality of argument. Thus, Lincoln's second Inaugural Address, or a speech by Martin Luther King Jr. or Desmond Tutu, whether explicitly religious or not, cannot be fairly called "religiously motivated."

The trouble with the language of motivation is that to characterize arguments by their motives is to identify something called a "motive" as distinct from the argument itself. To characterize some piece of discourse as "religiously motivated" is to condemn it, not because it is religious, but because it thereafter is known only in terms of its putative motivation, and not through what it is saying. An inquiry into motives can never be satisfied. It is a challenge for both religious discourse and that of liberal democracy to find a better way of talking about purpose than the current language of motivation.

A concern with motives is thus a third topos that makes religious argument simultaneously so powerful and so hard to hear in a democracy. To explore this difficult place a little more, I want to take as an example Robert Audi's claim that democracy excludes not only arguments with a religious content, but also those with a religious motivation:

> The motivation principle needed for a full articulation of standards of civic virtue is that since an argument can be tacitly religious without being religious in content, one might fail to adhere to the principle even in offering arguments that on their face are neither religious nor fail to provide adequate secular reason for their conclusion.[24]

I have two problems with Audi's claim. First, it really isn't about motivation at all. The language of motivation is just a stand-in for arguments that are, although they may appear not to be, religious. While Audi claims that we should bar religiously motivated arguments from democratic deliberation, he isn't really talking about motives but about implicit features of the argument that are no less real, and no less part of the argument itself, for being unstated. That seems to me an unproblematic use of the hermeneutics of suspicion, the possibility that interpretation is needed to understand an argument properly. What's wrong with laws demanding "equal time for creationism" is not their religious motivation but their religious substance and their probable religious effects. They fact that its proponents dishonestly disguise the religious content of creationism makes for more mistrust and less friendship, but the religious content is enough to vitiate such laws anyway.[25]

But my second problem with Audi's ban on religiously motivated argument cuts deeper. If an argument is a bad argument, then it fails regardless of motivation. On the other hand, if an argument does provide adequate secular reason, why should its religious "motivation" matter? In logic, a valid argument is not weakened by adding further premises. If "Socrates is a man; all men are mortal; therefore Socrates is mortal" is a valid argument, it is neither strengthened nor weakened by my adding that Socrates was a lousy husband. If there are adequate secular reasons for favoring "Sunday closing" laws, additional religious reasons or religious motives should not weaken those secular reasons. To the extent that we think about persuasion as reasoning, then, motivation should be irrelevant. To the extent that we look at the motives for persuasion, we cannot treat the given piece of persuasion as reasoning. A ban on inquiries into motives is therefore not only ethically appealing, but seems logically compelled. As in my example of the ideal scientist, motives are logically irrelevant. Therefore, to look at the motives of an argument is to regard it as something other than an argument.[26]

The crucial contrast that forces us to look at motives, and also to see how dangerous an inquiry into motives is, is the difference between reasoning persuasively and merely using reasoning in order to persuade. The issue is not then motivation so much as whether I hear you as arguing or as simply using argument to persuade me. If I think you are reasoning, I can disagree and still trust you. But if I think you are only using reasoning to persuade me, it is legitimate to ask about motivation just because the reasoning cannot be judged on its own. When reasoning is only one means among others that might be used to persuade me, then I would disarm myself if I looked only to the reasoning and not to why you were using it on me. The difference between arguing and merely using argument is crucial; it is difficult to discern; it is an always contestable boundary. That is why the language of motivation is both inadequate and necessary: inadequate for judging interesting cases of religious argument and necessary for excluding the uses of argument and religion in bad faith. The difference between arguing and merely using reasoning is similar to the difference between acting democratically and using democracy to further one's own ends.

If there is a motive distinct from the argument, then you are holding back from me. Since it is a reason for action, any motive could be made into a further premise within the argument, and you have not done so. You try to persuade me that the poor should get preferential treatment because of considerations of solidarity and eventual benefits to me from increased stability and productivity. In fact you are motivated to give preference to the poor because of a reading of Christian teachings. You think there is a more compelling argument, including a further premise, than the reasoning you offer to me. But you think that I would not accept the premise and therefore have to make do with a weaker argument. You can think that the secular argument, while incomplete, is good enough to motivate and justify a course of action against the alternatives, even though you can think of an even stronger argument. Your additional premise is not one that makes me turn against the policy—I don't think, "Since this is Christian, I'm against it." Your additional premise makes your conclusion neither stronger not weaker in my eyes, since I give it no value and hold it irrelevant. It is a reason for you, not for me. (It is the rhetorical equivalent of adding a tautology to a logical inference.) If, on the other hand, I translate your motives into premises and find the argument weaker, then I rightly reduce the credibility I give the argument. Knowing when to trust and when to be suspicious, when to be friendly and when to resist appeals in the name of friendship, is an additional challenge to listening to religious argument.

RELIGIOUS RHETORIC AND AUTHORITY

The final advantage of religious argument is that it is not only comprehensive, principled, and inclusive of purposes, but it is authoritative. You speak to me not as an equal, but as someone whose words carry power. Sometimes religious speakers themselves have authority and can back their arguments with sanctions, and sometimes it is the content of the religious argument that contains sanctions. In the first case I can be threatened with excommunication; in the second with eternal damnation. This makes religious arguments uniquely powerful.

It is for this reason, I think, that my students were so suspicious of the Roman Catholic bishop from St. Cloud. Aristotle says in the *Rhetoric* that the kind of character that is and ought to be the most authoritative source of belief comes from reasoning alone. The trust and friendship that makes true argument and persuasion possible comes from reasoning. My students could not attend to the bishop's words precisely because he was a bishop. Authority and power, rather than their being advantages of the religious speaker, are disadvantages insofar as they become sources of mistrust.

This is another dimension of the unique opportunities and dangers of religion and friendship. Friends can say things to me that no one else can. I regard the concern of a stranger for the fate of my immortal soul not as an act of friendly concern but as an act of impertinence.[27] But reasoning can draw on authorities without being authoritarian or an argument from authority. The third challenge to religious argument was how to argue and not just *use* argument. The final challenge is how to *use* authority and not be authoritative, without having authority substitute for reasoning.

The separation of rationality from authority, so that an appeal is judged on its own terms to be rational or irrational, regardless of its source and of the power behind the appeal, is a uniquely democratic achievement. Machiavelli argues in *The Prince* that "unarmed prophets" are always unsuccessful. In democracies today all prophets are unarmed, and consequently face a new challenge. It is only in modern liberal democracies that coercion needs justification and obedience is founded in consent. In his notorious characterization of religion as a "conversation stopper," Richard Rorty expresses the presupposition of democracy that "moral decisions that are to be enforced by a pluralistic and democratic state's monopoly in violence are best made by public discussion in which voices claiming to be God's, or reason's, or science's, are put on a par with everybody else's."[28] This is a novel position for most religions, and a serious test of their power to adapt to democracy. Religious argument is democratically trustworthy to the extent that it is not heard as authoritarian, which is to say, to the extent that it is heard as rational. Peculiarly modern problems of religious argument come from the fact that religious claims are always mediated, as all claims are, through consent. There are no divine sanctions for government except through consent. In a democracy, that is, religious arguments can provide truth, but not legitimacy. Since truth and legitimacy usually go together, it is a peculiar challenge to argue for truth recognizing that legitimacy comes not from truth, but from acceptance and agreement.

How to listen to a religious argument is similar to the issue of how to listen to one's parents as one gets older. From childhood through adolescence, parents usually are seen as authoritative, and can back their words with strong sanctions. In subsequent years their capacity to compel wanes. Do they therefore become just another voice, to be listened to when I like what they say, but ignored otherwise?

This last topos, especially, shows that there is an admission fee for anyone who seeks to gain a hearing in democratic deliberation. Religion and democracy are both transformed by the presence of religious argument. I don't want to minimize what is at stake.[29] My argument, of course, has affinities to traditional arguments that all religions in America must become forms of Protestantism with its emphasis on individuality and privacy. My point is a bit different, though. All religions in America must become rational through abandoning authority. They become more rational not by becoming less emotional or by losing faith, but by losing authority.

In this essay, I have presented a series of places of argument that show how religious argument, because of its unique powers, is both at an advantage and a disadvantage in democratic deliberation. I have presupposed that the burden of proof is on the religious speaker to show that I should listen to his discourse, and then worried about how to overcome that burden of proof. I am reminded of Machiavelli's problem in *The Prince*. The "new prince" seems at a permanent disadvantage to the hereditary monarch. All the hereditary ruler must do to stay in power is not mess up, while whatever made it possible for the new prince to usurp the throne makes it just as likely that others will overthrow him. By the end of *The Prince*, though, Machiavelli can claim that someone who follows its lessons will be more secure than the hereditary ruler: "The before-mentioned things, if prudently observed, make a new prince seem ancient, and render him at once more secure and firmer in the state than if he had been established there of old. For a new prince is much more observed in his actions than a hereditary one, and when these are recognized as virtuous, he wins over men more and they are more bound to him than if he were of the ancient blood" (chap. 24).

I present the analogy to suggest that where advantages and disadvantages lie is not so simple. Religious believers see themselves as an embattled and besieged minority engaged in a struggle with unfair rules against more powerful secular forces; and those who prefer a wall of separation—and again, I stress, this is a much larger class than the class of nonbelievers—similarly see themselves fighting against unequal odds. In such circumstances of mistrust, it may be useful to see the four topoi identified above as simultaneously advantages and disadvantages of religion in a democracy.

I cannot speak for the religious speaker, but I can speak for at least part of the audience of religious political discourse. Speaking religiously and listening to religious arguments are both hard work in a democracy. Religious rhetoric does not make heavier theoretical demands on an audience than any other political arguments do, but it does make heavy ethical demands. My four topoi require ethical work. The fact that it is difficult to be trusting and trustworthy suggests that such friendly arguments are more successful the closer they track free exercise rather than establishment considerations. Understanding alien voices is hard work, so hard that it may be impossible under the circumstances of political deliberation, with its limited time for decisions and need for simple and easily understood arguments. The more rational sites for political argument are often the occasions furthest removed from particular political decision.[30] It is my conclusion that the more rational places are the places where religious argument can more readily find a trusting audience. To return to where I started. I want to hear (some) religious arguments in a democracy because I want a community that aims at something more than agreement yet less than truth. Similarly, I am interested in a form of friendship that lies between the justice among strangers and the love within a family. Religious argument offers a concern with truth in democratic arguments where it is often lacking. That is both why I want to listen to religious argument and why it is so difficult to do so.

NOTES

1. See Michael W. McConnell, "State Action and the Supreme Court's Emerging Consensus on the Line between Establishment and Private Religious Expression," *Pepperdine Law Review* 28 (2001): 681–718 at 682: "The evil against which the Establishment Clause is directed is not religion, but government control over religion."

2. See Stephen Carter, *Culture of Disbelief* (New York: Basic Books, 1993), 45: "In truth, the seeming ubiquity of religious language in our public debates can itself be a form of trivialization—both because our politicians are expected to repeat largely meaningless religious incantations and because of the modern tendency among committed advocates across the political spectrum to treat Holy Scripture like a dictionary of familiar quotations, combing through the pages to find the ammunition needed to win political arguments."

3. Ibid., 230.

4. "What is essential is not that everyone shall speak, but that everything worth saying shall be said." Alexander Meiklejohn, *Political Freedom: The Constitutional Powers of the People* (New York: Oxford University Press, 1965), 26.

5. Thomas Nagel sees as characteristic of liberalism the distinction "between what justifies individual belief and what justifies appealing to that belief in support of the exercise of political power." Nagel, "Moral Conflict and Political Legitimacy," *Philosophy and Public Affairs* 16 (1987): 229. Others talk about the need to justify coercion.

The relation between what is a reason for me and what is a reason for others is at the heart of contemporary philosophical issues about what are called "internal" and "external" reasons.

6. Kent Greenawalt, *Private Consciences and Public Reasons* (New York: Oxford University Press, 1995), 6: "Basic principles of liberal democracy do not themselves resolve whether citizens and officials should exercise self-restraint about the grounds they use to resolve such questions. Desirable standards of public reason depend on history and the present composition of a political society." Michael Perry says that "persons with religious convictions about the good" should be free "to rely on those convictions." Perry, "Liberal Democracy and Religious Morality," *De Paul Law Review* 48 (1998): 112. But again the question: why should anyone listen? Nicholas Wolterstorff closes "Why We Should Reject What Liberalism Tells Us about Speaking and Acting in Public for Religious Reasons," in *Religion and Contemporary Liberalism,* ed. Paul J. Weithman (Notre Dame, Ind.: University of Notre Dame Press, 1997), 162–81 at 180, with a reorientation that is my point of departure: "Why not let people say what they want, but insist that they say it with civility? Why not concern ourselves with the *virtues* of the conduct of the debate rather than with the *content* of the positions stake out in the debate?" For me "civility" is not a matter of good manners and politeness, but of civic friendship.

7. See Donald Davidson, *Inquiries into Truth and Interpretation* (Oxford: Clarendon Press, 1984).

8. See Steven D. Smith, "Natural Law and Contemporary Moral Thought: A Guide for the Perplexed," *American Journal of Jurisprudence* 42 (1997): 320–21: "We can discern the promise and the predicament of contemporary natural law. The natural lawyer starts by criticizing, cogently, relativistic or conventionalist ethical positions. He continues by observing, correctly, that ethical systems which seek only to maximize 'subjective' values or goods miss much of what we understand 'morality' to be about. And he responds to this deficiency by emphasizing values or goods that are 'objective.' But in hypothesizing such entities, the natural lawyer severs goods from our language and understanding, in which things are 'good' to and for persons and as experienced by persons. The risk is that this separation will drain our moral discourse of comprehensible meaning, thereby rendering it a sort of sophisticated but empty word game.

"To put the point differently, our moral discourse is conducted by us, for better or worse, for our purposes and subject to our understandings. It would be arrogant and foolish to suppose that we are the center of the universe; but it is also futile to deny that we are, of necessity, the center of our universe. And what we are, again for better or worse, is persons—or 'subjects.' Consequently, the only kind of goods or reasons for acting that will enter our comprehension and command our attention will be, of necessity, 'personal' and 'subjective' in an important sense; the utilitarians are right about that much. So our dilemma is this: we want—and we appear to believe in—a morality that is more than the fulfillment of subjective desires (or, in other words, more than utilitarianism); but it seems that we cannot even comprehend goods or reasons for acting that are other than subjective."

See also Bryan Hehir, in an unpublished manuscript quoted in Perry, "Liberal Democracy," at 78: "When a religious moral claim will affect the wider public, it should be proposed in a fashion which that public can evaluate, accept or reject on its own terms. The [point] is not to vanish religious insight and argument from public life, [but only to] establish a test for the religious communities to meet: to probe our commitments deeply and broadly enough that we can translate their best insights to others."

We also encounter the two dimensions of charity in the badly named "originalism/ nonoriginalism" debate. Is the meaning we impute to the Constitution that which accords with what we think or with what we think some else—the authors, ratifiers, public at the time—thought. In "Rhetoric, Hermeneutics, and Prudence in the Interpretation of the Constitution," in *Rhetoric and Hermeneutics in Our Time*, ed. Walter Jost and Michael Hyde (New Haven: Yale University Press, 1966), 171–95, I trace Philip Bobbit's distinction of six modes of constitutional interpretation. Each could be read as a different form of charity, giving the best meaning to the Constitution. In much of life, charity and interpretation work smoothly and it would be tendentious to separate these choices or modes. But sometimes, as in the interpretation of alien voices, we are forced to make choices.

9. Richard Posner gets things exactly backward in *The Problematics of Moral and Legal Theory* (Cambridge: Harvard University Press, 1999), at 78: "Finnis and the other moralists who derive their moral codes from religious orthodoxy make a tactical mistake when they try to use reason to defend their beliefs. They play into the hands of their secular opponents, who want to make reason the only legitimate basis for making moral claims. Rather than playing on the opponents' turf, religious moralists should point out that secular moralists' views are founded as much as their own on faith, and that argument, understood as a form of rhetoric or theatre, occupies the same position in secular moral theory that liturgy does in religion." Posner's rhetorical policy is to have the religious advocate say, "Yes. I'm irrational and fall back quickly on faith. But so do you. So there."

10. These three claims organize the first six chapters of my *For the Sake of Argument: Practical Reasoning, Character and the Ethics of Belief* (Chicago: University of Chicago Press, 2004).

11. Jonathan Shay, *Achilles in Vietnam: Combat Trauma and the Undoing of Character* (New York: Atheneum, 1994), 180: "Democratic process embodies the apparently contradiction of *safe struggle.*" "Democratic process entails debate, persuasion, and compromise. These all presuppose the trustworthiness of words. The moral dimension of severe trauma, the betrayal of 'what's right,' obliterates the capacity for trust. The customary meanings of words are exchanged for new ones; fair offers from opponents are scrutinized for traps; every smile conceals a dagger.

"Unhealed combat trauma—and I suspect unhealed severe trauma from any source— destroys the unnoticed substructure of democracy, the cognitive and social capacities that enable a group of people to freely construct a cohesive narrative of their own future" (181).

12. See David Tracy, *Plurality and Ambiguity: Hermeneutics, Religion, Hope* (San Francisco: Harper and Row, 1988), 112: "Fundamental trust, as any experience can teach, is not immune to either criticism or suspicion. A religious person will ordinarily fashion some hermeneutics of trust, even one of friendship and love, for the religious classics of her or his tradition. But, as any genuine understanding of friendship shows, friendship often demands both critique and suspicion. A belief in a pure and innocent love is one of the less happy inventions of the romantics. A friendship that never includes critique and even, when appropriate, suspicion is a friendship barely removed from the polite and wary communication of strangers. As Buber showed, in every I-thou encounter, however transient, we encounter some new dimension of reality. But if that encounter is to prove more than transitory, the difficult ways of friendship need a trust powerful enough to risk itself in critique and suspicion. To claim that this may be true of all our other loves but not true of our love for, and trust in, our religious tradition makes very little sense either hermeneutically or religiously."

13. Greenawalt, *Private Consciences and Public Reasons*, 216–17.

14. See Kent Greenawalt, "Propter Honoris Respectum: Diverse Perspectives and the Religion Clauses: An Examination of Justifications and Qualifying Beliefs," *Notre Dame Law Review* 74 (1999): 1441: "If one focuses on legal rather than political or moral justification, the criteria of normative soundness may shift. For legal purposes, perhaps the civil peace justification need not now be persuasive in reality; it may be sufficient that people once believed it, or now believe it." Robert C. Post, *Constitutional Domains* (Cambridge: Harvard University Press, 1995), 174: "The First Amendment establishes a distinct domain of public discourse in order to implement our common belief in such values as neutrality, diversity, and individualism. It follows that the domain of public discourse will extend only so far as these values override other competing commitments, such as those entailed in the dignity of the socially situated self, in the importance of group identity, or in the necessary exercise of community authority. The boundaries of the domain of public discourse are located precisely where the tension between these competing sets of values is most intense, and where some accommodation must consequently be negotiated." Charles Larmore, "Pluralism and Reasonable Disagreement," *Social Philosophy and Policy* 11 (1994): 61: "Liberalism is a distinctively modern political conception. Only in modern times do we find, as the object of both systematic reflection and widespread allegiance and institutionalization, the idea that the principles of political association, being coercive, should be justifiable to all whom they are to bind. And so only here do we find the idea that these principles should rest, so far as possible, on a core, minimal morality which reasonable people can share, given their expectably divergent religious convictions and conceptions of the meaning of life. No longer does it seem evident—as it did, let us say, before the seventeenth century—that the aim of political association must be to bring man into harmony with God's purposes or to serve some comprehensive vision of the good life."

15. Stephen Gardbaum, "Liberalism, Autonomy and Moral Conflict," *Stanford Law Review* 48 (1996): 391.

16. Michael W. McConnell, "Five Reasons to Reject the Claim That Religious Arguments Should Be Excluded from Democratic Deliberation," *Utah Law Review* (1999): 650: "It is the very potency of democratic politics to induce compromise that moderation that causes me, as a religious person, to prefer that my church not engage in politics (except on the most compelling issues of justice, such as abortion and racial reconciliation). When groups identifying themselves with the gospel of Christ enter the political arena, and come to make political alliances and compromises, it is inevitable that they will blunt their religious witness." See too H. Jefferson Powell, *The Moral Tradition of American Constitutionalism: A Theological Interpretation* (Durham: Duke University Press, 1993), 277: "Christians cannot adopt the language of constitutionalism and remain faithful to their own social vision."

17. For a consideration of the liberal uses of empirical rhetoric, see Dan M. Kahan, "The Secret Ambition of Deterrence," *Harvard Law Review* 113 (1999): 413–500.

18. Kenneth L. Karst, "The First Amendment, The Politics of Religion and the Symbols of Government," *Harvard Civil Rights-Civil Liberties Review* 27 (1992): 503–530, 507–8: "Today, the risk of religious polarization does seem to have lessened in the resource-allocation context, where the issues can be seen as part of the everyday grist of the political mill: bargaining among a multitude of interests over the distribution of public resources to various uses—and thus to various groups. Issues concerning governmental deployments of the symbols of religion, however, have a far greater capacity to polarize, for at least two reasons. First, unlike the typical resource-distribution questions ('How much?' 'How soon?'), they are not the subject of multilateral negotiation and they do not invite compromise. Rather, they present yes-no questions that offer no middle ground. A group that has a clear-cut majority and places great importance on an issue of status dominance need not bargain with anyone about that issue. . . . Second, any such symbol has a diffuse meaning, and so serves as a handy referent for a whole world-view, a whole cultural group. It is easy for winners and losers alike to see the symbol not only as a statement about what the town or school stands for, but also as a recognition of who is in charge. . . . The surest way to polarize a community and keep it polarized is to provoke an all-or-nothing struggle centered on a religious group's status dominance."

19. "Democracy is a political system for people who are not sure that they are right." E. E. Schattschneider, quoted in John H. Ely, *On Constitutional Ground* (Princeton: Princeton University Press, 1996), 10. See also Posner, *The Problematics of Moral and Legal Theory,* 22: "If the only reason that virgins are hurled into volcanoes is to make crops grow, empirical inquiry should dislodge the practice. But when human sacrificers do not make falsifiable claims of the efficacy of the practice, so that the issue becomes a choice of ends rather than a choice of means to an agreed end (making the crops grow), our critical voice is stilled. Or rather, it becomes a voice expressing disgust—a reaction to difference— rather than a voice uttering reasoned criticism."

20. "One can always split an economic difference in two—and while half a loaf is better than no bread, half a child, as King Solomon long ago perceived, is not good at all. The same goes for half a religion, half a philosophy, or half a political pinciple." Peter F.

Drucker, "On the 'Economic Basis' of American Politics," *Public Interest* 10 (1968): 30, 35, quoted in Karst, "The First Amendment," 508.

See Jonathan Sacks, *One People? Tradition, Modernity and Jewish Unity* (London: Littman Library of Jewish Civilization, 1993), 147: "Modernity privatizes the religious domain. Liberal theologies, accommodating themselves to social and intellectual change, translate statements about external reality into propositions about believers themselves, and propositions about authority into the vocabulary of personal choice. Religious language, instead of describing a given external and objective order, now designates a chosen internal and subjective reality. Once this move is made, pluralism becomes an intellectual possibility. Statements of objective truth clash in a way that statements about subjective perception do not. When religion no longer contests the public domain, coexistence takes the place of conflict. Because ultimate realities have been internalized, religious movements can see their differences as matters of interpretation rather than truth." See also David Sidorsky, "Moral Pluralism and Philanthropy," *Social Philosophy and Policy* 4 (1987): 100: "The justification for religious tolerance was the similarity of value commitment in the other religion that deserved to be tolerated. In that sense, pluralism required the relegation to insignificance of such 'outward' or secondary aspects of religion as ritual, language, and form and style of worship, and appropriate appreciation of the 'inward' or major substance of moral value. In the parable of Lessing's play *Nathan the Wise,* which is paradigmatic for religious tolerance in the Enlightenment, the authentic magical ring transmitted over generations can only be distinguished from the counterfeit ring by its *moral* powers. All religions share, in this view, the *core* of ethical culture."

Marc Stern, "The Attorney as Advocate," *Texas Tech Law Review* 27 (1996): 1373: "Tolerance on public issues too readily becomes moral indifference. It is hard, and may be disingenuous, to insist that while I am opposed to abortion, and regard it (at least in many cases) as an unspeakable moral wrong, I am prepared to tolerate abortion in the name of other goods. This involves a weighing of competing harms, in which it is often too easy to downgrade the particular religious norm in favor of tolerance."

Jeremy Waldron, " 'Transcendental Nonsense' and System in the Law," *Columbia Law Review* 100 (2000): 42–43: "The separation of law and morality, and the refusal to associate the concept of law with any particular moral theory or social or political program is not just an abstract thesis in jurisprudence. It reflects the reality of almost every developed legal system—that lawmaking takes place in a context of moral disagreement and political competition. And that almost every modern legal system operates politically under the auspices of a multi-party state. Any identification of law with morality, therefore, would not be only theoretically tendentious, but politically poisonous, as each party would accuse the other of abandoning the rule of law simply by virtue of its attempt to implement its own program. Legal positivism is a jurisprudence ready-made for the multi-party situation, the situation in which different moralities and ideologies compete for possession of the commanding heights; other legal philosophies, which deny the separation of law and morality, either have to regard some of the parties in modern political competition as anti-legal or else water down the moral content that they associate with the concept of law to some rather agreeably anodyne values. The very formalism of the positivist account of sovereignty or rules of recognition, which many find distressingly 'thin' and bereft of substance, has its advantages precisely because, on the positivist account, law and the apparatus of lawmaking are understood in terms that are hospitable to various parties and ideologies (each of which, if it had the world to itself, would inject a different substantive content into the concept of law)."

21. Robert Bork, *The Tempting of America: The Political Seduction of the Law* (New York: Free Press, 1990), 124.

22. See Milner Ball, who argues that theology is irenic where legal language is coercive. Ball, *The Word and the Law* (Chicago: University of Chicago Press, 1993): "A commitment to treating others with equal respect forms the ultimate reason why in the face of disagreement we should keep the conversation going, and to that, of course, we must retreat to neutral ground."

23. Michael Walzer, "Drawing the Line: Religion and Politics," *Utah Law Review* (1999): 620.

24. Robert Audi, "Religious Values, Political Action, and Civic Discourse," *Indiana Law Journal* 75 (2000): 280. See also Larry G. Simon, "Racially Prejudiced Governmental Actions: A Motivation Theory of the Constitutional Ban against Racial Discrimination," *San Diego Law Review* 15 (1978): 1041 ff. Everything here turns on how one knows what counts as "the same action."

25. In a similar way, the justification given in law for inquiry into motives is not so much that motives are relevant, but that otherwise, acting on principles such as antidiscrimination would have consequences that are too far-reaching. "A rule that a statute designed to serve neutral ends is nevertheless invalid, absent compelling justification, if in practice it benefits or burdens one race more than another would be far reaching and would raise serious questions about, and perhaps invalidate, a whole range of tax, welfare, public service, regulatory, and licensing statutes that may be more burdensome to the poor and to the average black than to the more affluent white." *Washington v. Davis,* 426 U.S. 229, 248 (1976).

26. See Robert P. George, "Public Reason and Political Conflict: Abortion and Homosexuality," *Yale Law Journal* 106 (1997): 2484: "Rationalist believers do not claim on the basis of secret knowledge or special revelation that their beliefs are publicly justifiable by rational argument; on the contrary, they defend their views precisely by offering public justification, that is, rational arguments in support of the principles and propositions on the basis of which they propose political action. These arguments are either sound or unsound. If sound, there is no reason to exclude the principles and propositions they vindicate as 'illegitimate' reasons for political action. If unsound, then should be rejected—on rationalist believers' own terms—precisely for that reason."

27. See Post, *Constitutional Domains,* 63: "We indicate respect for a person by acknowledging his territory; conversely, we invite intimacy by waiving our claims to a territory and allowing others to draw close. An embrace, for example, can signify human

compassion or desire, but if it is unwelcome it can instead be experienced as a demeaning indignity. The identical physical action can have these two very different meanings only because its significance is constituted by the norms of respect which define personal space."

28. Richard Rorty, "Religion as Conversation-Stopper," *Common Knowledge* 3 (1994): 4.

29. See Walzer, "Drawing the Line," 624: "The authority structures of most of the world's religions are antithetical to those of liberal democracy, and so when we require believers to adhere to the rules of the political arena, we are requiring them to speak and act in unfamiliar ways. Nonetheless, all the major religions have traditions of argument that can be adapted to democratic use—as American Catholic bishops, black Baptist preachers, and liberal rabbis in their different fashions have shown. (Religious groups that refuse to adapt their arguments and join the democratic debate can opt for a sectarian existence—outside the political arena but still protected by its rules.)"

30. See David Hollenbach, "Civil Society: Beyond the Public-Private Dichotomy," *Responsive Community* 5 (1994–95), 22: "Conversation and argument about the common good . . . will not occur initially in the legislature or in the political sphere (narrowly conceived as the domain in which conflict of interest and power are adjudicated). Rather it will develop freely in those components of civil society that are the primary bearers of cultural meaning and value—universities, religious communities, the world of the arts, and serious journalism. It can occur wherever thoughtful men and women bring their beliefs on the meaning of the good life into intelligent and critical encounter with the understandings of this good held by other peoples with other traditions. In short, it occurs wherever education about and serious inquiry into the meaning of the good life takes place."

CHAPTER NINE

Freedom in Amartya Sen and Gustavo Gutiérrez

Religious and Secular Common Grounds

Javier Iguíñiz Echeverría

It is often supposed that those who base their views of the world on perceived religious truth and those who do not will be unable to engage in deep and mutual conversation, for their basic assumptions are just too different. In this essay Javier Iguíñiz Echeverría compares the views of Amartya Sen and Gustavo Gutiérrez on development and human freedom, finding them to share a very great deal in attitude, in fundamental concern, and in intellectual method, even though the former describes himself as without religion, while the latter is profoundly theological. This comparison is of interest and importance both in its own right and as an example of the way the theologically minded can meaningfully converse with those who are not; more than converse, establish a common project or program.

In the world of economists—and development thinkers and practitioners—it is well known that Amartya Sen (Nobel Prize 1998) considers that "development can be seen . . . as a process of expanding the real freedom that people enjoy" (Sen 1999, 3). In the world of theologians and religious social activists it is equally well known that Gustavo Gutiérrez introduced, particularly where religious and political concerns overlap, a new theological proposal defining development as "liberation." In his foundational book in 1971, after making a critical analysis of the mainstream concept of development, he suggests a change in perspective: "This humanistic approach attempts to place the notion of development in a wider context: a historical vision in which mankind assumes control of its own destiny. But this leads precisely to a change of perspective which—after certain additions and corrections—we would prefer to call liberation" (Gutiérrez 1973, 41).[1]

We find, then, the suggestion to replace the term "development" with "liberation"; however, Gutiérrez's main point is not to question the propriety of the former term, but to explore the depth and practical relevance of its meaning. For instance, "the issue of development does in fact find its true place in the more universal, profound, and radical perspective of liberation. It is only within this framework that *development* finds its true meaning and possibilities of accomplishing something worthwhile" (Gutiérrez 1988, 24).[2]

What lies behind this apparent coincidence or, at least, convergence between the approaches of these two thinkers to the meaning of development? In this essay I show that the convergence is not a superficial or accidental one, but that it is based on quite extensive common grounds.

DEVELOPMENT: EXTENDING FREEDOM, LIBERATING

The similarities suggested by the quotations given above seem to be confirmed as we further elicit what development means to each of the writers. In manifesto-style, Gutiérrez asserts that a "broad and deep aspiration for liberation inflames the history of mankind in our day, liberation from all that limits or keeps man from self-fulfillment, liberation from all impediments to the exercise of his freedom" (Gutiérrez 1973, 27).[3] In general terms, and independent of that historical accent, what is meant here by "liberation" seems to be exactly what Sen is talking about when defining "development" (Sen 1999, 36–37): liberation is a means, and the exercise of freedom, an end that requires the widest possible set of opportunities. Moreover, an important exercise of freedom is that which occurs in the act of liberation itself. While Sen is careful to distinguish between substantive and instrumental freedoms, on many occasions they work together.

In our real world, the exercise of freedom requires a process of liberation. "Development requires the removal of major sources of unfreedom: poverty as well as tyranny, poor economic opportunities as well as systematic social deprivation, neglect of public facilities as well as intolerance or overactivity of repressive states" (Sen 1999, 3). For Sen as for Gutiérrez underdevelopment is understood as a restriction on freedom. Sen will say that his "analysis . . . builds on these understandings, in an attempt to throw light on underdevelopment (seen broadly in the form of unfreedom) and development (seen as a process of removing unfreedoms and of extending the substantive freedoms of different types that people have reason to value)" (Sen 1999, 86; see also ibid., 36–37). For Sen, development is thus a process of liberation. Moreover, he insists that the act of liberating oneself is valuable in itself. Gutiérrez insists that the reaction to oppression is already liberation, and part of any solution. In any case, the exercise of freedom includes its use to conquer greater levels of freedom; and to liberate yourself, you must be somewhat free already.

The terms "development" and "freedom" or "liberation" can be related in different ways. Sen's proposal is to consider development *as* freedom. That can mean either that development is understood exclusively in terms of freedom, or that it relates as well to such other social goals as justice, peace, and the like. In my view, Sen opts for widening the meaning of freedom to put it in contact with such other broad spheres of life as economics, politics, and culture. A similar understanding is that of Denis Goulet (1995), for whom freedom is but one component of development, the others being sustenance and esteem. On the other hand, Gutiérrez's original proposal was to replace the concept of development entirely with that of liberation (Goulet 1996). The reason given was that development was a too narrowly "economistic" concept. But even more importantly, development was not capable of leading to the structural roots of the poverty problem and the understanding of the conflictive nature of a true liberation process. Finally, it was a poor way of putting into practice the Bible's call to social action and transformation, for it was assumed that the meaning of the term "development" was static. Once it was seen, however, that the concept itself could be widened, as in the case of Sen's proposal, the need to abandon the term "development" became less urgent.[4]

APPROACHES TO FREEDOM

In a dialogue between religious and nonreligious individuals, the reality and nature of freedom is an important topic. Someone on the religious side might say that God acts without being restricted by human action. Humans are passive intermediaries of God's will. People from a materialistic perspective can be heard to argue that there are laws and principles governing human behavior such that no space is left for human will. Through the work of Amartya Sen and Gustavo Gutiérrez, I explore the questions regarding the existence of freedom in the first part of this section. But its *meaning* in religious and nonreligious perspectives will need clarifying, and that is the topic of the second part.

How Free? How Plural? What Is Being Poor? A Theological Answer

In this part of the essay I put the burden on the religious side on three counts. One is the existence of freedom *vis-à-vis* God, another concerns freedom and pluralism, and the third count involves freedom and the radicality of the religious perspective against poverty. After all, the combination of a belief in an all-powerful God and the long tradition of religious ambiguity about poverty requires a comment.

The Mysterious Encounter of Two Freedoms
As a theologian, Gutiérrez has to deal with the presence of God in history. This in itself is a complex topic, and here I concentrate on the relation between the freedom of God and that of human beings. The nature of this freedom is important for a dialogue with nonreligious individuals. According to Gutiérrez, two things must be kept in mind when seeking to understand the freedom of God. The first is that "God's plan has its origin in the gratuitousness of creative love" (1987, 69). The second is the freedom of humans. Both freedoms are discussed in the book of Job, where the long-suffering Job repeatedly asks God: "Why am I suffering if I am innocent?"

God answers that his freedom transcends human rationality—in this case, our understanding of the proper relation between suffering and guilt. God is not predictable and the world with its wonders have been created out of pure and gratuitous love, but not with the aim that they should become objects for human understanding. The rain does not fall only where humans need it. There is no anthropocentric view of nature here; humans are not the center of the universe. Much less are they able to understand the will of God. The world has been created by God for the pleasure of it, with no contingent relationship to anything else; it is not the effect of any cause. And quoting Gutiérrez, "This is the only motive for creation that can lead to a communion of two freedoms" (Gutiérrez 1987, 71).

Humans must start thinking of God as free. So long as humans try to predict God's behavior, they are in fact limiting, or even eliminating, God's own freedom. Moreover, the explanation of human suffering that attributes it to sinfulness cannot be correct, for Job suffers yet is innocent. The suffering of the innocent, and even that of the non-innocent, escapes easy explanation. But there is another freedom involved here.

Specifically, "God wants justice indeed, and desires that divine judgment (*mishpat*) reign in the world; but God cannot impose it, for the nature of created beings must be respected," continues Gutiérrez, commenting on another part of the book of Job. Here, God provokes Job into asking him to rid the world of injustice. The lesson in God's refusal is that "God's power is limited by human freedom [and that] the all-powerful God is also a 'weak' God" (1987, 77). Therefore, from a theological viewpoint, it is necessary to think of human freedom as if it were not created by God. After all, "Human beings are insignificant in Job's judgment, but they are great enough for God, the almighty, to stop at the threshold of their freedom and ask for their collaboration in the building of the world and in its just governance" (1987, 79). If God stops at the threshold of individual freedom, why should believers not do likewise?

Plurality and Universality

In an address to the Peruvian Academy of the Spanish Language, Gutiérrez reflects on the plurality of languages as a positive trait of human life. Countering the usual reading of the passage in Genesis about the Tower of Babel, he asserts that the plurality of languages can be interpreted as an expression of the freedom of the oppressed *vis-à-vis* imperial homogeneity. In this light, the biblical text should be read as "the painful historical experience of a subjugated people." Therefore, while it is true that "we have here a rejection of the haughtiness of those building the city and the tower," it is also "a political attempt, totalitarian in nature, to dominate nature, to dominate people" (Gutiérrez 1999, 196, 197). According to contemporary interpretations "in the Book of Genesis as a whole the diversity of peoples and languages is presented as a great treasure for humankind and as desired by God" (198).

But, then, "what space remains for universality?" (200). Based on his previous work on Arguedas, a Peruvian novelist and anthropologist (1990, 50–55), Gutiérrez asserts that universality can be found in a provincial setting:

> "A provincial of this world," José María Arguedas calls himself at one point. The human universality toward which Arguedas moves, starting with the Peruvian Indian and *mestizo*, bears the mark of the suffering and hope, the anguish and gentleness of those who are sometimes regarded as human refuse. Far from limiting his perspective, this stamp

gives it breath and effective power. "In the sound of the *charango* and the *quena,* I shall hear *everything,*" he says as he finishes his *Ultimo Diario*? His is the concrete universality which, as Hegel said, is expressed in the singular. (Gutiérrez 1999, 200; also in Nickoloff 1996, 70)

Poverty: Nonvoluntary

The concept of poverty for both Sen and Gutiérrez is complex, and it is especially so from a religious perspective. At one important level, that of material poverty, the coincidence between the two is total. In both we find, in the words of Gutiérrez, "the lack of economic goods necessary for a human life to be worthy of the name." This author continues this way: "In this sense poverty is considered degrading and is rejected by the conscience of contemporary persons. Even those who are not—or do not wish to be—aware of the root causes of this poverty believe that it should be struggled against." To appreciate how he came to this common ground, however, it is useful to see how Gutiérrez clarifies ambiguities typical of the religious approach to this issue. Here I summarize the one that is most immediately relevant for our purposes—namely, that "Christians . . . often have a tendency to give material poverty a positive value, considering it almost a human and religious ideal." This apparently runs counter to "the great aspirations of persons today who want to free themselves from subjection to nature, to eliminate the exploitation of some persons by others, and to create prosperity for everyone."

To complicate things, "the matter becomes even more complex if we take into consideration that the concept of material poverty is in constant evolution. Not having access to certain cultural, social, and political values, for example, is today part of the poverty that persons hope to abolish." With open irony the author continues with a question: "Would material poverty as an 'ideal' of Christian life also include lacking these things?" (1988, 163).

Gutiérrez insists throughout his writings on the critical importance of the same idea of poverty analyzed by Sen: "What we mean by material poverty is a subhuman situation. . . . [T]he Bible also considers it in this way. Concretely, to be poor means to die of hunger, to be illiterate, to be exploited by others, not to know that you are being exploited, not to know that you are a person. It is in relation to this poverty—material and cultural, collective and militant— that evangelical poverty will have to define itself" (Gutiérrez 1988, 164). The point here is clear. Those who consider poverty an option freely assumed cannot avoid taking a stand with respect to the poverty that is not freely assumed, which is quantitatively and qualitatively the more important one. "[I]n the

Bible poverty is a scandalous condition inimical to human dignity and therefore contrary to the will of God" (165).

To summarize, freedom and poverty are contrary to each other, radically opposite. Sen often uses fasting as an illustration to establish its difference with nonchosen poverty. Fasting is undertaken freely, and those who fast voluntarily are not considered poor. In that sense "evangelical poverty," to put it simply, is not poverty.

Multidimensional Freedom

Having roughly sketched the concepts of development and liberation, I now want to uncover the fuller meaning of freedom as articulated both by Gutiérrez and by Sen. Again, my argument in this essay is that there are grounds for a dialogue between these two scholars and their positions regarding freedom. Any such dialogue, however, requires that we take into consideration the multidimensional nature of freedom, as articulated by both authors, and the theological commitments that are specific to Gutiérrez. While I show that there is commonality between Sen and Gutiérrez in their understanding the nature of freedom, I must elucidate the ways in which Gutiérrez's religious approach makes the task of locating a common ground both more and less difficult.

Gustavo Gutiérrez identifies three levels of liberation. The first is society's liberation from international political and economic structures, for which a necessary condition is the achievement of a greater national autonomy. The second level relates to the exercise of personal freedom. The third will emerge only as we explore a religious approach to the matter. Consider the following crucial passage:

> In the first place, *liberation* expresses the aspiration of oppressed peoples and social classes, emphasizing the conflictual aspect of economic, social and political process which puts them at odds with wealthy nations and oppressive classes. . . . At a deeper level, *liberation* can be applied to an understanding of history. Humankind is seen as assuming conscious responsibility of its own destiny. This understanding provides a dynamic context and broadens the horizons of the desired social changes. In this perspective the unfolding of all the dimensions of humanness is demanded—

persons who make themselves throughout their life and throughout history. The gradual conquest of true freedom leads to the creation of a new humankind and a qualitatively different society. This vision provides, therefore, a better understanding of what in fact is at stake in our times. . . . Finally, the word *development* to a certain extent limits and obscures the theological problems implied in the process designated by this term. On the contrary, the word *liberation* allows for another approach leading to the biblical sources which inspire the presence and action of humankind in history. In the Bible, Christ is presented as the one who brings us liberation. Christ the Savior liberates from sin, which is the ultimate root of all disruption of friendship and of all injustice and oppression. (Gutiérrez 1988, 24–25)

One way to understand this passage is to interpret the first liberation Gutiérrez mentions as freedom from dependence, exploitation, and oppression in general, the second as a freedom to expand one's self-understanding and potential beyond historical limits, and the third as a mandate to free oneself from egoism—that is, to love. The second of these three levels of liberation is most often neglected by Gutiérrez's critics. For him, however, "it is not enough that we be liberated from oppressive socio-economic structures; also needed is a personal transformation by which we live with profound inner freedom in the face of every kind of servitude" (1988, xxxviii).

The Freedom to Live Fully in a Democracy

To some extent, the distinction Gutiérrez makes among the levels of freedom resonates with Amartya Sen's thinking, although there are real differences as well. When Sen identifies the "unfreedoms," he includes in the first group being free from hunger and chronic malnutrition, from inadequate health services, and in general, what is the worst failure of all, from the "premature ends" suffered by the poor and women. This last point is recognized also by Gutiérrez and under much the same terms. The claim that people are dying "before it's time" is an extremely important aspect of his views on freedom.

Sen also recognizes that there freedoms proper to the civil and political realm—to democracy (Sen 1999, 15–17). Again, this is an important topic in Gutiérrez: "Freedom and democratic participation are inalienable rights of the human person: these matters are therefore of primordial importance for those in Latin America who are thinking of the construction of a new society" (Gutiérrez 1988, 186).

Subjectivity: The Risk of Accommodation and Evasion

An approach to the problem of freedom that focuses on subjective experience is recognized by both Gutiérrez and Sen, though each expresses reservations. On the one hand, Gutiérrez is concerned with the tendency of the individual not to see the conflictive nature of society and the struggle that is necessary to overcome poverty. On the other hand, in the context of an analysis of the standard of living, Sen is wary of subjective perceptions of reality in general, since very poor people tend to accommodate their feelings and aspirations to what they conceive it possible to achieve. The consequence, then, is that they might live "happily" in the midst or extreme poverty.

Delving further into the notion of the subjectivity of freedom, and owing to his studies in psychology and his pastoral work, Gutiérrez introduced a dimension that was quite rare in the structuralist-minded Latin America of the 1960s and 1970s and, perhaps, even today:

> But modern human aspirations include not only liberation from the *exterior* pressures which prevent fulfillment as a member of a certain social class, country, or society. Persons seek likewise an interior liberation, in an individual and intimate dimension; they seek liberation not only in the social plane but also on a psychological. They seek an interior freedom understood, however, not as an ideological evasion from social confrontation or as the internalization of a situation of dependency. Rather, it must be in relation to the real world of the human psyche as understood since Freud. (1988, 20)[5]

Sen is also sensitive to this aspect of subjective freedom, as revealed in his challenge to utilitarianism and in his perception of the need for more objective criteria to determine the quality of life than that presented by the poor themselves. "Consider a very deprived person who is poor, exploited, overworked and ill, but who has been made satisfied with his lot by social conditioning (through, say, religion, or political propaganda, or cultural pressure). Can we possibly believe that he is doing well just because he is happy and satisfied?" (Sen 1987, 8). Sen obviously distrusts self-perception, without more, as a reliable way to gauge the standard of living. Notable, too, is his observation that religion is a source for the individual's accommodation—or, resigned acceptance—of oppressive conditions.

For Sen, however, the subjective is not entirely absent. For instance, he repeatedly includes in his writings an expression by Adam Smith regarding the needs of the individuals: not to be "ashamed to appear in public" (Sen 1999, 74). Shame is a subjective feeling.

Structural Factors and Interrelations

For both Gutiérrez and Sen, individual freedom is conditioned by structural factors. From the first, these factors were the ones against which Latin American social and political movements of the 1960s and 1970s, armed and unarmed, were fighting. The goal was to replace national and international structures of power with more balanced ones. Agrarian reforms, nationalization of firms, wide-ranging social programs, and the like were to be launched after political independence was completed. Sen writes:

> [T]he freedom of agency that we individually have is inescapably qualified and constrained by the social, political, and economic opportunities that are available to us. There is a deep complementarity between individual agency and social arrangement. It is important to give simultaneous recognition to the centrality of individual freedom *and* to the force of social influences on the extent and reach of individual freedom. To counter the problems that we face, we have to see individual freedom as a social commitment. (1999, xi–xii)

Although some dimensions of freedom have greater importance than others, they all interact in complex ways to enrich and strengthen each other. In the case of Gutiérrez, he is not dealing with "three parallel or chronologically successive processes." Indeed, to him they are "three levels of meaning of a single, complex process" that are interdependent (1988, 25). For Sen, the interrelation is important because "the effectiveness of freedom as an instrument lies in the fact that different kinds of freedom interrelate with one another, and freedom of one type may greatly help in advancing freedom of other types" (Sen 1999, 37).

Liberation "from" and Liberation "to"

A key distinction drawn by Gutiérrez that I can only briefly mention here is that between "freedom from" and "freedom to." A formally similar distinction is also present in Sen, but it lacks an explicit proposal about what to do with the freedom acquired—namely, to love (Gutiérrez 1971: 58), a commitment Sen is not prepared to make. As Sabina Alkire reminds us when writing about Sen, "Capability is . . . a set of vectors of functionings, reflecting the person's freedom to lead one type of life or another . . . to choose from possible livings. It is the presence of this term 'freedom to'—the inherence of free choice in human development—that led Sen to name this distinctive approach the 'capability' approach" (1998, 7).

The concept and implications of freedom have been central in the works of both men whose thinking we have thus far explored. Given his close contact with social and political liberalism, this is not surprising in the case of Sen. As for Gutiérrez, the accentuation of freedom as an essential feature of religious doctrine may not be as commonly understood, but here it is absolutely clear: "[B]iblical faith, . . . besides being memory, is freedom: *openness to the future*" (Gutiérrez 1983, 12).

THE MORAL PERSPECTIVE

There are further striking similarities between Amartya Sen and Gustavo Gutiérrez. These have to do with how each positions himself vis-à-vis reality in terms of a worldview that sees reality as not value free—a worldview that encounters reality at a deeper level than that of its instrumental value. At least four aspects of such a worldview appear to be important.

The Poor

The poor figure prominently in the worldview of each thinker. Both Sen and Gutiérrez give priority to the study of the sociopolitical context of the poor and discuss alternative ways of liberating them. In the preface to a recent work, for example, Sen writes:

> We live in a world of unprecedented opulence, of a kind that would have been hard even to imagine a century ago. . . . And yet we also live in a world with remarkable deprivation, destitution and oppression. . . . Overcoming these problems is a central part of the exercise of development. (Sen 1999, xi, xii)

This resonates clearly with Gutiérrez's perspective. For instance, in analyzing social conflict—that is to say, class struggle—the poor are recognized as those who always suffer the most, from conditions they are powerless to overturn. "By the 'poor' I mean here those whose social and economic condition is the result of a particular political order and the concrete histories of countries and social groups" (Gutiérrez 1988, 156).

Motivation and Commitment

How are these parallel and sometimes converging themes part of a shared intellectual project? To understand the mutual enrichment of the interconnections between these two thinkers, it is necessary that we look behind their intellectual endeavors in order to see what drives them forward. The deepest motivation for both authors, again, is the poor, but crucially, not the "poor" as a category for sociohistorical analysis. Rather, their underlying concern is with the poor themselves, with their suffering, their fate. This motivation is "previous" to the intellectual analyses, which is to say that it is out of the moral dimension of solidarity and identification with the poor that the authors' work arise. In the context of a debate with those who regard the fight against poverty as beneficial for the nonpoor, Sen says clearly: "The first requirement of the concept of poverty is of a criterion as to *who* should be the focus of our concern" (Sen 1991, 9). Scientific inquiry comes only after their identification. That is why

the focus of the concept of poverty is on the well-being of the poor as such, no matter what influences affect their well-being. *Causation* of poverty and *effects* of poverty will be important issues to study in their own rights, and the conceptualization of poverty in terms of the conditions only of the poor does not affect the worthwhileness of studying these questions. (Sen 1991, 10)

The answer to the problem of poverty is not important only as part of a broader cultural or national agenda; the poor are the final end for whatever intellectual work is undertaken in their interest. For Sen, there is no value-free approach to the poverty problem.

Much the same can be said of Gutiérrez, who, among others, has contributed to the Catholic Church's call to making a "preferential option for the poor" (Nickoloff 1996, 12). That too involves an *a priori* identification with the poor and their struggle. Any instrumental value that the alleviation of poverty might have always follows this fundamental commitment.

The convergence of Sen and Gutiérrez on the primacy of the poor, however, also signals the differences between them, insofar as Gutiérrez grounds the option for the poor in God. This option is, above all, God's option out of his pure gratuitousness, not ours (Gutiérrez 1988, 24 ff.).

> The ultimate reason for commitment to the poor and oppressed is not to be found in the social analysis we use, or in human compassion, or in any direct experience we ourselves may have of poverty. These are all doubtless valid motives that play an important part in our commitment. As Christians, however, our commitment is grounded, in the final analysis, in the God of our faith. It is a theocentric, prophetic option that has its roots in the unmerited love of God and is demanded by that love. (Gutiérrez 1988, xxvii)

Our Exclusive Responsibility

That I am comparing in this essay a religious and a nonreligious perspective does not change much the answer to the question about our responsibility. Sen, for instance, recalls Bertrand Russell's once being asked "If God exists, what would you most like to ask him?" Russell responded: "Why did you give so little evidence of your existence?" Similarly for Sen, "certainly the appalling world in which we live does not—at least on the surface—look like one in which an all-powerful benevolence is having its way" (1999, 282). He goes on to say: "It is hard to understand how a compassionate world order can include so many people afflicted by acute misery, persistent hunger, and deprived and desperate lives, and why millions of innocent children have to die each year from lack of food or medical attention or social care."

The difficulty in experiencing God's presence amid suffering and poverty is not lost on Gutiérrez. It informs some of the most challenging aspects of his pastoral work:

> In our continent we pose for ourselves a lacerating question: How to say to the poor person, to the oppressed person, God loves you? Indeed, the daily life of the poor seems to be the result of the denial of love.[6] The absence of love is, in the final analysis of faith, the cause of social injustice. The question of how to tell the poor person "God loves you" is much greater than our capacity to answer it. Its breadth, to use a phrase very

dear to John of the Cross, makes our answers very small. But the question is there, unavoidable, demanding, challenging. (Gutiérrez 1999, 139–40)

The extensive suffering in the world makes religious faith difficult, while religions often show themselves to be troublingly compatible with oppressive social and polititcal structures that are involved in suffering. In any case, as Sen himself asserts, the responsibility for the poor transcends religious faiths:

This issue, of course, is not new, and has been the subject of some discussion among theologians. The argument that God has reasons to want us to deal with these matters ourselves has had considerable intellectual support. As a nonreligious person, I am not in a position to assess the theological merits of this argument. But I can appreciate the force of the claim that people themselves must have responsibility for the development and change of the world in which they live. One does not have to be either a devout or nondevout to accept this basic connection. As people who live—in a broad sense—together, we cannot escape the thought that the terrible occurrence that we see around us is quintessentially our problem. They are our responsibility—whether or not they are also anyone else's. (1999, 282)

This "somebody else" is more than a little important for religious people, but in Gutiérrez, human responsibility for whatever is human is absolutely clear from the beginning of his work. The first excerpt from his work quoted in this essay shows it. This impulse is expressed in the earlier Vatican II document *Gaudium et Spes* 55:

In each nation and social group there is a growing number of men and women who are conscious that they themselves are the architects and molders of their community's culture. All over the world the sense of autonomy and responsibility increases with the effects of the greatest importance for the spiritual and moral maturity of humankind. This will become clearer to us if we advert to the unification of the world and the duty imposed on us to build up a better world in truth and justice. We are witnessing the birth of a new humanism, where people are defined before all else by their responsibility to their sisters and brothers and at the court of history.

Immersion

The final aspect of the worldview we have been exploring is methodological, yet it is also social and personal, and relates to the need for involvement in the process of liberation. Gustavo Gutiérrez is widely known as a social activist (Nickoloff 1996, 2–5; Brown 1990, chap. 2). Sen, while a part of the rarefied world of academic intellectuals, is also an activist of sorts, speaking from and to the civil society: "I have, throughout my life, avoided giving advice to the 'authorities.' Indeed, I have never counseled any government, preferring to place my suggestions and critiques—for what they are worth—in the public domain" (Sen 1999, xiv). Both are active lecturers worldwide, and their writings often are free of technical jargon, making them available to a wide audience. That is why immersion in a life of political and social engagement is essential to an analytical exercise that has to include the ethical dimension. "Ethical truth is in and of human life; it can be seen only from the point of view of immersion" (Nussbaum and Sen 1989, 311).[7]

CONCLUSION

By exploring some of the work of Amartya Sen and Gustavo Gutiérrez on development and freedom, I hope to have shown that there is sufficient common ground for a dialogue on the topic between religious and nonreligious perspectives. The promotion of a greater social commitment is at the core of Sen's and Gutiérrez's work. On the other hand, I have shown that the theological elements in Gutiérrez's work are not an important barrier, or at least, not an insurmountable one, to such a dialogue. Freedom and plurality feature strongly in both authors' writings. The crucial connecting point is, however, the centrality of the poor as an intellectual and moral source of personal commitment.

A further analysis of these thematic commonalities, however, is likely to reveal differences that enrich each other's analysis, particularly concerning freedom. A fuller study of Sen's analysis of the sociocultural and political status of India, read against Gutiérrez's analysis of the same in Latin America, would clarify how their more precise proposals for social action are not identical. Future work is needed to explore these two cultures and the way each is led to accentuate different aspects of the social process.

Finally, and in spite of their common ground, I find that the differences emerging out of the dialogue between the secular and religious perspectives should also be the topic of future work. This paper is an invitation to that dialogue and that study.

NOTES

Ruth Abbey and Bilinda Straight made extensive and formal and substantive suggestions. For their helpful comments, I also thank Rosemary Thorp, Denis Goulet, and the participants in the Faculty Summer Workshop at the Erasmus Institute (University of Notre Dame, June 2000).

1. In this essay I mostly refer to the first English edition of *A Theology of Liberation* (1973), but sometimes I use the 1988 edition in Spanish. For some nonliteral quotations I use the first Spanish edition (1971).

2. The central place of liberation is well recognized. As John Paul II states: "Recently, in the period following the publication of *Populorum Progressio,* a new way of confronting the problems of poverty and underdevelopment has spread in some areas of the world, especially in Latin America. This approach makes *liberation* the fundamental category and the first principle of action." *Sollicitudo Rei Socialis: On Social Concern* 46 (1987).

3. It would be interesting to analyze the historical process to which the quotation refers. Recently it has been said that "[i]n the last years, in the big capital cities in the southern hemisphere, the word freedom rises great multitudes that previously only the word independence could congregate" (Hussein 1993, 19).

4. Both these views are clearly different from development for freedom, or freedom in order to develop. In both cases, one would be the instrument of the other, and while they may function this way, neither of the terms can be reduced to that role alone.

5. For a summary and new and further developments, see Gutiérrez 1999, 188–93.

6. I would have preferred: "the equivalent to a denial of love."—J.I.E.

7. "Sen and Nussbaum distinguish two forms of ethical inquiry about development. The externalist or Platonic model is one in which 'rational criticism is detached and external.' From a transcendent, and a-historical standpoint, the ethicist looks down and 'recommends certain values as best for the development and flourishing of a people' and excludes 'any influence from the beliefs of those people as to what lives are best to live, or from wishes as to the sort of lives they want to live." David A. Crocker, "Toward Development Ethics," in *Economics, Ethics, and Public Policy,* ed. Charles K. Miller (Oxford: Rowman and Littlefield, 1998), 320.

WORKS CITED

Alkire, Sabina. 1998. Operationalizing Amartya Sen's Capability Approach to Human Development: A Framework for Identifying "Valuable" Capabilities. Ph.D. diss., Magdalen College, Oxford University.

Brown, Robert McAfee. 1990. *Gustavo Gutiérrez: An Introduction to Liberation Theology.* New York: Orbis Books.

Goulet, Denis. 1995. *Development Ethics: A Guide to Theory and Practice.* New York: Apex Press.

———. 1996 [1971]. " 'Development'—or Liberation?" In Jameson and Wilber 1996.

Gutiérrez, Gustavo. 1971. *Teología de la liberación.* Lima: CEP.

———. 1973. *A Theology of Liberation.* New York: Orbis Books.

———. 1983. *The Power of the Poor in History.* New York: Orbis Books.

———. 1986. *La verdad los hará libres.* Lima: IBC-R-CEP.

———. 1987. *On Job: God-Talk and the Suffering of the Innocent.* New York: Orbis Books.

———. 1988. *A Theology of Liberation.* Rev. ed. New York: Orbis Books.

———. 1990. *Entre las calandrias: Un ensayo sobre José María Arguedas.* Lima: IBC-R-CEP.

———. 1999. *The Density of the Present: Selected Writings.* New York: Orbis Books.

Hussein, Mahmoud. 1993. *Vertiente sur de la libertad.* 2d. ed. Barcelona: Icaria and Antrazyt.

Jameson, Kenneth P., and Charles K. Wilber, eds. 1996. *The Political Economy of Development and Underdevelopment.* 6th ed. New York: McGraw-Hill.

Nickoloff, James B. 1996. *Gustavo Guitérrez: Essential Writings.* New York: Orbis Books.

Nussbaum, Martha, and Amartya Sen. 1989. "Internal Criticism and Indian Rationalist Traditions." In *Relativism, Interpretation, and Confrontation,* ed. Michael Krausz. Notre Dame, Ind.: University of Notre Dame Press. Taken from David A. Crocker, "Toward Development Ethics," in *Economics, Ethics, and Public Polic,* ed. Charles K. Wilber Lanham: Rowman and Littlefield, 1998), 320.

Sen, Amartya. 1987. *The Standard of Living.* Cambridge: Cambridge University Press.

———. 1988. "The Concept of Development." In *Handbook of Development Economics,* ed. Hollis Chenery and T. N. Srinivasan. Elsevier Science Publishers.

———. 1991. *Poverty and Famines: An Essay on Entitlement and Deprivation.* Oxford: Clarendon Press.

———. 1998. "Teorías del desarrollo a principios del siglo XXI." In *El desarrollo económico y social en los umbrales del siglo XXI,* ed. Louis Emmerij and José Núñez del Arco. Washington, D.C.: Banco Interamericano de Desarrollo.

———. 1999. *Development as Freedom.* New York: Knopf.

CHAPTER TEN

The Primary Enemy?

Monotheism and Pluralism

Ruth Abbey

Does a monotheistic religion necessarily commit its adherents to a view of the world that denies the reality and value of pluralism? So argues Stuart Hampshire, who claims that this kind of religion necessarily entails a single, and universal, conception of the good. In this essay Ruth Abbey argues that a deep commitment to monotheism is in fact compatible with a pluralism, showing in particular how Charles Taylor has brought both elements into productive tension, and in several domains: his moral philosophy, his philosophy of the self, and his politics.

> *The primary enemy [of pluralism] is monotheism.*
> —Stuart Hampshire, *Justice Is Conflict*

Social and ethical pluralism are central issues in much contemporary political theory.[1] This reflects the increasing reality of, and significance attached to, diversity within Western societies. It is also due in part to the influence of Isaiah Berlin's seminal work on the topic.[2] Berlin defines pluralism as "the conception that there are many different ends that men may seek and still be fully rational, fully men, capable of understanding each other and sympathizing and deriving light from each other" (1990, 11). Stuart Hampshire and Charles Taylor are two important contributors to current debates about the political ramifications of ethical and social pluralism, and both grapple with these questions in the wake of Berlin's writings.[3] Yet they reach startlingly different, indeed incompatible, conclusions about the relationship between religion and pluralism. In this essay I provide an overview of Hampshire's argument and present it as a foil to the pluralism of Charles Taylor. This contrast is grounded in Hampshire's claim that any variety of monotheism must entail an antipluralist stance. Because Christianity is the font of so much of his pluralism, Taylor's work frontally challenges Hampshire's proposition.

HAMPSHIRE: PLURALISM AND PROCEDURALISM

For a short work, Stuart Hampshire's *Justice Is Conflict* (2000a) is remarkably wide ranging and suggestive. It also reprises some of the themes of Hampshire's 1983 work *Morality and Conflict,* and is heavily indebted to his 1991 article "Justice Is Strife." These works testify to Hampshire's belief in the reality, durability, and irreducibility of ethical differences among groups and individuals within and between societies: "Conceptions of the good, ideals of social life, visions of individual virtue and excellence, are infinitely various and diverse, rooted in the imagination and in the memories of individuals and in the preserved histories of cities and of states" (2000a, xi. Cf. 1983, 141, 148). This conviction that pluralism is the natural condition of humans no doubt informs, and probably even explains, his perception of the ubiquity of conflict in social life. Or rather, Hampshire seems to suggest that even if conflict itself is not always erupting, the potential for it to do so is pervasive. In this regard, his position resembles the Hobbesian analysis of life in the state of nature where even if conflict is not always breaking out, its possibility is omnipresent.[4] Hampshire thus portrays the possibility of conflict not as some aberrant inflammation among otherwise harmonious individuals, but rather as the normal condition of diverse human beings. Another way in which he continues Hobbes's thinking is to locate conflict at two levels of human life: it exists as an inner, psychic reality and manifests itself in relations among human beings. As Hampshire sees it, "every soul is always the scene of conflicting tendencies and of divided aims and ambivalences, and correspondingly, our political enmities in the city or state will never come to an end while we have diverse life stories and diverse imaginations" (2000, 5. Cf. 34).

But this conception of humans as different from one another—and aware of their differences—with the attendant conflict that this always threatens is not the whole of Hampshire's picture. He identifies the human capacity for reason as a countervailing force, mitigating the centrifugal tendencies of pluralism. Thus for him social life expresses two separate but equal human capacities: the prolific imagination and the integrating intellect. While the imagination dwells in the realm of the particular, focusing on and enhancing differences among individuals, the intellect is a conciliating force, pushing toward consensus and making possible shared beliefs about how such diverse and divergent individuals should live together (2000a, x–xi, 20–21). Although at one point Hampshire associates the human ability to reason with the transcultural truths of logic and mathematics (2000a, 20), his focus is really the sort of practical reason and argument associated with legal reasoning: the ability to hear both sides of an argument, to weigh and measure competing claims, to consider the relevant evidence, and so on (2000a, 40, 80, 95–96).

In fact, the crucial feature of Hampshire's brand of proceduralism, which affords it legitimacy over and above the contentions dividing the disputants, is the fact that it is premised on and committed to "adversary reasoning" (2000a, xi). This involves a determination to hear both, or all, sides of an argument in as unbiased a way as possible. Hampshire locates this sort of reasoning at the core of justice. This explains his claim that justice is essentially procedural: it reigns when routine, generally accepted, and indeed respected processes exist for reconciling disputes. In a traditionally liberal move, he effectively promotes the priority of the right over the good: justice involves the creation and reproduction of a set of overarching rules and conventions within which the contending parties are willing to maneuver. At times he even calls this conception "justice as fairness," signaling his allegiance with the proceduralism of John Rawls.[5]

Because the sort of reasoning required for procedural justice (or adversary reasoning or justice as fairness) is born of the intellect, and because the intellect is the unifying, convergent aspect of the human personality, Hampshire can go on to claim that this sort of reasoning is a universal phenomenon. His logic can be reconstructed in the following way:

- procedural reasoning is the central aspect of justice;
- procedural reasoning is the fruit of the intellect;
- intellect is a universal human capacity;
- this sort of justice is universal.

Expressing his belief in the universality of procedural reasoning, he declares that "fairness in procedures for resolving conflicts . . . is acknowledged as a value in most cultures, places and times: fairness in procedure is an invariable value, a constant in human nature" (2000a, 4. Cf. xi, 36, 46, 52–53, 87). Conversely, the absence, or even occasional failure, of this type of reasoning always and everywhere betokens injustice (2000a, 17).

One of Hampshire's explanations for adversary reasoning's being such a universal phenomenon lies in the close connection he posits between inner and outer, or selfhood and politics. Just as pluralism and division are intrapsychic as well as social facts, so the weighing of pros and cons in an attempt to reach a fair conclusion is an internal process of deliberation as much as a public one. The self that deliberates with itself about the right decision or fair outcome is a microcosm of social procedures of adversary reasoning (2000a, 5, 7). Here Hampshire accepts the homologic structure of Platonic thought— the just polis is the just person writ large—but amends the content, replacing Platonic harmony with pluralist polyphony (2000a, 4).

Yet Hampshire vacillates about where the initiative lies in this relationship between the deliberative self and the adversary reasoning of politics. In the first part of the book he locates it in the public domain, so that the individual engages in intramural negotiations because she has witnessed and can emulate the public processes of adversary reason. Thus "the inner mental uses . . . duplicate" and are the "shadow" of . . . the observable public activities" (2000a, 7). Shortly after, the terms "shadow" and "duplicate" are again applied to inner deliberations and we read that "[t]he public situations . . . *give rise to* corresponding mental processes which are *modelled* on the public procedures" (2000a, 9 [emphasis added]). Some pages later the idea of inner processes of deliberation copying outer ones recurs: "[W]e learn to transfer, by a kind of mimicry, the adversarial pattern of public life and interpersonal life onto a silent stage called the mind. The dialogues are internalized, but they still do not lose the marks of their origin in interpersonal adversarial argument" (2000a, 11–12).

Later in the book, however, the impetus for adversary reasoning begins in the subjective realm, with the public processes being a consequence of the experience of inner deliberation. Consider Hampshire's claim that at "first hand we know about the reflective balancing of pros and cons from which we have to construct some degree of consistency in action and in attitude for ourselves, and for this reason we can recognize and respond to the contrarieties of political debate and public argument" (2000a, 72). The priority of inner deliberation is echoed in a later remark: "[E]veryone has adversaries within his own soul and is in this way already prepared to step out onto the political or legal stage and to argue his case. He has already rehearsed the fairness of a

statement followed by a rebuttal, followed by restatement, in his own thinking" (2000a, 93–94). At one point Hampshire seems to suggest that the family
is an important school for teaching or promoting the art of fair deliberation
(2000a, 95). If so, this falls neither into the category of introspection nor the
public realm. It also poses the further question of whether all families really
do this and what form of family might do it best.[6] These observations about
the shifting locus of initiative should not be mistaken for pedantry or queru-
lousness. An advocate of adversary reasoning, Hampshire acknowledges that
it can falter and even degenerate into violence, and therefore he presumably
wants to strengthen and foster it. It thus seems imperative that he indicate
whether it is learned initially through introspection or from exposure to public processes of deliberation,[7] for this will have consequences for arguments
about institutional design and should shape and direct the efforts put into its
consolidation.

While the sort of proceduralism Hampshire outlines is universal, it is not
only universal; it is inevitably colored by local particularities and historical
contingencies. In any society, the processes that provide a means of arbitrat-
ing conflict are themselves the outcome of compromises and the arbitration
of earlier conflicts (2000a, 40, 58). The fact that this sort of mechanism for dispute resolution has to be institutionalized is another way in which it will be
colored by local particularities. So the general principle of hearing the other
side can be realized in a variety of ways. Pluralism and particularism thus re-
enter the picture Hampshire sketches of justice as this second face of proceduralism (2000a, 54–55, 97).

Yet it is hard to know how this quintessentially liberal approach to justice
justifies the book's title. As the foregoing account of Hampshire's position
suggests, justice seems to be opposed to, rather than synonymous or coextensive with, conflict. The term "justice" encompasses the way different societies
instantiate the universal human capacity for reasonableness, fairness, and listening to the other side in procedures that come to be accepted by all members of society. The function of justice is to negotiate conflicts; it might not
always resolve and will never remove them, but its role is one of mediating
conflict rather than being conflict.[8] As I see it, the closest Hampshire's analysis comes to warranting the work's title is on those few but fascinating occasions when he suggests that there might be more to justice than the account
of proceduralism that occupies so much of the book. I detect evidence of two
related remainders in the book: first, when Hampshire distinguishes between
procedural and substantive justice and allows that fair procedures can coexist

with unjust conditions, and second, when he acknowledges that the justice of the procedures themselves can come into contention.

The most obvious way in which a conception of justice can exceed proceduralism appears in Hampshire's distinction between justice as substance and as process. He concedes, for example, that seemingly fair rules and conventions can oversee and regulate an unjust "game," citing the institution of slavery (2000a, 30). Elsewhere he departs from the standard proceduralist view that any outcome reached according to the canons of fair procedure is *ipso facto* fair by conceding that one can respect the procedures as just but deplore the outcome (2000a, 46). Both these scenarios suggest that proceduralism does not exhaust the demands of justice.[9] Yet Hampshire's aim is to persuade his readers that "fairness in procedures for resolving conflicts is *the fundamental kind of fairness*" (2000a, 4 [emphasis added]). One reason for the priority accorded to proceduralism seems to be its universality. As debates about substantive justice are subject to the sort of pluralism and particularism identified above, they are demoted to second-rate candidates for consideration in the analysis of justice. Although it is precisely these various and particular disputes that generate the need for proceduralism (2000a, 4–5), proceduralism is accorded primacy in Hampshire's hierarchy of justice, perhaps because it is less vulnerable to diversity. Hampshire also recommends that the best way to proceed with these substantive disputes about justice is to take the proceduralist route (2000a, 28). However, this recommendation becomes problematic in light of the second, related area of slippage between justice and proceduralism.

This second sign of slippage appears at those points when Hampshire acknowledges that the procedures themselves can become the object of debate about justice and can be susceptible to charges of injustice (2000a, 28–29, 97). In such cases, justice cannot simply be equated with the routine procedures of conflict mediation; rather the meaning of justice itself becomes contested. However, instead of exploiting this tension to enrich his understanding of justice, Hampshire resolves it by saying that when such disputes occur within a framework of debate, arbitration, and hearing the other side, they are still reflecting "the universal principle of adversary argument" (2000a, 29). Presumably when such disputes do not take place within some such framework, the situation degenerates into violence, coercion, and, dare I suggest, conflict.

The point of these remarks is not simply to register uncertainty about the fit between the book's title and its import. They also pose some questions about the extent of Hampshire's pluralism, for he seems not simply to point to the need for procedure to regulate diversity, but to privilege the universal over the particular in a more fundamental way. In fact, a close reading of his text reveals its reliance on a series of traditional binary oppositions, such as those between unity and diversity; intellect and imagination; procedure and substance; reason and passion; necessity and contingency; absolute and relative; universal and local. This set of contrasts not only underpins Hampshire's position but the burden of his argument prioritizes the former over the latter in each of these cases. For present purposes, what is especially revealing about this is not just that it shows Hampshire's pluralism to be more limited and qualified than it initially seems, but also that (with the exception of the priority of procedure over substance), these are just the sort of contrasts and priorities that would characterize the sort of religious approach to ethical and political reasoning that he is at such pains to repudiate. To defend this interpretation, it is necessary to review the reasons why Hampshire pits his own pluralist position so implacably against monotheism.[10] This review will also pave the way for a discussion of the ways in which Charles Taylor's work challenges Hampshire's assertions about religion and pluralism.

It is clear from the outset that Hampshire is striving for an approach to ethics and politics that does not rely on foundations (2000a, ix–x), and in this sense he can be seen as continuing the quest to articulate a postmodern defense of liberalism initiated by Richard Rorty.[11] Hampshire's criticisms of monotheism are best understood against the wider background of this loss of faith in foundationalism. Characterizing his preferred approach as "aggressively secular and liberal" (2000a, 51), he declares that the sort of pluralism he champions is utterly incompatible with monotheism. This is because monotheism necessarily yields ethical monism and moral universalism: because there is one God, there is a single conception of the good that must apply, and should be applied, to all (2000a, 42, 51).[12] When monotheism is accompanied by an image of God as the benevolent and omnipotent creator, it establishes the expectation that the (only) correct moral code will be complete, well ordered and internally consistent, unblemished by lacuna or contradiction (2000a, 70). From this perspective, the sort of ethical pluralism Hampshire celebrates signifies error and deviation. As he sees it, the "opposite of monotheism and of this mono-moralism is the recognition of polymorphous ideals and of diverse conceptions of the good, tempered by respect for the local conventions and rules of conflict resolution" (2000a, 52).[13]

Before embarking on a discussion of the ways in which the thought of Charles Taylor threatens Hampshire's stark opposition between monotheism and pluralism, let me briefly indicate some of the questions about religion generated from within Hampshire's own analysis. First, as a pluralist who revels in human diversity, Hampshire is surprisingly dogmatic about, and dismissive of, religion. At one point he refers to "those men [sic] of religion who are disgusted by the easy going tolerance of secular liberals" (2000b, 80), yet it seems that Hampshire is in little danger of earning their contempt. There is little of the easygoing or tolerant about his approach to monotheism. And what his earlier depiction of the "aggressively secular" adds in honesty and self-awareness, it does so at the cost of pluralism.

A related way in which Hampshire's hostility toward monotheism clashes with his profession of pluralism comes in his portrayal of values that are universal but negative. He observes that many different ethical outlooks or worldviews agree in defining certain experiences as evil and to be avoided or minimized when possible. These anathema include war, violence, physical suffering, poverty, starvation, and tyranny. Let us leave aside the fact that many of the monotheistic religions contain long-standing and significant traditions that deplore these same evils.[14] In Hampshire's estimation, human beings only fail to define these anathema as evil when laboring under some form of "false consciousness" such as religion (2000a, xii). This is clearly a mirror-image of the sort of moral universalism he decries in monotheism, albeit of the negative variety. Here Hampshire has to explain away as mistaken or deceived those who do not subscribe to his values and assessments.

This ready dismissal of religious interpretations of life is also at odds with his account of the role of feeling and imagination in human history and society, which are important sources and expressions of diversity. Discussing the multifarious products of the imagination, which explicitly include the moral imagination, he writes:

> These are activities that we expect to vary vastly in form and content in different places, in different social groups, at different times in history, and in distinguishable cultures. We not only expect the diversity; we positively demand it. Their diversity . . . helps to establish the identity of distinct populations and of cultures. (2000a, 20. Cf. 21)

Exempting religious interpretations of life from this wondrous fecundity seems not only historically and culturally insensitive but, from a theoretical standpoint, arbitrary.

TAYLOR: PLURALISM AND RELIGION

Whatever the internal inconsistencies in Stuart Hampshire's account of religion, a powerful external challenge to the antagonism he posits between monotheism and pluralism can be found in the thought of Charles Taylor. One of the enduring features of Taylor's work across its many departments has been an awareness and celebration of pluralism, and an obverse resistance to reductionism of problems and standardization or homogenization of solutions. Aristotle has been an important inspiration for Taylor's pluralism, but fittingly, it is not limited to a single source. He is increasingly drawing attention to Christianity as a wellspring for this too. A Catholic of ecumenical outlook, Taylor describes himself as "a Christian [who] finds greatness in some facets of Islam, Judaism, Buddhism" (1991, 241. Cf. 1994, 226, 229). As well as appreciating some of the goods of other religious traditions, Taylor promotes pluralism within Catholicism. He proposes that "a Catholic principle . . . is no widening of the faith without an increase in the variety of devotions and spiritualities and liturgical forms and responses to Incarnation" (1999a, 15). In this section I highlight the powerful pluralism in Taylor's moral theory, his theory of the self, and his political philosophy, indicating how he links each of these with the Christian tradition.

When it comes to moral theory, Taylor insists that the domain of the moral includes quite different goods: some are universal, others obtain within a more limited collectivity such as the nation, while yet others are more particular and individual to cultures or groups (1985, 244; 1997). As this suggests, he believes that in any person's life there is always a multiplicity of goods to be recognized, acted on, and pursued. These goods are not only plural in the numerical sense, they are plural in an ontological sense; they are of qualitatively different types from one another, and because of this cannot always be harmoniously combined, rank-ordered, nor reduced to some more ultimate or foundational good. In emphasizing the qualitatively different yet valuable things to be incorporated in a good or fully human life, Taylor's ontological pluralism is directed against the sort of ethical monism and reductionism of such doctrines as classical utilitarianism. In this he finds common cause with Hampshire, who, as noted, also attacks the monism and universalism of utilitarianism.

But for Taylor, individuals are not just faced with multiple goods: we must also confront the fact that some of the things worthy of affirmation are irreconcilable with others. "There is no guarantee that universally valid goods should be perfectly combinable, and certainly not in all situations" (1989, 61). This means that individuals must choose among a range of goods that vie for their allegiance or attachment in the knowledge that the goods not chosen are nonetheless worthy of affirmation. From this pluralist point of view, moral choices are hard and necessarily entail sacrifice and loss. Taylor describes modern human beings as "always in a situation of conflict between moral demands, which seem to them irrecusable, but at the same time uncombinable. If this conflict is not felt, it is because our sympathies or horizons are too narrow, or we have been too easily satisfied with pseudo-solutions" (1994, 213).

Little, if anything, in Taylor's approach to morality meets the expectation Hampshire derives from monotheism: that it will yield a single, complete, coherent and contradiction-free moral code and disdain ethical pluralism as error or deviation. Yet Taylor implies that because the monotheism of Judaism, Christianity, and Islam hold the Creator to have proclaimed creation to be good, there is much in the world to affirm. This also means that in forgoing some of these things, the believer is facing the loss of something genuinely good. Taylor contrasts this with the Stoic outlook, which tries to transvalue or reappraise those goods that cannot be realized as not worth having anyway. He provides a dramatic illustration of the contrast between the Stoic and monotheistic outlooks by comparing the death of Jesus with that of Socrates. What Jesus' passion in the garden communicates is that his imminent death will bring not only suffering, but also the loss of something valuable—his mortal life. Socrates' rationalism in prison conveys the opposite: dying is a relief and a release and the loss of mortal life is not worth mourning. At a more general level, Taylor describes the difference thus:

> The great difference between Stoic and Christian renunciation is this: for the Stoic, what is renounced is, if rightly renounced, *ipso facto* not part of the good. For the Christian, what is renounced is thereby affirmed as good—both in the sense that the renunciation would lose its meaning if the thing were indifferent and in the sense that the renunciation is in furtherance of God's will, which precisely affirms the goodness of the things renounced: health, freedom, life. Paradoxically, Christian renunciation is an affirmation of the goodness of what is renounced. For the Stoic, the loss of health, freedom, life does not affect the integrity of the good. On the contrary, the loss is part of a whole which is integrally good and couldn't be changed without making it less so. (1989, 219)

While this is by no means a comprehensive account of Taylor's approach to morality, it does convey some sense of its thoroughgoing pluralism and challenges Hampshire's depiction of monotheism as necessarily issuing in ethical monism.[15] More generally, Taylor believes that one of the important functions of philosophy is to bring to light the multiple goods by which modern individuals live, to show their plurality and different sources (1989, 105, 502). He hopes that one of the consequences of articulating this plurality will be to reduce the appeal of simplistic and reductionist normative theories that try to artificially harmonize different goods or that deny the reality of conflicting goods (1989, 107).

Further evidence of the relationship between Christianity and pluralism in Taylor's work comes in his approach to selfhood. A major portion of his chief work, *Sources of the Self*, traces the changing understandings of what it is to be a person that he identifies as pivotal in the history of Western thought and in the formation of the modern identity. The peculiarly modern Western self that Taylor constructs through his historical narrative is clearly a multifaceted one. As he says, "our identities . . . are complex and many-tiered" (1989, 28–29). In the complexities, ambiguities, and tensions that emerge from Taylor's portrait of the modern notion of selfhood, we witness his pluralism forcefully (1985, 273, 276–77, 287) and appreciate anew his claim that becoming aware of the multifariousness of the modern self should caution against reductionist or unitary theories of morality. In both cases he hopes that uncovering the complexity of the modern self and its different strands will free people from the tendency to deny and stifle the plurality of goods that modern selves effectively, if not always knowingly, affirm (1989, 112, 503, 511, 514, 520). Taylor thus shares Nietzsche's powerful awareness of the multiplicity and complexity of the modern self, but it seems that, for him, the most useful template for thinking about humans as inherently plural is theistic. Taylor claims, for example, that "human diversity is part of the way in which we are made in the image of God," and links this to the trinitarian view of God as three persons in one (1999a, 14–15).

Taylor's pluralism informs his view of politics as much as it does his moral theory and approach to selfhood. For him, politics always involves complexity and conflicts, and it is a dangerous fantasy to believe that any single principle or formula will be adequate in resolving these. The sort of decisionmaking involved in politics demands something closer to Aristotle's notion of practical wisdom than the appeal to any basic principle that can be invoked to resolve all disputes.

There are always a plurality of goods, vying for our allegiance, and one of the most difficult issues is how to combine them, how to adjudicate at the places where they come into conflict, or mutually restrict each other. I have no difficulty with the idea that offering the greatest scope for different modes of life and conceptions of the good is *an* important goal. I cavil at the idea that it can be *the* goal; that is, that it doesn't have at certain points to compose with other ends, which will require its limitation. (1994, 250 [emphasis in original])[16]

Christianity provides the inspiration not just for Taylor's thinking about pluralism but also for some of his solutions to the political dilemmas and conflicts this poses. A good illustration of this can be found in his analysis of democratic exclusion. While the progress of democracy over the centuries from ancient Athens to the present day can be seen as a process of increasing inclusion and widening franchise, Taylor also identifies a dynamic of exclusion in the logic of democracy (1998; 1999b). His argument runs as follows. In order for the democratic principle of popular sovereignty to be realized or even conceptualized, an entity, a people, that can rule itself is required. That body must be capable of common deliberation and the formation of a shared will. This need not require unanimity, but it does entail the idea that there is a will or opinion held by the majority of people that guides decisionmaking. In the modern world, this idea of the people, of the self-ruling collective entity, has typically been conceived as the citizenry of a state, and the state has typically been construed as a nation-state. With the rise of nationalism, the state has been seen as providing not only the forum for self-government, but as an important source of a common cultural identity. To describe this as the dominant idea is not to deny the reality of multicultural societies nor of nationalist and secessionist movements. However, secessionist drives serve to confirm this understanding of popular sovereignty by proposing that "we" belong to a different people from "you," our rulers, and that as a separate people we are entitled to rule ourselves.

As this point about secessionist impulses signals, democracy's conception of popular sovereignty requires a high degree of cohesion and mutual trust. Those who belong to the collective democratic entity must identify with it to some degree and so must identify with one another to some extent. They must be willing to listen to, and believe themselves to be heard by, their fellows. Yet according to Taylor, it is just this need for a cohesive common identity that generates exclusion in democratic societies. For example, an ethnic minority might see itself or be seen by others as not being part of the group. Immigrants might be compelled to assimilate to the dominant culture before they can be accepted as full participants in political society. Women or gay people or disabled ones might be seen as not really fitting into politics at the highest levels, and so on. Yet this dynamic of exclusion runs counter to the democratic ethos that emphasizes equality, participation, and rule by the people. Taylor summarizes the situation thus:

> Democracies are in a standing dilemma. They need strong cohesion around a political identity, and precisely this provides a strong temptation to exclude those who can't or won't fit easily into the identity which the majority feels comfortable with, or believes can hold them together. And yet exclusion, besides being profoundly morally objectionable, also goes against the legitimacy idea of popular sovereignty, which is to realize the government of *all* the people. The need to form a people as a collective agent runs against the demand for inclusion of all who have a legitimate claim on citizenship. (1999b, 156 [emphasis in original])

Democracy's logic of exclusion is not, however, insuperable, and in Western societies many groups are challenging the demand that they conform in order to belong. Taylor predicts that democracies will face the ongoing challenge of reinventing themselves and finding new ways of including minority groups. The understandable temptation in this context is simply to advocate the liberal ideals of individual rights, a neutral state, and the priority of the right over the good (1998, 151). But for Taylor, more of the same is too limited a response to accommodating increasing expressions of diversity. He believes that new understandings of democratic belonging and less rigid conceptions of citizenship will need to be forged (1998, 150–51). Inspired by the work of Wilhelm von Humboldt, he adumbrates an alternative model of democratic inclusion, one that celebrates the differences among groups and encourages citizens not simply to tolerate but to learn about and engage with one another, understanding that their differences enrich one another and the polity as a whole (1998, 153–54). For Taylor, the ideal underlying this model is the Christian one—that the fullness of humanity can not be achieved by any individual alone but only through interaction with others who realize different aspects of human potential (1998, 153).[17] Here we see another way in which

Taylor's awareness of and respect for diversity is informed by the Christian tradition.[18]

This gesture in a Humboldtian direction might seem like a rather loose response to the problem, but Taylor is suspicious of generalized remedies to such intractable problems and aware of the limited contribution philosophy can make. How any particular democratic polity reconciles belonging with diversity will depend on its own culture and complexion and cannot be decided from without (1998, 151).

CONCLUSION

This is not the first time an argument has been adduced about the role of religion in Charles Taylor's thought.[19] However, as Taylor becomes increasingly explicit about the nexus between his religious beliefs and his philosophy, long-standing and characteristic features of his outlook appear in a new light. One such enduring and typical feature of his thought is his concern with pluralism, and an examination of the different ways in which Christianity has shaped his pluralism shows just how crude is the antagonism Stuart Hampshire posits between them.

Of course, the connections Taylor draws between Christianity and pluralism do not demonstrate that monotheism never issues in an antipluralist stance. Hampshire's analysis might be apposite for some varieties of monotheism. But given that he presents the antithesis between monotheism and pluralism as a necessary one, his argument requires modification insofar as Taylor's argument has any substance. How persuasive Taylor's position is remains to be seen; at this stage his remarks about the relationship between Christianity and pluralism are preliminary and gestural. They need to be developed and defended. Even when or if Taylor elaborates on these claims, they will stand as one among many interpretations of the relationship between Catholicism and pluralism. He will never be licensed to speak for the whole of Catholicism, let alone the whole of Christianity. It should be apparent that Taylor is staking out a position within Catholicism that would be resisted and contested from many quarters within that tradition, let alone those outside it. What these observations portend is the need not only to resist the false alternative Hampshire forces on us between monotheism and pluralism, but to deconstruct that putative opposition in order to better appreciate the plurality within monotheistic religions. Only then can the debate about religion and pluralism usefully proceed.

So this is obviously not the last word on the link between religion and pluralism in Taylor's work. Precisely because he has only recently become more explicit about the way his religious beliefs have shaped his thought, analysis of their connection is only beginning. William Connolly, for example, is a self-identified post-Nietzschean who nonetheless expresses admiration for many aspects of Taylor's thought. He is sceptical, however, about how consistent and robust Taylor's pluralism is in the face of nontheistic moral sources (Connolly 2004). But Connolly makes no suggestion that the religious foundations of Taylor's thinking render it impossible for him to appreciate nontheistic views as moral sources worthy of respect, if not allegiance. He does not assert the sort of *a priori* contradiction between religion and pluralism *à la* Hampshire. On the contrary, Connolly is pointing to inconsistencies and weaknesses in Taylor's practice as a pluralist and urging him to become more consistent in this. He is not denying its very possibility.[20]

One way of explaining the clash between Hampshire and Taylor is to deploy the distinction between strong and weak ontology proposed by Stephen K. White (2000). From this vantage point, Hampshire has classified all monotheism as strong ontology, according to which the ontological foundations of a worldview determine its ethical recommendations in a clear, direct, and distinct way (White 2000, 6–7). While some theism does serve as strong ontology,[21] White suggests that Taylor is better understood as having a weak ontology. This means that his theism shapes and prefigures, but neither determines nor dictates, his political and ethical values (White 2000, 13, 43, 63).[22] White's distinction not only sheds light on the debate between Taylor and Hampshire, but also suggests how much is at stake in their disagreement about the relationship between religion and pluralism. The aim of his essay has simply been to show that when considering the relationship between monotheism and pluralism, it helps to follow Hampshire's prescription for justice and "hear the other side" (Hampshire 2008a, 8).

NOTES

1. For a useful overview, see Galston 1999.

2. See, e.g., his essay "The Originality of Machiavelli," in Berlin 1979. Berlin recounts the jolt he received from reading Machiavelli, because it became clear that republican

virtu was incompatible with Christian virtue. This led Berlin to entertain the possibility that certain valuable human goods were fundamentally incompatible with others. It dislodged his previous belief that "there could be no conflict between true ends, true answers to the central problems of life" (1990, 8).

3. Hampshire refers to Berlin's pioneering work on pluralism (2000, 34). Taylor describes Berlin as "an inspiring teacher and friend for many decades" (1994, 213). All three philosophers spent part of their career at All Souls College, Oxford.

4. See, e.g., Hobbes's depiction of the chronic uncertainty and insecurity of life in the state of nature in chapter 13 of *Leviathan*.

5. This emphasis on hearing both or all sides of the dispute, on considering claims and counterclaims, and weighing up available, credible evidence before reaching a conclusion makes Hampshire's discussion of the duel as an example of proceduralism and fairness anomalous (2000a, 18). Duels are, to be sure, marked by strict procedures, but the idea that they involve a consideration of both sides of the dispute seems false. Duels only make sense, insofar as they do at all, within an ethos that accords custom, ceremony, and the honor ethic pride of place. Rational negotiation about conflict and dueling appear mutually exclusive.

6. Hampshire's earlier work acknowledges the diversity of family structures (1983, 143). The consideration of whether different forms of the family prepare individuals differently for adversary reasoning would benefit from some engagement with these issues as they were raised by feminist liberal thinkers such as Mary Wollstonecraft and John Stuart Mill. See Abbey 1997, 1999 for discussions of this. Hampshire is not unique among contemporary thinkers to neglect this vital question. As Will Kymlicka observes: "These questions [of the nature of liberal education and child rearing] have been almost entirely neglected by recent liberal philosophers." (1989, 98 n.7). Gutmann 1987 is, however, a notable exception to this.

7. In a brief restatement of the book's central concerns, Hampshire refers to "the derivation of the habit of private reasoning (in the soul) from the habit of public reasoning (in the city)," which suggests that the initiative lies with the outer (2000b, 80).

8. Mark Lilla raises different questions about how apposite the book's title is. As the equation of justice with conflict originates with Heraclitus, Lilla contends that the darker side of the human passions should have been discussed by Hampshire (2000, 48–49).

9. Compare John Haldane's claim that Hampshire's concession that substantive injustices can be produced by just procedures "rather undermines the attempt to make the notion of fair procedures do much work—and that after all is the rationale of the book" (Haldane 2001, 92).

10. "Against Monotheism" is the title of chapter 2 of *Justice is Conflict*.

11. Although Hampshire, with his division of the self into imagination and intellect; his transcultural conception of adversary reason, and his belief in the symbiotic relationship between inner and outer deliberation, seems to have a thicker theory of the self than does Rorty.

12. Although Hampshire takes monotheism to be a sufficient condition of moral universalism, it is not, as his example of utilitarianism indicates, its necessary condition.

13. A similar logic seems to underpin Michael Walzer's discussion of self-criticism. He depicts a view of moral conscience as unitary to be one "according to which God's singular umpire, or someone else's, rules supreme." Shortly after he refers to "a single critic, standing in a privileged place, upholding a uniform and universal standard." He summarizes this outlook thus: "One God, one umpire: singularity is transitive" (1996, 97).

14. This was forcefully symbolized at the UK's inaugural Holocaust Memorial Day Celebration on January 27, 2001. Leaders from a raft of religious traditions lit candles with the wish that the attempted genocides of the twentieth century—Nazism, Bosnia, Rawanda, and Cambodia—would never recur.

15. See Abbey 2000, chap. 1, for a fuller account of Taylor's approach to moral theory. There I argue that his conception of "hypergoods" goes some way to mitigating his pluralism, but also contend that he sees hypergoods as part of the moral framework of some, rather than all, individuals.

16. His discussion of the reality and importance of what he calls "irreducibly shared goods" lends his political theory a counterpart of the ontological pluralism of his moral theory. What the phrase "irreducibly social goods" captures is a category of goods that cannot be disaggregated or decomposed into individual goods, but one that must be shared by two or more individuals. Some things can only be appreciated when they are understood as shared; some goods can only be realized in concert with others (1995, 127–45). Taylor's examples include love, friendship, frank and equal social relationships, and citizen self-rule.

17. A similar point was made by Jonathan Sacks, chief rabbi of Britain's Orthodox Jewry. Speaking at the inaugural Holocaust Memorial Day Celebration on January 27, 2001, he condemned ethnic violence and genocide. One of his criticisms was that they strove to defy the pluralism of human life, which is a diversity created by God. He prayed that humans could come to see God's image in those not made in their image. His words provide a glimpse into how another form of monotheism can provide a basis for the celebration of pluralism.

18. The Christian pluralism of the eighteenth-century German J.G. Herder is also important for Taylor's thinking. Herder is a pivotal figure in Isaiah Berlin's history of Western thought too (1990, 55, 74), but more despite, than because of, his religious premises. See Linker 2000 for an account of Herder's pluralism.

19. See, e.g., Baier 1988; Schneewind 1991; Skinner 1991, 146; Lane 1992; O'Hagan 1993.

20. For a useful overview of Connolly's position, see White 2000, 106–50.

21. In this context, White (2000, 7 n.9) contrasts the Catholicism of Alisdair MacIntyre with that of Charles Taylor.

22. Taylor in fact proposes such a flexible relationship between ontology and politics in "Cross Purposes in the Liberal-Communitarian Debate," in Taylor 1995. The political ramifications of his theism, however, are not discussed there.

WORKS CITED

Abbey, Ruth. 1997. "Odd Bedfellows: Nietzsche and Mill on Marriage." *History of European Ideas* 23(2–4): 81–104.

———. 1999. "Back to the Future: Marriage as Friendship in the Thought of Mary Wollstonecraft." *Hypatia: A Journal of Feminist Philosophy* 14(3) (Summer): 78–95.

———. 2000. *Philosophy Now: Charles Taylor.* Princeton: Princeton University Press.

Abbey, Ruth, ed. 2004. *Contemporary Philosophy in Focus: Charles Taylor.* New York: Cambridge University Press.

Baier, Annette. 1988. "Critical Notice" of C. Taylor *Philosophy and the Human Sciences: Philosophical Papers,* vol. 2. *Canadian Journal of Philosophy* 18:589–94.

Berlin, Isaiah. 1979. *Against the Current.* London: Hogarth Press.

———. 1990. *The Crooked Timber of Humanity.* Princeton: Princeton University Press.

Connolly, William E. 2004. "Catholicism and Philosophy: A Nontheistic Appreciation." In *Contemporary Philosophy in Focus: Charles Taylor,* ed. Ruth Abbey, 166–86. New York: Cambridge University Press.

Galston, William. 1999. "Value Pluralism and Liberal Political Theory." *American Political Science Review* 93(4) (December): 769–78.

Gutmann, Amy. 1987. *Democratic Education.* Princeton: Princeton University Press.

Haldane, John. 2001. Review of *Justice Is Conflict. Journal of Applied Philosophy* 18(1):91–94.

Hampshire, Stuart. 1983. *Morality and Conflict.* Cambridge: Harvard University Press.

———. 1991. "Justice Is Strife." *Proceedings and Addresses of the American Philosophical Association* 65(3) (November).

———. 2000a. *Justice Is Conflict.* Princeton: Princeton University Press.

———. 2000b. Letter to the editors. *New York Review of Books* (June 15): 80.

Kymlicka, Will. 1989. *Liberalism, Community and Culture.* Oxford: Clarendon Press.

Lane, Melissa.1992. "God or Orienteering? A Critical Study of Charles Taylor's *Sources of the Self.*" *Ratio* 5 (June): 46–56.

Lilla, Mark. 2000. "Philosophy for a Messy World: Review of *Justice Is Conflict.*" *New York Review of Books* (May 11): 48–50.

Linker, Damon. 2000. "The Reluctant Pluralism of J.G. Herder." *Review of Politics* 62(2) (Spring): 267–95.

O'Hagan, Timothy. 1993. "Charles Taylor's Hidden God." *Ratio* 6 (June): 72–81.

Schneewind, Jerome B. 1991. Review of *Sources of the Self. Journal of Philosophy* 88(8):422–26.

Skinner, Quentin. 1991. "Who Are 'We'? Ambiguities of the Modern Self. *Inquiry* 34:133–53.

Taylor, Charles. 1985. *Philosophical Papers II: Philosophy and the Human Sciences.* Cambridge: Cambridge University Press.

———. 1989. *Sources of the Self: The Making of the Modern Identity.* Cambridge: Harvard University Press.

———. "Comments and Replies." *Inquiry* 34 (1991):237–54.

———. 1994. "Reply and Rearticulation." In *Philosophy in an Age of Pluralism: The Philosophy of Charles Taylor in Question,* ed. J. Tully and D. Weinstock, 213–57. Cambridge: Cambridge University Press.

———. 1995. *Philosophical Arguments.* Cambridge: Harvard University Press.

———. 1997. "Leading a Life." In *Incommensurability, Incomparability, and Practical Reasoning,* ed. R. Chang, 170–83. Cambridge: Harvard University Press.

———. 1998. "The Dynamics of Democratic Exclusion." *Journal of Democracy* (October): 143–56.

———. 1999a. *A Catholic Modernity?* Edited by J. L. Heft. New York: Oxford University Press.

———. 1999b. "Democratic Exclusion (and Its Remedies?)." In *Multiculturalism, Liberalism and Democracy,* ed. R. Bhargava, A. K. Bagchi, and R Sudarshan, 138–63. New Delhi: Oxford University Press.

Walzer, Michael. 1996. *Thick and Thin: Moral Argument at Home and Abroad.* Notre Dame, Ind.: University of Notre Dame Press.

White, S. K. 2000. *Sustaining Affirmation: The Strengths of Weak Ontology in Political Theory.* Princeton: Princeton University Press.

CHAPTER ELEVEN

Is It Possible to Be Catholic and Modern in Latin America?

Observations from Chilean History

Sol Serrano

How should we think and talk about the relation between religion and modernity? In this essay Sol Serrano addresses this deep theme of much contemporary thought in the context of the history of Chile. The story begins with a direct conflict between the Catholic Church and liberal modernity, but is rather quickly complicated by tensions and conflicts within both groups. Elements within the church criticized paternalism toward the highly Catholic rural poor, for example, encouraging their movement into a more modern economy. At points the church defended human rights and democracy, which at other points it opposed. On the other side, modernists were split between capitalists and the Marxists who saw the origin of oppression in capitalism itself. And it has emerged over time that secularization, which the church naturally resisted, may have proven to be consistent with a revitalized religious life. The key to understanding these tensions and movements is a willingness to regard them as phenomena to be studied empirically, and this includes respect for the religious character of religious experience.

During his Parisian exile, Jose de San Martín—the general who won battlefield victories in the Rio de la Plata, Chile, and Argentina during the war for independence—said that Chile was proof that it was possible to be republican and speak Spanish. Similarly, it can be asked whether it is possible to be both Catholic and modern in a Latin American tongue. Much of our continent's literature would answer "no." In this essay, I do not seek to answer "yes" so much as to point out a difficulty many Latin American social scientists encounter when dealing with the relationship between Catholicism and modern culture. That difficulty, I argue, is largely due to thinking of religion solely in its ideological dimension, to mechanically identifying religion with culture, and to failing to acknowledge the legitimacy of religious experience as both autonomous and historical, subject to profound changes through mutually transforming dialogues with other expressions of culture.

This essay is written from my perspective as a historian, with a focus on Chilean history. I seek, however, to engage a broader debate, one central across Latin America—namely, the relationship between Catholicism and modernity. My aim in part is to make the debate more empirical and less ideological, and accordingly one in which the study of religious experience is carried out in the very cultural milieu in which it takes place, not from the standpoint of a presumed epistemology whose superiority is decided on *a priori*. I suggest that perhaps the modesty of the empirical method can contribute to a new perspective that will allow mystery to be respected and understood as mystery rather than simply as blindness.

ELUSIVE MODERNITY

The relationship between cultural identity and modernity in Latin America has engaged the region's intellectuals since independence from Spain in the early nineteenth century. The intention of the elites to build a modern nation based on popular sovereignty and capitalism had no native social roots. Independence itself was the result more of an external event—France's invasion of Spain—than of the internal maturing of demands for social and cultural change. The liberals who built the national states of the nineteenth century were very clear on this point. From the moderate Andrés Bello to the more hot-headed Jose Victorino Lastarria in Chile; Juan Bautista Alberdi, Domingo Faustino Sarmiento, and Esteban Echeverría in Argentina; Jose Maria Luis Mora and Carlos Maria de Bustamante in Mexico—they all explained this irony in terms of Spanish colonial domination and an uneducated population. The more radical among them pointed to the power of Catholicism. For liberal thought (mid-nineteenth century) and positivist thought (late nineteenth century), the church, with its unproductively managed properties, and religion, with its massive and superstitious practices, was one of the main obstacles to the modernization or progress of the continent.[1]

The Catholic Church in Spanish-speaking America was not pro-monarchy except at the time of independence itself, and the integralist form of conservatism was not strong within it; it was, however, completely pro-papacy, and it defended the unity of church and state and the supremacy of religion over the civil power. It also opposed freedom of worship and the process of secularization by which functions that were formerly under religious control, such as birth, marriage, or death, passed over to civil control. The specifically nineteenth-century conflict between Catholicism and liberalism—one side identified with the agrarian elites and the peasantry and the other with intellectuals, the emerging middle sectors, and artisans—was interpreted then and later as a conflict between the continent's cultural tradition and modern change.

The crisis of Latin American oligarchic society at the outset of the twentieth century also marked the crisis of the liberal and positivist elites who represented it. New intellectual currents sought to retrieve the value of what was native.[2] Intellectuals like the Cuban Jose Martí (1853–95) served as a paradigm for the appreciation of the vernacular culture and for the incorporation of the popular sectors into a democratic design for society. From another angle, the Uruguayan Enrique Rodó (1872–1917), a writer very much in the "academician" mold, left his mark on entire generation when he opted for the humanistic values of Spanish and Latin culture rather than the materialism of Anglo-Saxon culture. Essayists like the Mexicans Jose Vasconcelos (1881–1959) and Antonio Caso (1883–1940) exemplified opposition to the authoritarian and modernizing regime of Porfirio Díaz. In opposition to the scientific positivism proclaimed by the regime's defenders, they proposed a spiritual idealism embodied in the "cosmic race" of Latin America.[3]

The nationalistic essayists of the first half of the twentieth century were critical of the cultural disintegration of technological and secular modernity, although very few advocated religion as such. In his celebrated *The Labyrinth of Solitude,* Octavio Paz saw in pre-Colombian and Spanish Mexico a principle of integration based on myth and religion, while nineteenth-century liberalism only took into account the elites and had been unable to erect a principle of integration. This split was what the Mexican Revolution had sought to reverse.[4]

Starting in the 1950s, the role of social spokesperson for the continent shifted sharply from essayists to sociologists and economists. Assuming the paradigms of their own particular disciplines, notably the functionalism of sociology as practiced in the United States, they took a new look at the old themes of nineteenth-century intellectuals: how to build democracy and economic prosperity in the region. What once was called "progress" was now called "development," and Latin America was "underdeveloped." The United Nations agency ECLA (Economic Commission for Latin America) proposed a development model centered on inward industrialization and on expanding domestic markets with heavy state investment.[5] The sociological implication was that Latin America had to transform its structures in order to move from a traditional society—which was even described as "feudal"—to a modern society. Religion, specifically the traditionalism of Catholic culture, appears in this account to be one of the major impediments to this planned transformation. As laid out by Max Weber, the North Atlantic countries had developed under the influence of the individualism and thrift that were a part of the ethic of Protestantism, so different from the festive and collective ethic of Catholicism. The elites of Latin America were criticized for their lordly agrarian spirit as opposed to the innovating spirit of the capitalist entrepreneur. The agrarian structure with its semi-slave, illiterate, and plainly Catholic population, which was excluded from the market, symbolized backwardness.[6] Some within the Catholic Church made a similar analysis, criticizing paternalism toward the poor and encouraging their participation. In Chile, the first experience of agrarian reform was carried out by the church itself, on its own lands.[7] By contrast, dependency theory, grounded in Marxist structuralism, blamed the capitalism of the central countries for local underdevelopment.[8] Religion and the world of values in general were regarded as a reactionary smokescreen for hiding internal and external structural domination. As with nineteenth-century liberalism, the argument was not about religion itself but about how it operated with regard to social change; with the advent of social change, religion would disappear or become a purely individual matter.

Chile became a superb political laboratory for modernization theories with the advent of the administration of Eduardo Frei (1964–70) and the Christian Democrat Party, a Catholic party that had advocated social Catholicism since the encyclical *Rerum Novarum*. It was also a laboratory for the dependency theory under the administration of Salvador Allende (1970–73), the first Marxist government in the world to take office by election. But the modernizing experiences in a number of countries in the region ended in coups that ushered in authoritarian military regimes during the 1970s. The social sciences of the continent set about trying to explain this failure. One reason given was the abstract nature of the modernizing and revolutionary project and the failure to pay attention to the continent's cultural variables that account for its singularities. This was the same criticism that the early-twentieth-century essayists had made of nineteenth-century liberals. However, the assumption that modernization necessarily entailed secularization, that religion was more a residue from the past than a driving force, remained intact, or at least was not subjected to criticism. The role played by the Christian churches, and specifically the Catholic Church, in defending human rights and the central role of democracy in social thinking interrupted for a while the planned marriage between modernization and secularization.[9]

Only two currents of Chilean sociology, both of them Catholic, initiated a critique of secularization theories: one from culture-oriented Catholicism, and the other from liberation theology. While both criticized the historic and cultural vacuum of abstract theories of modernization, the culture-oriented critique raised as a counterposition the continent's cultural identity as a Catholic, baroque, and mestizo "ethos." This, it was argued, was forged in the seventeenth century on the basis of a ritual blend of the Spanish and the indigenous that remained in traditional popular religiosity and that had resisted the attempts at modernization begun by the Enlightenment and the liberal native elites. In opposition to the forms of enlightened modernity (the market, written culture, technology), the cultural critique has asserted the integrating blend of the American ritual and oral baroque. This amounts to a critique not only of secularization theories, but of secularization itself. For there is said to be an inherent, essential, and therefore irremovable contradiction between Latin American identity, defined as Catholic, and enlightened modernity.[10] This position thereby downplays the possibility that the liberal and democratic principles of political modernity and the formation of national states have in some manner permeated and changed Latin American culture. Moreover, if only popular religiosity expresses this baroque ethos, what happened with the other expressions of religion in modern culture? What is obvious is that this current, no matter how clear-eyed in its interpretation of colonial society, does not deal with the changes that religion undergoes in secularized culture.

The second current of Chilean sociology to criticize secularization theories has done so by demonstrating empirically that modernization and the changes expected to follow in its wake have not threatened the existence of religion. Indeed, as is the case with popular religion, they may have revitalized it. Religion is said to be a force not of domination and alienation of the oppressed, but of struggle and resistance on the part of the oppressed against their cultural enemies. In the words of one of its exponents, Cristián Parker: "Most recently, certain currents of theology and pastoral theory are attempting to rediscover, in traditional popular religion, the 'soul of the people'—the deeper Latin American identity, regarded as opposed to liberal Marxist secularism." The liberation current seeks to discern the germs of liberation in a religion of the oppressed that is a protest of the dominant culture.[11] Nevertheless, it is not only popular religion that proves the limits of secularization theories. Neither interpretation opens up the possibility of a Catholicism that takes on the values of liberal modernity, or simply takes into account the empirical fact that millions of Latin American Catholics live in a secularized world.

Catholic historiography has also offered its own critique of modernity and secularization. Indeed, this is one of the founding themes of traditional Chilean historiography, and in the twentieth century it separated conservatives from liberals. While both are identified with the formation of the national state and with the struggle for independence, they interpret the meaning of nineteenth-century history from opposed perspectives. Whereas for liberals the story is a political one that tells of the progressive expansion of freedom and tolerance—of gaining independence for reason from religious subjection, and of further separating state from church—for conservative historiography it is the story of the loss of power of the authoritarian central state, which dissolved into party factionalism (*partidismo*), initially liberal and then democratic. To the question why Chile was the first national state in the continent to become consolidated as such after independence, the answer is clear: because the conservative republic (1830–61) was the continuation of the centralized and authoritarian Spanish Catholic state, even though its foundation was not religious but legal. Chile's decline, so continues the conservative observer, comes not from the republic, but from secularization, from the separation of the religious and civil spheres, which is what allows for a pluralistic society. It is this liberal pluralism, described as "party factionalism," that undermines the foundations of state power, fractures national unity, and begins the decline. This "decline" view of the history of Chile in the twentieth century, which is critical of democracy, was prominent in Chilean intellectual circles and reached its point of greatest influence by providing ideological support to the military regime in its early days, although later it was clearly displaced by neoliberalism.[12]

The problem I would like to highlight is that, in Chile, both the modernizing currents and those opposed to them have agreed on one point: that secularization in the sense of the separation of the religious and civil spheres, and especially the independence of the latter, has meant a decline of religion in society—although for modernizers this decline has been insufficient, while for conservatives it has amounted to the decline of society itself. As Nestor García

Canclini notes for the region as a whole, "[T]he discussion fluctuates between dogmatic fundamentalisms and abstract liberalisms."[13] This debate has been so dramatically ideological in Chilean society that there has been no space for empirical study, the findings of which might lead both liberals and conservatives to reconsider their assumptions that secularization necessarily entails a decline of religion. As has been proposed by sociologist José Casanova, the "assumption that religion tends to disappear with gradual modernization has been proven to be false, and hence the historic processes of secularization must be studied and there is a need to rethink systematically the relation of religion and modernity and, more important, the possible roles religions may play in the public sphere of modern societies."[14]

Over the course of the twentieth century, the proportion of Christians in Latin America fell from 95.1 percent in 1900 to 92.2 percent in 1980; during that time Catholics declined from 92.3 percent to 88.7 percent, and Protestants rose from 1.5 percent to 3.2 percent.[15] That obliges Latin American social sciences to explain this phenomenon not only on the basis of the residue from colonial times, not only from the preponderance of the baroque, but also from the transformations of religion undergone as a result of modernization of the region.[16]

PUBLIC LIFE OF RELIGION IN THE REPUBLIC

The Spanish Catholic monarchy acknowledged the existence of two realms, religious and secular; and while each spoke and acted by its own authority, the former domain was superior to the latter. The foundation of the monarchical power was divine and the dominion of the Spanish crown over territories in the Americas was in accordance with concessions granted by the papacy. The crown for its part maintained the right to intervene in various areas of ecclesiastical government in exchange for the protection it afforded the church, whose own courts exercised coercive power, as during the Inquisition. Catholicism was a public religion in every sense. In Latin America, with the achievement of independence and the formation of sovereign representative states, this public character of religion came under attack. It would be a leading theme of the debate among liberals, conservatives, and the church hierarchy concerning the secularization of the state.

Religious freedom was not a cornerstone of emancipation-era thought in Chile or of its concept of sovereignty, probably because society was religiously homogeneous.[17] While there was no unanimity of opinion about the future to which the country should aspire, and though the more liberal figures called for tolerance to counter the inquisitorial spirit, most favored retaining the Catholic character of the state, and indeed all the constitutions of the other states in the region at the time enshrined it.[18] The maintenance of religious unity meant the prohibition of public worship of any other than the state religion. So stated the Constitution of 1833.[19] Hence, the public realm, whether of the state or civil society, was defined as Catholic and only Catholic. The private realm, on the other hand, was the domain of individual conscience. For even the staunchest partisans of religious unity recognized that no authority could penetrate the consciences and private opinions of citizens.

During the post-independence period there was tension and conflict between the Catholic Church and the state, but also negotiation in the context of a strongly regalist state and a clergy that retained hints of Gallicanism. After midcentury, however, the conflict widened to incorporate an emerging liberal call for a legislative agenda to consolidate the state's sovereignty, and hence to secularize it as the only source of the law. The first debate on this agenda, and one of the most emblematic, concerned the interpretation of Article 5 of the 1833 Constitution, which mandated tolerance of the worship practices of non-Catholics and allowed them to set up their own schools.[20]

As early as the 1820s, with the arrival of immigrants, primarily English and North American, in the port of Valparaiso, Protestant worship had been practiced in that city. The authorities followed a pragmatic policy that authorized Protestant places of worship as private space. Because this tolerance existed in practice, but not by legal mandate, it could be threatened by any possible collision with the law. This did, in fact, take place when Catholic Church leaders perceived what they took to be a growing alliance between liberal politicians and non-Catholics. Thus, in 1854, the archbishop of Santiago opposed the building of a Presbyterian Church, arguing that it was unconstitutional because the proposed church would be public rather than private. Construction was halted and the government reached an agreement with the Presbyterians that was both subtle and precarious: the church had to be behind a partition wall and the facade could not be visible from the street, it could not have a bell tower, and worship had to take place in utter silence.[21]

During constitutional debate on the matter, the discussion had turned on how the term "public" was interpreted in the restriction imposed by the Constitution on any other religious worship. Liberals thought that it should be interpreted in terms of property ("public" meant only what was state-owned), conservatives argued that it should be interpreted in terms of the public nature of access: every space that was not domestic was public and, therefore, a dissident (non-Catholic) rite could be practiced only in the intimacy of the home. The church hierarchy argued that confusion between "public" and "private" worship resulted from a prior confusion — namely, that freedom of conscience was the same as freedom of worship, or that the latter was a necessary consequence of the former.

> [F]reedom of conscience (cannot be understood) in the absurd sense that some attribute to it, namely as a right of a man to believe whatever he wants, to be a Muslim or Buddhist, to adore the sun like the Peruvians and the Persians, or wonderful Apis, like the Egyptians. . . . [T]he rational being has no right to believe whatever he likes, but the strict obligation to embrace the truth.

Intelligence could go astray and be at fault, but as long as it did not express it in deed or word, it was culpable only before God. "Society should look at this error as innocent . . . something else happens when the error goes outside; if it harms society the law can and must repress it."[22] Freedom of conscience did not entail freedom of worship precisely because one belonged to the private realm and the other to the public.

The church understood Roman Catholicism to be the sole religion, not only of the state, but of society. Nothing could be more alien to its mission and its history than to be restricted to the realms of state and individual privacy. Its public character was at the very heart of Catholic dogmas and ritual.

> For us Catholics, the church is the house of the Lord, a public place where the faithful meet to adore God who is present on his altars. We believe in the real presence of Jesus Christ. . . . But Protestants do not look at churches as places where they are sanctifying the presence of Christ. Hence they only serve for gathering to pray, read, and explain the bible; things that can be done perfectly well in a private house.[23]

Conservatives and the Catholic Church regarded acceptance of religious pluralism as the first phase of secularization. In opposition to religious unity, the liberals proposed one arising out of discussion and consensus — a unity, that is, built on the basis of representation, a popular sovereignty that granted political legitimacy to authorities chosen by the citizens. The conservatives never denied the value of popular sovereignty, and indeed, they appealed to it, claiming that they were a majority. Catholic women entered the fray, becoming the first women in the history of Chile to publish a newspaper, *El Eco de las Señoras*. Liberals believed it was written by priests.[24]

The solution reached was a clever political compromise: the Chilean Constitution was not revised, but an interpretative law was prepared allowing non-Catholics to have chapels and schools in "private spaces" (*recintos particulares*), which the 1857 Civil Code distinguished from public property. The public realm was thereby defined in terms of property, and the boundary line was drawn so that what was Catholic would be restricted to the state realm, while religious pluralism was accommodated as a domain of privacy within civil society.[25] After tolerance came laicising laws concerning the secularization of cemeteries in 1883 and the law of civil marriage and civil registry in 1884, thereby further narrowing the ambit of the public. If religious pluralism gained ground in civil society with the first step, it gained it in the state itself with the second.[26]

As the church experienced it, the growing separation of the public from the private realm meant that it was being expelled from the public domain, where it had figured so prominently, but was also being squeezed out of the private sector as the ultimate regulator of conscience. The separation between public and private forced it to "become Protestant." "One of the most dangerous illusions of the time in which we live," said the Chilean bishops after the laicising legislation was passed, "is that of believing that it is well to conceal religion, relegating it to the dark lavatory of individual conscience. . . . [I]n order for it to be loved, it must be known, and it is known only when it displays its divine excellences in public, and demonstrates its strength in the combats to which its enemies provoke it."[27]

The church had to continuously revise the way it understood its public character as this newly structured public domain took hold. To put it another way, the independence of the secular from the religious realm forced religion to become present in a new way. Opposed as it was to the formation of a pluralistic public sphere, Catholicism nevertheless had to participate in it with the instruments afforded by that sphere: equality before the law, freedom of expression, and freedom of association. It accordingly bolstered its presence in political society through the Conservative Party, which, as paradoxical as it might seem, was the party that pressed for the expansion of the vote to extend its representation, especially in the countryside, and advocated the electoral reform that established universal male suffrage in 1874; it was the party that advocated freedom of education and freedom of association, by invoking the rights that liberalism had succeeded in having enacted into law.[28]

Catholicism enhanced and transformed its organizational life. Religious brotherhoods were succeeded by mutual aid societies and workers credit unions. Following Vatican guidelines and the pastoral teaching of Pius IV and Leo XIII, the church encouraged the formation of organizations to combat Masonry and secularizing tendencies. The Catholic Union, which founded the Catholic University in 1888, was part of this new strategy. The church strengthened its educational network and set up its own newspapers and even its own banks. In these ways, Catholicism became privatized in the sense that it ceased being the sole religion of the state, but it continued its public role by participating in the debate on political society and civil society. This was the new public character of Catholicism in a secular state. It may help explain why Catholicism remained a powerful force in the fully secularized Chilean politics of the twentieth century, even before it became reconciled to many of the values of political modernity at Vatican II.

THE PRIVATIZATION OF BAROQUE CATHOLICISM

To emphasize the public character of Catholicism in a secular state does not mean denying its privatization. Catholicism in Chile did not become privatized in the way the liberals wanted: relegated to conscience and the church building. But it unquestionably lost some of its baroque public character as a consequence of the increasing importance of a market economy, science and technology, and industrialization and urbanization. It was also due to transformations within Catholicism itself. This trend has been the aspect of Chilean development least considered by historiography, and it must be examined to see how some behaviors and values, while undoubtedly modern, were not necessarily secularizing.

Toward the end of the nineteenth century, the Chilean church hierarchy signaled its fear that religion would be confined to the "dark lavatory of individual conscience" and its rejection of the social changes that seemed to be leading in that direction. But at the same time, and long before the rise of liberalism, it was wary of the profane excesses of baroque piety, especially among the ordinary people, but not only there. In the mid-eighteenth century, the Bourbon monarchy began a series of reforms to strengthen the central power of the monarchy and regalism in the church. It expelled the Jesuits, encouraged the reform of the religious orders and seminaries, revitalized learning, and sought by all means to discipline the ritual customs of the faithful. The results of that reform in Chile were weak. Although the ritualism of Tridentine Catholicism was deeply rooted in the region—this was the baroque—it had less effect in imposing a sense of religious discipline in the practice of the faithful. The church hierarchy reform measures in the nineteenth century included increasing the importance of the parish and of preaching, using the vernacular in the liturgy, reforming seminary studies and the convent life, encouraging congregations to be engaged in charitable works as a form of religious practice, and criticizing baroque religiosity. It is important to note that these reforms of the church were undertaken at the same time as the national state was taking shape. In this sense, the church was forced to face a new enemy: not far-away Protestantism but liberalism that posed a challenge close at hand.

The church resisted the spreading and deepening liberalism of the states throughout the continent. But along with it came something very important that has been little mentioned: the revitalization and education of the people through individual personal discipline—the value of self-control, work, and obedience. An extraordinary but little known example of this is the program of the archbishop of Santiago that brought to Chile French nuns devoted to an active life of missionary work. They began to arrive in the mid-nineteenth century to take responsibility for the education of upper-class women, setting up the National School of Teachers. They also were expected to deal with the emerging social problems of urban society: the sick, poor, and elderly who took refuge in hospitals and asylums; the sick who remained in their own homes; and prisoners, prostitutes, and vagrant women, whom they trained for craft work.

Until that time the only convents in Chile and Latin America had been contemplative. There was no precedent of religious women who went about on the streets, let alone who worked. The religious life of elite women was intensely ritual, but a small portion of them, influenced by traces of the Catholic Enlightenment, formed a society to support these new congregations. They thus became allies of the hierarchy in making these religious orders the model for female religious life.[29]

The encounter of the French nuns with Chilean society, with the church hierarchy and government authorities, with upper-class women and the poor of the city—all provide a uniquely rich illustration of the collision between two kinds of devotion: a collective, public, and emotional faith proper to the baroque, and a personalized, internalized, and austere faith proper to the

Counterreformation, or to an already assimilated Catholic Reformation, which had assumed the impact of the Enlightenment and rationalism.

To these French nuns, life in Chile seemed chaotic—from the way in which the cloister was observed in convents to the subhuman conditions in which the sick and criminals lived, the contempt for work among the upper-class girls, and the ceremonial pageantry practiced by all social sectors. By the late nineteenth century, the French religious women had established a firm footing for their work. They not only educated almost all upper-class women attending school, but they introduced a type of romantic piety, which while it was certainly emotional, avoided the excesses of baroque practices. Celebration of the month of Mary, first communion, devotion to the Immaculate Conception, the Sacred Heart, the Miraculous Medal, and the Virgin of Lourdes—all in time were to become a part of Catholic observance throughout the various social sectors and took their place alongside older devotions and feasts. The nuns organized rich and poor women into pious associations to maintain devotion to Mary and for works of charity, and they clearly displaced contemplative convents as the model of female religious life.

The statistics are truly astonishing. Whereas in 1849 there were three hundred contemplative religious women in Santiago, by 1899 there were only two hundred. More interestingly, the number of female vocations in the second half of the nineteenth century grew by 385 percent, from 356 in 1849 to 1,369 in 1889, on the basis of recruitment by the new congregations.[30] What declined was baroque piety and the type of convent that expressed it, while the new active model of congregation flourished and grew. These congregations signaled a tendency toward a more personalized and innerworldly faith, toward the feminization of religion, which was in keeping with many of the other changes that society was beginning to experience, such as industrialization, urbanization, and literacy.

Urbanization had a strong impact on the privatization of religion, driving religious practice from the public streets and consigning it to church buildings. Beforehand, God—literally for most Chileans—was believed to travel about the streets of Santiago and Valpariso and over winding rural roads whenever the Holy Viaticum was taken to the sick. The city would come to a halt as it passed. Passers-by knelt down, conversation stopped in houses, and in school the teacher maintained silence at the tinkle of the bell announcing it. But one day around 1860, in the noisy and bustling port of Valparaiso, a carriage failed to halt and splashed the consecrated Host. The bishop was left to ponder what was to be done under the new conditions of increasing urbanization signaled by this event, and declared that priests in parishes would henceforth visit the sick and dying carrying with them a consecrated Host in a small box inside a carrying case. The procession of the Holy Viaticum for visiting the sick was relegated to symbolic status and transformed into an annual feast, Quasimodo, celebrated to this day on the Sunday after Corpus Christi.

Business concerns also had a role in transforming the ritual practices of religion in the city. In Santiago after 1870, transport owners engaged church officials in extensive debates about whether public carriages ought to be suspended during the days of Holy Week. An agreement was reached that the suspension would apply only when the largest crowds were expected—for the "stations" on Holy Thursday, for example, and the procession to the Holy Sepulchre on Good Friday. Holy Week thus increasingly came to be celebrated inside the church's buildings, while the public life of the city became increasingly diverse and pluralistic. This pattern was continued, perhaps most emblematically, when the church was forced to stop its ringing of bells, which began to be confused with that of fire stations and schools. In these and other ways, religion in Chilean cities became increasingly privatized during the second half of the nineteenth century.

That said, however, the privatization of baroque Catholicism was incomplete, and many of its cultural expressions live on in Latin America. We need to recognize that in response to the separation of the religious and secular spheres, Chilean Catholicism maintained its public presence as one of the competing authorities in civil society. One could say that the privatization of baroque Catholicism gave rise to a new kind of public life of modern Catholicism.

NOTES

This essay appeared originally as "La privatización del catolicismo barroco y la publicidad del catolicismo moderno: Una mirada a la secularización en el caso chileno," *Revista Atenea,* no. 484, Universidad de Concepción, Chile (2001): 45–61, and is published here by permission.

1. John Lynch, *The Spanish American Revolutions 1808–1826* (New York: Norton, 1973); David Brading, *The First America: The Spanish Monarchy, Creole Patriots and the Liberal State, 1492–1867* (Cambridge: Cambridge University Press, 1991); Leslie Bethell, ed., *The Independence of Latin America* (Cambridge: Cambridge University Press, 1987).

2. Jean Franco, *The Modern Culture of Latin America* (Harmonsworth: Penguin Books, 1970).

3. Harold Eugene Davis, *Latin American Social Thought* (Washington, D.C.: University Press, 1961); José Luis Abellán, *La idea de América* (Madrid: Ediciones Istmo, 1972); Leopoldo Zea, *El pensamiento latinoamericano* (Mexico: Ariel Seix Barral, 1976).

4. Octavio Paz, *The Labyrinth of Solitude* (New York: Grove Press, 1961). First published in Spanish in 1950.

5. One of the main proponents of ECLA's economic model was the Argentine Raul Prebisch ("La periferia latinoamericana en el sistema global del capitalismo," *Revista Cepal* 13 [1981]). See Alfred Hirschman, ed., *Latin American Issues* (New York: Twentieth Century Fund, 1961).

6. The paradigmatic representative is Gino Germani, *Política y sociedad en una época de transición* (Buenos Aires: Paidós, 1969).

7. Brian Smith, *The Church and Politics in Chile: Challenges to Modern Catholicism* (Princeton: Princeton University Press, 1982).

8. André Gunder Frank, *Dependent Accumulation and Underdevelopment* (London: Macmillan, 1978).

9. Juan Francisco Marsal, *Dependencia e independencia. Las alternativas de la sociología latinoamericana en el siglo xx* (Madrid: Centro de Investigación Sociológica, 1979); Ignacio Sotelo, *América Latina: un ensayo de interpretación* (Madrid: Centro de Investigación Sociológica, 1980).

10. Pedro Morandé, *Cultura y modernización en América Latina. Ensayo sociológico acerca de la crisis del desarrollismo y de su superación* (Santiago: Cuadernos de Sociología, Pontificia Universidad Católica de Chile, 1984); Carlos Cousiño, *Razón y ofrenda. Ensayo en torno a los límites y perspectivas de la sociología en América Latina* (Santiago: Cuadernos de Sociología, Pontificia Universidad Católica de Chile, 1990).

11. Cristián Parker, *Popular Religion and Modernization in Latin American: A Different Logic* (Maryknoll, N.Y.: Orbis, 1996), 191–92.

12. The main exponents of conservative historiography are Alberto Edwards, *La fronda aristocrática,* 10th ed. (Santiago: Editorial Universitaria, 1987); Jaime Eyzaguirre, *Fisonomía histórica de Chile* (Santiago: Editorial Universitaria, 1948); Mario Góngora, *Ensayo histórico sobre la noción de Estado en Chile en los siglos XIX y XX,* 2d ed. (Santiago: Editorial Universitaria, 1986); Gonzalo Vial, *Historia de Chile,* 2 vols. (Santiago: Editorial Santillana, 1981). For a critical study of this historiography, see Renato Cristi and Carlos Ruiz, *El pensamiento conservador en Chile* (Santiago: Editorial Universitaria, 1992).

13. Nestor García Canclini, *Culturas híbridas* (Mexico: Editorial Grijalbo, 1990), 189.

14. José Casanova, *Public Religions in the Modern World* (Chicago: University of Chicago Press, 1994), 6.

15. Parker, *Popular Religion and Modernization in Latin American,* 57.

16. Recent literature in English on the matter include Carol Ann Drogus, "Religious Pluralism and Social Change: Coming to Terms with Complexity and Convergence,"

Latin American Research Review 35(1):261–70; Sarah Cline, "Competition and Fluidity in Latin American Christianity," *Latin American Research Review* 35(2):244–51.

17. Simon Collier, *Ideas and Politics of Chilean Independence, 1808–1833* (Cambridge: Cambridge University Press, 1967).

18. The constitutional texts may be found in Luis Valencia Avaria, *Anales de la República*, vol. 1 (Santiago: n.p., 1951).

19. According to Article 5: "The Religion of the Republic of Chile is Roman Catholic and Apostolic: with the exclusion of the public exercise of any other."

20. Simon Collier, "Religious Freedom, Clericalism, and Anticlericalism in Chile, 1820–1920," in Richard Helmstadter, *Freedom and Religion in the Nineteenth Century* (Stanford: Stanford University Press, 1997).

21. J. H. McLean, *Historia de la Iglesia Presbiteriana en Chile* (Santiago: Imprenta Universitaria, 1932), 17–18.

22. *Sesiones del Congreso Legislativo*, Deputies, 16 June 1865, session, 12.

23. Ibid.,15.

24. Erika Maza Valenzuela, "Catolicismo, anticlericalismo y la extensión del sufragio a la mujer en Chile", *Estudios Públicos* 58 (1995): 151; Ana María Stuven, "El Eco de las Señoras de Santiago. El surgimiento de una opinión pública femenina," in Horacio Aránguiz, ed., *Lo público y lo privado en la historia americana* (Santiago: Fundación Mario Góngora, 2000), 303–26.

25. On the establishment of religious freedom elsewhere in the continent, see Jean Pierre Bastián, ed., *Protestantes, liberales y francmasones. Sociedades de ideas y modernidad en América Latina, siglo XIX* (Mexico: Fondo de Cultura Económica, 1990); Fernando Armas Asin, *Liberales, protestantes y masones. Modernidad y tolerancia religiosa. Perú, siglo XIX* (Lima: Fondo Editorial, Pontificia Universidad Católica del Perú, 1998).

26. Sol Serrano, "La definición de lo público en un Estado católico," *Estudios Públicos* 76 (1999): 212–32.

27. "Pastoral colectiva sobre Relaciones entre la Iglesia y el Estado," *Boletín Eclesiástico* 9 (December 1884): 520.

28. Samuel Valenzuela, *Democratización vía reforma: la expansión del sufragio en Chile* (Buenos Aires: Editorial IDES, 1985).

29. A study of the French nuns and their arrival and work in Chile is Sol Serrano, *Vírgenes Viajeras. Diarios de religiosas francesas en su ruta a Chile* (Santiago: Ediciones Universidad Católica de Chile, 2000). The congregations that arrived in midcentury were the Sacred Heart of Jesus and Mary, the Sacred Heart of Jesus, the Sisters of Charity, the Good Shepherd of Angers, and the Sisters of Providence.

30. Ibid, 97.

CHAPTER TWELVE

Number, Shape, and the Nature of Space

An Inquiry into the Meaning of Geometry in Islamic Art

Carol Bier

The effort to understand religious art presents a special form of the problem of talking about religion. When an artist attempts to address the mystery that lies at the heart of all religion, he or she is representing what of necessity cannot be fully represented. Much of the meaning of the painting, or sculpture, or building must therefore lie outside the work itself, in its religious context — in the world of practice and belief in which the work is embedded and from which it takes much of its life.

In European art, religious meanings are traditionally personified and represented through figural images. In the arts of other cultures this is often not so, and the difficulty of understanding this kind of art is intensified if we view it, as we are naturally inclined to do, through a Western lens.

The arts of Islam present us with just such a situation. In this essay Carol Bier counters the trend that regards the geometric patterns of Islamic art as purely decorative. She shows that the Islamic visual tradition arose in response both to Greek mathematics and to philosophical discussions taking place within the Islamic world. She suggests that the repetitive aspects of geometric patterns express spiritual concerns in Islamic art, for both the maker and the viewer. In this sense, Islamic art is less representational than experiential in nature.

Approaching the study of art through the figural tradition (fig. 1a) privileges the arts of Western Europe, India, and China. Less well known in the academy are nonfigural arts of the Islamic world (fig. 1b), whose mathematical aspects

FIGURE 1A. Eugene Delacroix, *Odalisque*, ca. 1827–28, painting, France. Photograph © Fitzwilliam Museum, University of Cambridge. Reproduced by permission.

help create a beauty of form, pattern, and structure.[1] This essay takes as its starting point an approach to Islamic art that from the beginning assumes a cultural equity—that neither Islam, nor the Western tradition, is in any sense culturally superior to the other *a priori*.

Historically, both Islamic art and Western art have been concerned with form, space, and light both in depicting the human form (fig. 1a) and in the approximate repetition of particular shapes (fig. 1b). And both Western art and Islamic art invoke systems of proportion established by the invariant relationship of a circle to its diameter. The Western canon's paradigm for that proportionality is Leonardo da Vinci's *Vitruvian Man* (fig. 2a), in which a human male is set within a circle, establishing a system of proportion; for Islamic script styles, the circle is visually articulated as the measure of proportion (fig. 2b).[2]

Introductory surveys of art history generally characterize Islamic art as non-representational, aniconic, and ornamental, in contrast to the Western tradition.[3] The "ornamental" is often viewed as decorative, ancillary to content,

FIGURE 1B. Wall panel with geometric pattern, tenth century; painted ceramic, Nishapur, Iran (39.40.67). All rights reserved, The Metropolitan Museum of Art. Reproduced by permission.

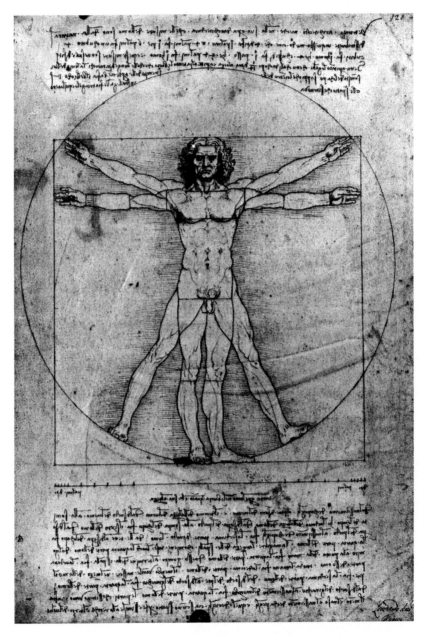

FIGURE 2A. Leonardo da Vinci, *Canon of Proportion* (also called *Vitruvian Man*), ca. 1492, drawing, Venice. Courtesy of Alinari / Art Resource, NY.

FIGURE 2B. Ibn Muqla (886–940) devised a system of proportions for Arabic scripts based on a circle, which was refined by Yaqut al-Musta'simi (d. 1298–99) (after Necipoglu 1995, 105, fig. 92a). By permission of Gulru Necipoglu.

and generally devoid of meaning apart from the intent to beautify; repetition is seen essentially as meaningless.[4] But exploring Islamic art from a different perspective—that of its mathematical components and pattern-making processes—shows that geometric pattern has for centuries had significant meaning both for its makers and for its viewers.

FIGURAL AND GEOMETRIC ART

Since the Renaissance the figural tradition has been central to the production and the reception of Western art (Freedberg 1989). In the classical, Hellenistic, and Roman periods, portrayal of the human figure was paramount for sculptural subjects, funerary works, and official imagery in coins. Eventually, this Western standard shaped the development of the field of art history as a discipline.[5]

The Western preoccupation with figural form and pictorial imagery is mimetic representation by means of portraiture, narrative, or icon. But if one looks at the human figure from another point of view, figural form might be seen as an appropriate subject for the exploration of form itself, defining it as a subject by examining the effects of light and by attending to the depiction of spatial dimension and volume. This approach would help establish the cultural equity to which we are committed, making it possible to value and appreciate Islamic art on an equal footing with Western art. In the process, a similar set of goals and artistic values might be discerned in the two cultures.

Representations of the Day of Judgment is an apt point of departure for questioning the primacy of the figural narrative in Western and Islamic art. The Day of Judgment and the weighing of the souls is a theme encountered in the tympanum (fig. 3a) of a Romanesque church, with visual depictions of biblical passages. In Islamic art, the same subject is also expressed visually (fig. 3b), but rather than use pictorial narrative or figural representation to convey the theme, it is depicted through the medium of language. The Taj Mahal, dating from the seventeenth century, is a funerary monument constructed by Shah Jahan to commemorate the death of his wife, Mumtaz Mahal. A geometrically conceived three-dimensional structure octagonal in plan, it has four main niches facing to the outside. Surrounding each niche is an inscription in Arabic, depicting in a cursive script passages from the Qur'an concerning the transition from the now to the hereafter and describing the Day of Judgment (Begley 1979).

FIGURE 3A. Tympanum of cathedral, ca. 1130, Romanesque style, Autun, France. Photo courtesy of Walter B. Denny.

FIGURE 3B. View of Taj Mahal, 1630s, Agra, India. Photo courtesy of Walter B. Denny.

FIGURE 4A. Raphael, *School of Athens* (1510–11), fresco, *Stanza della Segnatura,* Vatican. Courtesy of Alinari / Art Resource, NY.

To highlight the differences between these approaches, compare Raphael's *School of Athens* (fig. 4a) with an illustration from a Turkish manuscript depicting an Ottoman astronomical observatory (fig. 4b). The *School of Athens* presents a richly built architectural setting with numerous arches and a dome open to the sky. Viewers of the painting (or its reproduction) can almost feel the atmosphere; it is airy and alive, with breezes flowing freely; people converse in small groups. At the center, beneath an arch and walking toward the viewer, engaged in animated conversation, are Plato and Aristotle, each carrying a book (*Timeo* and *Ethico,* respectively). By contrast, to a viewer steeped in Western conventions of perspective, the Turkish illustration at first looks flat, without spatial dimension. But soon the thoughtful viewer can begin to recognize how the ground plane rises, distinguishing foreground and background by a vertical plane. This is comparable in Western contexts to the theatrical stage, in which "upstage" is back and far, while "downstage" is at the front, closer to the audience. In the Ottoman miniature, what is in the foreground is positioned lower; what is set higher signifies distance, as in a tilted

FIGURE 4B. Book illustration depicting astronomers' observatory, ca. 1581–82, Istanbul. Istanbul University Library, MS F. 1414, fol. 57r. Reproduced by permission.

stage. As depicted in the illustration, astronomers are engaged in various activities, displaying the equipment of their observatory, which includes a quadrant, sextant, astrolabe, and celestial globe. It is often lost on Western viewers that, by this planar method of spatial representation, the importance of what is depicted in the background is equal to that in the foreground—that is, there is no loss of potential information or importance in what is represented from afar, whereas the drawing in perspective necessarily loses detail and significance as the plane recedes to a vanishing point.

Contemplating these works in comparison with one another, one might reasonably speculate that among the books stacked horizontally at the back of the observatory would be the very same books depicted in the *School of Athens*. That is because the entire corpus of Greek scientific works from the classical period and late antiquity was avidly translated into Arabic in the early Islamic period, and that body of philosophical and scientific knowledge was passed down within the Islamic scientific community, just as the parallel inheritance is conveyed in Raphael's painting.[6] That same body of knowledge also passed into Europe as it was translated from Arabic into Latin from the twelfth century on, serving as the basis for later developments in the Renaissance when classical texts were sought in their original languages.[7]

There are other points of contact that link the West and Islam along a historical continuum of positive contact and exchange, the Crusades notwithstanding. But in the case of Islam today, the first challenge to establishing an attitude of cultural equity is to overcome negative stereotypes: terrorism, religious fanaticism, and the lack of women's rights are what first come to mind on the part of many Westerners when asked about Islam. Indeed, many are not aware that Islam shares a Judeo-Christian heritage and that it is of the same monotheistic tradition (Peters 1982). The god of the Muslims ("Allah," in Arabic) is the same god as that of Christians and Jews.

Art offers a lens through which we may peer at other cultures; it offers an opening to an awareness of diverse values, beliefs, and concepts, as well as an insight into how similar values, beliefs, and concepts are expressed in different ways by diverse cultures. The prevalence of geometric pattern in Islamic art offers particularly significant possibilities for bridging differences and exploring similarities. The spatial relationships expressed through geometry are the same throughout the world; geometry is equally accessible to all peoples. Grabar (1992, 152–53) first raised the paradox of geometric pattern in Islamic art: if geometry is equally accessible, why was it selected as an artistic subject primarily in Islamic art and not in the arts of so many other peoples? The same

question, surprisingly, might be rephrased in light of the prevalence of the figural tradition in Western art: why, if we are all human beings, has there been
so much greater a continuing fascination with the figural form in Western
art than in the arts of many non-Western cultures? Or, why was perspective as
understood in the Renaissance as the "true" way of seeing not readily adopted
in the arts of other cultures? The answer to each of these questions, surely, lies
embedded in the particular historical circumstances out of which individual
cultures emerge.

THE EMERGENCE OF GEOMETRIC PATTERN IN ISLAMIC ART

This essay explores how and why geometric pattern in Islamic art emerged
within that civilization in the ninth and tenth centuries, and did so with such an
intensity and far-flung proliferation that its presence could be found throughout the Islamic world of the time, from Spain to India, and ever since. Just what
historical circumstances contributed to the significant development of these
mathematical aspects of Islamic art in a manner that so distinguishes it from
other traditions of art?

Islam was born, through revelation, into a world of ongoing discourse. At
the time of its advent in Arabia during the seventh century, intellectual activity
centered in Alexandria in Egypt, Damascus in Syria, Jundishapur in Iran, and
in Constantinople, capital of the Byzantine empire. At Jundishapur, efforts to
compile all knowledge were taking place under the patronage of the Sasanian
ruler, Khosro I. With the growing strength of Christianity in a pluralistic world
of Jewish monotheism, Zoroastrian dualism, and pagan polytheism, discourse
focused on humankind and nature, the nature of God, and the cosmos, continuing to draw heavily from the transmitted works of Plato and Aristotle, filtered as they were through the neo-Platonism of the Alexandrian school and
Christian theologians. In the year 529, the Byzantine emperor Justinian had
closed the philosophical school in Athens and forbidden worship of the Olym-
pic gods. This outward triumph for Christianity drove scholars from Greece
to other established centers of learning in Egypt, Syria, and Iran.

Muhammad was born in Arabia around the year 570. In his middle years,
over a period of decades, he received a series of revelations that comprise the
Qur'an. God spoke to Muhammad in Arabic through the intermediary of the
archangel Gabriel. The God of the Qur'an is the same as that of the Christians and Jews, but with attributes emphasizing that he neither begets nor is

begotten. He is the first and the last, the beginning and the end. The year one in the Islamic calendar marks the emigration of Muhammad from Mecca to Yathrib, a town to the north, with a small band of followers. There, his teachings drew a larger following of converts from Judaism and Christianity, and from among the pagan Arab tribes as well. Yathrib became known as Madinat al-Nabi, or City of the Prophet, but the prophet returned to Mecca triumphant, and established himself in the kaaba, a building associated by tradition with Abraham, whom Muslims hold to be the first monotheist. The kaaba, cubic in form (as its name in Arabic suggests) remains to the present day as the physical focal point for prayer and pilgrimage for Muslims throughout the world.

Over the course of the first hundred years of its history, Islam developed through conquests and conversion into an empire comprising a plurality of races and ethnicities, languages, and nationalities. These were unified by the political dominion of a new monotheistic religion, based on an acceptance of the revelations in Arabic received by Muhammad, who was proclaimed to be the last—or, the "seal"—of the prophets. Within the diversity encompassed by the dramatic expansion of the emergent Islamic civilization, Arabic became accepted as the language of intellectual and religious discourse, and Islamic culture rapidly became recognizably urban and intellectual.

GEOMETRY IN DISCOURSE

By the eighth century of our era, there arose as part of Islam's rapid expansion an ambitious movement that in time would seek to translate into Arabic the full repertory of Greek scientific works. The translation movement had as a patron the Abbasid court in Baghdad from the middle of the eighth century (see note 6). The elevated role of geometry is perhaps suggested by the early description of Baghdad as "laid out with a circular plan as if drawn by a compass." In ninth-century Baghdad, the Abbasid ruler, al-Mamun, continued this patronage by establishing the *Bayt al-Hikma*, or House of Wisdom, where all the knowledge of humankind would be collected. Greek scientific writing and Indian sources were sought and edited. All of the works of Aristotle, Euclid's *Elements*, Archimedes' *On the Sphere and Cylinder*, and Appollonius's *Conics* were among the key works translated (Joseph 1992). Much attention was devoted to Aristotelian notions of the one and the many and to the study of form, matter, and meaning. During this period of intense exploration of mathematics and philosophy, Muslims articulated an understanding of trigonometry, formulating new ways of describing the proportional relationships expressed by sine, cosine, and tangent. In the tenth century, al-Khwarizmi wrote the mathematical text *Al-Jabr wa'l Muqabala,* which was later translated into Latin, retaining its title, from which we derive the word "algebra." In it, al-Khwarizmi addresses the notions of restorations and balancing; from his name in Latin (Algorismus), we have the word "algorithm."[8]

This blend of neo-Platonism and the Aristotelian tradition continued to serve as a font for contemporary discourse among philosophers (in Arabic, *falasuf*), and this melded into what became the Islamic form of debate (*kalam*) advocated by the theologians (*mutakallimun*). The amalgamation of Aristotelian and Platonic ideals was actively propagated by philosophers in the Arab realm. Geometry, an area of intellectual inquiry that was theoretical but had practical implications, was an integral part of the curriculum in the natural sciences, which included mathematics. To the Greek corpus of scientific works, including those dealing with geometry, were added works from India, which addressed numeration and introduced to the Islamic world what have come to be known as "Arabic numerals." To the numbers was added zero as a place holder.

During these early years of Islamic history, therefore, it is clear that learning was extolled and philosophy was considered the head of the sciences. This lasted into the eleventh century, when traditionalist forces installed an Islamic orthodoxy that ran counter to the rationalist philosophical tradition that had so informed earlier Islamic science and mathematics, but that now was considered suspect for having arisen in foreign cultures.

GEOMETRY IN ISLAMIC ART

Geometric pattern is not immediately apparent in the earliest works of Islamic art. But from the middle of the eighth century, and throughout the ninth and tenth centuries, key components of Islamic art developed that would sustain its unity to the present day, in spite of the diversity of cultures, ethnic identities, and regional traditions that fall under the general rubric "Islam." Among the most notable monuments in which geometric pattern predominates are the eighth-century floor mosaics of the palace and bath at Khirbet al-Mafjar near Jericho (fig. 5a) and the eleventh-century brick work in several tomb towers

FIGURE 5A. Floor mosaics, eighth century, Khirbet al-Mafjar near Jericho. Photo courtesy of Walter B. Denny.

on the Iranian plateau (fig. 5b). One might also cite ninth- and tenth-century carved stucco architectural decoration from sites in Iran (Nishapur, Chal Tarkhan, Neyriz), Afghanistan (Balkh), and Egypt (Ibn Tulun mosque in Cairo), which are stylistically related.[9]

Those who study Islamic art have assessed the proliferation of geometric pattern in a variety of ways. One approach, represented by the work of Critchlow (1976), El-Said (1993), and Abas (1995), is documentary and analytical; its goal is to reveal the spatial relationships of two-dimensional patterns and their implied underlying grid structures. This approach emphasizes the practical aspects of pattern-making—through the use of a compass and straight edge—by which all Islamic patterns may be effected. The analytical drawings in Bourgoin's *Arabic Geometrical Patterns* (1973) present two-dimensional patterns that Bourgoin documented in Cairo in the late nineteenth century. Representing a second approach to the study of Islamic art, Critchlow (1976) takes his documentation and analysis a step further, suggesting that the patterns reflect a cosmological understanding. This approach is also advocated by Bakhtiar (1976) and Ardalan and Bakhtiar (1973), whose analyses articulate

FIGURE 5B. Brick patterns, eleventh century, tomb tower at Kharraqan, Iran. Photo courtesy of David Stronach.

a spiritual quest on the part of the pattern-makers: enduring spiritual meaning is attributed to geometric forms and can be discovered through the practice of the craft that creates them.

A third approach to geometric patterns in Islamic art sees them in terms of their political function and context. This focus on political motivation is adopted by Necipoglu (1995) and Tabbaa (1991), and to some extent by Grabar (1992). In their analyses, historical circumstances are the primary factors influencing choice in the adoption of geometric forms of patterning. For example, Necipoglu's compilation of ornament and Islamic architecture seeks to interpret eleventh-century geometric patterns as expressions of dynastic identity, functioning as a form of dynastic propaganda (Necipoglu 1995, 96–99, 108–9, 192). Tabbaa focuses on the early Islamic development of proportional styles of calligraphy, in particular the style originated by Ibn Muqla around the year 1000 (fig. 2b), identifying the role of new conventions as a tool for the restoration of orthodoxy in eleventh-century century Baghdad, the Abbasid capital (Tabbaa 1991, 141–45).

Among other approaches, Chorbachi (1989) relates Islamic geometric patterns to the development of mathematical ideas and expressions, and the growth of mathematical thinking within the early Islamic realm. At the other end of the spectrum of meaning in ornament is the reception of Islamic ornament in Europe of the nineteenth century. Necipoglu articulates the assumptions that underlie the work of Owen Jones's *Grammar of Ornament*, attributing universal and timeless qualities to patterns regardless of their cultural origin, a method by which Jones attempts to develop laws of design equivalent to the laws of science (Necipoglu 1995, 64 n.16). Jones's approach explores patterns as visual expressions of design principles with universal application, rather than as systems of signification with cultural associations and contextual meanings.

None of these studies, however, has sought to explain the proliferation of geometric patterns from the eighth through the eleventh centuries as visual analogues to Islamic ideas or ways of thinking that were central to the philosophical debates of the time, although Necipoglu (1995, 96) does suggest the relevance of historical circumstance more generally. Yet this was a period of intense dialogue concerning man's relationship to the universe, and who we are in relation to larger forces of nature and the cosmos. Many philosophers of the East engaged in that discourse, offering commentaries on the translated works of Plato, Aristotle, and other writers, drawing on the heritage of classical antiquity. The Greek inheritance was readily received among the newly established Muslim intellectual elites. Arab and Islamic work in geometry appropriated and expanded on this body of classical material, leading to developments in algebra and trigonometry, and to an increased understanding of optics.

THE MATHEMATICS OF SPACE AND FORM

Several developments in Islamic art and architecture from the eighth to the eleventh centuries suggest a link during this period with a heightened interest in the mathematics of space and form. The articulation of patterned brickwork (fig. 5b) in tomb towers on the Iranian plateau (Demavand, Radkhan, and Kharraqan), and the proliferation in Islamic monuments from Spain to India of *muqarnas,* the internal segmentation of vaults, may be cited as particularly deserving scrutiny.[10]

Plato's *Timaeus* and Islamic Art

One seemingly coincidental, but I think crucial, point of reference and comparison warrants close attention here—namely, the relationship between Plato's ideal triangles (*Timaeus* 53–54) and El-Said's system of proportion in Islamic art based on $\sqrt{2}$ and $\sqrt{3}$. In a thesis published posthumously, El-Said (1993) puts forward an intriguing analysis of Islamic geometric patterns, according to which most patterns may be classified as belonging to a "root two system," (fig. 6a) or a "root three system" (fig. 6b). The difference between the patterns has to do with whether they are based on a square or a triangular grid. "Root two" describes the unit of proportion established by the diagonal of a square, which has a length of $\sqrt{2}$ in relation to the unit length of each side. "Root three" describes the unit of proportion established by the altitude of an equilateral triangle, which has a length of $\sqrt{3}$ in relation to the unit length of half the side of an equilateral triangle. Based on these two systems of proportion, a line of any magnitude may be established to generate patterns at different scales with the same proportional relationships. Once the craftsman determines a generating unit and a mode of iteration, the pattern may be carried through from conception to completion (El-Said 1993, 14).

Not quite twenty-five hundred years earlier, in what is one of the more difficult passages of his late dialogue *Timaeus,* Plato proposed two ideal triangles. One is the right isosceles triangle, with one right angle and two angles of 45°;

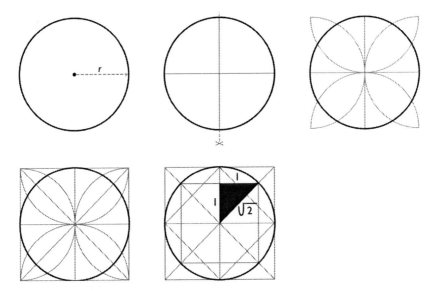

FIGURE 6A. El-Said's "Root Two" system of proportion, based on a right isosceles triangle. Contructions by Marina Meyerson.

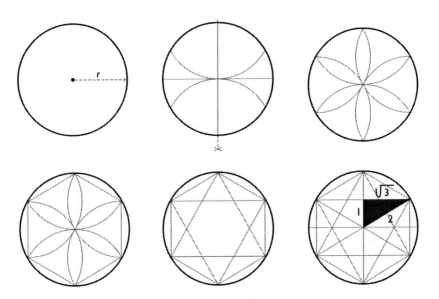

FIGURE 6B. El-Said's "Root Three" system of proportion, based on one half an equilateral triangle. Constructions by Marina Meyerson.

the other is half an equilateral triangle (thus, a triangle with angles of 30°, 60°, and 90°), with one side half the length of the hypotenuse. As Plato describes it:

[53] All solids again are bounded by planes, and all rectilinear planes are composed of triangles. There are two basic types of triangle, each having one right angle and two acute angles: in one of them these two angles are both half right angles, being subtended by equal sides, in the other they are unequal, being subtended by unequal sides. . . . We must proceed to inquire what are the four most perfect possible bodies. . . . [54] Of the two basic triangles, then, the isosceles has only one variety, the scalene an infinite number. We must therefore choose . . . the most perfect of this infinite number. If anyone can tell us of a better choice of triangle for the construction of the four bodies, his criticism will be welcome; but for our part we propose to pass over all the rest and pick on a single type, that of which a pair compose an equilateral triangle. It would be too long a story to give the reason, but if anyone can produce a proof that it is not so we will welcome his achievement. So let us assume that these are the two triangles . . . one isosceles and the other having a greater side whose square is three times that of the lesser.[11]

Plato immediately applied his ideal triangles to the construction of four three-dimensional solids (cube, tetrahedron, octahedron, and icosahedron), which we have come to call the "Platonic solids" (along with the dodecahedron, each face of which is a pentagon). El-Said's triangles, in contrast, are used to explain patterns in two-dimensional space. The apparent coincidence of Plato's pair of ideal triangles and El-Said's dual system is interesting. At first consideration, this suggests what might seem an unlikely proposition—namely, that Plato's work influenced Islamic art directly, in spite of the temporal and spatial distances. Another view might grant that although Plato was no doubt right,[12] there may have been an independent discovery in the Arab and Islamic realms of the tenth century. A third possibility is that Plato proposed his ideal triangles in the fourth century b.c. without proof, in order to expound on forms in three-dimensional space, and that the significance of these triangles in two-dimensional space was not fully understood until many centuries later, when it was formulated visually by Islamic artisans.

Plato's *Timaeus* is neither an easy text nor is it considered to be primarily a mathematical work. As a cosmology, it has been studied and commented on more often in relation to theological issues and to its creation story, in which the universe and everything in it is attributed to one supreme deity. Recognized for its influence on Christian thought, especially in light of its appropriation by the Scholastics, the *Timaeus* has become a major text of Western civilization. A quick glance at classical Islamic sources establishes that the text of the *Timaeus* was known to the Arabs in the tenth century, as it is listed among the dialogues of Plato in the *Fihrist* of al-Nadim, a compendium of contemporary sources (Dodge 1970, 593). Unfortunately, no copy of this translation survives, but there are numerous references to its subject matter among Islamic philosophical works (Walbridge 2000, 84–96).

The chief protagonist in Plato's dialogue is Timaeus himself. He expresses excitement but also confusion over how to go about defining three-dimensional space, and struggles to come up with a vocabulary for its description (Plato 1977, 24). Commentators as early as Aristotle sought to explicate the relevant passage about receptacles, forms, and motion (Claghorn 1954, chap. 2). Since Aristotle, numerous scholars continued the attempt with surprisingly different interpretations. In the sixth century, Simplicius sought to explicate and summarize the various opinions of his predecessors (Urmson 1992). If we approach Plato's ideal triangles from the perspective of two-dimensional space, perhaps it will become clear that Plato understood more than many later commentators.

Pattern-Making Exercises to Cover the Plane

Circles of equal radius, like pennies, naturally combine in one of two ways when tightly packed. One way of packing yields centers that form a triangular grid (fig. 7a); six circles surround every penny, all contiguous. This is the tightest possible packing in two dimensions; it has a three-dimensional analogue that in mathematics is the basis for Kepler's conjecture of 1611 that the tightest way to pack spheres of equal size is in a pyramidal cannonball formation. The proof for this conjecture had been sought by mathematicians for nearly four hundred years before being proposed in 1998 by Thomas Hales of the University of Michigan.[13] The other method of tight-packing (fig. 7b) yields centers that form a square grid; here, only four pennies touch every penny. In comparison to the triangular tight-packing, one can see that the spaces between the pennies packed in a square grid are greater.

In either system of tight-packing, the operative unit of measurement is the diameter of the penny. The proportional relationship of diameter to circumference is invariant (symbolized by the Greek letter π, so one can readily

FIGURE 7A. Tight-packed pennies form a triangular grid.

FIGURE 7B. Tight-packed pennies form a square grid.

see the implications of tight-packing for circles with equal diameters of any size. Such basic mathematical considerations underlie the play of pattern in Islamic art (Bier 2000). Furthermore, the underlying proportional relationships in each method are determined by the square root of three for the triangular tight-packing, and by the square root of two for the square tight-packing, relating this exercise both to El-Said's analysis and to Plato's proposition of ideal triangles.

The patterns that can be elaborated on these two grid systems (square and triangular) are explored with intensity in Islamic art. By selecting centers in a triangular grid, one can establish a rhombic or a hexagonal grid. By connecting centers to form lines and angles, or highlighting curves, many seemingly complex patterns may be generated from simple algorithms. The triangular grid lends itself to six-pointed stars and hexagons; the square grid may yield eight-pointed stars and cross forms. Lines and angles may then be established to create more relationships of stars and polygons. Further connecting lines or obliterating lines produces interlaced patterns. Through such intensive play with seemingly inexhaustible possibilities, one can begin to recognize aspects of intricacy, ambiguity, and complexity that are, in essence, simple. These interrelationships are fundamental to the production of patterns. They may result from the iterative manipulation of a single module, with only one or two variables of form, color, orientation, or placement. Increasing the complexity of the module increases the apparent complexity of the entire pattern.

Making Patterns

Art that relies on the principles of pattern-making forces the artist to engage in processes over which he has little control. Decisions may be made at the level of design; but once it is decided how the design will be manipulated to form a pattern, the laws of symmetry prevail until the symmetry is broken. The artist thus participates in a process by which number and pattern, unit and shape, are united integrally in visual forms. By participating in the processes of pattern-making, an artisan may quickly become familiar with the principles of applied geometry without ever needing to know or understand the symbolic or formulaic expression of iterations and algorithms, or the geometric relationships they represent.

The artistic production of repeated patterns may become deeply meaningful as meditation for the individual pattern-maker, who is enmeshed in a process at once unitary and systemic, in which mindlessness and mindfulness become one. The process of repetition itself constrains the individual within the laws of symmetry, while allowing full expression of the self. Because of the nature of the process, the pattern-maker may achieve a meditative state while engaged in pattern-making. But a similar effect may also be experienced by a viewer of the completed pattern. By contemplating a pattern, exploring the various relationships of its parts and uncovering the inherent ambiguities of its visual expression, it is possible to move beyond a level of cognition that depends on visual perception and optical recognition alone.

Several recent works touching on geometry in Islamic art have questioned the role and relationship of mathematician to artist (Özdural 1995, 1996; Grabar 1992). The craft of the artist is assumed, but what of his or her mathematical knowledge? How might mathematical knowledge have been transmitted to artisans and craftsmen who created the monuments that have endured to this day? From the careful study of geometric patterns in Islamic art, it can be argued that little mathematical knowledge is required to make what appear to be complex patterns from simple algorithms (El-Said 1993, 14). Once a generating unit and its mode of iteration have been determined, it is the process of pattern formation that carries the craftsman from conception to completion.

Apart from the sequences involved in constructions using a compass and straight edge, the processes of pattern formation differ in the various media. For example, the use of ceramic tile may entail incising, cutting, and glazing, while for a pile carpet, the patterns are effected by counting and repeating sequences of knots (pieces of colored yarns, wrapped around pairs of warps). On a page in an illuminated manuscript, patterns may actually be constructed using a compass and straight edge, then filled in with a pen or brush, using pigments and various techniques for gilding. For carved stucco, the pattern may be first constructed using a compass and straight edge, then carved and painted. Alternatively, blocks may be carved first and the stucco molded or stamped in a manner similar to the printing of patterns on cloth. For pattern-woven textiles, an entirely different technique is utilized, one in which a model is established to effect mechanical repetition at the loom by calculated manipulations of warp and weft. It should be clear that each technology affects the process through which relationships are established between number and shape. The resulting visual effect in a work of art is far removed—and yet integral with—the temporal processes of pattern formation.

One of the primary characteristics of pattern is that it is both unitary and systemic. The physical and visual effects of pattern-making as a process of iteration thus connect the maker to an implication of infinity. When making a pattern, the maker is engaged in a process that is itself limited by the laws of nature. Symmetry allows for repetition, but only according to certain principles (Bier 1997).

This discussion, then, is not so much about the *role* of geometry in Islamic art as it is about *geometry* in Islamic art, and the reasons for its presence. The questions are not about decoration and ornament, but about surfaces and the plane, about units and repeats, about properties of the circle and the nature of space. It has not been adequately recognized that these forms, no matter how basic they are understood to be today, were new to the artistic repertory of pattern-making from the eighth to the eleventh centuries, during which time they were critical to the exploration of the mathematical properties of space in two and three dimensions in the Islamic world.

THE MEANING AND METAPHYSICS OF NUMBER AND SHAPE

The fifty-one epistles of the *Ikhwan al-Safa* (Brethren of Purity) deal with number and geometry (Netton 1982; Nasr 1964). The brethren emphasized "one" as indivisible, a unit synonymous with "thing" (*shay*). Multiplicity arises from the addition of one to one in succession. The work of the brethren explored the relations among algebra and geometry, ethics, Aristotelian logic, physical and corporeal questions, the intellect, and ways of knowing God. They acknowledged their predecessors, especially Nichomachus of Gerasa and Pythagoras, in the study of number, which, they argued, can lead to knowledge of the soul and ultimately to the knowledge of God, which is possible only through thought (Fakhry 1997, 58). They declared that "knowledge of number with its laws, nature, kinds, and properties ... will obviously be familiar with the number of created things, together with reason for their present qualities and why they are neither more nor less than they are" (Netton 1982, 10). From contemplation of multiplicity, an individual's self-knowledge will yield recognition of a human being's intermediate position; "knowledge itself is intermediate between total ignorance and omniscience" (Fakhry 1997, 58).

The Brethren of Purity justified a relationship between revelation and rational thought as described by Fakhry (1997, 59):

The human mind, according to the Epistles, is unable to grasp the highest realities such as God's essence or His majesty, the form of the whole universe, or even the intelligible forms, as separated from matter. Nor are individuals able to grasp such philosophical questions as the origination of the universe and the cause of its coming into being, or the mode of existence proper to created entities in the higher or lower worlds. If the knowledge of all those realities cannot be attained through reason, the individual's only recourse is assent to the teachings of the prophets, who received their inspiration from God.

For the brethren, there was no conflict between religion and philosophy. I argue below that this metaphysical link—relating the individual to origins, existence, space, and extent—lies at the heart of geometric pattern in the period of formulation of Islamic art.

From the ninth and into the eleventh century, Mu'tazili rationalists held political favor in Baghdad, the Abbasid capital. They held that reason could demonstrate the existence of God, and that a rational knowledge of God was possible (Martin and Woodward 1997, 9–12). They also accepted the historical context of revelation, and argued for ethical accountability to God. Such interpretations ran counter to more traditional views, which emphasized the "uncreatedness of the Qur'an" and the power of divine will. The Islamic world was thus divided between those who defended the power and role of reason (the Mu'tazilites) and the defenders of faith (the Ash'arites). Geometry and pattern, with its inherent implication of the infinite, could serve both sides.

Seeking the earliest use of the concept of *logos,* Detienne in his provocative work on the *Masters of Truth in Archaic Greece* proposes that "on the one hand, *logos* was seen as an instrument of social relations. . . . Rhetoric and sophistry began to develop the grammatical and stylistic analysis of techniques of persuasion. Meanwhile, the other path, explored by philosophy led to reflections on *logos* as a means of knowing reality: is speech all of reality? If so, what about the reality expressed by numbers?" (Detienne 1996, 17). If the question were posed today, "How can knowledge be verbalized?" no one would disagree that it is through *logos,* the word, whether spoken or written. But what if we pose the question differently and ask, "How can knowledge be visualized?"

In the context of the discourse from the eighth to the eleventh centuries, can we perhaps view geometric pattern in Islamic art as a representation of the rational intellect, and thereby perceived as proof for the existence of God? Patterns provide a system of natural laws that exist outside the individual, but within which an individual may situate herself. They force acknowledgment and acceptance of those laws, which are "external" to the individual, yet allow within the structure of those laws the participation of the individual as maker or viewer. Is pattern nonrepresentational? Or is it representational at the deepest meaning as a metaphorical statement of relationships, of existence, of the cosmos—as a reality itself that expresses realities beyond that which can be merely seen?

Rather than practical applications of a theoretical formulation, patterns during this period might better be seen as practical formulations that later gave rise to theoretical applications. The play with visual forms in the Islamic world between the eighth and eleventh centuries, then, may be seen as removed from theory, but related to discourse. The then contemporary discourse is neither critical nor documentary; it is about ideas of theory and reality, limits and conceptions, magnitudes and relationships—the metaphysics of number and shape. It is a discourse of correspondences, into which these visual forms fit as graphic expressions of geometric realities that predate human manipulation or intellectual intervention. In the late twelfth century, Ibn al-Arabi directly relates geometry to God, "God is both the center point (*nukta*) and the circumference (*muhit*)," citing the divine names of the First and the Last, the Manifest and the Non-Manifest (Chittick 1998, 224), hinting already at an accepted understanding of the qualities of the circle, and a recognition of the significance of manipulating number and shape.

If one considers the cultural environment for this development, it is possible to put forward the intriguing hypothesis that pattern play in Islamic art elaborated on the geometry transmitted from the Greeks, combined with the arithmetic absorbed from India. The Hindu numbers counted from one to nine, making a decimal system of base ten, with zero as a place holder. These were transmitted throughout the Islamic world and eventually to Europe, where they came to be called "Arabic numerals." The combined inheritance of Indian reckoning (Joseph 1992, 311–16; Saidan 1978; Levey and Petruck 1965) and Greek geometry allowed the Muslim craftsmen to conscientiously exploit the potentiality of the relationships among numbers (arithmetic) and shapes (geometry).

The earliest Islamic art did *not* demonstrate a proclivity for geometric patterns. Rather, as the early monuments reflect, it was heir to a rich mix of preexisting artistic traditions—those of the late Roman and early Christian eras; the Byzantine Greeks; and the Jews and Persians of late antiquity in Mediterranean lands and beyond (Grabar 1973). But beginning in the eighth century, a clearly defined Islamic aesthetic asserted itself from Spain to India, characterized by planar patterns consisting of tessellations, stars and polygons, interlaced patterns, and three-dimensional segmented structures—*muqarnas*—that had internal divisions within a vaulted structure. This centuries-long development can be described as the movement from the *formation* of Islamic art to its *formulation*.

In the course of its development, Islamic art reflected a deconstruction of artistic design elements and an identification of universals of number and shape, newly applied to the construction of patterns. Form and pattern were at first not understood as number theory and pattern theory, but were treated as having a potential for intellectual exploration beyond mere repetition. In the arts of the Islamic world beginning in the eighth century, visual analogues to then contemporary discourse can be seen to emerge. By this interpretation, both Islamic art and philosophy of the time expressed ontological concerns regarding human beings, the rational intellect, and the nature of God. This trend continued until the restoration of orthodoxy in the eleventh century (Makdisi 1990).

Eventually Islamic decorative arts entered into the European realm in the middle of the nineteenth century (Jones 1842–45 and Jones 1868). By then, Islamic art influenced European art under the rubric of "Oriental exoticism." The meaningfulness of Islamic patterns, charged with significance in their classical Islamic context, co-mingled with the visual appeal of the European decorative arts tradition, so that the Islamic forms lost their metaphysical subtexts, from which they were already quite far removed. Owen Jones's *Grammar of Ornament* both consciously and conscientiously sought a rational language to describe ornament in a manner appropriate to industrial technologies, neglecting the deeper significance of this kind of art in its original cultural contexts.

I have argued in this essay for the recognition of a creative moment in the history of a developing civilization—around the year 1000, with antecedents as early as 750 of the common era—that produced a new understanding of the structuring of space through the use of number and shape. The construction of patterns in Islamic art became charged with new meanings—mathematics and physics were at one with metaphysics, theology, and art—and provided a rich source for artistic exploration throughout the Islamic world from Spain to India. Disciplinary boundaries, as we know them today, were fluid or nonexistent. The resulting cultural synthesis can be likened to other great moments of civilization—the fifth century B.C. in Athens, or the Renaissance in Italy—moments of great intellectual energy coupled with dramatic cultural advancement.[14]

The tenth and eleventh centuries within the Islamic world have been characterized both as a golden age and as an age of great transition (Richards 1973). However it is understood, I contend that the crucial development of the time was not a new conceptualization of space generally nor a new utilization of space, but rather a new understanding of two-dimensional space that connects with the metaphysics of number and shape. This new understanding found expression in the many designs on buildings and objects in which any unit and an algorithm for its repetition function together within the laws of nature. The subject of representation, then, may be seen as the pattern itself. What seems significant is that any visual form may serve the same function, allowing a full exploration of the processes of pattern-making. This realization was exploited in the formulation of Islamic art to create a plethora of geometric patterns and visual forms that express the understanding of oneself in the cosmos, either as pattern-maker or viewer.

EPILOGUE

The subjects of this discourse, both verbal and visual, persist to the present. But the locus today has shifted to the concern of theoretical physicists with the nature of space and time, as well as to more recent attempts to bridge science and religion, and contemporary explorations into the relationship of man and the universe (Huggett 1999; Brisson and Meyerstein 1995). Today, within the academy, there is an effort to break down disciplinary boundaries. Yet in order to succeed in this process, we need to allow ourselves opportunities to reintegrate our ways of thinking, learning, and knowing. Crucial, I believe, to a renewed understanding across the bounds of individual disciplines is a renewed respect for humankind and its relationship to forces greater than self. The striving for a single unified theory, a new gnosis, may be prefigured in medieval Islamic art by the visually explicit understanding of number, shape and the nature of space.

NOTES

This essay has benefited from the comments of Jerry Cooper, Claudia Brittenham, and Bilinda Straight, each of whom I wish to thank for their insightful suggestions.

1. Figural arts of the Islamic world are not considered in this essay. For discussion of the proscription against figural images in Islamic art, see Freedberg 1989, 55.

2. Ibn Muqla (886–940 A.D.), "master of the proportioned script," is considered by many to be the father of Islamic calligraphy (Tabbaa 1991, 122). He defined a system of proportion for the first canonical Islamic script style; his and all subsequent cursive scripts are based on the circle as the measure of proportion (Grabar 1992, chap. 2).

3. Islamic art, although still practiced today, is generally placed in the context of the Middle Ages. See H.W. Jansen, *History of Art,* 3d ed. (New York: Abrams, 1986), 242–54; Frederick Hartt, *Art: A History of Painting, Sculpture, Architecture,* 3d ed. (New York: Abrams, 1989), 349–68; Hugh Honour and John Fleming, *The Visual Arts: A History,* 3d ed. (Englewood Cliffs: Prentice Hall, 1991), 296–316. The third editions of these works, although generally better balanced and more accurate with regard to Islam than earlier editions, still retain a Eurocentric stance, including some negative prejudice in comparing Islam with Christianity. Honour and Fleming present early Islamic art only, and that in a section entitled "Art & the World Religions" (i.e., non-European).

4. Although Ernst Gombrich (1979) sought to correct this judgment, he identified three principle roles for ornament: framing, filling, and linking, none of which position ornament as the *subject* of representation. Freedberg (1989, 54–82) specifically confronts the notion of aniconism (the rejection of figural imagery) and its implications for the absence of meaning.

5. The cultural dominance and biases of a Western European perspective is addressed by Robert S. Nelson, "The Map of Art History," *Art Bulletin* 79(1) (1997): 28–40. The parallel hegemony of Enlightenment thinking in the social sciences is discussed by Ruth Abbey, *Philosophy Now: Charles Taylor* (Princeton: Princeton University Press, 2000), chap. 5.

6. For discussion of the translation of the Greek scientific corpus into Arabic, see Gutas 1998; Peters 1968; Rosenthal 1990, 1994.

7. The contribution of Arabic sources and Islamic science to the Renaissance is recognized in Sarton 1952. The study of optics and conics, for example, dramatically affected later developments in the Renaissance, leading in part to the artistic evolution of perspective (Panofsky 1997). Damisch (1994), however, sees this development as culturally specific to time and place, from an exclusively Western vantage point.

8. For a summary of al-Khwarezmi's contributions to European mathematics, see Victor J. Katz, *A History of Mathematics: An Introduction,* 2d ed. (Reading, Mass.: Addison-Wesley, 1998), 240–49, passim. See also J. L. Berggren, *Episodes in the Mathematics of Medieval Islam* (New York: Springer-Verlag, 1986), 6–9.

9. Illustrations are easily accessible in any of several general surveys of Islamic art, See Sheila S. Blair and Jonathan M. Bloom, *Islamic Arts* (London: Phaidon, 1997); Richard Ettinghausen, Oleg Grabar and Marilyn Jenkins-Madina, *Islamic Art and Architecture, 650–1250,* 2nd ed. (New Haven: Yale University Press, 2001); Robert Hillenbrand, *Islamic Art and Architecture* (London: Thames and Hudson, 1999).

10. An overview of the development of this form is provided by Yasser Tabbaa under the entry "Muqarnas" in *Dictionary of Art* (London: Macmillan, 1997), and in an article, "The Muqarnas Dome: Its Origin and Meaning," *Muqarnas* 3 (1985): 61–74.

11. Page references to the *Timaeus* are to the 1578 edition of Stephanus; translation here is by Desmond Lee in Plato 1977, 73–75; see also Cornford 1997, 212–16; Taylor 1928, 361–72.

12. Even today, the triangles available for purchase in specialized stores serving the drafting needs of architects, engineers, and artists are the right isosceles triangle and the 30°-60°-90° triangle. But we would not presume by the coincidence that these are Platonic triangles, rather, perhaps, that Plato hit on something fundamental to our conceptualization of nature and the built environment.

13. Simon Singh, "Mathematics 'Proves' What the Grocer Always Knew," *New York Times,* 25 August 1998, F3, col. 1.

14. For a brief survey of linked advances in geometry and art since the Renaissance, see Ivins 1964, 105–10. For a broader view of relationships between art and the physics of space, see Shlain 1991.

WORKS CITED

Abas, Syed Jan, and Amer Shaker Salman. 1995. *Symmetries of Islamic Geometrical Patterns.* Singapore: World Scientific.

Ardalan, Nader, and Laleh Bakhtiar. 1973. *The Sense of Unity: The Sufi Tradition in Persian Architecture.* Chicago: University of Chicago Press.

Bakhtiar, Laleh. 1976. *Sufi: Expressions of the Mystic Quest.* New York: Thames and Hudson.

Begley, Wayne. 1979. "The Myth of the Taj Mahal and a New Theory of Its Symbolic Meaning." *Art Bulletin* 61(1):7–37.

Bier, Carol. 1997. "Symmetry and Pattern: The Art of Oriental Carpets." Available at http://mathforum.edu/geometry/rugs. The Math Forum and The Textile Museum.

———. 2000. "Circles and Centers: A Review Article." *Middle East Studies Association Bulletin* 34(1), 56–68.

Bourgoin, J. 1973. *Arabic Geometrical Pattern and Design.* New York: Dover.

Brisson, Luc, and Walter Meyerstein. 1995. *Inventing the Universe: Plato's Timaeus, the Big Bang and the Problem of Scientific Knowledge.* Albany: State University of New York Press.

Chittick, William C. 1998. *The Self-Disclosure of God: Principles of Ibn al-Arabi's Cosmology.* Albany: State University of New York Press.

Chorbachi, W. K. 1989. "In the Tower of Babel: Beyond Symmetry in Islamic Design." *Computers and Mathematics with Applications* 17:751–89. Reprinted in I. Hargittai, ed., *Symmetry 2: Unifying Human Understanding.* New York: Pergamon.

Claghorn, George S. 1954. *Aristotle's Criticism of Plato's* Timaeus. The Hague: Nijhoff.

Cornford, Francis M. 1997. *Plato's Cosmology: The* Timaeus *of Plato.* Indianapolis: Hackett.

Critchlow, Keith. 1976. *Islamic Patterns: An Analytical and Cosmological Approach.* London: Thames and Hudson.

Damisch, Hubert. 1994. *The Origins of Perspective.* Translated by John Goodman. Cambridge: MIT Press.

Detienne, Marcel. 1996. *The Masters of Truth in Archaic Greece.* New York: Zone Books.

Dodge, Bayard, ed. and trans. 1970. *The Fihrist of al-Nadim: A Tenth Century Survey of Muslim Culture.* 2 vols. New York: Columbia University Press.

Fakhry, Majid. 1997. *A Short Introduction to Islamic Philosophy, Theology, and Mysticism.* Oxford: Oneworld.

Freedberg, David. 1989. *The Power of Images: Studies in the History and Theory of Response.* Chicago: University of Chicago Press.

Gombrich, E. H. 1979. *The Sense of Order: A Study in the Psychology of Decorative Art.* Ithaca: Cornell University Press.

Grabar, Oleg. 1973. *The Formation of Islamic Art.* New Haven: Yale University Press.

———. 1992. *The Mediation of Ornament.* Bollingen Series XXXV/38. Princeton: Princeton University Press. [See esp. chap. 3: "The Intermediary of Geometry."]

Gutas, Dimitri. 1998. *Greek Thought, Arabic Culture: The Graeco-Arabic Translation Movement in Baghdad and Early Abbasid Society (2nd–4th/8–10th Centuries).* London: Routledge.

Huggett, Nick, ed. 1999. *Space from Zeno to Einstein.* Cambridge: MIT Press.

Ivins, William M., Jr. 1964. *Art and Geometry: A Study in Space.* New York: Dover.

Jones, Owen. 1842–45. *Plans, Elevations, Sections and Details of the Alhambra.* London: O. Jones.

———. 1868. *The Grammar of Ornament.* London: Bernard Quaritch.

Joseph, George Gheverghese. 1992. *The Crest of the Peacock: Non-European Roots of Mathematics.* New York: Penguin Books.

Levey, Martin, and Marvin Petruck, trans. 1965. *Kushyar ibn Labban, "Principles of Hindu Reckoning."* Madison: University of Wisconsin Press.

Makdisi, George. 1990. *History and Politics in Eleventh-Century Baghdad.* Brookfield, Vt.: Variorum.

Martin, Richard C., and Mark R. Woodward, with Dwi S. Atmaja. 1997. *Defenders of Reason in Islam: Mu'tazilism from Medieval School to Modern Symbol.* Oxford: Oneworld.

Nasr, Seyyed Hossein. 1964. *An Introduction to Islamic Cosmological Doctrines. Conceptions of Nature and Methods Used for its Study by the Ikhwan al-Safa, al-Biruni and Ibn Sina.* Cambridge: Belknap Press, Harvard University Press.

Necipoglu, Gulru. 1995. *The Topkapi Scroll—Geometry and Ornament in Islamic Architecture.* Santa Monica: Getty Trust Publications.

Netton, Ian Richard. 1982. *Muslim Neoplatonists: An Introduction to the Thought of the Brethren of Purity (Ikhwan at-Safa').* London: Allen and Unwin.

Özdural, Alpay. 1995. "Omar Khayyam, Mathematicians, and *Conversazioni* with Artisans." *Journal of the Society of Architectural Historians* 54(1) (March): 54–71.

————. 1996. "On Interlocking Similar or Corresponding Figures and Ornamental Patterns of Cubic Equations." *Muqarnas* 13:191–211.

Panofsky, Erwin. 1997. *Perspective as Symbolic Form.* New York: Zone Books.

Peters, F. E. 1968. *Aristotle and the Arabs: The Aristotelian Tradition in Islam.* New York: New York University Press.

————. 1982. *Children of Abraham: Judaism, Christianity and Islam.* Princeton: Princeton University Press.

Plato. *Timaeus and Critias.* Translated by Desmond Lee. London: Penguin Books.

Richards, D. S., ed. 1973. *Islamic Civilization 950–1150. Papers on Islamic History III.* Oxford: Cassirer.

Rosenthal, Franz. 1990. *Greek Philosophy in the Arab World.* Brookfield, Vt.: Variorum.

————. 1994. *The Classical Heritage in Islam.* London: Routledge.

El-Said, Issam. 1993. *Islamic Art and Architecture: The System of Geometric Design.* Edited by Tarek El-Bouri and Keith Critchlow. Reading, UK: Garnet Publishing.

Saidan, A. S., trans. 1978. *The Arithmetic of al-Uqlidisi: The Story of Hindu-Arabic Arithmetic as Told in Kitab al-fusul fi al-hisab al Hindi, by Abu al-Hasan, Ahmed ibn Ibrahim al-Uqlidisi, Written in Damascus in the Year 341 (A.D. 952/3).* Boston: Reidel.

Sarton, George. 1952. *A History of Science.* 2 vols. Cambridge: Harvard University Press.

Shlain, Leonard. 1991. *Art & Physics: Parallel Visions in Space, Time, and Light.* New York: William Morrow.

Tabbaa, Yasser. 1991. "The Transformation of Arabic Writing: Part 1, Qur'anic Calligraphy." *Ars Orientalis* 21:119–48.

Taylor, A. E. 1928. *A Commentary on Plato's* Timaeus. Oxford: Clarendon Press.

Urmson, J. O., trans. 1992. *Simplicius: Corollaries on Place and Time.* Ithaca: Cornell University Press.

Walbridge, John. 2000. *The Leaven of the Ancients: Suhrawardi and the Heritage of the Greeks.* Albany: State University of New York Press.

CHAPTER THIRTEEN

Liminal Pedagogy

The Liberal Arts and the Transforming Ritual of Religious Studies

Jeffrey J. Kripal

In the classroom both students and teachers must face the question how they are to talk about religion, especially the religions of others. In addition to the dangers of patronization on the one hand or "going native" on the other, which are themes in several of the essays in this book, there is the question of the impact of the study of religion on one's own beliefs, or disbeliefs. If the religious commitments of others are talked about as real possibilities for sensible and wise people—possibilities one could imagine sharing—what is to be the effect of that on oneself?

Here Jeffrey Kripal shows how he raised and addressed this question in his classroom at Westminster College, where many of his students were lifelong and relatively unquestioning Christian believers. As the reader will see, he has a way of making the question of their own attitudes and commitments central to the experience of his students, at once insisting on its reality and importance and respecting the autonomy of the student who must ultimately make the choice for himself or herself.

You find yourself able to pass over from the standpoint of your life to those of others, entering into a sympathetic understanding of them, finding resonances between their lives and your own, and coming back once again, enriched, to your own standpoint.
—John Dunne

But simply because the academic study of religion is neutral vis-à-vis competing religions' claims does not mean that it is value-free. The study of religion can never be value-free because the very existence of the discipline depends on this value: the development of a worldview that cherishes a neutral position vis-à-vis the various religions as well as an ability to see the internal

coherence and logic that empowers each of them. This value is emphatically rejected by at
least some segments of all major religions. . . . [Thus o]ne should feel that sexist, racist,
ethnocentric, and religious chauvinisms, if present, are being threatened by the academic
study of religion. . . . It is rarely possible to conclude one's studies carrying the same opinions
regarding religious, ethnic, class, gender, and cultural diversity with which one began.
—Rita Gross

A rather long time ago, about one hundred years to be inexact, a Belgian anthropologist by the name of Arnold van Gennep noticed something particular
about many of the initiation rituals of different cultures. They tended to follow a tripartite pattern: moving from an initial state of separation from society through a transitional period and into a final state of incorporation back
into the community.[1] Much later, the American anthropologist Victor Turner
picked up on van Gennep's tripartite structure and decided to focus on what
we might call the "existential" and "social transformational" possibilities of this
movement. He thus extended the model into his well-known reflections about
the "liminal" qualities of van Gennep's transition state, a chaotic but creative
condition defined for Turner by paradox, ambiguity, and bivalency, and an attending, often radically egalitarian, social experience that Turner called "com-
munitas."[2] I propose that the same model can be used to understand and appreciate what often happens in the liberal arts' religious studies classroom.

I stole the idea from Bryan Rennie, my colleague at Westminster College,
where we both taught the history of religions. (I have since moved to Rice University, where I no longer teach this particular course.) I can't recall whether it
was something he said to me one day, or whether it was something I saw in
one of his own syllabi. It doesn't really matter, I suppose. The idea was simple
enough: to develop an introductory course on the comparative study of religion
along the lines of a ritualized initiation, to take the students—consciously,
intentionally, systematically—through the stages of pre-ritual stability, ritual
liminality, and post-ritual reconstitution. Is not this what essentially happens
anyway when a group of students are confronted over an extended period of
time in an already pluralistic setting with worlds of meaning radically different than their own? And is this not, in some broad cultural sense, the spirit
behind a four-year liberal arts college experience? Why not make this implicit
process more explicit? At least then, I thought, I could be more honest about
what in fact I was trying to accomplish in the classroom.

This essay is a collection of stories about what happened when I decided to
teach religious studies in a small liberal arts setting in just this way. There are

some happy endings here, and some sad ones. There are pedagogical conclusions on my part, and more than a few questions. I proceed in three steps. First, I trace the barest outlines of my own pedagogical training as a more or less direct outcome of my own education: I teach as I was taught. Second, I reflect on the general patterns that define being a professor of religion at a small American liberal arts college. What does it feel like? What does it involve emotionally, professionally, religiously, socially? Finally, I focus on a single course I taught, the introductory course in comparative religion, outlining in some detail its structure, spirit, content, and general effect on the students. This final exercise, I hope, will give me a concrete way of embodying and performing the seeming random reflections that preceded it. We move, then, from life to theory to praxis.

THE TEACHER TAUGHT:
OR BLAMING OTHERS FOR MY PEDAGOGY

One teaches very much as one has been taught, which is another way of saying that one learns one's pedagogy by stages from people, usually from people whom one loves. Wendy Doniger, my own graduate mentor, puts it this way: "Though I have lived a rather bookish life, all that I ever learned I learned for the love of some person, so I must tell the story of my intellectual odyssey in terms of the people who changed my life."[3] I learned my first and perhaps most important lessons about pedagogy from my high school mathematics teacher, James Fraser. Jim loved mathematics as an exquisitely beautiful form of pure knowledge, as a virtual Platonic vision in the high school classroom (and he knew more than a little about Plato; I even recall the philosopher's bust looking down on us from a dusty shelf). If there is such a thing as the pure love of knowledge for its own sake, and I think there is, Jim had it. Happily, he also had the ability to communicate it to his students.

Jim's love of mathematics and learning in general was contagious, in the best sense of that term, if also mischievous and creative. I remember his showing the class a film on the geometry of the fourth dimension; it made absolutely no sense to any of us, especially since he wouldn't show us the title run, that is, the first few seconds of the film that would have included a title or subject, and adamantly refused to tell us what it was about. He thought we could figure it out on our own. We couldn't. If my memory serves me here, it was only years later, long after I had graduated, that he told me what the film was about, and then only because I took the trouble to ask him.

From Jim I also caught a passion for learning, a sense of intellectual beauty and simplicity, and a pedagogical penchant for the quirky and silly. Among other antics, Jim liked to quickly shuffle his feet from side to side while keeping his legs stiff, giving the impression of his floating across the blackboard, which he covered with a ridiculous amount of colored chalk, equations, and number problems each day. He would do almost anything to keep hold of our hormone-compromised attention spans.

My second important lesson I learned in the seminary from the monks of Conception Abbey, who taught me, as much by example as by what they said in the classroom and in the confessional, the Thomistic conviction that the search for truth can be fearless and bold and holy, since the truth (including New Testament criticism and Freudian psychology, both of which I first learned from them) cannot possibly contradict God, because God made the human mind and instilled in it a passion for knowledge. If, then, the truth and God do appear to contradict one another, it is our image or idea of God that must change, not the truth (which is never perfect but always preferred). And as our perceptions of truth change—and they will change, if we are honest and brave—so too must our visions of God and our understandings of religion.

It was once more a monk who refused to take me back as his spiritual directee my senior year, lest I remain dependent on him, and who encouraged me not to join the monastery but to go to graduate school where I could pursue my quest(ion)s in freedom and honesty, outside, if necessary, both the daily discipline of monastic life and the doctrinal parameters of the church itself. Both outsides, it turned out, were in fact necessary. I will never forget a story this same monk told me about a Renaissance biblical scholar (I forget the man's name, but it doesn't matter—it is the story that counts). He had been imprisoned for refusing to stop teaching about contradictions in the Pentateuch and what these might suggest about the texts' very human histories. He was, in other words, an early pioneer in what would much later become historical criticism of the biblical texts. After his long imprisonment, the scholar returned to his podium in the university and picked up exactly where he left off, with the texts' contradictions and what these might suggest about their human histories, as if nothing at all had happened.[4]

The human mind is sacred, "immeasurable" as Emerson put it centuries later in his "Divinity School Address" at Harvard.[5] This mind's truth, moreover, is often greater than the equally historical and bounded church, and if the church thought it was God, well, then it was mistaken and needed to be corrected, prison or no. Truth is holy, even and *especially* when it feels sacrilegious.

"Offensive," after all, is often nothing more than a misleading name for "truth beyond the present tradition" or for an insight someone does not like. It is a fearful and ultimately vain attempt to end discussion, not begin it anew.

The same monk who refused to accept me as his spiritual directee for one last year also encouraged me to go the University of Chicago to study the history of religions. I did. I arrived at the Divinity School knowing virtually nothing about the school, its faculty, or the comparative study of religion. All I knew was that I wanted to study the relationship between sexuality and mystical experience (years of anorexic suffering linked to my own sexual repression, the Catholic discipline of celibacy, and some psychologically astute monk-counselors had made the issue particularly salient for me),[6] and that something the Hindu tradition called "Tantra" seemed an especially good way to begin asking questions (and getting a very different set of answers). It is often said in India that when the disciple is ready the guru appears. I was certainly ready, and the guru did indeed appear. Actually, there were many gurus, too many really. Ed Dimock, the doyen of Bengali studies in America at that time, his health failing, agreed to conduct a private tutorial with me and one other student on Tantra in Bengal. There were days the two of us walked into his office only to find Ed stretched out on a couch, too weak to sit up but still willing to talk about the Bengali materials he loved so deeply. Ed died a few years ago. His student, Clint Seely, an expert on Bengali literary history, would teach me Bengali and mentor me through the years of my dissertation. Within another religious and cultural world, the historian of Christianity Bernard McGinn taught me how to think about the philosophical, theological, epistemological, and erotic dimensions of Christian mysticism. Indeed, Bernie went so far as to help a small coterie of us form our own private study group on mysticism. We gathered every other week to discuss another article or book, always with him there to guide us.

But probably no one played a more important role in my graduate training than the mythologist and historian of religions Wendy Doniger. The fit was not obvious, least of all to us. I was a hick from Nebraska, a rather shy, small-town, Catholic boy from an even smaller Catholic seminary of which I am certain that she had never heard. Wendy, on the other hand, was a sophisticated, cosmopolitan woman from an accomplished New York Jewish family with two Ph.D.s to her credit, one from Harvard and one from Oxford. She had read more languages than I could name. And, perhaps most strikingly, she had a certain undeniable charisma: when I sat in her office, I thought I could feel the hair on my head blow back in a wind of intellectual energy emanating from her. We were very different. But we had very similar questions to ask of life and religion. We wanted to know about sexuality. She had applied her questions to world mythology, particularly Hindu mythology and, a bit later, to Greek, Roman, Christian, Jewish, and contemporary popular materials. I would apply mine to the history of mysticism, particularly Hindu and Christian mysticism. But there were many connections, and she taught me—as much by her presence and writings as by anything she said in class—how better to ask my questions and advance my own personal answers. The truth of the matter is simple: I doubt very much whether I could have asked, much less answered, the questions I did with her at Chicago anywhere else in the country. Wendy gave me a freedom others would have certainly tried to deny me, and that has made all the difference. I could not have been "me" on the page without her.

Finally, there was Aditi Sen, my Bengali teacher in Calcutta. Aditi came from a noble Indian intellectual heritage. Her grandfather, for example, was Dinesh Chandra Sen, the great Bengali literary historian whose massive *History of Bengali Language and Literature* inspired me during my studies there. Aditi had studied comparative literature and was now in charge of tutoring American students at the American Institute of Indian Studies in Calcutta. That year, I was the only one. In a word, Aditi taught me about culture, or, in a few more words, about the multiplicity and complexity of culture. Because of her—and I mean Aditi as a whole person—I never again thought of culture, any culture, as monolithic, as "one thing." I, after all, had had the good fortune of learning my Calcutta primarily from an elegant, educated, Westernized woman (a rare treat indeed, since the genders are kept quite distinct in the public culture), and so I knew perfectly well that the Calcutta of the streets, or of the press, or of the temples, or of the politicians (each world controlled more or less by men) was not the only Calcutta, and maybe not even the most important. Aditi taught me, in other words, about cultural pluralism, even within a "single" culture of a kind that, I now knew, does not really exist and probably never did.

PROFESSING RELIGION

Two scenes.

Scene One. I always dread it. I'm on a plane or at a social gathering and someone asks me what I do. "I am a college professor," I admit, fully aware of what will come next. "What do you teach?" There it is. The big question. I once heard the evangelical sociologist Tony Campolo beautifully describe his own version of the dilemma. He's on an airplane, and the passenger next to him asks, "What do you do for a living?" Campolo explained that he has two options. If he feels like chatting, he says, "I'm a sociologist," and the conversation takes off from there, almost always in an animated fashion. If, however, he does not feel like talking, he replies, "I'm a Baptist preacher," and that pretty much ends the conversation. As Richard Rorty has said, religion is a conversation stopper. The situation is similar, if perhaps not quite so drastic, for the religion professor. "What do you teach?" I've tried them all: "religion," "religious studies," "the history of religions," "comparative religion." They all kill the conversation. Eyes glaze over as memories of Sunday School class, CCD, uncomfortably hard pews, or damning sermons filled with incomprehensible beliefs invade my would-be interlocutor's brain. I have barely opened my mouth, and I am already condemned, more or less identified with that minister, priest, or church. The situation is seldom any better for the religiously committed or devout: no bad memories here, just lots of suspicions (most of them accurately placed) on me. Sometimes I try to throw a wrench into this neuronal machine of memory and hesitancy and admit what I really do: "I teach gender and religion, which you are free to translate as 'sex and religion.'" That either really works, or it really doesn't.

I hate these public spaces.

Scene Two. "What are the three things your mother told you never to talk about in public?" I ask my gender and religion class on the first day. "Sex, religion, and politics," they answer, after more than a little prodding from me. "That's all we'll be talking about for four months now. Get ready."

The Call and the Red Chair

When I joined the Westminster faculty in 1993, I was hired under two general rubrics: Asian Studies and Roman Catholic Studies. The combination may have been unusual, but the logic was not: the Department of Religion and Philosophy was simply trying to fill its major gaps, and it was given one position with which to do this. These two areas of concentration, moreover, made good sense, since the college at that point lacked anyone with graduate training in the study of Asian cultures, and, although Westminster College is a church-related institution with strong and proud ties to the Presbyterian Church U.S.A., it actually has more Catholic students than Presbyterian students and, again, had no one on the faculty with the training to address this tradition either historically or theologically. I thus understood my calling at

Westminster to be threefold: (1) to introduce into the curriculum a more concentrated and academically rigorous treatment of Asian religions, particularly Hinduism and Buddhism; (2) to address the large Catholic body on campus, primarily through classroom lectures but also through my personal presence in the department; and (3) to fulfill both of these tasks in a way that was respectful of and in dialogue with the Presbyterian faith-heritage of the college. Whether I had actually fulfilled any of these objectives nine years later, when I left, I leave to my former colleagues and administrative superiors to decide. From my perspective, one thing is crystal clear: it was a wonderfully rewarding experience trying.

My first week on campus was not particularly encouraging, though. I had missed the faculty orientation workshop in order to deliver a paper at the Parliament of World Religions in Chicago and so found myself sitting in the library, waiting to visit with the head librarian, who would fill me in on what I had missed the previous week. As I sat in a big red leather chair innocently reading the *Chronicle of Higher Education* (or was it *People Magazine*?), I was approached by a stately looking elderly woman. She had seen my picture in the local paper in an article on the new faculty and was here to quiz me. Was I a minister? No, I told her. Was I a Christian? I did my undergraduate training at a Catholic seminary and think at least partly out of that tradition, I told her. She took that as a no. What would I teach? General introductory courses in the comparative study of religion and, I hoped, some new courses on Hinduism and Buddhism. That's about the last thing I said. From then on, it was all her, as she proceeded to tell me that these were not "real" religions. There was only one religion, and that was Christianity. What I think she really meant, though, was that there was only one religion, and that was Presbyterian Christianity and, if push comes to shove, it was her particular, highly idiosyncratic, millenialist interpretation of Presbyterianism, maybe even her local church filled with people who looked exactly like her. No "heathen" here.

I said nothing in reply. I was young. I was green. And, to be honest, I was caught completely off guard. I did, however, share the story with numerous colleagues and administrators, and they all knew immediately whom I was talking about. Their responses were important, as it was clear to me that this woman represented a significant voice from within the tradition but by no means a central one. My later experience at the college after that only confirmed this: again and again, despite its often very conservative past that would have nothing to do with the likes of me (part Catholic, part Hindu, interested in religious forms of sexuality), Westminster showed itself to be warmly supportive of a cosmopolitan, widely inclusive, deeply human vision of its mission. If it was once exclusivistic in its approach to what we foolishly call "non-Christian" religions, it no longer was. Pluralism, as an ideal if not a reality, was now the order of the day. Consequently, I felt welcomed and at home there. I may have sat uncomfortably within the general worldview of the institution's history—just whose history would I sit comfortably in?—but it was a familiar and comfortable sort of uncomfortableness, a kind of gracious invitation to sit down there in that place and with those people, red leather chair or no.

Reputation and Resistance

My first semester was my most difficult teaching experience, but not, I think, because I was especially inexperienced (that goes without saying). Rather, it was because I did not yet have a "reputation" on campus. Every professor has one, whether or not he or she is aware of it. The dormitory halls and campus quads resonate with innumerable oral traditions about this or that class or professor. And when one is teaching introductory classes on religion, not to have such a reputation is a difficult thing, since there is no "filtering mechanism" at work to ensure a relatively capable and ready classroom. Without a reputation, students take a professor's classes not because they are drawn to them for their content or reported spirit (the oral traditions, I suspect, are quite accurate), but out of pure experimentation or hope, much of it in vain. Whatever social benefits such painful exercises might bring to us as a culture, it is still a difficult thing to teach comparative creation myths to students who believe in the literal, "scientific" truth of Genesis 1–3, or New Testament criticism and the psychology of religion to students who want to "save" you or hear that, yes, Freud really was a pervert and quack. I am reminded here of a funny story Elisabeth Schüssler Fiorenza, who teaches New Testament feminist criticism at Harvard Divinity School, tells about a friend leading an adult education class in a Catholic parish who raised the historical fact that Jesus was a Jew. This apparently was more than the pious parishioners could process. "But the Blessed Mother for sure is not," an exasperated listener finally responded.[7] Along similar lines, just how much learning can one expect to accomplish in a course like "Understanding the Bible" when the primary text's very first lines—"In the beginning . . ."—inevitably elicit such statements as "I don't believe in evolution" or "This is not what my minister says"?

Quite a bit really, for such honest faith statements force the learning community to encounter the tough questions of authority and truth, religion and science, history and myth, unexamined belief and critical reflection. This is the power and social importance of teaching religious studies at an undergraduate level: you are right there with individuals, just as they are emerging from the often unquestioned worldviews of their individual adolescences and subcultures, that is, their families and faith communities. A few of these individuals will learn to think for themselves, to question and to doubt, to begin to be free. Granted, almost certainly, this brave intellectual independence, like college itself, may be short-lived, if indeed it develops at all. Nevertheless, there is a space here for it to show itself and grow, if the student so chooses. Still, how much more can be accomplished if these matters are more or less resolved before the students walk into the classroom. How much more pleasant and exciting a class can be if the majority of the students are not numbed into silence by the embarrassing loquacity and predictable objections of the most close-minded person in the room. This is what a "reputation" can win a teacher—the blessed absence of ignorance, fear, and bigotry. I am perfectly aware that it is our responsibility as teachers to struggle with just these kinds of resistance, and that objections are central to the health and vitality of critical discourse, and indeed I have spent a good share of my teaching (and writing) career on just these sorts of "front lines." But that is all the more reason for taking joy and pleasure in pedagogical contexts in which one does not have to spend the entire course at square one, that is, with the patently obvious but passionately denied truths that sacred texts have histories and saints have bodies.

Freud in the Classroom

Although in eight years at Westminster I taught but one course on the thought of Sigmund Freud, a January-term course titled "Freud and the Study of Religion," I talked about Freud quite a bit in the classroom and with my colleagues. The results were often either dramatic or funny, or, much in the spirit of Freud, more than a little of both, as if our lives were written out from those two forms of Greek theater, the tragedy and the comedy. In terms of the dramatic (very much minus the humor), I once lectured on Freud's *Introductory Lectures on Psycho-analysis*. As I got into the topics of dream interpretation, sexual trauma, and the family romance, a female student in the back row became increasingly interested (and agitated). She insisted on talking to me after class every day, and as we talked her topic became more and more defined, and more and more troubling. She wanted to tell me about her dreams. I listened. A certain recurring dream, it turned out, always involved her father, whom she could only see from the waist up in the dreams. He would come to her in these dreams, and she would get very upset. As we talked more, she confessed to me that her father had been fondling her breasts for years, and that she no longer wanted to go home. I stopped her there and explained to her that I was not a therapist and so could not adequately help her with these issues. I encouraged her to see the therapist on staff at the college as soon as possible. For days she refused, until I offered to accompany her to the counselor and sit in with her for the first session. This we did. Freud had opened up a way for her at least to begin to deal with her own painful past. I do not know what came of the therapy. I do not know if she took this way. Perhaps she did. I suspect that she did not.

At other times a student might be very willing to think and act on Freudian thought but be unable to find sufficient social or familial support to make it stick. Consider, for example, that powerful mix of psychoanalysis and feminism first named and appropriated in Juliet Mitchell's classic *Psychoanalysis and Feminism* and now more or less common within gender studies.[8] Here the social and psychological structures of patriarchy are minutely analyzed, and we can catch a glimpse of how things might be very different were our children socialized differently and provided with less oppressive and dualistic reality systems. For example, I routinely taught the above-mentioned "Gender and Religion" at Westminster, often to adult students. The class was usually filled with women, who came to the subject with decades of lived experience at being disempowered but little or no ability to name or understand the social and religious structures that undergird it all and make it seem so "natural," if not divinely revealed. They often became quite excited and enthusiastic as they began to see what had happened, how much sense a feminist model could make of religion, and how things could in fact be different. The stunning reversal of human procreation in the Adam and Eve story (with the woman "birthed" from the man), the male code of the biblical covenant cut directly into the penis through the ritual of circumcision, Jesus' rather clear rejection of the family, his radical call to become castrated for the kingdom (eunuchs were both powerful figures in ancient royal administrations and often assumed to be homosexually active), and his easy and quite culturally scandalous familiarity with women (not to mention prostitutes), the potentially alienating absence of female divinities within the Western monotheisms, the sexlessness of the Virgin Mary in Catholic thought, the European witch trials, the Muslim veil, the social effects of polygyny, and the widespread traditional refusal to educate women or allow them access to scriptural knowledge—these are powerful truths to profess and hear. Tragically, however, when adult female students go back to their homes and churches and try to effect some real change, their efforts are often almost immediately crushed by the very institutional structures and readings of Scripture they have been studying and learning to see as constructed rather than as "natural" or "revealed." They are effectively disempowered again. In my experience at Westminster, female students sometimes emotionally broke down in class or in private with me. In some ways, the class had made their situation worse, for they now saw injustice more clearly but, for no fault of their own, found themselves in situations in which they simply could do nothing concrete about it. At least before the course they could not see their own suffering so clearly: the opium was gone now, at least until they could forget again. But could they?

What is a teacher to do in such a situation, especially when he knows that, in other instances (which he can never predict), the student will be able to act on what he or she learns and effect real personal or even social change? I had these students as well at Westminster, and I could tell many stories here. Should one stop professing truth as one sees it because this truth may create more suffering for some? The practice of freedom is a poignant discipline, filled with real human suffering, the teacher's included. I see no way around this. It is not always an easy thing to be liminalized, to be dissolved for a moment.

At other times, teaching Freud can be light-hearted, if still revealing. One of my funniest memories of teaching undergraduates at Westminster involves a tie (I, by the way, love ties—the only remotely interesting thing a man can wear in this culture). I had been lecturing on Freud to a class of first-year students. We had discussed, among other things, the (in)famous connection between long oblong objects and phallic meanings in Freud's thought, and we somehow got on the subject of ties, those incredibly odd silk objects that men in our culture insist on hanging from their heads to their waists, as if to link the penis and the head. It was not a particularly serious conversation, more playful than anything. The next day, a student came to class with his suit jacket buttoned tight. Towards the middle of class, he asked if he could show the class his, well, tie. As we all turned our eyes toward him, he opened his jacket to reveal a tie with a perfect (and very large) penis on it. No symbol here. If ties were not phallic before Freud, they certainly have become so after him. I am not sure what this incident taught us about the intricacies of Freudian thought, but I am absolutely certain that it was pedagogically productive, not to mention memorable, primarily for the energy and community feeling it released in the form of laughter.

Peter Berger once wrote a book about humor as a humble form of transcendence, laughter being one of those "rumors of angels" the sociologist detected in human social life.[9] Someone should write a book about humor and pedagogy. Laughter opens the mind and the heart and joins people together across the chasms of their own solipsisms. Certainly those who cannot laugh at themselves, at sex, and at their most cherished beliefs (which always involve both themselves and sex) are unable to study religion critically. They are stuck, usually very angry, almost always insecure, and not at all fun to be around. And, of course, they always hate Freud, that man who reminds us of way too much.

THE INITIATION

But it is not Freud who sat at the center of our comparative religious studies curriculum at Westminster. Rather, it was the spirits of Max Müller, Wilhelm Dilthey, Rudolf Bultmann, Paul Tillich, John Hick, and Mircea Eliade, or differently, it was the thought-worlds of the comparative study of religion, textual hermeneutics, biblical criticism, comparative theology, history of religions, and postmodernism. This is a rather pedantic, name-dropping way of saying that it was the problems and promises of religious pluralism that defined most of our teaching, at least within that branch of our departmental curriculum that we called "the history and philosophy of religion." At the core of this enterprise was a course titled "Understanding Religious Experience and Expression." The course was new when I arrived in 1993, the brainchild of a forward-looking adjunct instructor and a visionary chair of the department (Bob VanDale). It was originally designed, I think, to avoid the two reigning paradigms in the introductory course: the "world religions model" in which one proceeds, world civilization by civilization, through the five or six "great world religions," and the Eliadean "pattern model," in which the focus is instead on comparative themes or patterns in the history of religions (creation myths, initiation, sky gods, purity systems, and the like). In some ways, the course was even more insanely ambitious in its scope than either of the two traditional models, as it tried to incorporate a little of both in its approach: the "parts" of specific religious worlds are studied in their integrity, and the "whole" of this or that pattern is traced through the different worlds. The logic comes directly from Dilthey: it is impossible to understand the whole (religion) without looking at the parts (the religions), just as it is impossible to understand the individual parts without looking at them in the context of the whole. The most famous expression of this comparative spirit in the study of religion is certainly Max Müller's appropriation of an insight original to the linguist's study of languages: "He who knows one knows none." Of course, matters are significantly more complicated than this, but "Understanding Religious Experience and Expression" was an undergraduate introductory course, not a graduate seminar or dissertation defense. If we could impress on the students this general comparative insight and some awareness of the immense complexity and diversity (and yet vague unity) of human religious experience, then we would have accomplished our purpose.

I tried to do this through a semester of four ritual movements: (1) an opening series of lectures on what the study of religion involves (and, just as importantly, does not involve) called "Preparing for the Initiation," during which I asked the students to write a brief paper defining their worldviews and, by implication, themselves, with the stated understanding that one must be self-reflexively aware of the general outlines of one's world before one can enter those of others; (2) a long section called "Encountering the Worlds: Entering the Chaos," in which we explored together both the major religious traditions of the world and the general patterns (initiation, creation myth, sacrifice, purity/impurity, eschatology, and so on) that define these worlds; (3) "Ordering the Worlds: Emerging from the Chaos to Recreate the World," in which I provided the students with four different ways to make sense of the bewildering religious pluralism we had been encountering all semester (more on this below); and, finally, (4) a concluding section called "Applying the Categories," in which the students were expected to use their new-found categories of comparison to compare some religious theme in both their own religious world and at least one other (for example, death in Methodism and Theravada Buddhism, or doctrines of God in Catholicism and Hinduism). This was all announced immediately at the first meeting of the course, actually on the first page of the syllabus, which read as follows:

> Many of us have seldom thought deeply and critically about our own religious worlds: how they are symbolically structured, how myth and ritual function in them, how they are rooted in historical processes that stretch back for centuries, how they employ violence to reach their theological or practical ends, and, perhaps most importantly, how they relate to other religious worlds that operate with radically different practices, deities, and beliefs. This course is designed to provide the student

with both an "open forum" and the categories necessary to ask such questions in a way that is intelligent, honest, and true to the historical record of humanity's religious experience. In the course of the class's four parts, the student will be expected to: (1) define his or her own religious world; (2) enter and analyze the "other worlds" of humanity's religious traditions; (3) emerge from this experience with a tentative stance on the plurality of religious forms; and (4) use this stance and the categories learned in the class to present a group project and write a specifically comparative essay.

On the first day of class I made it quite clear to the students that my pedagogical goal for most of the course (all of part 2) would be to confuse them, to disorient them, to shake the very foundations of their worlds. This, I pointed out, was neither ill intentioned nor designed to trick them: it was a direct function of the stunningly complex, indeed baffling reality of religious pluralism in human history. It is the history of religions itself that is disorienting, confusing, dissolving, maddeningly ambiguous. As a historian of religions and a professor of religion, it was my job to communicate as much of this richness and ambiguous confusion (pick your term) that I could. The students began the course mouthing the usual comfortable platitudes—"All religions are basically the same." "Religion is about morality and how to be a good person." For four months we explored the religions' contradictory answers to the same existential questions (Is there a divine source? What happens to us when we die? Why do we suffer? What is the soul? What is the purpose or goal of human life). We also engaged in extended studies of both religious altruism and violence, developed a keener sense of what can only be called "cultural relativism," and discussed religion's formative influence on human sexuality (and vice versa). After all of this, few students left quite so comfortably with the same platitudes. The world was much richer and complicated. Nothing is black and white. Nothing.

Certainly the most crucial part of the course occurred when the students finally emerged from this long confusion, this liminal period of "Entering the Chaos," and were asked to make some sense of it all now. I made it clear that I was looking for no "right answer" (although I was also perfectly clear about my own pluralistic positions when they asked me—and they always did), and that they would not be graded on which option they take. In a series of lectures, we defined and discussed the following four answers to the religious pluralism we had been exploring all semester:

Exclusivism: the rejection of other worlds based on the categories of one's own world (for example, "Buddhists are going to hell because they do not accept Jesus Christ," or "Good Christians will be reincarnated as better Hindus").

Inclusivism: the acceptance of other worlds based on the categories of one's own world (for example, "Buddhists can go to heaven," or "Christians can achieve nirvana").

Pluralism: the potential acceptance of all worlds as cultural approximations of the sacred ("Heaven," "nirvana," "God," "Brahman," and so on are all symbols that have arisen in particular human societies to capture a sacred reality that in the end transcends and escapes them all).

Reductionism: the reduction of religious phenomena to nonreligious phenomena ("Religious experiences are products of natural psychological processes and experiences that meet certain emotional needs," or "Religious phenomena are products of social processes and projections of a particular society's codes and needs that are designed to produce social consistency and stability").

We went through each of these options carefully, exploring the potential social and psychological benefits and dangers of each. It is easy, for example, to see the psychological power of exclusivism, to understand how seductive it must be to believe, to really believe, that one has the answers to life's deepest questions, and that these answers are stable and final. The walls are high here, the in-group feels confident and secure (or so we are made to believe), and the parking lots are full. But at what social cost? Pluralism (or reductionism) makes far better sense of religious history, but just how does one believe as a pluralist? One's walls are so low here that they disappear altogether, and with them goes any hope for a close-knit community, or so it seems. Little wonder that the majority of students (and mainline churches) opted for some form of inclusivism, in essence a halfway house that avoids the feared extremes of both exclusivism and pluralism. As for reductionism, its different forms are extremely powerful, and we are all reductionists at times, particularly with other people's religious experiences (that peyote, those "possessions" that look a lot like schizophrenia), but here we leave religion altogether and enter a secular worldview, a move that was emotionally impossible for most of my students. And then there was the problem of ethics and cultural relativism. It is easy to be pluralistic about doctrines of God—whether or not "He" has a son, how many there are, even whether or not God exists. But what about those questions regarding abortion, female (or male) circumcision, and systematic social discrimination based on race, gender, or sexual orientation? Exclusivism enters through the back door again as ethical conviction. Most of us, it seems, pass through any number of exclusivistic, inclusivistic, pluralistic, and reductionistic modes, often no doubt within the same hour.

And lest the discussions veer off in some civil but intellectually vacuous direction, I played the provocateur and brought the students back with some intentionally disturbing "hard questions" aimed primarily at their own religious heritages (and if I were teaching a classroom of Muslims or Hindus or Jews, I would, of course change the questions to "provoke" their own, equally ambiguous histories). So to my primarily Christian audience:

1. Where are you going when you die? Where is a Hindu going when he or she dies? How do you know you will not be reincarnated?

2. If you were born in Sri Lanka, you would most likely be a Buddhist or Hindu now, with convictions and beliefs as sincere and strong as your particular Christian convictions and beliefs. How do you explain that?

3. How is the statement "A Hindu is going to hell" any different than "Blacks are inferior"? Are not both forms of bigotry and ignorance, one couched in religious language, the other in racial terms?

4. "Revelation" and "Bible" are often invoked to "prove" the superiority of Christianity, but the other traditions have their own revelations and sacred scriptures. Why are their "Bibles" wrong and yours right?

5. Highly educated, economically successful Americans tend to belong to "liberal" denominations, whereas less educated, less economically successful Americans tend to belong to "conservative" or "fundamentalist" denominations. What, if anything, does this mean?

6. Muslims understand the Christian Scriptures much as Christians understand the Jewish Scriptures: as something their own tradition "fulfills," "corrects," "completes," or "supersedes." Why is this move acceptable in the Christian case and not in the Muslim one? How might a Jewish believer read these theological moves?

And my personal favorite:

7. Psychological studies of religious belief among white Americans have consistently found positive correlations between religious piety and "ethnocentrism, authoritarianism, dogmatism, social distance, rigidity, intolerance of ambiguity, and specific forms of prejudice against Jews and blacks."[10] Explain.

It was up to the students, of course, to assess what all of this means, or could mean. It is important, though, to keep in mind here that, with a few very rare exceptions, such a course represented the first time in a student's life that he or she was not only asked but encouraged to think critically, openly, and publicly about religion. Unlike academics in, say, chemistry or American history or English literature, those of us in religious studies are always introducing; in essence, we have nothing to build on, since there is no stable place in the elementary or high school public curricula where religion is addressed, not as a confessional truth, but as a legitimate object of humanistic and social-scientific study. "You want me to do *what?*" the first-time students ask with darting eyes. "Can I really say this?" their faces shout. Yes, exactly. One of my former students, shocked by the freedom the course induced, explained how he was kicked out of his high school Bible school class for asking too many questions. Another student, this one an adult female, told how she was silenced in her church when she insisted on praying "Our Mother, who art in heaven." The classroom is not and must not be such a constricting space.

It is this very promise of religiously understanding oneself within a larger pluralistic world, however, that can also become problematic for some students, who quite accurately read the comparative approach to religion as potentially (if not actually) threatening to their exclusivistic understandings of religion and truth. If there is a pedagogical problem that I regularly encounter in the classroom, it is how to remain faithful to academic standards and work compassionately with individuals whose worlds such standards can easily (and probably should) call into serious question. But this is a problem, I would argue, that is inevitable, understandable, and, in the end, positive and creative. Why? Because any genuine understanding of another faith demands an emotional and intellectual openness, however tentative, to that other world of belief and practice. There can be no understanding without some measure of sympathy, no transformation without some temporary and imaginative passing over, as the theologian John Dunne put it so beautifully at the beginning of this essay. Moreover, as Rita Gross points out in my other opening epigraph, our very practice of comparing religions in the classroom assumes an egalitarian spirit, a willingness to subsume very different practices (like the Catholic Mass and the Hindu puja) into a single comparative category (like ritual). If this openness and this initial egalitarianism are emotionally threatening, they are also absolutely necessary, for without these risks (and they are risks) of the deepest sort there can be no understanding, no tolerance, no education in the root meaning of that world, to lead out, in this case, from one's own brief twenty-year-old world into the much larger universe of humanity's religious history.

After such an experience, my Westminster students were effectively living in a more vast, more complex, more ambiguous, more mysterious, and yet somehow more understandable world. And that in itself can be a religious experience. Consider, for example, the following comments taken directly from my course evaluations for "Understanding Religious Experience and Expression":

> I learned a lot about myself as well as about those around me. This is probably the first class that has really changed me and helped me to realize who I was.

> This course really helped me examine my own faith and the way in which I view others' faiths. Prior to the course, I didn't have sufficient knowledge of world faiths, and to be honest, I did not really care to. I thought that my own faith was good enough. Now, however, the beliefs of others have affected how I look at my own, and I have obtained tolerance. I view myself as a pluralist, and in this way this course is the most valuable I've ever had.

> I feel that I am a better person because of this course. This class has been a religious experience. An extremely valuable religious experience. I used to dread the fact that we are required to take a religion course. Now I am glad that it was required.

Of course, not every student was so affected. I have had students, so distraught over being told that there are other sacred worlds to live in, break down and cry, either during class or afterward. Others have voiced their objections to my superiors or in the same student evaluations of the course. One student, for example, wrote: "The class was a challenge to the Western/Christian ideals [that I] held, which made me mad but, [it] was beneficial because it made me think."

But some of the most critical evaluations I have received come from my "Understanding the Bible" course I teach. I have often said that it is relatively easy to teach religious studies through Asian religions in the American classroom, since there are far fewer people to offend with basic historical information and critical methods common in the academy, but often considered scandalous or demeaning in the public cultures of the religions. Theoretically, for example, I could stand up in front of a typical American classroom and go on for some time about the likely dating of the Vedas, the Indo-European hypothesis, or the sexuality of this or that Hindu saint (all of which would conflict considerably with common Hindu opinion on these matters), and no one would flinch. But as soon as I get up and do the same with Christianity, the historical Jesus, and the Catholic saints (and I did this *all the time* at Westminster College, as I do it now in my most recent writings), the sparks fly. In many ways, then, it could be said that it is more fruitful to teach religious studies with the religious material of the host culture: the stakes are higher, the critical approaches more salient, the energy greater. Hence my desire to teach "Understanding the Bible" as well as "Religions from Asia" at Westminster.

"Understanding the Bible" involved a quick trip through the entire Bible, with an emphasis on historical-critical readings of specific texts, the history of biblical scholarship, the four-source theory, the historical Jesus scholarship, and the history and politics of canon formation. It was a very difficult ride for conservative students with a literal bent. One student accused me of being "condescending" (and perhaps I was, but I am also reminded of the adult female student who, after hearing me take a positive position on evolution, insisted on labeling me "opinionated"—name-calling, essentially an implicit ad hominem argument, is an all-too-easy way to dismiss an important challenge to one's world view). Another student felt that "Christians who believe in the Bible were in many cases indirectly or directly ridiculed" in the lectures. I doubt very much that I intentionally ridiculed anyone, and I deeply regret doing so if I did. But I am certain that I was hard, and intentionally so, on literalist, ahistorical approaches to the biblical texts, and I can easily see how such a class could be experienced as a kind of ridiculing. What always has to be challenged in such circumstances, though, is the implicit conflation of "Christians who believe in the Bible" with "Christians like me who read the Bible literally." In the end, I have to admit that religious studies is often threatening, at least to any and all understandings of "religion" that restrict all legitimate meanings of that word to "my religion." Rita Gross is right. Religious studies is something of a scandal to many people's worldviews, and it should remain so: "one should feel that sexist, racist, ethnocentric, and religious chauvinisms, if present, are being threatened by the academic study of religion."[11]

A CONCLUDING THOUGHT

I do not want to be taken as saying that academics and professors of religion do not have their own biases, blind spots, and prejudices, which in turn need to be challenged by their students and readers and put on the public table for open discussion and debate. We are fallible human beings, like everyone else. There thus can be no substitution for self-reflexivity and radical self-criticism—in the end, this is what constitutes the cultural value of the critical study of religion. At its best, the discipline is always there, to call into question, to doubt, to provoke, to catalyze further reflection. This, I think, is what we should ultimately be about in the academy. Put differently, we might say that as intellectuals we belong on the margins of all religions, in the in-between, in the liminal, a marginal space that is somehow, paradoxically, also at the very center of contemporary public culture. This marginal center or central margin is where we teach. This is also where we, with our students, are transformed. This is where we should dwell, however uncomfortably.

NOTES

1. Arnold van Gennep, *Rites of Passage* (Chicago: University of Chicago Press, 1960).

2. Victor Turner, *The Ritual Process: Structure and Anti-Structure* (Chicago: University of Chicago Press, 1969).

3. Wendy Doniger, "From Great Neck to Swift Hall: Confessions of a Reluctant Historian of Religions," in Jon R. Stone, ed., *The Craft of Religious Studies* (New York: Palgrave, 2000), 36.

4. Much the same occurred in our own era, when, after a year of being officially silenced by Rome, Thomas Fox, the Dominican theologian (later turned Episcopalian priest) and pantheistic mystic, returned to the podium at an event designed to commemorate the end of his silencing and dryly began with something to the effect of "Now, as I was saying before I was rudely interrupted, . . ."

5. Ralph Waldo Emerson, *Emerson on Transcendentalism,* ed. Edward L. Ericson (New York: Ungar, 1986), 87.

6. I tell this story in some detail in *Roads of Excess, Palaces of Wisdom: Eroticism and Reflexivity in the Study of Mysticism* (Chicago: University of Chicago Press, 2001).

7. Elisabeth Schüssler Fiorenza, *In Memory of Her* (New York: Crossroad, 1985), 105–6, referenced in Marcus J. Borg, *Meeting Jesus Again for the First Time: The Historical Jesus and the Heart of Contemporary Faith* (New York: HarperSanFrancisco, 1994), 39 n.3.

8. Juliet Mitchell, *Psychoanalysis and Feminism: A Radical Reassessment of Freudian Psychoanalysis* (New York: Basic Books, 2000 [1974]).

9. Peter Berger, *A Rumor of Angels* (New York: Doubleday, 1970).

10. David M. Wulff, *Psychology of Religion: Classic and Contemporary* (New York: John Wiley and Sons, 1997), 223. Wulff's entire section "Religion and Social Attitudes" (220–43) is required reading for anyone who assumes that religious belief and practice necessarily lead to prosocial behaviors and humanitarian attitudes; quite the contrary in many cases. For a fuller look at this issue from a historical perspective, with a measure of hope, see R. Scott Appleby, *The Ambivalence of the Sacred: Religion, Violence, and Reconciliation* (Lanham, Md.: Rowman and Littlefield, 2000).

11. Rita Gross, *Feminism and Religion* (Boston: Beacon Press, 1996), 13.

CHAPTER FOURTEEN

The Unbearable Intimacy of Language and Thought in Islam

Ebrahim Moosa

Although Westerners may have the impression that Islam is and always has been dominated by a radical fundamentalism that finds all meaning and value unproblematically articulated in an ancient sacred text, as Ebrahim Moosa here observes there have in fact long been real differences within the Muslim community concerning the nature of language, including sacred language, and the proper modes of its interpretation. In this essay Professor Moosa explores in particular the ways in which the influential eleventh-century thinker, al-Ghazālī, addressed the fundamental issues of the origin of language (divine or human?); the development and change of language (how possible if language is divine in origin?); and the nature of interpretive authority (self-evidence or the judgment of the community of Arabic speakers?). It is most fitting to close this book with this essay, for it emphasizes simultaneously the deep pluralism that is the hallmark of the conversation the book seeks to capture and continue, especially the continuity across religious traditions of the most basic questions of language, meaning, and authority.

A whole mythology is deposited in our language.
—Ludwig Wittgenstein, *Remarks on Frazer's* Golden Bough

But we do not think in words. Or rather, we sometimes think in words. Words are scattered archipelagos, drifting, sporadic. The mind is the sea. To recognize this sea in the mind seems to have become something forbidden, something that the presiding orthodoxies, in their various manifestations, whether scientist or merely commonsensical, instinctively avoid. Yet this is the crucial parting of the ways. It is at this crossroads that we decide in which direction knowledge will go.
—Roberto Calasso, *Literature and the Gods*

Public discussions about Islam are often reductive, hiding more than they are supposed to reveal. Talk about "Islamic fundamentalism" might give comfort to those who like to talk in ideological keystrokes, but it remains a problematic category precisely because it also carries an unusual and complex political freight. For surely, literalism and fundamentalism are trends that are also pervasive in Jewish, Christian, Buddhist, and Hindu traditions; yet many political pundits and commentators present fundamentalism as unique to Islam.

What most people avoid talking about is the heightened political conflict, dramatized by the attacks on September 11, 2001, and subsequent events that manifest hegemonic Euro-American dominance being met by Muslim resistance. The latter is a political resistance that draws on religious resources and cultural memories of a variety of Muslim societies. And since religio-political discourse is an anomalous category in Euro-America, "political Islam," "Islamic fundamentalism," or "militant Islam" are identified as problems. Of course each of these categories have complex narratives and mean different things in Western and Muslim contexts. This is not the place to discuss the interface of religion and politics. Suffice it to say that those of us who examine cultural formations are ignorant at our peril if we fail to account for the political battles that are shaping the languages of the cultures in question.[1]

That caveat notwithstanding, it is equally true that within Muslim communities there are ensembles of critical issues being debated that, because they do not make for tantalizing and sensational headlines, do not enjoy the serious scholarly scrutiny they deserve. For at least a century, Muslim thinkers have been struggling with the impact of modernity on the premodern Muslim traditions, especially the way modern modes of thinking affect the inherited values and practices of tradition. Unique challenges arise when the forces of social change and history disrupt values stemming from tradition. So, for instance, when tradition reasserts itself in the lives of contemporary Muslims as alternative political proposals informed by Islamic political and legal traditions, these initiatives clearly trigger fears in outsiders and pose challenges to those who embrace Islamic discourses.

Some of these fears are sensationally mediated through malevolent representations of Islam. Most Muslim law (*sharī'a*) is held up as an anachronism by outsiders and insiders alike (for good humanitarian reasons), but it is equally ubiquitous as a ground of attack against Muslims. In many instances, it is crude abuses of Islamic law by demagogues that are held out as typical, as the trials of women charged for adultery in Nigeria under *sharī'a* law in recent years has so painfully demonstrated.

Within Muslim communities certain brands of politics that draw on a legacy of Islamic law and politics also exacerbate certain fears. The critical questions animated by such concerns explore how inherited values can adapt to radically changed societies. Furthermore, they ask how these laws and values can be applied to people with altered communal and individual subjectivities. This line of questioning assumes that norms, values, and subjectivities always undergo change within the fabric of a coherent tradition. With the advent of modernity and colonialism, however—and especially with the subsequent Euro-American "colonialization" of power—Muslim traditions, institutions, and practices were radically ruptured and have since being struggling to gain coherence.

In the search for coherence and meaning, some Muslim thinkers have attempted to mend the breach by reading anew their traditions in a conversation with modern traditions. Central to such a project is the question how revealed teachings evolve and interact with historical change. It is in the reading of traditions, whether modern or premodern, that the issues of language and interpretation are paramount. Practitioners of Islam today, as well as in the past, devote a remarkable amount of energy to the interpretation of texts. The single most important issue in modern Islam, in my view, is the ideological contest over who has the authority to produce meaning from canonical texts and how the right to interpret is to be executed.

A good part of the debate centers on how the documents of tradition, such as the normative teachings of the Prophet Muḥammad known as the *sunna* (normative tradition) and the Qur'ān, are to be validly interpreted as sources for practical norms. Adherents to the two major divisions within Islam, the Sunnī and Shīʿa, already disagree over what should be accepted as supplementary authoritative sources. Perhaps two examples will give some sense of the scale of issues involved. For the Sunnīs the consensus decisions of the scholars of the community have binding authority, but for the Shīʿa it is the authority of the hereditary successors (*imāms*) from the line of descendants of the Prophet's daughter Fāṭima that has finality. Second, among the Sunnīs, at least for those within the canonical tradition, the use of reason in rule-making is limited to syllogistic and analogical modes of reasoning, whereas among the Shīʿa inductive modes of reasoning are permissible. In short, traditions have their own rules by which they are made and unmade, a very important part of which has to do with how one understands words, expressions, meanings, and language.

In part, normative authority within the Muslim intellectual tradition is derived from texts, language, and interpretation as they coalesce within social realities. In fact, language, theory, and interpretation are interdependent. Language is the primary constituent for the formation, preservation, and transformation of a tradition. Reductive analyses often characterize religious traditions as caught in a tension between the polar opposites of "modernizers" and "conservatives": proponents of new knowledge against defenders of old wisdom. Whenever we describe battles over authority in religion, there is a predisposition to consider the views of our opponents to be literalist or narrow while preserving for ourselves the privilege of advancing sophisticated figurative readings. As questionable as such "us versus them" thinking may be on other grounds, it also obscures larger epistemological issues. An intellectual tradition, like an organism, develops a life of its own. In the process, it generates an armory of weapons for use in defending itself against forces—real or imagined—that may threaten it. In literate societies, the major weapon of defense is language itself.

That debates over language are prominent very early in the history of Islam is borne out by two major developments that brought into sharper focus the centrality of the disputes. One was the encounter of the Arabian tradition from the eighth century onward with other intellectual traditions of the Fertile Crescent, and the competition generated as a result of its mingling with Greek, Indic, and later Persian intellectual traditions.[2] The second concerned the politics of knowledge: around the eleventh century, the institutions of intellectual production and knowledge within Muslim societies became subject to ideological "spin" for political ends.

While these developments cannot be ignored, overall a healthy cultural tension sustained the conversational encounter between the emergent and not-so-monolithic Arabicate/Islamicate cultures, on the one hand, and the multiple Greek philosophical and scientific heritages, on the other, starting as early as the eighth century. While the tenor of the debate often betrayed xenophobic and essentialist overtones, each against the other, it is interesting to note that the Muslim term describing Hellenic knowledge does not frame it as foreign knowledge. In fact, it marks knowledge chronologically, though not privileging antique learning, by describing the learning of the Greeks as the "knowledge of the ancients" ('ulūm al-awā'il). In some circles, of course, this term earns as much popularity as it gains notoriety in others. If anything, the tension between the Arabicate/Islamicate epistemic system and the non-Arabicate epistemologies, which existed cheek by jowl in the emerging and cosmopolitan Islamic empire, is extraordinarily productive. What we call "Islamic civilization" today would have been a mere shadow of itself without such fecund mixing and creativity.

During the eleventh century A.D. — corresponding to the fifth century of the *hijrī* calendar—a crisis gripped the intellectual heartlands of the then Muslim world. Perhaps it resembled the havoc the Sophists produced in Greek society many centuries earlier.[3] Muslim political authorities gradually began to take control of the production of knowledge in order to bolster their authority. The pretext then, as it is today, was that draconian measures had to be adopted in order to defend the empire against the barbarians, and especially against internal dissenters and subversives, who were often portrayed as more dangerous than the external enemy. What leavened the body politic, and the disciplines of knowledge, was the twin reflex of authoritarianism and the colonialization of knowledge. Disciplines such as logic, dialectical theology, philosophy, and linguistics became the site and battleground where this ideological struggle was played out. The religious sciences proper, such as the sciences related to the exegesis of the Qur'ān and Islamic law, were not immune from such developments.

Dialectical theologians, jurists, and others—always eager to pursue a variety of intellectual agendas—entered the fray by creating sharp distinctions between purely rational sciences and nonrational or authority-based disciplines. Not long thereafter, zealously held ideological commitments were translated into theories and doctrines. Polemics flourished at the expense of the integrity of language and its use. Language was always where conflict first surfaced, because words have to do the work for everyone. If words or utterances have coherent and logical relations with defined meanings within ordinary language use, then whatever this coherence may be, it is transformed in the hands of polemicists and ideologues who have to "pay the words extra" for the additional services rendered.[4]

In order to map the relationship between language and the interpretations of religious texts that inspire talk about religion, I explore below some of the ideas of the twelfth-century Muslim thinker Abū Ḥāmid al-Ghazālī (d. 505/1111), demonstrating how his approach to language frames his hermeneutic and thought. It is important first to note that a kind of mythopoetics that inform the imagination of the Arabic language also subtly shape the production of meaning. Ernst Cassirer reminds us that language and myth are near of kin: their proximity is like two different shoots from the same root.[5] This is even more significant when one considers the fact that the Arabic language is viewed as an auspicious and sacred language in the Muslim religious imagination. Why? The reason is that the Prophet Muḥammad came from an Arabian milieu in which the divine speech (*logos*) became manifest. The point I want to make, however, is somewhat different. I argue that language itself is a substrate within which all thought occurs. It is actually the poetics of language that provides the elasticity that enable religious traditions to flourish in their multiplicity and tenacity.

MYTHOPOIESIS OF ARABIC

Myths similar to those supporting the importance of the Hebrew language also coalesce around Arabic. Each of these languages develops its privileged position by being imbued with divine Revelation. One effect of this claim is that the revealed Scripture in Arabic is held to be not only unique, but also untranslatable, a notion that sparked some controversy in early Islam.[6] More importantly, the myth of origination sheds light on the metaphysical narrative that underpins meaning in this language.

In Eden, the story goes, Adam spoke Arabic. When he sinned and was expelled, he lost his ability to speak Arabic and thus began to speak Syriac.[7] Another narrative states that during the childhood of humankind, Adam and his progeny all spoke a language God had taught them. But as the progeny grew up and then separated from each other, each group chose a different language for itself.[8] It is for this reason that there is a plurality of languages.

The prolific Egyptian commentator of the Qur'ān and authority on prophetic traditions, Jalāl al-Dīn al-Suyūṭī (d. 911/1505), citing an earlier chronicler, 'Alī b. Muḥammad al-Ḥasan Ibn 'Asākir (d. 571/1176), tells the story about the beginnings of language, an epoch of human history that starts with the Tower of Babel.[9] In these Muslim accounts, linguistic unity only appears to have existed in the Edenic paradise. After the Fall of Adam, languages multiplied. There is, however, no nostalgia over the shattering of linguistic unity.

Another account, traced to the Prophet Muḥammad, explains how Arabs came to speak the language of paradise on earth:

> When God assembled all creatures (*khalā'iq*) in Bābil (Babel) he sent a wind [to announce a meeting]. Everyone who had gathered in response to the call eagerly inquired as to why they were invited. A caller then

announced: "Whoever has the West to his right, and the East to his left and faces the Inviolable House (*al-bayt al-harām*) [Ka'ba in Makka] as his orientation, to him is given the language of the people of heaven." One, Ya'rūb b. Qaḥṭān then rose [and was addressed and given the Arabic language].[10]

According to the legend Ya'rūb was the first person to speak the Arabic language. In a similar fashion the wind announces that whoever does so and so, to him will belong a given language, until some seventy-two languages are delegated to an equal number of persons.[11]

The cosmogonic myth of Babelian provenance has tentative connections to the cosmogony of language in Arabia. Ismā'īl (Ishmael), the son of the prophet Ibrāhīm (Abraham)—an ancestor to the Ishmaelite Arabs—apparently forgot his ancestral language.[12] One must assume this happened after his father Abraham abandoned him and his slave mother Hagar in the Arabian wilderness on God's command. During this wilderness exile, Ismā'īl began to speak a new language that turned out to be Arabic. Details in the Muslim accounts state that the young Ismā'īl learned Arabic at the age of fourteen and was taught by means of divine inspiration (*ilhām*).[13]

Muslim sources state that the primordial Ishamaelite Arabic vanished over time. Several observe that differences between the primordial Ishmaelite Arabic and the Arabic of the Qur'ān are so enormous that they may be regarded as two different languages. However, we are also told that elements of the primordial Arabic do reappear in later Arabic.[14] Thus, with the advent of Islam, not only is the primordial link between the Arabs and Abraham restored by way of Ishmael and Muḥammad, but so too are elements of the primordial Ishmaelite Arabic introduced by the Prophet himself.

Muḥammad, it is reported, used some idiomatic expressions that were unfamiliar to his contemporaries. This trait was not viewed as odd language use, but rather as highly eloquent. One measurement of eloquence among pre-Islamic and early Islamic Arabic speakers was to use language that was free from the corrupting influences of foreign tongues. So when the Prophet, who is held up as an exemplar of eloquence, showed traces of this primordial Ishmaelite Arabic in his own speech, he was understood to be drawing on this memory of pristine language use. This understanding is based on a comment made by 'Umar b. al-Khaṭṭāb, the second successor to the Prophet as caliph, who once asked: "Oh Messenger of God! Why is it that you are the most eloquent among us, whereas [we know as a matter of fact that] you had never left our midst?" To which the Prophet replied: "The language of Ismāʿīl became entirely obliterated. So Gabriel, on whom be peace, brought it to me and made me memorize it; and so I remembered it."[15]

In this way the prelingual and cosmic primordiality of the language is affirmed, since the Qurʾān is brought to the Prophet on the wings of the angel Gabriel. Corroboration of this is found in a report, where the Prophet says: "My community was shown to me in water and clay; and, I was taught all the names, in exactly the same way that Adam was taught all the names."[16] The word "community" here includes the linguistic community. Other reports reinforce the claim that the Prophet is "unconditionally the most eloquent of all creation" and Arabic is the best of all languages.[17] Arabic then surpasses all other languages by its merit, perfection, and superiority. This cumulative mythical and edificatory narrative informs the language theories held by some of the early Muslim interpreters.

The Tower of Babel myth, as narrated in the Muslim tradition, does not signify catastrophe, nor does it express nostalgia for linguistic unity. Actually, it heralds the birth of new languages and advances linguistic diversity. As Jacques Derrida points out, the myth goes beyond establishing the "irreducible multiplicity of tongues." Rather, it denotes human imperfection given the imperfection of human language. This "incompletion, the impossibility of finishing, of totalizing, of saturating," Derrida explains, is the inability of our symbolic systems to copy artifacts in the same way that an architectural construction or an architectonics reaches completion.[18]

The nature of language makes its flourishing possible since it continues to struggle with its own incompleteness. Muslim discourse on language eschews monolithic singularity of idioms and stresses instead the multiplicity of idioms. In part, certain passages of the Qurʾān explicitly frame this linguistic diversity. Among the signs of God, the Qurʾān says, is "the diversity of your tongues and colors: for in this indeed are messages for all who are possessed of [innate] knowledge."[19] Neither is a single community a desideratum. "If God willed," the Qurʾān states, "you would have been made into a single people."[20] Other passages are similar: "And had your Sustainer so willed, He could surely have made all people into a single community (*umma*): but [he willed otherwise, and so] they continue to hold divergent views."[21]

Here the term *umma* denotes not a nation but a community or group (*jamāʿa*), as this word allows such polyvocality, according to Ghazālī.[22] Commentators of the Qurʾān are unanimous that the Scripture only hypothetically poses a single confessional community, in order to demonstrate what divine omnipotence could achieve but chose not to. Diversity and plurality are thus ingrained in the texture of the tradition and constitute a desirable goal. If a single confessional community is not viewed as an ideal, then a single linguistic community similarly is not part of a divine scheme. Different moral communities envisage different languages as well as different ways of understanding language and meaning.

ORIGINS OF LANGUAGE

It is the origins and nature of language, however, more than the plurality of languages, that have exercised Muslim thinkers. Language is significant for several reasons, but mostly because it is the revelatory medium in which the sacred text, the *verbum dei*, is spoken once and for all. And most of the authoritative writings that explicate the sacred texts are also written in Arabic. Muslim jurists in particular, notes Bernard Weiss, have a greater interest in linguistic matters than do jurists in other legal systems.[23] In part, this has to do with the fact that Islamic law is not legislated and codified and that jurists must interpret source materials that are not written in a legal idiom. Rather, law and ethics are derived from narrative discourses, which in turn are subject to analysis and the distillation of meaning through elaborate rules of language. In the Muslim legal tradition, as in other traditions, everything that jurists utter is regulated, conditioned, and channeled by language. As Michel Villey has pointed out in another context, it is not sufficient to say that language is the instrument of the jurists, without adding that this instrument, like all techniques, dominates them. "Language is a *servant-maitresse,* and in reality, language is itself knowledge; its vocabulary and syntax are modes of thinking about the world, of carving out a structure of the world; of our science, our language constitutes the first half."[24]

Muslim jurists would find little to disagree with in Villey's assessment. One of the most important discussions in Islamic legal theory falls under the rubric of "linguistic premises" (*al-mabādī al-lughawīya*). So important is the question of language that one notable jurist, Abū al-'Abbās Ibn al-Qāṣṣ (d. 335/946) went so far as to claim that language was one of the sources of law.[25]

While one could choose from a number of sources to illustrate the issues surrounding language, I focus here on Ghazālī's discussion of the relationship between language, meaning, and interpretation.[26] He, like many thinkers before him, grapples with each of the two fundamental positions that can be taken on the origins of language: language is either (1) a product of divine intervention and authorized by Revelation (*tawqīfī*) or (2) established by human conventions (*istịilāḥī*).[27] The first of these includes the conviction that the divine intervenes through nature or instructs the essential sounds or words through a medium such as an angel or a prophet.[28]

On the origins of language Ghazālī is very subtle. He never explicitly tells his readers whether he favors the divine origins theory or the idea that language is a product of human conventions. Many Muslim scholars before him were equally elusive on the matter. Ghazālī's approach is to propose three possible scenarios depicting the origin of languages and to construe two sets of arguments—one hypothetical and the other factual. In the hypothetical argument, all three scenarios are possible. The first pictures language as having been invented by man, and that humanity has continued to develop its languages autonomously. In the second scenario, language is seen as the product of a divine intervention either by direct creation or by Revelation and transmittal to humans by different modes of instruction. The third scenario combines the other two by proposing that the most elementary units of language are divine in origin, but that humans invented the rest.[29] Here Ghazālī echoes the view of a predecessor in the Shāfiʿī law school, Abū Isḥāq al-Isfarāyīnī (d. 418/1027) who suggested this compromise view of the third scenario.

The factual arguments Ghazālī provides are quasi-theological. For instance, his assertion that language has divine origins bears a close resemblance to the natural origins of language theory. The Eternal Power, he explains, is not incapable of creating sounds and letters that are heard by either one person or a group. The same Power can also create knowledge in these persons in order that they may discern that certain sounds and letters signify certain meanings and designated things.[30] This, of course, is at the heart of the naturalistic approach.

Ghazālī goes further, however, stating that God is capable of creating a common motivation in the minds and actions of rational people (*compotes mentis-'uqalāʾ*), so that they independently discover the need to communicate with each other. Thus when social necessity forces them to satisfy that need, it is almost instinctive that they invent a language in order to sustain their interactions and social relations. This process is very similar, he says, to the way a parent teaches a language to a child, or the way a mute expresses himself or herself by means of signs.

Of course Ghazālī is quick to admit that there can be no unequivocal way to make a conclusive finding on the origins of language. Claims that are asserted for any one argument, he admits, are neither rationally conclusive nor supported by scriptural authority.[31] Ghazālī is also not convinced by those who suggest that the divine origins of language has a foundation in the Qur'ān. Some protagonists of this view offer as proof the verse stating: "And He [God] taught Adam all the names." Not only does he point out that this verse is open to multiple interpretations, but it does not amount to demonstrable proof.[32]

A close reading of Ghazālī suggests, in the end, that he is not persuaded by the theory of the divine origins of language. For some unarticulated reason, however, he equivocates, repeating both sides of the argument, and finally aligns himself with a large group of Muslim thinkers who suspend judgment on this contentious issue altogether. He also thinks that speculation is indulgent and fruitless.[33] Perhaps, as Bacon said in a different context, the conundrum about the divine origins of language is akin to a holy vestal: dedicated to the gods but infertile, pious but of no use. For the entire debate would in time lose its importance within Muslim theology, particularly after the heady disputes over the nature of the Qur'ān as created or uncreated divine speech in the tenth and eleventh centuries. And it is not until the late nineteenth and twentieth centuries that faint echoes of the relevance of language and Revelation could again be heard.

I think that the underlying reason Ghazālī hedges on this matter is strategic. He was fully aware of the connections that existed between the divine origins theory and a contentious theological position. The Ash'arī theological school with which he was aligned opposed the view of the Mu'tazilīs, pietist rationalists influenced by Stoic ideas, who asserted that all speech, including the Qur'ān, was the product of human creativity. The debate about the created or uncreated nature of God's speech, namely the Qur'ān, like the debate about the divine and human nature of Christ, had explosive consequences. For Ghazālī to side with the Mu'tazilīs on the matter of the origins of language could have resulted in his intellectual suicide, for he would be espousing a theological contradiction if he believed in the uncreated Qur'ān and not believe in the divine origins of language.

Even if Ghazālī held firm convictions on the origins of language, therefore, he could not openly favor the theory that language was created by humans. His rivals would have concluded him to be a crypto- Mu'tazilī, even if the identity of his outlook with those of the Mu'tazilīs was more a matter of coincidence than one of a shared rationale for their common conclusion. But the divine origins theory also buttressed the thesis that language and words have objective meanings, something that Ghazālī could not subscribe to in an unqualified manner. On this matter as well, prudence counseled that his ambivalence be reflected as neutrality.

Ghazālī seems to incline to the view that the operation of language, as opposed to its origins, is entirely a matter of environmental determinism. But he avoids the charges leveled at some of the Muʿtazilīs thinkers who believed that the origins of language was in history and that language was not a transcendental reality. The assumption in Muʿtazilīs thinking was that each nation or community first arose in a native "environment" where it developed its mores and other traits specific to that milieu, and then "got together," so to speak, to produce a language. On this understanding, it is possible that at some stage human beings could have been fully developed in all respects of the mind, but without a language.

Ghazālī stops short of attributing to language the quality of personal agency, yet at the same time he avoids saying that it is the result of some external agency. He implicitly endorses the idea that languages possess an internal principle of development, a kind of organic entelechy that impels its emergence. For him the two options, divine or human origins of language, are inadequate explanations. Both approaches assume the prior existence of a language, whether in the ability of humans to comprehend a divine instruction or their capacity to communicate with each other in a language they are already supposed to know. Language is indeed the one element that distinguishes humans as rational beings. To claim that a fully developed human could exist without language would, in the words of Herder, be tantamount to turning "men into animals," the flagrant error, he believed, Condillac and Rousseau had committed in this regard.[34]

There is a reason why Ghazālī invests language with an internal principle of development. Language, he suggests, is not merely a spectator or a medium of expression in the system of thinking; rather it is integral to the thought process itself. Ghazālī was fully aware that this relationship of language (articulated sound and words) and thought (intelligible sense and meaning) was a contentious one. In the century immediately preceding Ghazālī, a famous debate took place that highlighted different ways of imagining language. The debate between the Nestorian Christian Mattā (Matthew) bin Yūnus al-Qunnāʾī (d. 328/940), a translator of philosophical texts from Syriac to Arabic, and Abū Saʿīd al-Sīrāfī (d. 368/979), a philologist, dialectical theologian, and jurist, had implications for the way we understand the world as mediated by the word.[35]

Ghazālī would attempt to straddle both sides of that debate by favoring the determinative role of the linguistic community as well as the role of logic in trying to make sense of intelligible statements and meanings.

THEORY OF SIGNIFICATION

All of the preceding discussion—from the mythopoeia of the Arabic language to the theories about its origin and related issues—bear on a matter of great significance: the alleged transparency and interpretive nature of meaning. The myths and the theological debates about Arabic, and language in general, are based on the fact that language is a given entity. This "givenness" of language establishes the relationship of an expression or a word to a meaning in a way that makes meaning predictable. Now we can understand why mythography labored so hard to link the Arabic of the Prophet Muḥammad to Ishmaelite Arabic, and also why the divine origins theory of language, in relation to the uncreated nature of the Qur'ān, was so important: they preserve the primitive "givenness" of both the speech of God, namely the Qur'ān, and the teachings the Prophet (Sunna). Thus it was important theologically to maintain that language's meaning is given, lest it be said that God did not make his will and intention sufficiently clear to humanity.

Behind the debate over the origins of language, therefore, lurk the more vexing problems related to the issue of meaning. For some it was a source of comfort that God originates language: meaning is given, transparent, and objective. Such meanings are secure and stable by divine fiat and authority. All that is required for humans to discover language's meanings and intentions is to follow the correct method of analysis and interpretation. There are others, however, who also take words and their meanings seriously, but for whom those meanings are not so much given and predetermined as they are jointly constructed by the reader and the text. But if humans have a role in originating and authorizing words and meanings, then language can be subverted by subjective meaning and impure human designs.

From very early on Muslim jurists succeeded in welding the interpretation of the source texts to a pragmatics of language and a theology of interpretation. No one was more successful than Muḥammad bin Idrīs al-Shāfi'ī (d. 204/820), who marked out the foundations for the pragmatics of language in the juristic arena and, in the process, valorized Arabocentricity. In his famous *Epistle* (*al-Risāla*) on legal theory, Shāfiʿī with great systematic rigor provides an argument for the unrivaled coherence of the Arabic language.

The challenge for Shāfiʿī is to reveal the intertextual hermeneutic between the Qurʾān and the prophetic reports (*ḥadīth/sunna*) for juridical purposes. The hermeneutical device that he employs to unravel this interpretive labyrinth is his creative use of a Qurʾānic term *al-bayān*, meaning "to elaborate." In doing so he hardly need justify the use of this term, since the Qurʾān states that God is the one who teaches humans the art of "making things clear" (*bayān*). It is this art of knowing how to clarify things that Shāfiʿī finds compelling because it is sanctioned by Revelation and at the same time is central to his hermeneutical project. The term *bayān* thus resonates with a sense of "elucidation," "elaboration," and "to make clear." *Bayān*, he explains, "is a collective term for a variety of meanings which have common roots but different ramifications."[36]

Shāfiʿī's notion of *bayān* as a form of "perspicuous elucidation," as Majid Khadduri translates the term, is akin to Wittgenstein's notion of "perspicuous presentation"—a method of understanding that enables one to see the intermediate links and formal connections between different parts of a whole field of ideas, and ultimately of facts.[37] For Wittgenstein something is "perspicuous" not only because of the way that different parts connect, but also in view of the fact that the meaning "points to some unknown law."[38] This is integral to Wittgenstein's understanding of language as a grammar or network of meanings and ideas, perhaps better described as a "pictorial image." For ultimately the way we perceive and represent the world is by some pictorial image in our minds, even if we are not aware of it.[39]

Muslim jurists, including Shāfiʿī, have done exactly that: to clarify and present the various parts of a complex picture of ideas in an intelligible manner. The sum total of Revelation, Shāfiʿī states, includes various dimensions or aspects that literally constitute "the many faces (aspects) of perspicuous declaration (*wujūh al-bayān*)."[40] Revelation, whether the Qurʾān or the prophetic reports, literally have "faces" (*wujūh*) or registers of interpretation that must be addressed in an intelligible fashion. But Shāfiʿī's point would be lost if we do not also hear him to say that these varieties of registers are actually part of the Revelation itself, for they are assigned and given.

Shāfiʿī's hermeneutical strategy became the paradigmatic model in Islamic law, where language acquired both an opacity and translucence of brilliant clarity and instrumentality. In his hands the performative aspect of language is limited to various predetermined registers of meaning. Nothing by way of unanticipated, unpredictable, and unimaginable meaning can be derived from the source texts since in his view there is a perfect fit between the patina of the language and the interpretive method. Of course, it goes without saying that any unpredictable meaning that bolsters the ideology of the hegemonic interpretive community would be viewed as intended, if not acceptable, while anything contrary would be rejected.

LANGUAGE AND MEANING

Shafiʿī cast long shadows, and it is against this backdrop that Ghazālī has to negotiate the implications of his views on language. How a word ought to be used, Ghazālī states, is related to the idea of original positing (waḍʿ), the assignment of a particular phonemic configuration to a meaning.[41] Knowledge of both vocabulary and grammatical principles concerning the use of words and expressions, as both Bernard Weiss and Muḥammad Ali point out, is essential in communication.[42] At the same time words not only have designated meanings, but they are also the product of certain preconcerted determinations made by a communal tradition (tawqīfī) that regulates the inherited practices of language use. A mere social institution or analogical deduction cannot credibly invent such uses.[43]

Ghazālī maintains that, in theory, the Arabic-speaking people have the final authority in determining the meaning of words. Of course, privileging the Arabic-speaking interpretive community in this way is a consequence of a more dogmatic formulation of language use, namely, adherence to the indexical meanings of established words (waḍʿ). Every word signifies a specific semantic meaning or indexical symbol, irrespective of context, analogy, or reason. A favorite rhetorical catchphrase is: "analogy is not applicable in language" (lā qiyās fī al-lugha).[44] In the final analysis, for Ghazālī it is the conventions of the linguistic community and their assignation of meanings to an articulated sound that determines the standard for language use.[45] In this context Ghazālī's next statement makes eminent sense. "Indeed," he says categorically, "language [as form] is about assigning expressions to meanings (waḍʿ) in its entirety, as well as the determination of a communal tradition (tawqīf); [but] it [language] does not adhere to analogy as a matter of principle."[46] Ghazālī here puts forward a representational theory of language in which there is a one-to-one correspondence between signs and their extralinguistic real-world referents. It remains to be seen whether he believes that some kind of intrinsic meaning inheres in those real-world referents independent of human action and thought.

Asserting the primacy of the Arabic-speaking community of the Prophet as the final arbiter for meanings is not without problems. For how does such a theory account for the linguistic changes the community undergoes over the centuries? This question challenges all traditions that rely on texts authored centuries ago. Would the most recent use of indexical meanings be authoritative or would only the earliest sense of the words that correspond to the time of the origination of the text be authoritative? The Muslim Revelation, in addition to poetic truths and symbolic language, also pertains to many detailed aspects of everyday life—ranging from rules governing marriage and divorce, war, and criminal penalties to practices of ritual cleanliness and inheritance. Typically, the Qur'ānic themes that regulate these social transactions are culturally specific, that is, these very same practices have different cultural equivalents in non-Arabicate communities. Similarly, even within Arabicate society these practices have undergone dynamic changes, an evolution that the Madīna school of law of Mālik has jealously guarded and preserved.

The history of the Qur'ān is the best illustration of this evolution. The Revelation in Madīna, the city to which the Prophet migrated after receiving Revelation in Makka for nearly thirty years, introduces amendments and changes on specific practices, largely due to the fact that the economic and sociopolitical context of Madīna differed so substantially from that of Makka. Of course, the issue whether God transforms his will in history became an agonizing question for theologically minded Muslims. In its wake was spawned the view that altogether denied that a later Revelation could repeal an earlier one, even though the majority of Muslim scholars hold that abrogation and repeal does occur.[47]

Repeal of certain portions of the revealed text has proved to be so controversial precisely because it affects the idea of normativity. It calls into question the process in which norms are framed in authoritative speech (which later become texts), which in turn is affected by the vagaries of language. But deriving ethical values from speech/texts independent of the experience of the community creates another peculiar problem for normativity—what I call a "text-dependent ethics," an ethics informed mainly by texts that is peculiar to urbanized and modern literate societies. Here ethics becomes a text-fetish, in which practically all consideration is given over to questions regarding the authority of texts but little interest is given to the experiences of living communities and traditions. In modern interpretations of Islam these are particularly challenging questions. Not only have our notions of authority, community, and political order undergone shifts from previous assumptions, but even the way we imagine texts is different, due to major economic, cultural, and political shifts. In certain modern interpretations of Islam the emphasis is exclusively on the text of Qur'ān with little place for other sources and tradition.

This is very different from how the Qur'ān has traditionally been imagined and interpreted. The Qur'ān in the Muslim imagination, says Ghazālī, is an "all-encompassing ocean from which derives the knowledge of the ancients and the moderns."[48] While he acknowledges that the Qur'ān has the potential to provide all kinds of knowledge, one must understand that knowledge in this case is derivative. In other words, knowledge here is not something simply given, but is sought after and involves labor. For Ghazālī is aware of the fact that the number of Qur'ānic verses that provide teachings are limited, whereas the number of possible contingencies in human life are unquantifiable. Future events can thus not be circumscribed by a finite set of statements.[49] One of the strategies that Ghazālī employs is to test the elasticity of language by way of the analogical imagination and, in so doing, he "plough[s] over the whole of language" as Wittgenstein remarked.[50]

For Ghazālī too, the propositional aspect of language, its indexical meaning of words, is important, for without an element of agreement on meanings communication is impossible. In one of his shorter treatises, Ghazālī stresses the importance of proficiency in the various aspects of language and deems it "an extraordinary instrument" and the "foundation of all foundations."[51] Language also has an instrumental value insofar as it mediates our understanding of the revealed sources, whether the source is the Qur'ān, the reports of the Prophet, or everyday social and scientific realities.

One may be forgiven for thinking that, given the emphasis Ghazālī placed on the opacity of indexical meanings and on the definitive role of the linguistic community, language is merely an instrument. It is true that normative discourse relies greatly on propositional speech, but it cannot do so exclusively. In order for jurists to approximate the intention of the one who reveals the norm—namely, God—they must engage the performative aspect of language. Ghazālī is indeed prepared to explore the complex ways in which the intention of the speaker and author affects the meanings of words. Therefore, he does not hesitate to explore the constructed nature of language and meaning formation in speech that provide its performative character. Here "performative" means the social and contextual circumstances of the interpreter. Language is not imagined, as James Boyd White points out, as a set of propositions but as a "repertoire of forms of action and of life."[52] Much of the meaning of words is derived from the tones, the inflections, and gestures used as well as the context in which they are uttered. We could view "languaging" as a kind of dance, says White, where it is not the truth value of a gesture or performance that counts but its appropriateness to context.[53] So, we might say that when Ghazālī repeatedly asks us to analyze any discourse, he is proposing that we attend to the dance of the "intended meanings" (ma'ānī) of expressions. These intended meanings must be fathomed before one tries to configure what individual words signify.[54] In other words, the intended meaning of speech, in his view, is more than just the sum total of individual words.

The rhetoric of intentionality in language is hard to suppress in Ghazālī's writings, for it assumes different guises. In one instance he says: "One who considers the realities of these words may become bewildered by the multiplicity of the words and imagine many meanings. But the one to whom the realities are unveiled will make the intended meanings (ma'ānī) a foundation (asl) and make the vocables (words) subservient to it."[55] He elsewhere notes that by following the "correct method" one will know when not to search for meanings in words. In those cases the interpreter should "first ascertain the intentions (ma'ānī) and only consequently (secondly) contemplate the words."[56] Neither should one succumb to formalism and become obsessed with terminologies, he says, since this would obstruct one from getting to the heart of the matter. "All these stray ideas stem from the ignorance of several groups who seek the essential realities (al-haqā'iq [proper sense]) from vocables (alfāz)," Ghazālī observes. "So they stumble in this regard due to the errors that stem from the multiple human terminologies construed from words."[57]

Note that in the preceding passages Ghazālī approaches the issue of language with less emphasis on the propositional character of language than on the importance of the intentions behind words and how they are put to work. Meaning here resides in the performative gesture of words. And, in so doing, they defy the strict logic governing word use and preassigned meanings. Ghazālī insists almost ad nauseum that one must first come to terms with the intention of the speaker before analyzing the words themselves. Failing to correctly understand the speaker's intention can result in serious misinterpretation of speech. This is especially true when a word has several referents such as homonyms and figurative usages. Because the real intention of the speaker only surfaces in actual speech, it is critically important that, as part of the speech act, the hearer first discern what specific meaning the author had in mind.

The way intentions formed in the psyche are disseminated into speech is, according to Ghazālī, analogous to the way images are construed in dreams.[58] Just as the intention in a speech act determines how ideas are verbalized—how thoughts (*khayāl*) are expressed—similarly the full meaning of images in a dream become apparent only during wakefulness, when the intentionality lying behind those images is measured against real-life experiences.[59]

John Searle approaches the intentionality of speech acts by pointing out the necessary distinction between *intrinsic* and *derived* intentionality.[60] The first of these applies when, for example, we speak about ourselves, saying: "I am thirsty." Here, the intentionality is intrinsic to the self-understanding and expression of the speaker. Derived intentionality, on the other hand, underlies our "speech" when we use words, sentences, pictures, diagrams, graphs, and the like to make meaningful statements about the world. According to Searle, all linguistic meaning depends on and reflects derived intentionality.[61] The crucial difference between the two is that intrinsic intentionality is *observer-independent*, whereas derived intentionality is *observer-dependent*.

I would argue that when Ghazālī claims that linguistic meaning is not identical to the speaker's words he is pointing us in the direction of Searle's derived intentionality. What the speaker is understood to be saying is observer-dependent: it is the observer, the reader, and the interpreter who imbue the individual words used in expressions with the critical nuance necessary to reveal the intentions of the speaker. In a poststructuralist or Derridian idiom, one could say that the process of signification causes a *differance*, a deferral of meaning, as well as a difference in meaning, insofar as the words signify something more than their originally assigned meanings.

This gap between signification and understanding is also the space in which multiple intentions can be both deposited and divined. Ghazālī alerts us to the need to search for the intentions behind words and expressions as they are deployed in context-specific speech acts and discourses. In any field of possible meanings, Ghazālī forcefully argues, it is not detached reason that directs the selection of a specific meaning. Rather, it is the play of the rules of language and/or the force of authority that shapes the field of meaning.[62] Ghazālī in this way proposes that there is an intimate bond between language, authority, and the construction of meaning.

DECODING RELIGIOUS DISCOURSE

Ghazālī's theory of linguistic meaning has been criticized for overextending the process of interpretation. His fondness for figurative interpretation when there is no self-evident or compelling reason to divert us from the literal meanings has particularly been a target for criticism. A few examples illustrate the point.

A teaching of the Prophet Muḥammad documented in a report (*ḥadīth*) reads: "Angels do not enter a home in which there is a dog."[63] Most scholars understand this statement plainly to mean dogs as we know them are prohibited from the interior of the home. Ghazālī, however, provides an esoteric and figurative interpretation of this teaching. The human heart, he explains, is the locus of angels, or if you like, the place where angelic forces coalesce. All negative human qualities and habits such as anger, concupiscence, envy, jealousy, arrogance, and narcissism are like angry barking dogs. "How will angels enter it [the heart] when it is occupied by dogs?" Ghazālī asks.[64] Given the animality that dogs represent, this quality is antithetical and injurious to the purification of the heart and self-fashioning. "And God does not make the light of knowledge enter the heart," he adds, "except by way of angels."[65] In another place, he writes that whether one imagines a house made of clay or thinks of an animal as a dog, the report must be read in such a way that "home" is understood as a "house of religion" (*bayt al-dīn*). The home of religion, he says, is the heart; at times dogs overwhelm the heart, and on other occasions angels prevail.[66]

When asked by his interlocutors whether he believed the house referred to in the report to be one made of brick and mortar, and the dog the canine we commonly know, Ghazālī's reply is in the affirmative. He explains: "One can explore what we have observed, in order to deduce the understanding to which we have drawn your attention, so that you can then proceed to that to which we have alluded."[67] There is no objection to such an interpretive move, provided the rules of interpretation and logic support it. The other proviso is that a figurative interpretation should not conflict with any of the principles of the revealed law (*sharī'a*) or violate the sensibilities of those who are spiritually enlightened.

Ghazālī justifies his interpretation of the report, for example, by arguing that a synoptic and cumulative view of other teachings attributed to the Prophet make it manifestly clear that human hearts are the "homes" that God built with his own hands.[68] Furthermore, he points out that knowledge flourishes in the human heart. His interpretations, he goes on to argue, do have hermeneutical backing and he makes an intertextual argument drawing on other texts for support. Ghazālī mounts such a defense for his interpretation in spite of the fact that it goes against the plain meaning of the text and clashes with the established consensus position of the law schools regarding dogs in the homes. Ghazālī justifies his position by pointing out that his interpretation does not deny the literal meaning of the text. Instead, he claims that his interpretation is a gloss and an insight that he derives from the prophetic report.

Another example is a passage in the Qur'ān where the Prophet Abraham makes a prayer for himself and his Ishmaelite offspring. Addressing God, Abraham beseeches: "Preserve me and my offspring from the worship of idols."[69] What outrages some of Ghazālī's critics is that he interprets "idols" to mean the love of gold and silver.[70] Why does Ghazālī interpret the passage in this way when, from the plain meaning of the text, it is clear that Abraham is concerned with the possibility of his progeny succumbing to idolatry? It becomes clear that Ghazālī interprets idolatry to be a form of crass materialism, and idols were in fact often made out of precious materials. So in that sense his interpretation is not far off. But his detractors argue that he goes against the assigned meanings of words and, therefore, is taking liberties beyond a tolerable limit.

What would justify his figurative interpretation of idols? Ghazālī's eighteenth-century Indian commentator, Murtaḍā al-Zabīdī (d. 1205/1791), who settled in Egypt, writes that Ghazālī may have connected the verse with another report from the Prophet that reads: "Wretched is the slave ('abd) of the dīnār [ancient gold currency] and dirham [silver currency] and the servant of the belly."[71] Now the connector between the Qur'ān passage and the prophetic report is that both are concerned with worship. In the one it is the worship of idols and in the other the worship of wealth. The verb and noun used in both texts is ya'bud and 'abd, meaning "to worship" and "servant," respectively. Just as Abraham fears that his progeny should worship idols and therefore prays for protection from idolatry, the Arabian Prophet fears that his followers should become servants of materialism. Ghazālī, in his interpretation, says Zabīdī, makes a legitimate intertextual connection between idolatry and materialism and therefore it is a valid form of exegesis.

In Ghazālī's view it is imperative in the interpretive act to make such mental cross-overs (i'tibār) and intertextual references. In fact, the Arabic word I here translate as "cross-over" is the root word 'a-b-r, which means "to bridge," "to cross over," and "to do mental consideration" (*I'tibār*) as part of the process of relating one thing to the other. Here he does come up against the majority of those thinkers who continue to insist on language's propositional character and indexical signification as the sole form of linguistic meaning.

But the insistence on unmediated understanding of meaning can be said to be true of many contemporary interpreters of Muslim law. This outlook is bolstered by a totalitarian thinking induced by modern practices and technologies that claim for themselves a universal scope. For such proponents, language is just an accidental vehicle that transmits messages without being implicated in the content of the message or the precise linguistic mode of its transmission. Language on this theory depends for its existence, says White, "on chains of reasoning, deductive or inductive in character, that are external to itself and context."[72] Its fundamental presumption is that every experience, every idea, can be translated into any language, which in turn implies that all knowledge, all truth, is universal—"transparent" in the sense that it is independent of the historical conditions of time and place. This reductionist approach to language was not always the prevailing mood of Muslim scholarship. In previous centuries, as Bernard Weiss has pointed out, language was an active agent in the construction of the moral and ethical universe of Islam.[73]

I have shown that Ghazālī does understand the process of interpretation to involve translation, but it is translation of a sort that is sensitive to linguistic contexts and fully exploits the capaciousness of language. Ghazālī seems to have realized that if knowledge produced five centuries earlier were to make any sense for him, then it required a substantive translation, namely, a certain amount of intertextual interpretation or connection to new data as well as cultural adaptation. All authentic translation at least seeks to reproduce the structure of the alien discourse within the translator's own language. In addition, each translator not only gives voice to the intention of the original statement, but also supplements the original with his or her own contextual experiences. This is very different from a translation that merely recasts one statement into another linguistic context without showing any awareness of the organic transformation of the translated text and its meaning.

Ghazālī offers us a place of enunciation from where one can reengage language in its performative sense. Many of the words we use are not just signs in the sense of signals, but rather symbols. Ghazālī would certainly be in accord with Susanne Langer's assertion that when we "talk about things" we frequently use language symbolically.[74] The role of symbolic language is not that of a mere "announcer" of what is, a mere describer of facticity. Symbols substitute for signs to serve as reminders of the meaning of past experiences and ideas, and to imaginatively anticipate a future. Wittgenstein tells us that "to imagine a language means to imagine a form of life."[75]

Without doubt, the two kinds of language described above—propositional language, on one hand, and symbolic and performative language, on the other—do not exist in their pure forms in everyday life. Both are at work in imperfect relation to each other. Sometimes it is necessary to act as if language were factually transparent, such as when talking about street names, ascertaining a day of the week, or stating the time or day in the month. Here language is merely descriptive of a presumptively shared world. At other times, however, to glean the full meaning of a speech act requires that we broaden our understanding of language so as to recognize its participation in shaping and producing meaning. Therefore, we have to shift our attention in order that we may come to see language as having its own reality and see its uses as forms of life, with all the myriad complexities that life entails.

NOTES

1. See Mahmood Mamdani, *Good Muslim, Bad Muslim: America, The Cold War and the Roots of Terror* (New York: Parthenon, 2004).

2. See Lenn E. Goodman, "Ordinary and Extraordinary Language in Medieval Jewish and Islamic Philosophy," *Manuscrito: Revista Internacional de Filosofia* 11(1) (April 1988): 57–83; Goodman, "Jewish and Islamic Philosophy of Language," in *International Handbook of Contemporary Research,* ed. Marcelo Dascal and Dietfried Gerhardus (Berlin: Walter de Gruyter, 1992), 34–55.

3. See 'Abd al-Salām al-Musdī, "al-Tawḥīdī wa su'āl al-lugha," *Fuṣūl* 14(3) (Kharīf 1995): 126–57, esp. 143–44.

4. See Winnifred Fallers Sullivan, *Paying the Words Extra: Religious Discourse in the Supreme Court of the United States* (Cambridge: Harvard University Press, 1994).

5. Ernst Cassirer, *An Essay on Man: An Introduction to Philosophy of Human Culture* (New York: Doubleday, 1953), 142.

6. Abdul Latif Tibawi, "Is the Qur'an Translatable?" *Muslim World* 52 (1962): 4–16.

7. Jalāl al-Dīn al-Suyūṭī, *al-Muzhir fī 'ulūm al-lugha wa anwā'ihā,* ed. Muḥammad Ahmad Jād al-Mawlā, 'Alī Muḥammad al-Bajāwī, and Muḥammad al-Faḍl Ibrāhīm, 2 vols. (Cairo: Dār Iḥyā'al-Kutub al-'Arabiyya/'Īsā Bābī al-Ḥalabī, 1971), 1:30.

8. Ibid., 11.

9. Ibid., 32.

10. Ibid., 32.

11. Umberto Eco, *The Search for the Perfect Language,* trans. James Fentress (Oxford: Blackwell, 1997), 74, points out that Isidore of Seville circulated a fanciful account of seventy-two existing languages and elaborated a series of etymologies that made him a laughing stock of scholars ever since. Isidore may not have been the only one to hold this conviction; many Muslim scholars have believed that there were seventy-two languages at one point.

12. Suyūṭī, *al-Muzhir,* 33.

13. Badr al-Dīn al-Zarkashī, *al-Baḥr al-muḥīt fī uṣūl al-fiqh,* ed. Muḥammad Muḥammad Tāmir, 4 vols. (Beirut: Dār al-Kutub al-ʿIlmiyya, 1421/2000), 1:398.

14. Suyūṭī, *al-Muzhir,* 32–33, citing a report of Muḥammad b. Sallām al-Jumaḥī (d. 232/845–46).

15. Ibid., 35.

16. Ibid.

17. Ibid., 209, 321.

18. Jacques Derrida, "Des Tours de Babel," in *Acts of Religion,* ed. Gil Anidjar (New York: Routledge, 2002), 104.

19. Qurʾān 30:22.

20. Qurʾān 5:48; also see ibid., 2:213; Abū al-Qāsim Jār Allāh Maḥmūd b. ʿUmar al-Zamakhsharī, *al-Kashshāf ʿan ḥaqāʾiq al-tanzīl wa ʿuyūn al-aqāwīl,* 4 vols. (Beirut: al-Dār al-ʿIlmiyya, n.d.), 2:298.

21. Qurʾān 11:118.

22. Abū Ḥāmid al-Ghazālī, "Kitāb Ādāb Tilāwat-al-Qurʾān," in *Iḥyāʾ ʿUlūm al-Dīn,* 5 vols. (Beirut: Dār al-Kutub al-ʿIlmiyya, 1421/2001), 1:275.

23. Bernard Weiss, "Language and Law: The Linguistic Premises of Islamic Legal Science," in *In Quest of Islamic Humanism: Arabic and Islamic Studies in Memory of Mohamed al-Nowaihi,* ed. A. H. Green (Cairo: American University Press, 1984), 16.

24. Michel Villey, preface to "Le Langage du Droit," *Archives de Philosophie du Droit* 19 (1974): 1.

25. Zarkashī, *al-Baḥr,* 1:12.

26. In deliberating the origins and nature of language, Ghazālī, along with a number of other Muslim theorists, anticipated the work of Johann Gottfried Herder (1744–1803) by nearly seven centuries. Like Ghazālī, Herder struggled with creationist versus conventionalist positions. See Johann Gottfried Herder, *Essay on the Origin of Language,* ed. and trans. John H. Moran and Alexander Gode (New York: Ungar, 1967).

27. Abū Ḥāmid al-Ghazālī, *al-Mustaṣfā fī ʿilm al-uṣūl,* 2 vols. (Beirut: Dār al-Kutub al-ʿIlmiyya, 1403/1983), 1:319.

28. Rafīq al-ʿAjam, ed., *Mawsūʿa muṣṭalaḥāt uṣūl al-fiqh ʿinda al-muslimīn,* 2 vols. (Beirut: Maktaba Lubnan, 1998), 1:506.

29. Ghazālī, *al-Mustaṣfā,* 1:318.

30. Ibid., 1:319.

31. Such a report would be called *mutawātir,* which is to say categorical, on the grounds that it is supported by consecutive and unimpeachable testimony and transmitted authority is called *sam'.*

32. Ghazālī, *al-Mustaṣfā,* 1:319. Ghazālī says that while either of the propositions regarding the origin of language might be argued to be true, language must in either case preexist human creation either through a divine imperative or by means of a creation that was instrumental in the production of a primitive language prior to Adam.

33. Ibid., 1:320.

34. Herder, *Essay,* 103.

35. Abū Ḥayyān al-Tawḥīdī, *Kitāb al-Imtā 'wa al-mu'ānasa,* ed. Aḥmad Amīn and Aḥmad al-Zayn, 3 vols. (Beirut: Manthūrāt Dār Maktaba al-Ḥayāt, n.d.), 1:104–28. This debate was translated with an introduction by D. S. Margoliouth in "The Discussion between Abu Bishr Matta and Abu Sa'id on the Merits of Logic and Grammar," *Journal of the Royal Asiatic Society* (1905): 9–129; for an excellent discussion of this debate, see Muhsin Mahdi, "Language and Logic in Classical Islam," in *Logic in Classical Islamic Culture,* ed. G. E. Von Grunebaum (Wiesbaden: Otto Harrassowitz, 1970), 51–83.

36. Majid Khadduri, *al-Shafi'ī's Risāla: Treatise on the Foundations of Islamic Jurisprudence* (Cambridge: Islamic Texts Society, 1987), 67; Muḥammad bin Idrīs al-Shāfi'ī, *al-Risāla,* ed. Aḥmad Muḥammad Shākir (Cairo: Dār al-Turāth, 1399/1979), 21.

37. Ludwig Wittgenstein, *Remarks on Frazer's* Golden Bough, ed. Rush Rhees, trans. A. C. Miles (New Jersey: Humanities Press, 1979), 8e.

38. Ibid., 8e, 9e.

39. Ibid., 9e.

40. Khadduri, *Treatise,* 67; al-Shāfi'ī, *al-Risāla,* 21.

41. Ghazālī, *al-Mustaṣfā,* 1:338.

42. Bernard Weiss, "Medieval Muslim Discussions of the Origin of Language," *Zeitschrift der Deutschen Morgenlandischen Gesellschaft* 124 (1974): 33–41; Muḥammad M. Yunus Ali, *Medieval Islamic Pragmatics* (Richmond [UK]: Curzon, 2000), 15–40.

43. See Aziz al-Azmeh, *Arabic Thought and Islamic Societies* (London: Croom Helm, 1986), 116.

44. Ghazālī, *al-Mustaṣfā,* 2:5, 2:10 ("Inna al- qiyās bātil[un] fī al-lugha li annahā tuthbatu tawqīf[an]"); see also ibid., 2:39 ("wal lughatu tuthbatu tawqīf[an] wa naql[an], la qiyās[an] wa istidlāl[an]").

45. Early Muslim thinkers thought of language as a necessary instrument of social intercourse. A colleague of Ghazālī during their student says in Nisapūr—Abū al-Ḥasan 'Alī b. Muḥammad b. 'Alī, better known as Ilkiyā al-Harrāsī (d. 504/1110), a renowned Shāfi'ī jurist of his time—explained that when human beings recognized the need for community and coexistence, they also realized the need to form a habitat in which to live. Civilization (*tamaddun*), the development of crafts and skills together with the need for language stemmed from such felt needs to develop social existence, see Suyūtī, *al-Muzhir,* 26.

46. Ghazālī, *al-Mustaṣfā,* 1:324.

47. *Encyclopaedia of Islam,* EI 2, s.v. *badā',* ed. H.A.R. Gibb et al. (Leiden: E.J. Brill, 1986).

48. Abū Ḥāmid al-Ghazālī, *Jawāhir al-Qur'ān,* 5th ed. (Beirut: Dār al-Āfāq al-Jadīda, 1411/1990), 8.

49. Abū Ḥāmid al-Ghazālī, "*al-Qisṭās al-Mustaqīm,*" in *Majmū'a Rasā'il al-Imām al-Ghazālī* (Beirut: Dār al-Kutub al-'Ilmiyya, 1406/1986), 33; Abū Ḥāmid al-Ghazālī, *al-Faḍā'ih al-Bāṭiniyya,* ed. 'Abd al-Raḥmān al-Badawī (Cairo: al-Dār al-Qawmiyya li al-Tibā'a wa al-Nashr, 1282B/1964), 88.

50. Wittgenstein, *Remarks,* 7e.

51. There has been some dispute among scholars of Ghazālī whether the *Risāla al-Ladunniyya* can be attributed to him. Although Subkī, a major biographer of Ghazālī, along with a number of other modern scholars do not include it among those works attributed to Ghazālī, other scholars have found credible evidence supporting that attribution. A sixth-century manuscript dating back to shortly after Ghazālī's death listed his other works such as *Munqidh* and *Qisṭās,* including the *Risāla al-Ladunniyya.* See 'Abd al-Rahmān al-Badawī, *Mu'llafāt al-Ghazālī,* 2d ed. (Kuwait: Wakāla al-Matbū'āt, 1977), 270. Some scholars like Asin Palacios think Ghazālī's text resembles parts of Muhī al-Dīn Ibn 'Arabī's treatise on the soul, and therefore dismiss it as an authentic text of Ghazālī. Joseph McCarthy has since come across a manuscript that suggests that the *Risāla al-Ladunniyya* predates Ibn 'Arabī, see Badawī, above. Also see Margaret Smith's translation of this treatise, "al-Risālat al-Ladunniyya by Abū Ḥāmid Muḥammad al-Ghazālī (450/1059–505/1111)," *Journal of the Royal Asiatic Society–Part II* (April 1938): 177–200, *Part III* (July 1938): 353–74; Abū Ḥāmid al-Ghazālī, "al-Risāla al-Ladunniyya," in *Majmū'a Rasā'il al-Imām al-Ghazālī* (Beirut: Dār al-Kutub al-'Ilmiyya, 1406/1986), 98.

52. James Boyd White, *Justice as Translation: An Essay in Cultural and Legal Criticism* (Chicago: University of Chicago Press, 1990).

53. Ibid., xii.

54. The word *ma'nā,* pl. *ma'ānī,* has different uses in Arabic. In the most elementary and commonly used sense, it is the meaning assigned to a word. Of course, here it is the dictionary meaning that corresponds to the indexical assignment of meanings to words. But there is also another way in which the word *ma'nā* is used, especially in its plural form. Ghazālī frequently uses the word in this other sense where it means the "intention" in the mind of the speaker or the author. In this instance *ma'nā* is synonymous with *murād* (intended) and *maqṣūd* (sought after).

55. Abū Ḥāmid al-Ghazālī, *The Niche of Lights/Mishkat al-Anwar: A Parallel English-Arabic Text,* trans., intro., and annot. David Buchman (Provo: Brigham Young University Press, 1998), 26.

56. Abū Ḥāmid al-Ghazālī, *al-Iqtiṣād fī al-i'tiqād* (Cairo: Matba'a Muḥammad 'Alī Subayḥ wa Awlāduhu, 1390/1971). "Wa idhā am'anta al-naẓar wa ihtadayta as-sabīla 'arafta qaṭ'an anna akthar al-aghālīṭ nasha'at min ḍalāl man ṭalab al-ma'ānī min al-alfāẓ, wa laqad kāna min ḥaqqihi an yuqaddira al-ma'ānī awwalan thumma yanẓur fī al-alfāẓ

thāniyan. Wa yaʿlam annahā isṭilāḥāt lā tataghayyar bihā al-maʿqūlāt wa lakin ḥurima al-tawfīq, ustudbira al-ṭarīq, wa nukila ʿan al-taḥqīq" (13).

57. Abū Ḥāmid al-Ghazālī, *Iḥyā' ʿUlūm al-Dīn*, "Kitab al-ʿIlm," bayān tafāwut al-nufūs fī al-ʿaql (Beirut: Dār al-Kutub al-ʿIlmiyya, 1421/2001), 1:87.

58. Abū Ḥāmid al-Ghazālī, "al-Maḍnūn bi hi ʿala ghayri ahlihi," in *Majmūʿa Rasā'il al-Imām al-Ghazālī* (Beirut: Dār al-Kutub al-ʿIlmiyya, 1406/1986), 125.

59. Ibid.

60. John R. Searle, *Mind, Language and Society* (New York: Basic Books, 1998), 92.

61. Ibid., 93.

62. Ghazālī, *al-Iqtiṣād*, 23. Ghazālī explains that the use of a word cannot be justified by reason, but only by the conventions of the linguistic community and the authority of Revelation.

63. Ghazālī, *Iḥyā'* "Kitab al-ʿIlm," 1:51; see also Ghazālī, *Mīzān al-ʿamal*, ed. Sulaymān Dunyā (Cairo: Dār al-Maʿārif, 1964), 342.

64. Ghazālī, *Iḥyā'*, 1:51.

65. Ibid.

66. Ghazālī, *Mīzān al-ʿamal*, 342.

67. Ghazali, *Iḥyā'*, "Kitāb al-imlā," 5:23.

68. Ibid., 5:22.

69. Qur'ān 14:35.

70. See Murtaḍā al-Zabīdī, *Ithāf sādāt al-muttaqīn bi sharḥ iḥyā' ʿulūm al-dīn*, 14 vols. (Beirut: Dār al-Kutub al-ʿIlmiyya, n.d.), 1:50.

71. Ibid.

72. White, *Justice as Translation*, x.

73. Bernard Weiss, "Language and Tradition in Medieval Islam: The Question of al-tarīq ila maʿrifat al-lugha," *Der Islam* 61 (1984): 91.

74. Susanne K. Langer, *Philosophy in a New Key: A Study in the Symbolism of Reason, Rite and Art* (New York: Mentor Books, 1958), 37.

75. Quoted in White, *Justice as Translation*, ix.

CONTRIBUTORS

RUTH ABBEY is associate professor of political science at the University of Notre Dame. Among her recent works is *Charles Taylor* (Princeton, 2004).

CLIFFORD ANDO is associate professor of classics, history, and law at the University of Southern California. His most recent book is *Roman Religion* (Edinburgh, 2003).

R. SCOTT APPLEBY is professor of history and John M. Regan Jr. Director of the Joan B. Kroc Institute for International Peace Studies at the University of Notre Dame. He is the author most recently (with Gabriel A. Almond and Emmanuel Sivan) of *Strong Religion: The Rise of Fundamentalisms around the World* (Chicago, 2003).

LUIS E. BACIGALUPO is professor of medieval philosophy, philosophy of religion, and ethics, and is the director of the Office for Social Responsibility at the Pontifical Catholic University of Peru. His most recent publication is a 2004 article on individual freedom in the law review *Arequipa*.

CAROL BIER is research associate at The Textile Museum in Washington, D.C. She teaches at the Maryland Institute College of Art and the master of liberal arts program at Johns Hopkins University. Her most recent publication is *The Persian Velvets at Rosenborg* (Copenhagen, 1995).

WAYNE C. BOOTH (1921–2005) was George M. Pullman Distinguished Service Professor Emeritus in the Department of English Language and Literature, the Committee on Ideas and Methods, and the College, at the University of Chicago. His most recent book was *The Rhetoric of Rhetoric: The Quest for Effective Communication* (Malden, Mass., 2004).

PATRICK J. DENEEN is Markos and Eleni Tsakopoulos-Kounalakis Associate Professor of Government at Georgetown University. He is the author of *The Odyssey of Political Theory* (Lanham, Md., 2000) and *Democratic Faith* (Princeton, forthcoming).

JAVIER IGUÍÑIZ ECHEVERRÍA is professor of economics at the Pontifical Catholic University of Peru. His most recent book is *Desarrollo; Libertad y Liberación en Amartya Sen y Gustavo Gutiérrez* (Lima, 2003), which expands on the essay presented in this volume.

EUGENE GARVER is Regents Professor of Philosophy, St. John's University. His most recent book is *Living with Thought: A Confrontation with Aristotle's Ethics* (Chicago, forthcoming).

JEFFREY J. KRIPAL is J. Newton Rayzor Professor and Chair of Religious Studies at Rice University. His most recent book is *Roads of Excess, Palaces of Wisdom: Eroticism and Reflexivity in the Study of Mysticism* (Chicago, 2001).

SABINE MACCORMACK is Theodore Hesburgh C.S.C. Professor in Arts and Letters at the University of Notre Dame. Her most recent book is *On the Wings of Time: Rome, the Incas, Spain, and Peru* (Princeton, forthcoming).

EBRAHIM MOOSA is an associate professor of Islamic studies and director of the Center for the Study of Muslim Networks at Duke University. He is the author of *Ghazālī and the Poetics of Imagination* (Chapel Hill, 2005).

SOL SERRANO is professor of Chilean history at the Pontifical Catholic University of Chile. Her most recent book is *Virgenes Viajeras* (Santiago, 2000).

BILINDA STRAIGHT is assistant professor of anthropology at Western Michigan University. Her first book, *Miracles and Extraordinary Experience in Northern Kenya* (Pennsylvania, in press), is about the religious experience of the Samburu of northern Kenya.

JAMES BOYD WHITE is Hart Wright Professor of Law, professor of English, and adjunct professor of classics at the University of Michigan. His most recent book is *Living Speech: Resisting the Empire of Force* (Princeton, forthcoming). He has addressed the issues of the present book most notably in "Talking about Religion in the Language of the Law," in *From Expectation to Experience* (Michigan, 2001) and in *How Should We Talk about Religion?* (Erasmus Occasional Paper, 2001).